Functional and Concurrent Programming

Functional and Concurrent Programming

Core Concepts and Features

Michel Charpentier

♦♦ Addison-Wesley

Boston • Columbus • New York • San Francisco • Amsterdam • Cape Town
Dubai • London • Madrid • Milan • Munich • Paris • Montreal • Toronto • Delhi • Mexico City
Sao Paulo • Sidney • Hong Kong • Seoul • Singapore • Taipei • Tokyo

Cover Image: echo3005 / Shutterstock

For information about buying this title in bulk quantities, or for special sales opportunities (which may include electronic versions; custom cover designs; and content particular to your business, training goals, marketing focus, or branding interests), please contact our corporate sales department at corpsales @pearsoned.com or (800) 382-3419.

For government sales inquiries, please contact governmentsales@pearsoned.com.

For questions about sales outside the United States, please contact international@pearsoned.com.

Visit us on the Web: informit.com/aw

Library of Congress Number: 2022946382

ISBN-13: 978-0-13-746654-2
ISBN-10: 0-13-746654-4

1 2022

To Karen and Andre

Contents

List of Listings

List of Figures

Foreword by Cay Horstmann

In my book *Scala for the Impatient*, I provide a rapid-fire introduction into the many features of the Scala language and API. If you need to know how a particular feature works, you will find a concise explanation and a minimal code example (with real code, not fruits or animals). I assume that the reader is familiar with Java or a similar object-oriented programming language and organize the material to maximize the experience and intuition of such readers. In fact, I wrote the book because I was put off by the learning materials at the time, which were disdainful of object-oriented programming and biased toward functional programming as the superior paradigm.

That was more than a decade ago. Nowadays, functional techniques have become much more mainstream, and it is widely recognized that the object-oriented and functional paradigms complement each other. In this book, Michel Charpentier provides an accessible introduction to functional and concurrent programming. Unlike my Scala book, the material here is organized around concepts and techniques rather than language features. Those concepts are developed quite a bit more deeply than they would be in a book that is focused on a programming language. You will learn about nontrivial and elegant techniques such as zippers and trampolines.

This book uses Scala 3 for most of its examples, which is a great choice. The concise and elegant Scala syntax makes the concepts stand out without being obscured by a thicket of notation. You will particularly notice that when the same concept is expressed in Scala and in Java. You don't need to know any Scala to get started, and only a modest part of Scala is used in the code examples. Again, the focus of the book is concepts, not programming language minutiae. Mastering these concepts will make you a better programmer in any language, even if you never end up using Scala in your career.

I encourage you to actively work with the sample programs. Execute them, observe their behavior, and experiment by making changes. I suggest that you use a programming environment that supports Scala worksheets, such as Visual Studio Code, IntelliJ, or the online Scastie service. With a worksheet, turnaround is quick and exploratory programming is enjoyable.

Seven out of the 28 chapters are complete case studies that illustrate the material that preceded them. They are chosen to be interesting without being overwhelming. I am sure you will profit from working through them in detail.

The book is divided into two parts. The first part covers functional programming with immutable data, algebraic data types, recursion, higher-order functions, and lazy evaluation. Even if you are at first unexcited about reimplementing lists and trees, give it a chance. Observe the contrast with traditional mutable data structures, and you will find the journey rewarding. The book is blessedly free of complex category theory that in my opinion—evidently shared by the author—requires a large amount of jargon before yielding paltry gains.

The focus of the second part is concurrent programming. Here too the organization along concepts rather than language and API features is refreshing. Concurrent programming is a complex subject with many distinct use cases and no obvious way of teaching it well. Michel has broken down the material into an interesting and thought-provoking sequence of chapters that is quite different from what you may have seen before. As with the first part, the ultimate aim is not to teach you a specific set of skills and techniques, but to make you think at a higher level about program design.

I enjoyed reading and working through this unique book and very much hope that you will too.

Cay Horstmann
Berlin, 2022

Preface

Before you start reading this book, it is important to think about the distinction between programming *languages* and programming language *features*. I believe that developers benefit from being able to rely on an extensive set of programming language features, and that a solid understanding of these features—in *any* language—will help them be productive in a variety of programming languages, present or future.

The world of programming languages is varied and continues to evolve all the time. As a developer, you are expected to adapt and to repeatedly transfer your programming skills from one language to another. Learning new programming languages is made easier by mastering a set of core features that today's languages often share, and that many of tomorrow's languages are likely to use as well.

Programming language features are illustrated in this book with numerous code examples, primarily in Scala (for reasons that are detailed later). The concepts, however, are relevant—with various degrees—to other popular languages like Java, C++, Kotlin, Python, C#, Swift, Rust, Go, JavaScript, and whatever languages might pop up in the future to support strong typing as well as functional and/or concurrent programming.

As an illustration of the distinction between languages and features, consider the following programming task:

> *Shift every number from a given list by a random amount between* -10 *and* 10*. Return a list of shifted numbers, omitting all values that are not positive.*

A Java programmer might implement the desired function as follows:

Java

```java
List<Integer> randShift(List<Integer> nums, Random rand) {
  var shiftedNums = new java.util.ArrayList<Integer>(nums.size());
  for (int num : nums) {
    int shifted = num + rand.nextInt(-10, 11);
    if (shifted > 0) shiftedNums.add(shifted);
  }
  return shiftedNums;
}
```

A Python programmer might write this instead:

```python
                                                                    Python
def rand_shift(nums, rand):
    shifted_nums = []
    for num in nums:
        shifted = num + rand.randrange(-10, 11)
        if shifted > 0:
            shifted_nums.append(shifted)
    return shifted_nums
```

Although they are written in two different languages, both functions follow a similar strategy: Create a new empty list to hold the shifted numbers, shift each original number by a random amount, and add the new values to the result list only when they are positive. For all intents and purposes, the two programs are the same.

Other programmers might choose to approach the problem differently. Here is one possible Java variant:

```java
                                                                    Java
List<Integer> randShift(List<Integer> nums, Random rand) {
    return nums.stream()
        .map(num -> num + rand.nextInt(-10, 11))
        .filter(shifted -> shifted > 0)
        .toList();
}
```

The details of this implementation are not important for now—it relies on functional programming concepts that will be discussed in Part I. What matters is that the code is noticeably different from the previous Java implementation.

You can write a similar functional variant in Python:

```python
                                                                    Python
def rand_shift(nums, rand):
    return list(filter(lambda shifted: shifted > 0,
                       map(lambda num: num + rand.randrange(-10, 11), nums)))
```

This implementation is arguably closer to the second Java variant than it is to the first Python program.

These four programs demonstrate two different ways to solve the original problem. They contrast an imperative implementation—in Java or in Python—with a functional implementation—again, in Java or in Python. What fundamentally distinguishes the

programs is not the languages—Java versus Python—but the features being used—
imperative versus functional. The programming language features used in the imperative variant (assignment statements, loops) and in the functional variant (higher-order
functions, lambda expressions) exist independently from Java and Python; indeed, they
are available in many programming languages.

I am not saying that programming languages don't matter. We all know that, for
a given task, some languages are a better fit than others. But I want to emphasize
core features and concepts that extend across languages, even when they appear under
a different syntax. For instance, an experienced Python programmer is more likely to
write the example functional program in this way:

```
                                                                    Python
def rand_shift(nums, rand):
    return [shifted for shifted in (num + rand.randrange(-10, 11) for num in nums)
            if shifted > 0]
```

This code looks different from the earlier Python code—and the details are again unimportant. Notice that functions `map` and `filter` are nowhere to be seen. Conceptually,
though, this is the same program but written using a specific Python syntax known as
list comprehension, instead of `map` and `filter`.

The important concept to understand here is the use of `map` and `filter` (and more
generally higher-order functions, of which they are an example), not list comprehension.
You benefit from this understanding in two ways. First, more languages support higher-
order functions than have a comprehension syntax. If you are programming in Java, for
instance, you will have to write `map` and `filter` explicitly (at least for now). Second,
if you ever face a language that uses a somewhat unusual syntax, as Python does with
list comprehension, it will be easier to recognize what is going on once you realize that
it is just a variation of a concept you already understand.

The preceding code examples illustrate a contrast between a program written in plain
imperative style and one that leverages the functional programming features available
in many languages. I can make a similar argument with concurrent programming. Languages (and libraries) have evolved, and there is no reason to write today's concurrent
programs the way we did 20 years ago. As a somewhat extreme example, travel back
not quite 20 years to 2004, the days of Java 1.4, and consider the following problem:

> Given two tasks that each produce a string, invoke both tasks in parallel and
> return the first string that is produced.

Assume a type `StringComputation` with a string-producing method `compute`. In
Java 1.4, the problem can be solved as follows (do not try to understand the code; it is
rather long, and the details are unimportant):

```java
                                                          ─── Java ───
String firstOf(final StringComputation comp1, final StringComputation comp2)
    throws InterruptedException {
  class Result {
    private String value = null;

    public synchronized void setValue(String str) {
      if (value == null) {
        value = str;
        notifyAll();
      }
    }

    public synchronized String getValue() throws InterruptedException {
      while (value == null)
        wait();
      return value;
    }
  }

  final Result result = new Result();
  Runnable task1 = new Runnable() {
    public void run() {
      result.setValue(comp1.compute());
    }
  };
  Runnable task2 = new Runnable() {
    public void run() {
      result.setValue(comp2.compute());
    }
  };
  new Thread(task1).start();
  new Thread(task2).start();
  return result.getValue();
}
```

This implementation uses features with which you may not be familiar (but which are covered in Part II of the book).[1] Here are the important points to notice:

- The code is about 30 lines long.

- It relies on *synchronized* methods, a form of locking available in the Java Virtual Machine (JVM).

---

[1] One reason such old-fashioned features are still covered in this book is that I believe they help us understand the richer and fancier constructs that we should be using in practice. The other reason is that the concurrent programming landscape is still evolving and recent developments, such as virtual threads in the Java Virtual Machine, have the potential to make these older concepts relevant again.

- It uses methods `wait` and `notifyAll`, which implement a basic synchronization scheme on the JVM.

- It starts its own two threads to run the two tasks in parallel.

Fast forward to today's Java, and reimplement the program:

```Java
String firstOf(StringComputation comp1, StringComputation comp2, Executor threads)
    throws InterruptedException, ExecutionException {
  var result = new CompletableFuture<String>();
  result.completeAsync(comp1::compute, threads);
  result.completeAsync(comp2::compute, threads);
  return result.get();
}
```

Again, ignore the details and observe these points:

- The code is much shorter.

- Class `Result` is gone. It implemented a poor man's form of a *future*, but futures are now available is many languages, including Java.

- Synchronized methods are gone. The code does not rely on locks anywhere.

- Methods `wait` and `notifyAll` are gone. Instead, `CompletableFuture` implements its own synchronization, correctly and efficiently.

- No thread is created explicitly. Instead, threads are passed as an argument in the form of an `Executor` and can be shared with the rest of the application.

There is one more difference between the two variants that I want to emphasize. In the newer code, the two `Runnable` classes have disappeared. They have been replaced with an odd-looking syntax that did not exist in Java 1.4: `comp1::compute`. You may find this syntax puzzling because method `compute` seems to be missing its parentheses. Indeed, this code does not invoke `compute`, but rather uses the method itself as an argument to `completeAsync`. It could be written as a lambda expression instead: `comp1::compute` is the same as `() -> comp1.compute()`. Passing functions as arguments to functions is a fundamental concept of functional programming, which is explored at length in Part I, but finds frequent uses in writing concurrent code as well.

Here's the point of this illustration: You can still write the first version of the program in today's Java, but you shouldn't. It is notoriously difficult to get multithreaded code correct, and it is even more difficult to get it correct *and* make it efficient. Instead, you should leverage what is available in the language and use it effectively. Are you making the most of the programming languages you are using today?

As a trend, programming languages have become more abstract and richer in features, a shift that makes many programming tasks less demanding. There are more concepts to understand in Java 19 than there were in Java 1, but it is easier to write correct and efficient programs with Java 19 than it was with Java 1. Feature-rich programming languages can be harder to learn, but they are also more powerful once mastered.

Of course, what you find hard or easy depends a lot on your programming background, and it is important not to confuse simplicity with familiarity. The functional variants of the Java and Python programs presented earlier are not more complicated than the imperative variants, but for some programmers, they can certainly be less familiar. Indeed, it is more difficult for a programmer to shift from an imperative to a functional variant (or vice versa) within Java or Python than it is to shift from Java to Python (or vice versa) within the same imperative or functional style. The latter transition is mostly a matter of syntax, while the first requires a paradigm shift.

Most of the advantages of current, feature-rich, programming languages revolve around functional programming, concurrency, and types—hence the three themes of this book. A common trend is to provide developers with abstractions that allow them to dispense with writing nonessential implementation details, and code that is not written is bug-free code.

Jumps and gotos, for instance, were long ago discarded in high-level programming languages in favor of structured loops. But many loops can themselves be replaced with functional alternatives that instead use a standard set of higher-order functions. Similarly, writing concurrent programs directly in terms of threads and locks can be very challenging. Relying on thread pools, futures, and other mechanisms instead can result in simpler patterns. In many scenarios, you have no more reason to use loops and locks than you have to write your own hash map or sorting method: It's unnecessary work, it's error-prone, and it's unlikely to achieve the performance of existing implementations. As for types, the age-old dichotomy between safety—being able to catch errors thanks to types—and flexibility—not being overly constrained in design choices because of types—is often being resolved in favor of safe *and* flexible type systems, albeit complicated ones.

This book is not a comprehensive guide to everything you need to know about functional and concurrent programming, or about types. But to leverage modern language constructs in your everyday programming, you need to become familiar with the abstract concepts that underlie these features. There is more to applying functional patterns than being aware of the syntax for lambda expressions, for instance. This book introduces only enough concepts as are needed to use language features effectively. There is a lot more to functional and concurrent programming and to types than what the book covers. (There is also a lot more to Scala.) Advanced topics are left for you to explore through other resources.

Why Scala?

As mentioned earlier, most of the code illustrations in this book are written in Scala. This may not be the language you are most familiar with, or the language in which you plan to develop your next application. It is a fair question to wonder why I chose it instead of a more mainstream language.

Scala is a programming language that aims to combine object-oriented and functional programming, with good support for concurrency as well.[2] It is a hybrid language—also called a multi-paradigm language. In fact, all three versions of the random shifting program already written in Java and in Python can be written in Scala:

```scala
                                                              ──── Scala ────
def randShift(nums: List[Int], rand: Random): List[Int] = {
  val shiftedNums = List.newBuilder[Int]
  for (num <- nums) {
    val shifted = num + rand.between(-10, 11)
    if (shifted > 0) {
      shiftedNums += shifted
    }
  }
  shiftedNums.result()
}

def randShift(nums: List[Int], rand: Random): List[Int] =
  nums.view
    .map(num => num + rand.between(-10, 11))
    .filter(shifted => shifted > 0)
    .toList

def randShift(nums: List[Int], rand: Random): List[Int] =
  for {
    num <- nums
    shifted = num + rand.between(-10, 11)
    if shifted > 0
  } yield shifted
```

The first function is imperative, based on an iteration and a mutable list. The next variant is functional and uses `map` and `filter` explicitly. The last variant relies on Scala's `for`-comprehension, a mechanism similar to (but more powerful than) Python's list comprehension.

You can also use Scala to write a concise solution to the concurrency problem. It uses futures and thread pools, like the earlier Java program:

```scala
                                                              ──── Scala ────
def firstOf(comp1: StringComputation, comp2: StringComputation)
           (using ExecutionContext): String = {
  val future1 = Future(comp1.compute())
  val future2 = Future(comp2.compute())
  Await.result(Future.firstCompletedOf(Set(future1, future2)), timeout)
}
```

---

[2]Different incarnations of Scala exist. This book uses the most common flavor of Scala, namely, the one that runs on the JVM and leverages the JVM's support for concurrency.

Given the book's objectives, there are several benefits to using Scala for code illustrations. First, this language is feature-rich, making it possible to illustrate many concepts without switching languages. Many of the standard features of functional and concurrent programming exist in Scala, which also has a powerful type system. Second, Scala was introduced fairly recently and was carefully (and often beautifully) designed. Compared to some older languages, there is less historical baggage in Scala that can get in the way when discussing underlying concepts. Finally, Scala syntax is quite conventional and easy to follow for most programmers without prior exposure to the language.

Nevertheless, it is important to keep in mind that programming language features, rather than Scala per se, are the focus of this book. Although I personally like it as a teaching language, I am not selling Scala, and this is not a Scala book. It just happens that I need a programming language that is clean and simple in all areas of interest, and I believe Scala meets these requirements.

Target Audience

The target audience is programmers with enough experience to not be distracted by simple matters of syntax. I assume prior Java experience, or enough overall programming experience to read and understand simple Java code. Concepts such as classes, methods, objects, types, variables, loops, and conditionals are assumed to be familiar. A rudimentary understanding of program execution—execution stack, garbage collection, exceptions—is also assumed, as well as basic exposure to data structures and algorithms. For other key terms covered in depth in the book, the glossary provides a basic definition and indicates the appropriate chapter or chapters where the concept is presented.

No prior knowledge of functional or concurrent programming is assumed. No prior knowledge of Scala is assumed. Presumably, many readers will have some understanding of functional or concurrent concepts, such as recursion or locks, but no such knowledge is required. For instance, I do not expect you to necessarily understand the functional Python and Java programs discussed earlier, or the two Java concurrent programs, or the last two Scala functions. Indeed, I would argue that if these programs feel strange and mysterious, this book is for you! By comparison, the imperative variant of the number-shifting program should be easy to follow, and I expect you to understand the corresponding code, whether it is written in Java, Python, or Scala. You are expected to understand simple Scala syntax when it is similar to that of other languages and to pick up new elements as they are introduced.

The syntax of Scala was inspired by Java's syntax—and that of Java by C's syntax—which should make the transition fairly straightforward for most programmers. Scala departs from Java in ways that will be explained as code examples are introduced. For now, I'll highlight just three differences:

- *Semicolon inference.* In Scala, terminating semicolons are inferred by the compiler and rarely used explicitly. They may still appear occasionally—for instance, as a way to place two statements on the same line.

- *No "return" needed.* Although a `return` keyword exists in Scala, it is seldom used. Instead, a function implicitly returns the value of the last expression evaluated in its body.

- *Significant indentation.* The curly braces used to define code blocks can often be inferred from indentation and are optional. The first Scala `randShift` variant can been written:

```scala
──────────────────────────────────────────────────── Scala ──
def randShift(nums: List[Int], rand: Random): List[Int] =
  val shiftedNums = List.newBuilder[Int]
  for num <- nums do
    val shifted = num + rand.between(-10, 11)
    if shifted > 0 then shiftedNums += shifted
  end for
  shiftedNums.result()
end randShift
```

When indentation is used to create blocks, markers can be added to emphasize block endings, but they are optional. An even shorter version of the `randShift` function takes the following form:

```scala
──────────────────────────────────────────────────── Scala ──
def randShift(nums: List[Int], rand: Random): List[Int] =
  val shiftedNums = List.newBuilder[Int]
  for num <- nums do
    val shifted = num + rand.between(-10, 11)
    if shifted > 0 then shiftedNums += shifted
  shiftedNums.result()
```

In this book, code illustrations rely on indentation instead of curly braces when possible and omit most end markers for the sake of compactness. I expect readers to be able to read imperative Scala code in this form, like the preceding function.

How to Read This Book

I believe that the primary value of this book lies in its code illustrations. To a large extent, the text is there to support the code, more than the other way around. The code examples tend to be short and focused on the concepts they aim to illustrate. In particular, very few examples are designed to perform the specific tasks you need to solve in your daily programming activities. This is not a cookbook.

Furthermore, concepts are introduced from the ground up, starting with the fundamentals, and expanding and abstracting toward the application level. The code that you might find to be the most applicable is found in the later chapters in each part of the book. I have found this progression to be most conducive to a solid understanding of features, which can then be translated into languages other than Scala. If you feel that the early topics are well known and the pace too slow, please be patient.

This book is designed to be read in order, from beginning to end. Most chapters—and their code illustrations—depend on ideas and programs presented in earlier chapters. For instance, several solutions to the same problem are often presented in separate chapters as a way to illustrate different sets of programming language features. It is also the case that Part II on concurrent programming uses concepts from Part I on functional programming.

While this makes it near impossible to proceed through the contents in a different order, you are free to speed through sections that cover features with which you are already familiar. Material from this book has been to used to teach undergraduate and graduate students who are told that, as long as the code makes sense, they are ready to move on to the next part. It is when code starts to look puzzling that it is time to slow down and pay closer attention to the explanations in the text.

There are several ways you can safely skip certain parts of the contents:

- Chapter 15 on types can be skipped entirely. Elsewhere in the book, several code examples make simplifying assumptions to avoid intricate concepts such as type bounds and type variance. A basic understanding of Java types, including generics (but not necessarily with wildcards) and polymorphism, is sufficient.

- Any "aside" can be safely ignored. These are designed as complementary discussions that you may expect to find, given the book's topics (and I would not want to disappoint you!), and they can sometimes be lengthy. They are rarely referred to in the main text, and any of these references can be ignored.

- Any "case study" chapter can be skipped. I would not necessarily recommend that you do so, however, because the case study code is where features are put together in the most interesting ways. However, no concept or syntax needed in a later part of the book is ever introduced in a case study. The main text does not refer to code from the case studies, with one minor exception: Section 10.8 refers to a binary search tree implementation developed in Chapter 8.

Additional Resources

The book's companion website is hosted at https://fcpbook.org. It contains additional resources, a list of errata, and access to the code illustrations, which are available from GitHub. The code examples were compiled and tested using Scala 3.2. The author welcomes comments and discussions, and can be reached at author@fcbbook.org.

Acknowledgments

I want to thank past and present colleagues for the encouragements that got me started and for their feedback on the early stages of this project. Some were confident I had something to say (and could say it) before I realized it myself.

A special thanks to my students, who went through various iterations of the material that ended up in this book. They were my guinea pigs. More times than I care to admit, I subjected them to frantic improvisation because a feature suddenly needed for that day's lecture was only going to be introduced as part of the following week's discussion. (To arrange hundreds of code examples in a consistent order is harder than it looks.) With last minute changes before every class, students got used to, in their own words, "handouts and slides on which the ink is not quite yet dry."

Some of the ideas for code illustrations in this book were gathered over a period of thirty years, during which time I refined them by writing and rewriting many implementations in a variety of programming languages. As much as I'd like to specifically thank the original authors of these examples, I can't remember all the sources I've used, I don't know which of them were original, and I feel it wouldn't be fair to mention some names but not the others. Nevertheless, I don't claim to have invented all the examples used in this book. The code is mine (including bugs), but credit for program ideas that originated elsewhere should go to their creators, whoever they are.

It is truly scary to think what this book would have been if I had been left on my own. Whatever its current flaws, it was made astronomically better with the help of my editor, Gregory Doench, and his production team. They were very patient with a first-time author who clearly didn't always know what he was doing.

My feelings toward anonymous and non-anonymous reviewers is mixed. Without a doubt, they helped improve the book but at the cost of extending my prison sentence every time I was hoping to get paroled. I am thankful for their help—feedback from Cay Horstmann, Jeff Langr, and Philippe Quéinnec, and long email discussions with Brian Goetz, in particular, come to mind—but I cannot say I always welcomed their input as unmitigated good news. I had been warned that writing a book like this was a major undertaking but not that I would have to write it four times.

Which brings me to my deepest gratitude. It goes to my family, who showed angelic patience as I kept promising to be done "by next month" for more than a year. They must have grown tired of "the book" repeatedly getting in the way of our family life. Indeed, I'm amazed that my wife didn't pick up the phone one day, call my editor, and notify him: "That's it. The book is finished. Done. Today. Now."

About the Author

Michel Charpentier is an associate professor with the Computer Science department at the University of New Hampshire (UNH). His interests over the years have ranged from distributed systems to formal verification and mobile sensor networks. He has been with UNH since 1999 and currently teaches courses in programming languages, concurrency, formal verification, and model-checking.

Part I

Functional Programming

Chapter 1

Concepts of Functional Programming

There is no universally accepted definition of functional programming, but all can agree that it involves programming with functions. This chapter is an overview of some of the characteristics of a functional programming style. It argues that these characteristics all are, with varying degrees, a consequence of choosing to program in terms of functions.

1.1 What Is Functional Programming?

The idea of programming with functions is not new. The concepts behind functional programming have been around since at least the programming language Lisp (late 1950s), or even since λ-calculus (1930s) at a more theoretical level. In recent years, concepts of functional programming have seeped from truly functional programming languages, like Haskell and ML, into mainstream, general-purpose languages like Java, Python, and Kotlin. You may use these added functional programming features in various ways, depending on the application domain and your personal preferences. Developers who discuss the pros and cons of functional programming often focus on the characteristics that are the most advantageous or disadvantageous to them. As with other aspects of programming and programming languages, people can become very opinionated, and arguments are often heated as to what functional programming is and is not.

You may hear that functional programming is centered around higher-order functions and lambda expressions. Or you might read an introduction to functional programming that talks at length about recursion. Or an opinion that functional programming is all about immutability. Or lazy evaluation.

This chapter is a brief exposition of my own view, which could be summarized as: *all of the above*. At the core of functional programming is the idea of programming with functions, and I hope to convince you that many of the programming characteristics often associated with a functional programming style, like those just mentioned, follow more or less directly from this use of functions. Apparent conflicts in definitions are often only choices of which facets to emphasize, and in what order.

This book does not assume prior knowledge of functional programming. The chapters that follow will define the terminology that is only briefly mentioned here (higher-order and recursive functions, lambda expressions, immutability, lazy evaluation), alongside a few other terms like tail recursion, pattern matching, and algebraic data types. You are not expected to understand all these concepts from this chapter. Rather, the idea is to point out that they are all somewhat related. The details come later.

1.2   Functions

Functions are a well-established mathematical concept: A function associates every value from a set with a unique value from another set (both sets may or may not be the same). The first set is often referred to as the *domain* of the function and the second as its *range* or *codomain*. Functions are said to *map* values from the domain to values from the codomain, and functions are sometimes called *mappings*. Functional programming is rooted in a yearning to write programs in terms of constructs that approach mathematical functions.

This mathematical notion of function does not necessarily coincide with what a `function` keyword might do in a programming language, or what you think of when you decide to implement a "function" in your favorite language. Instead, you need to think back to the functions you saw in your high-school algebra class. In that sense, $f(x) = \sqrt{x}$ and $g(x) = x^2 - 1$ are functions (on real numbers), while Java's sorting method `Arrays.sort` is not.

Why? The Java method sorts an array by rearranging its contents. By doing so, it *modifies* the array; it does not map it to another value. In mathematics, functions do not modify anything. What is there to modify, anyway? The number 4 is a value; $\sqrt{4}$ is another value, also a number; and so is $4^2 - 1$. Functions map values to values, but values are not modified. Using $\sqrt{4}$ or $4^2 - 1$ in a larger expression does not "modify" the number 4, whatever that would mean. Similarly, a sorting *function*—as opposed to Java's `Arrays.sort`—would map an array value to another, sorted array value, but would not modify its input array in any way.

A core principle of functional programming is to organize code in terms of functions that do not modify anything. Consider, for instance, these two Java "functions":

```Java
String firstString1(List<String> strings) {
  return strings.get(0);
}

String firstString2(List<String> strings) {
  return strings.remove(0);
}
```

Both return the first string of a list of strings (assuming the list is not empty). Seen as functions, they are equivalent: For any non-empty list of strings x, the strings `firstString1(x)` and `firstString2(x)` are the same.[1] However, the `firstString2` function also removes the first string from the list—thus modifying the list—while `firstString1` does not.

---

[1] This assumes that list x implements the `remove` method, which technically is optional in Java.

As this Java example illustrates, functions that modify some object and functions that do not are often indistinguishable from their signatures: `firstString1` and `firstString2` both take a `List<String>` argument and return a value of type `String`. Instead, programmers are expected to rely on good naming and documentation—including possibly annotations—to help emphasize that a function-like construct also modifies the state of a system. For instance, the two functions in the preceding example could be named `getFirstString` and `getAndRemoveFirstString`, respectively.

The starting point of functional programming is to rely, as fundamental organizational blocks of code, on functions that produce new values but do not modify existing data in any way. State modifications, when necessary, are performed elsewhere in ways that are unambiguous—that is, not through constructs that look like functions.

Aside on λ-Calculus

When discussing functions, notations from a typical algebra class are somewhat ambiguous. One might write $f(x) = x^2 - 1$ as a way to define function f. Then, $f(2)$ is used to represent the value obtained by applying function f to the number 2. In the same way, $f(y)$ is f applied to variable y. However, by itself, $f(x) = (x - 1)(x + 1)$ is far from clear. Is this a (re)definition of f? Or is it a theorem about an existing function f, one stating that $f(x)$ is always equal to $(x - 1)(x + 1)$?

λ-Calculus (where λ is the Greek letter *lambda*) is a theory of functions developed in the 1930s and serves as one of the mathematical foundations of functional programming. In λ-calculus, the definition of f and the corresponding theorem would be stated unambiguously. The definition of f could be written as $f = \lambda x.\, (x^2 - 1)$; the application of f to number 2 would be $f\,2$; and the general theorem would be $f\,x = (x - 1)(x + 1)$ (assuming a standard notation for arithmetic operations).

This book focuses on practical programming, so it does not discuss λ-calculus in any depth. It should be said, though, that many core ideas of functional programming find their roots there. For instance, in λ-calculus, functions and data are terms of the same algebra. This naturally leads to the notion of functions as values, which is explored in Chapter 9. *Currying* (Section 9.2) is tied to the fact that all functions in λ-calculus are single-argument functions. Addition, for instance, would be defined as $\lambda x.\, \lambda y.\, (x + y)$, which is a function of a single argument (x) that returns another function $\lambda y.\, (x + y)$ of a single argument (y). Other aspects of functional programming are often discussed in terms of λ-calculus. Hybrid programming languages, for example, sometimes discuss the relationship between *methods* and *functions* (Section 9.6) in terms of the η-conversion, which states that $\lambda x.\, f\,x$ and f are equivalent. (In programming language terms, you can think of it as the equivalence between the function that applies method `f` and method `f` itself.)

The debt of functional programming to λ-calculus is nowhere more evident than in the terminology used for *function literals* (Section 9.3): They are often expressed as "*lambda expressions*," and `lambda` is actually a keyword used to define such functions in languages like Ruby and Python.

1.3   From Functions to Functional Programming Concepts

Many of the programming concepts and features presented in the first part of this book follow quite naturally from the decision to organize code in terms of functions. First, the idea of functions that do not modify anything can be generalized to the broader notion of *immutable* data, which cannot be modified at all. Functional programming often involves applying functions to compute immutable values from other immutable values, such as when you apply $\sqrt{\ }$ to (immutable) number 4 to produce (immutable) number 2. Function `firstString2` given earlier can modify its input list because Java lists are (often) mutable. By contrast, Scala lists are immutable:

```
                                                              Scala
def firstString(strings: List[String]): String = ...
```

It does not matter how the function is implemented: You can know for sure that it does not modify the given list of strings, because the list simply cannot be modified. (Immutability is discussed in Chapters 3 and 4.)

What about performance? Won't immutable lists force the costly creation of new lists as the state of a system evolves? Not necessarily. New immutable lists can often share data with existing lists and be created with minimal copying and memory allocation. Other data structures also have this property. They are typically defined in terms of *algebraic data types*, and functional programming languages often implement a notion of *pattern matching* to better support programming with such types. (Algebraic data types and pattern matching are the topic of Chapter 5.)

Another important observation about immutability is that code that produces an immutable value from another immutable value gains nothing from being repeated multiple times. This is critical, because it means that, in a purely functional approach to programming, loops are useless. Indeed, if the body of a loop does not change the state of a system in any way, executing it ten times instead of one (or even zero times) makes no difference. If you are used to imperative programming, you may find the idea of programming without loops quite mystifying. It is actually a frequent mistake, when first learning functional programming, to try to use a functional computation as the body of a loop. Instead, functional programming makes heavy use of *recursion*, not only as a replacement for loops, but also as a natural way to process algebraic data types that are recursive in nature, like trees. (Recursion is discussed at length in Chapters 6 to 8, and used throughout the book.)

From the centrality of functions in functional programming emerges another idea, that of functions as values. In functional programming languages, functions are regular values, which can be stored in collections, or used as arguments and return values of other functions. This gives rise to the concepts of *higher-order functions* and of *function literals*, often expressed in terms of *lambda expressions*. (Higher-order functions, function literals, and lambda expressions are the topics of Chapters 9 and 10.)

Since, in functional programming, functions can be used as values, you can sometimes replace an explicit argument with a function that can compute this argument, thus delaying the evaluation of the argument until it is needed. The argument is then said to be *lazily* evaluated. By the same token, functions can also be stored inside data structures to implement lazily evaluated types, such as *streams* and *views*. (Lazy evaluation is covered in Chapters 12 and 14).

Finally, handling failures by throwing and catching exceptions becomes inadequate in programs that embed their control flow in higher-order functions. Instead, faults and errors are better treated in functional programming as regular values—of well-chosen types, defined for this purpose. (Chapter 13 discusses functional error handling.)

1.4 Summary

It is not uncommon for tutorials and overviews to answer the question *What is functional programming?* by emphasizing one or more of the characteristics highlighted in this chapter. You might hear that functional programming is all about recursion, or all about immutability, or all about higher-order functions and lazy evaluation. In truth, all these ideas are important, and all follow from the central principle of using functions as the primary notion of computation. The concepts briefly mentioned here are thoroughly explored in the first part of the book (Chapters 2 to 14) through small code illustrations and longer case studies.

Chapter 2

Functions in Programming Languages

The simplicity of mathematical functions is often enriched in programming languages with features that facilitate their use as programming abstractions. Some of the most common features are discussed in this chapter. Hybrid languages, which combine functional and object-oriented programming, typically distinguish between operators, methods, and functions and define mechanisms to bridge all three. Additionally, type parameterization, optional arguments, and variable-length arguments are commonly used to define templates that represent families of functions.

2.1 Defining Functions

Most programming languages offer a mechanism to structure code in terms of functions. You define a function by giving it a name, and by specifying its arguments and return value. For example, a simple absolute value function can be defined in a variety of languages:

Java
```java
int abs(int x) {
  if (x > 0) return x; else return -x;
}
```

JavaScript
```javascript
function abs(x) {
  if (x > 0) return x; else return -x;
}
```

Python
```python
def abs(x):
    return x if x > 0 else -x
```

Kotlin
```kotlin
fun abs(x: Int): Int = if (x > 0) x else -x
```

```
──────────────────────────────────────────────── Scala ──
def abs(x: Int): Int = if x > 0 then x else -x
```

These five definitions show many similarities. For instance, the body of the function is exactly the same in Java and in JavaScript, and also in Kotlin and in Scala. However, you might also notice several differences:

- A function is introduced in Java without a keyword. By contrast, JavaScript uses `function`, Kotlin uses `fun`, and Python and Scala use `def`.

- Java, JavaScript, and Python all use the keyword `return` to return a value. Kotlin and Scala do not (at least in this example).

- The body of the function is delimited by curly braces in Java and JavaScript. Python uses indentation. For a function body as simple as the absolute value, the Kotlin and Scala variants use nothing. (When defining more complex functions, Kotlin uses braces and Scala uses braces or indentation.)

- Types are handled differently: Java uses a "`type variable`" syntax, while Kotlin and Scala use "`variable: type`." More noticeably, JavaScript and Python do not mention types at all.

- The languages use a different syntax to test whether input `x` is positive. Some rely on parentheses; some don't. Some include a `then` keyword; others don't. More importantly, the Python, Kotlin, and Scala variants use "`if`" as an expression, with a value. The Java and JavaScript variants do not.

Some of these differences are trivial matters of syntax. Developers are expected to seamlessly navigate such minor variations when switching languages. You may write `def` a few times as you start programming in Kotlin, but it should not take long to adjust to writing `fun` instead. Other dissimilarities run deeper and will be revisited (typing strategies are discussed in Chapter 15, and the use of conditionals as expressions is discussed in Chapter 3). This book uses mostly Scala—with some Java—in its code illustrations. You may already be familiar with one or the other language—more often Java than Scala, I suspect—but should quickly get used to both as you read the code examples.

2.2　Composing Functions

Imperative code tends to rely heavily on sequential composition:

```
──────────────────────────────────────────── pseudocode ──
doOneThing(...);
doAnotherThing(...);
```

The two functions `doOneThing` and `doAnotherThing` are executed in sequence, one then the other. When functions are used as functions—mechanisms to produce values from values—as opposed to acting in some way on the state of an application, they need to be composed differently. Let's supplement the absolute value function with a second function, `dots`, for the purpose of an illustration:

```scala
def dots(length: Int): String = "." * length
```

This function creates a string of dots of a specified length. It can be combined with the absolute value function to produce the string `"..."` from the number `-3`:

```scala
dots(abs(-3)) // the string "..."
```

Functions are composed by using the output of a function as the input to another function. Note that I did not use sequential composition and did not write:

```scala
abs(-3);
dots(-3);
```

which would not have the desired effect. For sequential composition to work, function `abs` would need to change a number (into its absolute value) before `dots` uses it to build a string. This would work:

```scala
num = -3;
num = abs(num);
dots(num); // the string "..."
```

However, this pattern cannot be expressed without introducing a variable `num`. You need to store the effects of the first part of the sequence somewhere and tell the second part where to find them.

Functions can be composed more easily because their effects are local. Ideally, a function only needs to know its input and does nothing more than produce an output (see the discussion of pure functions in Chapter 3). This makes it possible to compose functions into larger functions, for which functional programming languages define specific operators:

```scala
(dots compose abs)(-3) // the string "..."
(abs andThen dots)(-3) // the string "..."
```

Functions `abs` and `dots` are composed, and the composed function is then applied to the argument `-3`. By contrast, you cannot compose two sequential code fragments into one without tying them together by mentioning explicitly what is being transformed by the first part so the second part can use it, which is the role of variable `num` in the preceding example.

If you are new to functional programming, you may find expressions like `dots compose abs` or `abs andThen dots` somewhat mystifying. Instead of being applied to arguments, functions `abs` and `dots` look like they are themselves arguments to the operators `compose` and `andThen`. Indeed, this is exactly what is happening, and Chapters 9 and 10 are dedicated to this very important feature of functional programming.

NOTE

Function `dots` breaks down if `length` is negative. To keep the code excerpts short and focused on the concepts being illustrated, I deliberately omit all argument validation throughout the book. As a reader, you are asked to assume that arguments have reasonable values and have been validated elsewhere.

2.3   Functions Defined as Methods

As a programming language, Scala is said to be *hybrid*, or *multi-paradigm*, because it aims to combine concepts from object-oriented and functional programming. This makes it well suited for the purpose of this book but also slightly complicates the discussion of function definition.

As a functional language, Scala offers various mechanisms to define functions. But, because it is also an object-oriented language, it uses the notion of methods as well. The same can be said of other hybrid languages, such as Kotlin. Technically, the Scala implementations of `abs` and `dots` in Section 2.2 are methods, not functions. Both functions and methods can be used as code structuring devices, but they are not always equivalent.

There is no need to get sidetracked here by a lengthy discussion of the differences between functions and methods—I have heard that even the Scala language specification does not use these terms in a consistent way. As we delve more deeply into our exploration of functional programming, some differences will be discussed (see, in particular, Sections 2.5 and 9.4). For now, I loosely use "function" as a term for a programming language construct with input arguments and an output value, which includes Scala methods.

2.4   Operators Defined as Methods

Programming languages not only have functions (and methods) but also tend to use operators when building expressions. For instance, all five absolute value implementations use a binary operator ">" in the expression `x > 0`, and a unary operator "–" in the expression `-x`.

Scala uses methods with symbolic names to implement almost all its operators. For instance, both ">" and "–" are implemented as methods. The expression x > 0 invokes a method ">" on an object x with argument 0. It could be written as x.>(0), but there really is no reason to do so. Instead, some languages let you use an infix notation when invoking methods, which makes perfect sense for methods defined with symbolic names. This includes your own user-defined methods:

```
                                                              Scala
class Node:
    def --> (that: Node): Edge = Edge(this, that)
    ...
```

Listing 2.1: Example of a method defined with a symbolic name.

Given this definition, the expression a --> b can be used to create an edge between two nodes a and b. In effect, you have defined an operator "-->". In addition, you can sometimes specify that a method with a regular name can be used as an operator:

```
                                                              Scala
class Node:
    infix def to(that: Node): Edge = Edge(this, that)
    ...
```

Listing 2.2: Example of a method defined for infix invocation.

Given this definition, you can build an edge between a and b with the expression a to b.

2.5 Extension Methods

To further complicate matters—as if having to distinguish between functions, methods, and operators was not enough—programming languages often define features that bridge all three concepts. For example, functions, defined as methods, sometimes benefit from being invoked as methods instead of functions. (You read that right.) It might be that a function, say f(x,y,z), is better used as a method of its first argument: x.f(y,z).

Extension methods are a powerful mechanism that makes it possible to seemingly add methods to an existing type. They exist in a variety of programming languages, including Scala, Kotlin, C#, and Swift. They let you craft an existing function onto a type as an additional method.

As an illustration, assume that a function of two arguments has been defined (as a method) to shorten strings:

```
                                                              Scala
def shorten(str: String, maxLen: Int): String =
    if str.length > maxLen then str.substring(0, maxLen - 3) + "..." else str
```

This function can be invoked as follows:

```scala
shorten("Functional programming", 20) // "Functional progra..."
```

If desired, you can make this function look like a method of the **String** type by defining an extension:

```scala
extension (str: String)
    def short(maxLen: Int): String = shorten(str, maxLen)
```

Listing 2.3: Example of a method added to a type by extension.

With this extension in scope, a new method **short** can now be invoked on strings:

```scala
"Functional programming".short(20) // "Functional progra..."
```

Hybrid languages like Scala or Kotlin define other bridges between functions and methods. In Chapter 9, we will see a conversion that operates in the opposite direction: It lets you use a method where a function is expected.

2.6   Local Functions

Chapter 1 kicked off with the claim that the starting point of functional programming is the structuring of code in terms of functions. As a result, functional programs are often built from numerous small functions that target specific tasks. Most languages that support a functional programming style let you define functions within functions. Not that there is any reason to do so, but you could also write the absolute value function this way:

```scala
def abs(x: Int): Int =
    def max(a: Int, b: Int): Int = if a > b then a else b
    max(x, -x)
```

Listing 2.4: Example of a local function defined within another function.

This variant implements the absolute value of x as the largest of x and -x. It uses a local function max, defined inside function abs. In Scala, a block of code is an expression and has a value. A block's value is the value of the last expression evaluated in the block— max(x, -x) in this example—which is why no **return** keyword is needed. Blocks are delimited by curly braces, but braces can often be omitted if you use proper indentation, as in Listing 2.4.

An important property of local functions is that they can access the arguments and local variables of their enclosing function. As an even quirkier definition of absolute value, you could write:

```scala
                                                                                Scala
def abs(x: Int): Int =
  def maxX(a: Int): Int = if a > x then a else x
  maxX(-x)
```

Note how local function `maxX` uses variable `x`, which is not one of its arguments.

2.7   Repeated Arguments

Many programming languages support a notion of *repeated* or *variable-length* arguments, sometimes known as *"varargs."* The best-known example of a variable-length arguments function is `printf`. After a format string, the function takes an unspecified number of arguments:

```scala
                                                                                Scala
printf("%d bottles of beer\n", 99);      // prints the string "99 bottles of beer"
printf("%s: $%.2f\n", "total", 12.3456); // prints the string "total: $12.35"
```

Developers can define their own functions with repeated arguments:

```scala
                                                                                Scala
def average(first: Double, others: Double*) = (first + others.sum) / (1 + others.size)
```

Listing 2.5: Example of a function with variable-length arguments.

Here the * in the signature indicates that the argument `others` can appear 0 or more times. The following are all valid calls to function `average`:

```scala
                                                                                Scala
average(1.0, 2.3, 4.1)
average(10.0, 20.0)
average(10.0)
```

You can think of this feature as a mechanism used to define a family of functions: a one-argument `average` function, a two-argument `average` function, a three-argument `average` function, etc. This is also true of optional arguments and type parameters, which are described next.

2.8   Optional Arguments

Optional arguments are another feature that is available in many languages. They allow programmers to specify a default value for an argument, making this argument optional when you apply the function:

```scala
def formatMessage(msg: String,
                  user: String = "",
                  withNewline: Boolean = true): String =
  val sb = StringBuilder()
  if user.nonEmpty then sb.append(user).append(": ")
  sb.append(msg)
  if withNewline then sb.append("\n")
  sb.result()
```

Listing 2.6: Example of a function with default values for some of its arguments.

In this function, the `user` string defaults to the empty string, and the `withNewline` flag defaults to true. All of the following are valid calls of this function:

```scala
formatMessage("hello")               // "hello\n"
formatMessage("hello", "Joe")        // "Joe: hello\n"
formatMessage("hello", "Joe", false) // "Joe: hello"
```

2.9   Named Arguments

You may have a need to invoke the `formatMessage` function to format a message with no user and no newline:

```scala
formatMessage("hello", false) // rejected by the compiler
```

This does not work because the function expects a string as the second argument, not the Boolean false, which should be the *third* argument. To get around this difficulty, you need to specify the name of the argument explicitly:

```scala
formatMessage("hello", withNewline = false) // "hello"
```

With explicit names, arguments can be reordered arbitrarily. All of the following calls are valid:

```Scala
formatMessage(msg = "hello", user = "Joe")
formatMessage(user = "Joe", msg = "hello")
formatMessage(user = "Joe", withNewline = false, msg = "hello")
```

Even when they are not strictly necessary, you can sometimes rely on argument names to improve code readability:

```Scala
formatMessage("Tweedledee", "Tweedledum") // which is user and which is message?
formatMessage(msg = "Tweedledee", user = "Tweedledum") // clearer

Writer("/var/log/app.log", true) // what is true?
Writer("/var/log/app.log", autoflush = true) // clearer
```

2.10 Type Parameters

In many typed programming languages, functions can be parameterized by types. What this means is that a function not only uses typed arguments, but the types of these arguments (and the type of the return value) are themselves arguments of the function. This is known as parametric polymorphism, sometimes referred to as *generics* (Java) or *templates* (C++). Consider function `first`, which returns the first element of a pair:

```Scala
// DON'T DO THIS!
def first(pair: (Any, Any)): Any = pair(0)
```

Argument `pair` has type `(Any, Any)`, which represents pairs of any types—`Any` being the type of everything in Scala. The function can be applied to a pair of integers, as in `first((1, 2))`, or a pair of strings, as in `first(("A", "B"))`. The problem with this definition of `first` is that its return type is `Any`. When you apply `first` to a pair of integers, the function returns a value of type `Any`. This value happens to be an integer, but the type information is lost:

```Scala
first((1, 2))                      // has type Any
first((1, 2)) + 10                 // rejected by the compiler
first(("egg", "chicken"))          // has type Any
first(("egg", "chicken")).toUpperCase // rejected by the compiler
```

You might be tempted to get around the difficulty with a *typecast*:

```scala
// DON'T DO THIS!
first((1, 2)).asInstanceOf[Int] + 10                    // 11
first(("egg", "chicken")).asInstanceOf[String].toUpperCase // "EGG"
```

This is the wrong solution. A better approach is to use a type parameter in the definition of function `first`:

```scala
def first[A](pair: (A, A)): A = pair(0)

first((1, 2))                       // has type Int
first((1, 2)) + 10                  // 11
first(("egg", "chicken"))           // has type String
first(("egg", "chicken")).toUpperCase // "EGG"
```

Listing 2.7: Example of a function parameterized by a type; contrast with Lis. 2.8.

The function now has a type parameter `A` and produces a value of type `A` from a pair of type `(A, A)`. Adding `[A]` to the definition of function `first` makes `A` a (type) variable of the function. The name is irrelevant. You could define `first` as

```scala
def first[Type](pair: (Type, Type)): Type = pair(0)
```

but it is customary to use single-letter variables, like A, B or T.

Each instantiation of type `A` in Listing 2.7 results in a different function: `first[Int]` is a function that works on a pair of integers, `first[String]` is a function that works on a pair of strings, etc. When the expression `first((1, 2))` is compiled, type `A` is inferred[1] by the compiler to be `Int`, and the value returned by the function is thus of type `Int`, which is why the expression `first((1, 2)) + 10` is type-correct. In cases where type inference is unable to decide a type parameter, you can set it manually, as in `first[Int]((1, 2))` or `first[String](("egg", "chicken"))`.

Why is the use of type parameters preferable to typecasts? The main benefit is that a mistake, such as `first((1, 2)).toUpperCase`, will be caught at compile time. If you use a typecast instead, `first((1, 2)).asInstanceOf[String].toUpperCase` will only fail at runtime (by throwing a `ClassCastException`). The mistake could remain undetected until you write a test that exercises this code path.

Note that the expression `first((1, "chicken")) + 10` still cannot be compiled. The reason is that the compiler needs to infer a type `A` that is compatible with the

---

[1] Type inference is a mechanism by which a compiler calculates (infers) type information that is not provided explicitly by a programmer. It is discussed in Section 15.5.

integer 1 and the string "chicken". The compiler sets A to be Any,[2] the only type that contains both values. To better handle heterogeneous pairs, you can modify function first to use two type parameters:

Scala

```scala
def first[A, B](pair: (A, B)): A = pair(0)
```

Listing 2.8: Example of parameterization by multiple types; contrast with Lis. 2.7.

The expression first((1, "chicken")) + 10 can now be compiled, after the compiler infers types A=Int and B=String. Similarly, first(("egg", 2)).toUpperCase is a valid expression, with types A=String and B=Int.

Type parameterization is a powerful feature that you should use as often as possible. If you find yourself frequently testing and casting types at runtime, it could be a sign of inadequate leverage of type parameterization. Step back, and see if adding type parameters to functions, methods, or classes could help you avoid the typecasts.

2.11   Summary

- All mainstream programming languages implement at least one code-structuring abstraction that can be used to represent a function. In languages that favor object-oriented programming, many functions are implemented as methods.

- The role of a function is to produce output values from input values. Accordingly, functional code is typically structured in terms of function composition, in which the output of a function is used as the input of the next function.

- In addition to functions and methods, programming languages may rely on operators, often applied in prefix or infix notation. Some languages use symbolic names to implement some or all of their operators as functions or methods.

- Functions often rely on other, intermediate functions in their definition. In some languages, it is possible to define local functions within functions. A local function can access the arguments and local variables of its enclosing function directly, which simplifies its signature and improves code legibility. (This is similar to the use of local classes in object-oriented languages.)

- For increased flexibility, functions may use named arguments, repeated arguments (also called variable-length arguments or *varargs*), or default values. Some languages, such as Scala, Kotlin, and Python, implement all three mechanisms, while others, such as Java, support repeated arguments but not named arguments or default values.

---

[2]Technically, the type inferred by the Scala compiler is Matchable, a strict subtype of Any, but you can think of it as Any for all practical purposes.

- In typed languages, functions can often be parameterized by types, making it possible for developers to write code templates that implement multiple functions of different signatures. Effective use of type parameterization helps reduce the need for runtime type checks and typecasts and the risk of runtime exceptions they carry.

Chapter 3

Immutability

Functional programming is inspired by mathematical functions, which are not contingent on any notion of mutation, or state change, or variable assignment. A functional programming style favors immutable data. Imperative code based on mutation is replaced with programs that combine immutable values into expressions. In particular, series of immutable values are used as a substitute for the mutable data structures typical of imperative programs.

3.1   Pure and Impure Functions

Mathematical functions were characterized earlier as mappings of values from an input set to values in an output set. For instance, an absolute value function maps integers (of any sign) to non-negative natural numbers. Programming language functions are constructs that *can* represent mathematical functions, but they are not limited to this purpose. You can implement the mathematical absolute value function as a function of your favorite language—as we did earlier in Java, JavaScript, Python, Kotlin, and Scala[1]—but you can also write "functions" that perform I/O, interact with users and devices, block threads, or modify the state of an application is some arbitrary way.

At this point, I need to introduce some terminology to avoid writing about functions and "functions" for the remainder of the book. A standard way to refer to a programming function that represents a mathematical function is to say that the function is pure. Pure functions are characterized by two properties. First, their output is entirely determined by their input. In particular, when invoked multiple times on the same input, a pure function always produces the same output.[2] Second, pure functions do not modify the state of a system (or the state of its environment). These modifications are known as side effects: In addition to producing an output value, as is proper for a function, code with side effects modifies existing data. Functions that do not satisfy these two properties are said to be impure. Most programming languages let you write both pure and impure functions.

---

[1] The functions from Chapter 2 do not implement the mathematical absolute value function because their domain is not the infinite set of integers with the usual addition and subtraction operations, but rather a different set of 32-bit values with 2's complement arithmetic. Still, they implement a mathematical function, just not the standard absolute value.

[2] *Input* here is to be understood as an input *value*. When invoked multiple times on the same mutable object, a pure function could still produce different outputs because the object—and thus the input—has changed.

As an example of code that fails to satisfy the first property of pure functions, consider function `format`:

— *Scala* —
```scala
var prompt = "> "

def format(msg: String): String = prompt + msg
```

This function's behavior depends on the value of the external variable `prompt`. As a result, it might produce different outputs when you call it multiple times on the same input:

— *Scala* —
```scala
format("command") // "> command"
prompt = "% "     // change the prompt
format("command") // "% command"
```

Function `format` produces two different strings from the same input, making it impure.

As an illustration of the second characteristic of pure functions—the absence of side effects—recall function `firstString2` from Chapter 1, rewritten here in Scala (but still using Java lists):

— *Scala* —
```scala
import java.util

def firstString2(strings: util.List[String]): String = strings.remove(0)
```

This function returns the first string from its input list but also has the side effect that the value is removed from the list, making the function impure.

A function can even be impure by breaking *both* purity constraints:

— *Scala* —
```scala
var lastID = 0

def uniqueName(prefix: String): String =
    lastID += 1
    prefix + lastID

uniqueName("user-") // "user-1"
uniqueName("user-") // "user-2"
```

This function has the side effect of modifying variable `lastID`, on which its own computation depends, so it fails to meet both of the requirements needed to be pure. By contrast to these examples, function `firstString1`, which returns a string without removing it from the list, is pure (assuming that method `get` on a Java list is pure, which it is for standard list implementations).

Note that the two reasons that a function might be impure—side effects or dependency on external mutable state—are closely related. Both stem from the notion of mutable state: A function can be impure because of its own mutations, or because it is impacted by the mutations of other functions. In particular, in a program that consists entirely of functions free of side effects, all the functions are pure.[3] Mutation is the source of impurity.

3.2 Actions

Both functions `firstString1` and `firstString2` return the first string of a list, but `firstString2` also removes the string from the list as a side effect. A third variant of the function is possible, one that removes the first string, but does not return it:

```scala
def removeFirstString(strings: util.List[String]): Unit = strings.remove(0)
```

This function uses the same implementation as `firstString2`, but its return type is different: `Unit` instead of `String`. For a programmer new to functional programming, `Unit` is an unusual type. There is only one value of type `Unit`, typically referred to as *unit*, and represented in Scala by the token "`()`".

As a function, `removeFirstString` is not very useful: From its return type, you already know that the function will return *unit* before you even call it. So why call it as all? For its side effect of removing the first string from the list.

Type `Unit` is used when a function has nothing useful to return and is defined solely for the purpose of exploiting its side effects. Such functions are sometimes called procedures. In this book, I use the simpler and shorter term *action* instead of procedure, but this is not standard terminology. By choosing `Unit` as the return type, you can make it clear to the user that a function has side effects. Indeed, a function with return type `Unit` and no side effects would truly be useless.

Several hybrid languages rely on the `Unit` type to ensure that all methods are functions: Every method returns a value, even if this value is sometimes useless. As an older language, Java uses the notion of `void` methods, which do not return anything, and thus are not functions, not even peculiar ones. In Java, `removeFirstString` would be a `void` method, making it clear that it is invoked only for the purpose of exerting a side effect.

You can make your code less surprising by relying as much as possible on actions and pure functions. Take, for example, class `java.util.Arrays`. All its methods are either actions like `sort` or `fill` or `setAll`, which modify their input but return no value, or pure functions, like `binarySearch` or `hashCode` or `equals`, which return a new value without side effects.

Functions that include side effects but are not actions, like `firstString2`, tend to be more confusing. In particular, impurity is not obvious from the function's signature, since

---

[3]For this reason, "pure" is sometimes used loosely to mean "free of side effects."

a meaningful pure function could be defined with the same signature. This could lead you to call a function without being aware of its side effects, with adverse consequences. In other words, it is an easy mistake to use `firstString2` with the implementation of `firstString1` in mind.

Still, impure functions have their uses. When something has clear side effects—there is no way it could be a pure function—an action can safely be replaced by a function that returns something useful. For instance, the Java method `add`, which clearly adds a value to a set, also returns a Boolean:

Java

```
Set<String> set = ...;
if (set.add("X")) {
  // "X" was added and was not already in the set
} else {
  // "X" was already in the set, which was left unchanged
}
```

You can rely on the value returned by `add` to know if an element was indeed inserted into the set, or if the element was already in the set and did not need to be added.

A Boolean value is not the only choice that makes sense for an adding function. Scala's set method "+=", for instance, returns the set itself, making it possible to chain operations:

Scala

```
val set: Set[String] = ...
set += "X" -= "Y"
```

String "X" is first added to the set. Method "+=" returns the set itself, on which method "-=" is then applied to remove string "Y".

Note that method "-=" also returns the set, but in this example, the value being returned is ignored. In other words, "-=" is used here as if it were an action. When the return value of a function with side effects is ignored, I will sometimes refer to the function simply as an action instead of the more cumbersome "impure function used as an action."

In summary, there are three possible variants for a "first string" function:

Scala

```
// pure function, cannot be used as an action
def getFirstString(strings: util.List[String]): String = strings.get(0)

// impure function, can be used as an action
def getAndRemoveFirstString(strings: util.List[String]): String = strings.remove(0)

// action, cannot be used as a function
def removeFirstString(strings: util.List[String]): Unit = strings.remove(0)
```

Listing 3.1: Pure function versus impure function versus action.

The pure function has no side effects, while the action does not return any meaningful value. The impure function is a combination of both. You can argue that it is the most powerful and versatile combination, but it is also the most susceptible to bugs if used erroneously—that is, as if it were a pure function.

3.3 Expressions Versus Statements

While imperative programming is characterized by the use of statements, functional programming relies instead on expressions. Statements *do* things for the purpose of updating a mutable state. In contrast, expressions *are* things: They are values. In the code examples in Section 3.1, `prompt = "% "` and `lastID += 1` are statements;[4] `prompt + msg` and `prefix + lastID` are expressions.

Expressions are used in every programming style, including imperative. Languages that aim to support functional programming, however, typically give expressions a preeminence they do not have in imperative languages. In particular, functional programming languages tend to include additional mechanisms that are well suited to expressions. For instance, we have already seen that a code block in Scala is also an expression, equal to the value of the last expression in the block. In C or Java, a code block has no value and cannot be used as an expression.

As another example, consider conditionals. If you are used to imperative programming, you are familiar with `if-then-else` as a construct used to select statements based on a Boolean condition:

Java

```
if (num > 100) println("large"); else println("small");
```

Listing 3.2: Example of `if-then-else` as a statement; contrast with Lis. 3.3.

This code is a statement that prints `large` for large numbers and `small` for small numbers. It is not an expression. Java's `if-then-else` is ill suited to combine expressions. If `f` and `g` are pure functions, the code

Java

```
if (condition) f(x); else g(y);
```

is silly: It evaluates either `f` or `g` depending on a condition, but since these functions have no side effect, it might as well do nothing. To be effective, a Java `if-then-else` must involve statements, for instance via assignments or actions:

Java

```
if (condition) r = f(x); else someAction(g(y));
```

---

[4]In C or Java, the statement `prompt = "% "` is also an expression, with value `"% "`. Like impure functions, statements that are also expressions can be a source of confusion. In more recent languages, such as Scala or Kotlin, `prompt = "% "` is used only as a statement. As an expression, it has type `Unit` and is useless.

By contrast, `if-then-else` in a functional programming language is used to select *expressions* based on a Boolean condition, and it is itself an expression:[5]

Scala
```scala
if num > 100 then "large" else "small"
```

Listing 3.3: Example of `if-then-else` as an expression; contrast with Lis. 3.2.

This line is a value, of type `String`, that is equal to either `"large"` or `"small"` depending on the condition. You can use this value anywhere a string might be used:

Scala
```scala
(if num > 100 then "large" else "small").toUpperCase
"the number is " + (if num > 100 then "large" else "small")
println(if num > 100 then "large" else "small")
```

In the last line of this example, the `if-then-else` expression is used as the input to action `println`. This has the same effect as the Java program in Listing 3.2, but proceeds differently: Instead of selecting between two print statements, `if-then-else` is used to select between two strings, and the selected string is printed. Of course, nothing prevents you from using `if-then-else` to combine expressions with side effects. The behavior of Listing 3.2 can also be achieved in Scala as follows:

Scala
```scala
if num > 100 then println("large") else println("small")
```

This is still an expression, but its value—*unit*—is useless. The expression is evaluated only for its side effect.

As an expression, `if-then-else` makes no sense without the `else` part, which is typically required in a functional programming language. However, `if-then` (with no `else`) does make sense when using actions. As a hybrid language, Scala implicitly substitutes `else ()` for a missing `else` clause when `if-then-else` is used imperatively.

Another fundamental construct used in imperative programming to combine statements is the `while`-loop (and its `for`-loop and `do`-loop derivatives). Although they are useful with statements, loops make little sense with expressions: The repeated evaluation of a pure function is pointless. When shifting from imperative to functional programming, such ineffective loops can be replaced with either recursion (Chapters 6 and 7) or higher-order functions (Chapters 9 and 10).

3.4   Functional Variables

The most fundamental statement is the assignment statement, often denoted as "=", or sometimes as ":=". It is the most common source of side effects. All the side effects in the code illustrations so far have been caused by assignments, either directly (for

---

[5]Functions `abs`, `max`, and `shorten`, in Chapter 2, use `if-then-else` as an expression.

example, to modify variables `prompt` and `lastID`) or indirectly (for example, inside the implementation of list method `remove`). A functional programming style aims at eliminating side effects so as to write programs in terms of pure functions. Not surprisingly, this means targeting the assignment statement for elimination (or at least much reduced usage).

If you look closely at the Scala examples so far, you'll notice that I have introduced some local variables with the keyword `val`, and others with the keyword `var`. You may also notice that the `var` variables were used as the targets of assignment statements, but the `val` variables were not. Indeed, the distinctive difference between the two is that `val` is used to proscribe assignments:

```
Scala
val two = 2
val three = two + 1
two = two + 1 // rejected by the compiler
```

What `val` really does is give a name to an expression. Despite similarities in the syntax, you are better off thinking of `val two = 2` as giving the name `two` to the value 2, rather than as *assigning* 2 to *variable* `two`. Because of its `val` definition, `two` is not an ordinary variable in the C or Java sense. In particular, it cannot be reassigned with a different value. If you attempt to write this kind of assignment, such as `two = two + 1` or `two = 3`, the compiler will reject it as a "reassignment to `val`" error.

As a consequence of this restriction, `two` and 2 are now equivalent expressions; wherever the name `two` appears (within the scope of the `val` declaration), it means 2. This property is known as *referential transparency*: The expressions `two` and 2 are interchangeable, and one can always be substituted for the other. You do not need to carefully parse code to see if `two` is being modified somewhere, because it cannot be changed. This would not be true if `two` was introduced as a reassignable variable, using `var`. Then it could be initialized with 2 at the beginning of the program but have another value by the time it is used inside a later expression.

Names introduced using `val` are often said to be functional variables. You might also see them being referred to as *immutable*, *non-reassignable*, or *assign-once* variables. Functional programming languages rely heavily on this notion of variables. Hybrid languages might complement functional variables with old-fashioned, reassignable variables. In Scala, the declaration `var two = 2` assigns the value 2 to the name `two`, but the variable can later be updated via assignment statements like `two = 3` or `two += 1`, and the referential transparency property is lost.

If you are new to functional programming, you may find the idea of programming without assignments quite puzzling. Still, if you want to practice with a functional programming style in a language that supports both types of variables, you should strive to maximize your use of functional variables. Purists might even consider any use of an assignment statement to be a "code smell," but pragmatic users of hybrid languages will know when reassignable variables are warranted, and when they are better avoided.

As an illustration, consider the problem of parsing a command-line option to set a verbosity level: 0 is the default level, -v sets it to 1, and -vv sets it to 2. An imperative programmer could implement this as follows:

```
                                                           ── Scala ──
var verbosity = 0
if arg == "-v" then verbosity = 1
else if arg == "-vv" then verbosity = 2
```

This sets `verbosity` to the desired value, but the variable is reassignable, and there is no referential transparency. Could `verbosity` be declared as a `val` instead? A programmer used to a more functional style would implement the calculation in this way:

```
                                                           ── Scala ──
val verbosity = if arg == "-v" then 1 else if arg == "-vv" then 2 else 0
```

The trick is to use `if-then-else` functionally, as an expression, and then to set `verbosity` to the value of that expression, once and for all.

If your experience has been mostly with imperative programming, you may find the first version easier to understand. It does take a little time to get used to thinking in terms of expressions instead of statements. As a trend, however, many programming languages offer improved support for programming with expressions. Java, for instance, retrofitted its `switch` statement in version 14 to become an expression. You could use it to implement the parsing example:

```
                                                           ── Java ──
final int verbosity = switch (arg) {
   case "-v"  -> 1;
   case "-vv" -> 2;
   default    -> 0;
};
```

In Java, `final` is used to prevent variable reassignment. If you use the earlier imperative approach to define `verbosity`, you won't be able to mark it as `final`.

3.5   Immutable Objects

Declaring a variable using `val` guarantees that the name continues to refer to the same value while in scope. However, if this value is a mutable object, the object itself might still change (as in Listing 2.6, for instance). To get the full power of referential transparency, you need to use `val` to refer to *immutable* values.

An object is immutable, also called *functional* or *persistent*, if its own state cannot be changed. Many common Java types, such as `String` and `BigInteger`, define immutable objects. You are probably already familiar with the benefits of using immutable objects, such as for avoiding aliasing issues or facilitating inter-thread sharing. A functional programming style emphasizes their use even more, a pattern sometimes known as functional–object-oriented programming.

Like defining `val` variables or thinking of `if-then-else` as an expression, using and designing immutable objects may require some adjustment if you come from an imperative programming mindset. You will need to get used to different interfaces and programming patterns.

Consider sets as an example. The Scala standard library implements both mutable and immutable sets. If you come from a Java or Python background, mutable sets feel completely natural:

```scala
val set = Set("A", "B") // a mutable set
set += "C"
// set is now {A,B,C}
```

The action `set += "C"` modifies the set by adding `"C"` to it. Alternatively, you can rewrite the example using an immutable set, stored in a mutable variable:

```scala
var set = Set("A", "B") // an immutable set
set = set + "C"
// set is now {A,B,C}
```

Instead of a "+=" method that modifies the set, immutable sets define a "+" method that creates a new set from an existing set. The set on which method "+" is applied is not modified—it is immutable.

Avoid the common mistake of using persistent structures with a mind frame that expects mutability:

```scala
// DON'T DO THIS!
var set = Set("A", "B") // an immutable set
set + "C"
// set is still {A,B}
```

Here, method "+" is used as if its effect was to modify a set by adding an element. But that is not what the method does. Instead, a new set is created—and not used—and variable `set` is unchanged, so it is still equal to the set $\{A, B\}$.

3.6   Implementation of Mutable State

To be able to "add" C to an immutable set $\{A, B\}$, I had to store the set in a `var`, not a `val`. A variable defined as a `val` on an immutable set cannot be modified in any way. The mutable set, in contrast, can be stored in a `val`: The set itself is modified, and the variable is never reassigned.

Often, you have a choice between an immutable type in a `var` and a mutable type in a `val` as means to implement the same mutable state. Both approaches have their merits and weaknesses. In general, using immutable structures leads to easier data sharing and reuse, but mutable structures can have slightly better performance, and can also facilitate the delegation of thread-safety in concurrent programming (see Section 19.5). Scala uses methods named "+=" and "-=" on many mutable types to make both variants look similar:

```scala
                                                          Scala
val set = Set("A", "B") // a mutable set
set += "C" // a call to method +=; that is, set.+=("C")
// set is now {A,B,C}

var set = Set("A", "B") // an immutable set
set += "C" // a reassignment of a var; that is, set = set + "C"
// set is now {A,B,C}
```

The similarity makes it easier to switch from one approach to the other. However, it can also be a source of confusion:

```scala
                                                          Scala
var set = Set("A", "B") // a set of unknown type
set += "C" // is this a call to += or a reassignment of a var?
```

A common practice in Scala is to use immutable types by default: Set, unqualified, usually refers to a persistent set. To use mutable types, you need to import them explicitly. Use a strategy that makes it clear that a mutable type is being used:

```scala
                                                          Scala
val set1 = Set(1, 2, 3)

import scala.collection.mutable
val set2 = mutable.Set(1, 2, 3)

import scala.collection.mutable.Set as MutableSet
val set3 = MutableSet(1, 2, 3)
```

In this code, set1 is immutable, while set2 and set3 are mutable. Importing scala.collection.mutable.Set without renaming—as I did earlier in the chapter—is considered bad practice.

NOTE

For convenience and readability, I often use, throughout the book, formulations like "an element is added to/removed from the set" or "the list is reversed" or "the kth value is replaced," even when referring to persistent structures. These statements are intended to mean "a new set is created with an element added/removed," "a new list is created containing all values in reverse order," etc.

3.7 Functional Lists

The most widely used persistent data structure in functional programming is the functional list. Either a list is empty (no elements) or it consists of a first value (called the *head*), potentially followed by more values (the *tail*). Every list can be built from two primitives: the empty list and an operator that combines a head element with an existing list. Traditionally, the empty list is called "nil," and the operator is called "cons." This terminology dates back to the days of Lisp, with the list [1,2,3] being built as follows:

```
                                                                   Lisp
(cons 1 (cons 2 (cons 3 nil)))
```

The nested expression starts with the empty list `nil`, uses `cons` to build the list (cons 3 nil), which is the list [3], then uses `cons` again to add 2, then 1, in front of the list. The head of the final list is 1; its tail is the list (cons 2 (cons 3 nil)).

Languages of the ML family popularized the use of the infix operator ":·:" to represent `cons`. It is also being used in more recent languages like F# and Scala. The Lisp code just given can be written in Scala as follows:

```
                                                                   Scala
1 :: 2 :: 3 :: Nil
```

Again the head of the list is 1, and its tail is 2 :: 3 :: Nil.

For convenience, languages define factory functions to build lists. You can build the list [1,2,3] in Lisp as (list 1 2 3) and in Scala as List(1, 2, 3). Scala also defines a function `List.empty` that returns `Nil`; I sometimes use this version for clarity and better type inference. However, it is essential to keep in mind the `nil`/`cons` structure of functional lists for at least two reasons.

First, building a new list from an existing list does not, in general, require a full copy of the original list. This is because different lists can often share data. As an illustration, consider the three lists a, b, and c defined as follows:

```
                                                                   Scala
val a = List(1, 2, 3)   // the list [1,2,3]
val b = 0 :: a          // the list [0,1,2,3]
val c = a.tail          // the list [2,3]
```

The memory allocation of these three lists looks something like Figure 3.1. Although the three lists together contain nine values, there are only four cells allocated in memory, thanks to data sharing between a, b, and c. Because lists are immutable, this sharing is harmless. The same is true, to some degree, of other persistent data structures. The method "+" used earlier on an immutable set does not make a full copy of the set. If largeSet contains 1 million elements, largeSet + x is a new set that contains 1 million and one elements, but the two sets share the vast majority of the memory allocated to implement them.

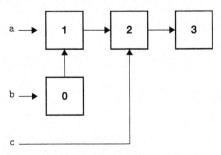

Figure 3.1 Functional lists memory sharing.

Another consequence of this data sharing is that, on functional lists, *both* the head and the tail methods are efficient, constant-time operations—typically, a single pointer dereference. As long as you can express an algorithm in terms of head and tail, lists make a reasonable implementation choice. Be aware, however, that other list operations may not be as fast. Methods such as last and length, for instance, require a computing time that is proportional to the length of the list, and methods such as appended or concat need to copy the entire list.

The second reason the head/tail structure of functional lists is important is that the tail of a non-empty list is itself a list. In consequence, many computations on lists can be implemented efficiently using recursion. Chapter 7 is dedicated to recursive programming with lists.

3.8 Hybrid Designs

In a purely functional programming approach, all functions are pure, and all values are immutable. There is nothing wrong with that—and plenty that is good—but sometimes programmers prefer a more hybrid approach that combines pure functions and values with actions and mutable objects. If you are used to an imperative programming style, you can start using some functional programming features without committing to a fully functional design. In particular, there are some benefits from relying on immutable values when building mutable objects, and vice versa.

In a hybrid application that combines pure functions, impure functions, and actions, you need to worry about possible side effects when calling functions that are not under your control. The beauty of immutable values is that they can be shared safely, knowing that no unexpected side effect can modify them.

As an illustration, consider an application that keeps track of registered users in a mutable set:

```scala
type Directory = mutable.Set[String]

def register(dir: Directory, user: String): Unit = dir += user
```

Listing 3.4: A directory as a mutable set; contrast with Lis. 3.5.

Users are added via a **register** action, which modifies the set.

Now suppose that you need to call a function that is not under your control—say, **newRegistrations**, which calculates the set of newly registered users, given an earlier directory:

```scala
val yesterdayDir: Directory = ...
val todayDir: Directory    = ...
register(todayDir, "new user 1")
register(todayDir, "new user 2")
val todayReg = newRegistrations(todayDir, yesterdayDir)
```

The problem here is that function **newRegistrations** is not necessarily pure. It could be implemented as follows:

```scala
def newRegistrations(newDir: Directory, oldDir: Directory): Directory =
  newDir.subtractAll(oldDir)
```

This implementation removes from the set **newDir** every user already in the set **oldDir**, and returns **newDir**. The return value is correct, but the set **newDir** has been modified.

Because you worry that **newRegistrations** could be implemented like this, you need to make sure that the directories you pass as arguments will not be modified. So, you end up calling **newRegistrations** on copies of your directories:

```scala
val todayReg = newRegistrations(toDayDir.clone(), yesterdayDir.clone())
```

Unless you know for sure that `newRegistrations` does not modify its arguments,[6] you cannot dispense with the calls to `clone`, sometimes known as *defensive copies*. The sad part of this story is that it also possible—likely, even—that `newRegistrations` is implemented as a pure function. In that case, the defensive copies are entirely wasted.

Wasted defensive copies are actually quite common[7] in large applications that depend on a multitudes of libraries. You can avoid them by using immutable directories instead:

Scala

```scala
type Directory = Set[String]

def register(dir: Directory, user: String): Directory = dir + user
```

Listing 3.5: A directory as an immutable set; contrast with Lis. 3.4.

Registration relies on a pure function that produces a new set of registered users, but does not modify its input. You can use an immutable directory in an application as follows:

Scala

```scala
val yesterdayDir: Directory = ...
var todayDir: Directory     = ...
todayDir = register(todayDir, "new user 1")
todayDir = register(todayDir, "new user 2")
val todayReg = newRegistrations(todayDir, yesterdayDir)
```

Function `newRegistrations` can be called on directories directly, without cloning—immutable sets do not even have a public `clone` method in Scala. There is no danger of a side effect inside `newRegistrations` modifying them: They are immutable!

Note that the application is not written in a functional style: It uses assignment statements as side effects and sequential composition to chain modifications. Still, the imperative code benefits from using immutable directories by avoiding unnecessary defensive copies.

You might argue that no one in their right mind would implement the function `newRegistrations` by modifying the input set. Maybe. But can you rely on a stance that all libraries should use reasonable code? In an ideal world, you would depend on documentation to confirm that `newRegistrations` has no side effects. But how often have you found library documentation to be deficient?

---

[6]This includes tomorrow's implementation of the function. So, if the function is not under your control, checking the source code is not enough. You need some guarantees, typically in the documentation, that the function not only *is* but *will remain* pure.

[7]It can also be the case that you are calling a method that stores its arguments and makes its own defensive copies because it worries that the arguments might be modified after the call. In the worst case, you may end up cloning objects both on the calling side and inside the code that is called. Paradoxically, sharing immutable objects often results is less memory allocation, not more.

3.9 Updating Collections of Mutable/Immutable Objects

As noted earlier, a non-reassignable variable can refer to an immutable object or a mutable object. In the same way, an immutable structure, like a functional list or a persistent set, can contain mutable or immutable objects. This has an impact on how you update a state that uses those structures.

Consider the following scenario as an illustration. Data is represented as immutable lists of Load objects. Each Load object has a weight, which can be reduced by one. A mutable variant of Load implements two methods:[8]

```scala
                                                                — Scala —
trait Load:
    def weight: Int     // current weight
    def reduce(): Unit  // reduce load weight by one
```

Listing 3.6: Example of a mutable type; contrast with Lis. 3.7.

An application needs to perform an operation that reduces the weight of all the loads in a list by one. You can implement it as follows:

```scala
                                                                — Scala —
def reduceAll(loads: List[Load]): List[Load] =
    for load <- loads do load.reduce()
    loads
```

Even though the list is immutable, its contents are being modified. However, the same list, containing the same objects, is returned.

Alternatively, you could implement loads as an immutable type:

```scala
                                                                — Scala —
trait Load:
    def weight: Int    // current weight
    def reduced: Load  // a reduced load, with a weight reduced by one
```

Listing 3.7: Example of an immutable type; contrast with Lis. 3.6.

The weight method is unchanged from before. However, since loads are now immutable, the reduce action is replaced with a reduced function without side effects, which produces a new load with a reduced weight. You can no longer implement the function reduceAll by modifying the loads. Instead, new load objects must be created and then

---

[8]Traits can be used in Scala to define public interfaces. They can do more, like "mix-ins," but they are used only as interfaces in this book.

stored into a new list. You can replace the `for-do` syntax with a `for-yield` syntax that does just that:

```scala
def reduceAll(loads: List[Load]): List[Load] = for load <- loads yield load.reduced
```

Method `reduced` is applied to all the loads in the list but, since it has no side effects, the loads do not change. Instead, all the new load objects that are created by `reduced` are assembled into a new list, which is returned. In general, `for-yield` applies a function to a collection of values and returns a new collection with the outputs.[9] The function being applied is typically pure.

3.10 Summary

- The responsibility of a function is to calculate an output value from one or more input values. While doing so, functions should refrain from depending on an external mutable state and from modifying anything in a system (or its environment) through side effects. This includes modifying the function's arguments, if they are mutable.

- Functions that adhere to this contract are said to be pure. A functional programming style emphasizes the use of pure functions as often as possible.

- Programming with pure functions is programming with values: Output values produced by functions are used as input arguments to other functions. This results in a programming style centered on expressions instead of statements. Programming languages that support a functional style often reflect this choice in their control structures. In Scala, for instance, `if-then-else` is an expression, and so are code blocks.

- In functional programming, the main use of variables is to name expressions. The resulting names are variables in the mathematical sense, as in "let x be $\sqrt{2}$ in ...." They are not variables in the C/Java sense of memory locations that can be reassigned. Hybrid languages make use of both kinds of variables: functional (non-reassignable) variables and traditional, imperative (reassignable) variables. In Scala, these variables are introduced by the keywords `val` and `var`, respectively.

- Functional programming and object-oriented programming can be combined into a functional–object-oriented programming style that centers on immutable objects, also called functional objects. Methods on a functional object are not used to modify the object, but rather to produce a new object.

---

[9]The `for-yield` syntax is somewhat particular to Scala, although other languages define similar constructs. The more universal way to implement this transformation is to use a higher-order function called `map`. See Section 10.9 for a discussion of `map` and its relationship with `for-yield`.

- Immutable objects can be used as components to implement other objects, which can be mutable or immutable. Because the underlying objects are immutable, references to them can be freely shared across class/method boundaries, eliminating the need for defensive copies.

- Mutable objects, in particular, can be implemented in terms of reassignable fields that refer to immutable objects, or in terms of fields—usually non-reassignable—that refer to other mutable objects. Using immutable objects in reassignable fields tends to make data sharing easier—for example, making it harmless to publish references on an object's internal data.

- In functional programming libraries, data structures are often implemented as immutable values (possibly objects). Conceptually, data is added to a structure by creating another structure, but the previous structure is unchanged. For this reason, immutable data structures are sometimes called persistent. The most common persistent structure in functional programming is the functional list. A non-empty list consists of a first value, called the head, potentially followed by a list of more values, called the tail.

- Head access and tail access are efficient, constant-time operations on functional lists, and do not involve copying. Other persistent data structures, such as sets and maps, also implement fast adding and removing operations that do not require copying the entire collection.

- Functional programming languages define standard operations to process collections of immutable values. To those, hybrid languages add operations to process collections of mutable objects. In Scala, these operations are available through a `for-do` and `for-yield` syntax.

Chapter 4

Case Study: Active–Passive Sets

To help cement the ideas explored in Chapters 1 to 3, this first case study develops several variants of a small program. The functionality to be implemented is a structure that keeps track of the states of a collection of objects. Each element from the collection can be in an *active* or *passive* state. States can be queried, and changed from passive to active, or from active to passive. The state of the entire collection can also be queried and modified by global operations that activate or deactivate all the elements. The service is implemented in a classic object-oriented style, a purely functional style, and a hybrid style that uses functional objects.

4.1 Object-Oriented Design

Consider first a standard, object-oriented implementation—nothing functional here. An `ActivePassive` class is parameterized by the type of active/passive elements. It is implemented in terms of a mutable set, `activeSet`, used to represent the subset of elements that are active—elements outside the set are passive. Initially, all the elements are passive, and this set is empty.

```scala
class ActivePassive[A](elements: Set[A]):
  private val activeSet = mutable.Set.empty[A]

  def isActive(elem: A): Boolean = activeSet.contains(elem)

  def isPassive(elem: A): Boolean = !isActive(elem)

  def allActive: Set[A] = activeSet.toSet

  def allPassive: Set[A] = elements diff activeSet

  def isAllActive: Boolean = activeSet.size == elements.size

  def isAllPassive: Boolean = activeSet.isEmpty

  def activate(elem: A): Unit = activeSet += elem

  def deactivate(elem: A): Unit = activeSet -= elem
```

```
def activateAll(): Unit = activeSet ++= elements

def deactivateAll(): Unit = activeSet.clear()
```

Listing 4.1: Object-oriented active-passive sets, using underlying mutable sets.

This class uses two fields: `elements`, an immutable set (initialized in the constructor), and `activeSet`, a mutable set, initially empty. Methods `isActive` and `isPassive` are implemented in terms of lookups in `activeSet`: An element is active if it is found, and inactive if it is not found.[1] A user can retrieve the set of all currently active elements by calling method `allActive`. This method makes a copy of the mutable `activeSet` using method `toSet`, which returns an immutable set.[2] To produce a set of all inactive elements, you need to calculate the set difference between `elements` and `activeSet`, which is done with method `diff` in Scala. Method `isAllActive` must return true exactly when all the elements are active—in other words, when `elements == activeSet`. Since `activeSet` is always a subset of `elements`, this is equivalent to the faster test `activeSet.size == elements.size`. Implementing `isAllPassive` is simpler: Just test if `allActive` is empty. To activate an element, you add it to the (mutable) set `activeSet`. To deactivate an element, you remove it from the set. To activate all the elements, you add the entire `elements` set to `activeSet`. To deactivate all the elements, you simply clear the `activeSet`.

Instances of class `ActivePassive` are mutable: They change when elements are activated or deactivated. The implementation in Listing 4.1 relies on a mutable set, but you could implement a mutable `ActivePassive` class using immutable sets instead. Listing 4.2 shows this version.

Scala

```
private var activeSet = Set.empty[A]

def allActive: Set[A] = activeSet

def activate(elem: A): Unit = activeSet += elem

def deactivate(elem: A): Unit = activeSet -= elem

def activateAll(): Unit = activeSet = elements

def deactivateAll(): Unit = activeSet = Set.empty
...
```

Listing 4.2: Object-oriented active-passive sets, using underlying immutable sets.

---

[1] As always, argument checking is omitted. It is assumed that `isActive`, `isPassive`, `activate`, etc., are always called on members of the `elements` set.

[2] In Java, you could avoid the copy by returning an immutable wrapper on the mutable set—`Collections.unmodifiableSet(activeSet)`—but Scala has no such mechanism in its standard library.

Method `allActive` is simpler than before: You can just return a reference on field `activeSet` instead of having to copy the set. This works because `activeSet` is an immutable set, and returning a reference to it is harmless. The code for methods `activate` and `deactivate` looks unchanged but is actually compiled differently. Instead of calling methods `+=` and `-=` on a mutable set, you are now creating a new immutable set and reassigning field `activeSet` with it. (The similarity in this syntax was discussed in Section 3.6.) Methods `activateAll` and `deactivateAll` are implemented without any set operation. They simply (and efficiently) reset field `activeSet` with the value `elements`, or with an empty set. The other methods (`isActive`, `isPassive`, `allPassive`, `isAllActive`, and `isAllPassive`) are unchanged.

In summary, there are two ways you can define `activeSet` to implement a mutable active–passive set:

```scala
private val activeSet = mutable.Set.empty[A]  // in Listing 4.1
private var activeSet = Set.empty[A]          // in Listing 4.2
```

In one case, you activate/deactivate elements by modifying a mutable set. In the other case, you do it by building a new immutable set and reassigning a mutable field.

4.2 Functional Values

Let us now put on our functional programmer hat and rewrite the active–passive example entirely in terms of pure functions and immutable values. We need some type to represent `ActivePassive` values. A typical functional approach is to use pairs:[3]

```scala
opaque type ActivePassive[A] = (Set[A], Set[A])
```

The first set in a pair represents the entire collection; the second set is the subset of active elements. Both sets are immutable. All the remaining code is written as functions:

```scala
private def elements[A](ap: ActivePassive[A]): Set[A]  = ap(0)
private def activeSet[A](ap: ActivePassive[A]): Set[A] = ap(1)

def createActivePassive[A](elements: Set[A]): ActivePassive[A] = (elements, Set.empty)
```

---

[3]Because of the keyword `opaque`, this definition makes the types `ActivePassive[A]` and `(Set[A], Set[A])` distinct. This prevents you from using a `(Set[A], Set[A])` value by mistake as an argument to a function that expects `ActivePassive[A]`, and vice versa. In particular, you avoid the risk of calling an active–passive function with a pair that does not represent an active–passive set—that is, one in which the second set is not a subset of the first set.

```scala
def isActive[A](ap: ActivePassive[A], elem: A): Boolean = activeSet(ap).contains(elem)

def isPassive[A](ap: ActivePassive[A], elem: A): Boolean = !isActive(ap, elem)

def allActive[A](ap: ActivePassive[A]): Set[A] = activeSet(ap)

def allPassive[A](ap: ActivePassive[A]): Set[A] = elements(ap) diff activeSet(ap)

def isAllActive[A](ap: ActivePassive[A]): Boolean =
  elements(ap).size == activeSet(ap).size

def isAllPassive[A](ap: ActivePassive[A]): Boolean = activeSet(ap).isEmpty

def activate[A](ap: ActivePassive[A], elem: A): ActivePassive[A] =
  (elements(ap), activeSet(ap) + elem)

def deactivate[A](ap: ActivePassive[A], elem: A): ActivePassive[A] =
  (elements(ap), activeSet(ap) - elem)

def activateAll[A](ap: ActivePassive[A]): ActivePassive[A] =
  (elements(ap), elements(ap))

def deactivateAll[A](ap: ActivePassive[A]): ActivePassive[A] =
  (elements(ap), Set.empty)
```

Listing 4.3: Functional active–passive sets.

The querying functions are similar to the corresponding methods used in the object-oriented implementations. They differ by the use of an explicit argument `ap` instead of implicitly using `this`:

```scala
// in Listings 4.1 and 4.2
def isAllActive: Boolean = activeSet.size == elements.size

// in Listing 4.3
def isAllActive[A](ap: ActivePassive[A]): Boolean =
  activeSet(ap).size == elements(ap).size
```

Because active–passive sets are now immutable, the operations that activate or deactivate elements change more substantially. They now need to create a new value: a new active–passive pair that differs from the previous one by having some elements activated or deactivated. Notice that the signatures are different from before: Instead of `Unit`, they now have `ActivePassive[A]` as their return type. For instance, to activate a single element `elem` in function `activate`, you create a new active set, `activeSet(ap) + elem`, and use it to make a new active–passive pair. Two private functions are added to access pair elements so as to avoid writing all the code in terms of `ap(0)` and `ap(1)`, which would be error-prone. Finally, the class constructor from the object-oriented variants is replaced with a `createActivePassive` function.

All the functions used in the implementation are pure, and active–passive values are used by function composition. Instead of

```scala
ap.activateAll()
ap.deactivate(A)
ap.deactivate(B)
```

in an object-oriented design, you write

```scala
deactivate(deactivate(activateAll(ap), A), B)
```

in the functional variant.

4.3   Functional Objects

In a hybrid programming language, you can combine the choice of immutable values (as in the functional implementation) with the use of methods instead of functions (as in the object-oriented implementations). In this functional–object-oriented approach, active–passive values are immutable objects:

```scala
class ActivePassive[A] private (elements: Set[A], activeSet: Set[A]):
  def this(elements: Set[A]) = this(elements, Set.empty[A])

  def isActive(elem: A): Boolean = activeSet.contains(elem)

  def isPassive(elem: A): Boolean = !isActive(elem)

  def allActive: Set[A] = activeSet

  def allPassive: Set[A] = elements diff activeSet

  def isAllActive: Boolean = activeSet.size == elements.size

  def isAllPassive: Boolean = activeSet.isEmpty

  def activate(elem: A): ActivePassive[A] = ActivePassive(elements, activeSet + elem)

  def deactivate(elem: A): ActivePassive[A] = ActivePassive(elements, activeSet - elem)

  def activateAll(): ActivePassive[A] = ActivePassive(elements, elements)

  def deactivateAll(): ActivePassive[A] = ActivePassive(elements, Set.empty)
```

Listing 4.4: Functional–object-oriented active–passive sets.

The `ActivePassive` class is back, but defined differently. Both fields, `elements` and `activeSet`, are now immutable sets and are never reassigned.[4] As a consequence, active–passive objects are never modified. Instead, activation and deactivation methods return a new active–passive set, as in the functional variant. To activate an element, for instance, you create a new `activeSet`, as in Listing 4.3, but instead of using it to build a new pair, you wrap the set into a new `ActivePassive` instance. Internally, each new active–passive set is built using a private, two-set constructor. Users, however, can only use a single-set public constructor (`def this` in the source code). This makes it impossible for them to create nonsensical objects in which `activeSet` is not a subset of `elements`.

As with the functional variant, these active–passive sets rely on function composition, but you write the code with a method-call syntax. Instead of

```Scala
deactivate(deactivate(activateAll(ap), A), B)
```

you now write

```Scala
ap.activateAll().deactivate(A).deactivate(B)
```

As a final note, be aware that mutable and immutable variants typically use different function and method names. To better highlight differences and similarities, I used the same names in all the variants. In practice, the functional variants should use names consistent with the fact that values are immutable. We saw, for instance, that mutable sets in Scala use a method `+=`, while immutable sets use `+`. Similarly, arrays have a method `update`, while lists have a method `updated`. Here, the immutable variant of `ActivePassive` in Listing 4.4 would have been better written using `activated`, `deactivated`, `allActivated`, and `allDeactivated` instead of `activate`, `deactivate`, `activateAll`, and `deactivateAll`.

4.4   Summary

The point of this case study is to illustrate the differences between mutable and immutable data. There are really two variants of the active–passive sets here: Listings 4.1 and 4.2, on the one hand, and Listings 4.3 and 4.4, on the other hand. The first two implement a mutable variant, the last two an immutable variant.

The fact that Listing 4.1 relies on mutable sets while Listing 4.2 uses immutable sets is an implementation choice. From a user standpoint, the two `ActivePassive` classes are equivalent. In the same way, Listing 4.3 is expressed in terms of pairs and functions, while Listing 4.4 uses a class and methods instead. It slightly changes how you write code—for example, `activate(ap, A)` versus `ap.activate(A)`—but underneath,

[4]In Scala, fields introduced in the constructor are implicitly `val`, unless you use `var` explicitly.

both implementations are the same. They both represent active–passive sets as pairs of immutable sets, either using a built-in pair type, or our own, two-field `ActivePassive` class as a wrapper. Both implementations share the same fundamental property that active–passive sets are immutable, and activation/deactivation always creates a new set.

When using a true functional programming language, you are likely to write this immutable variant directly in terms of functions. However, with a hybrid object-oriented/functional language, using functional objects is an attractive option that arguably results in cleaner code than a purely functional implementation.

You may wonder about the relative performance of each implementation—the question of performance always comes up when discussing immutability. Immutable active–passive sets incur two performance costs:

- Activation and deactivation of elements require the allocation of a new wrapping container for the two sets—either a pair or an instance of class `ActivePassive`. Discarded pairs, sets, and wrappers also create additional work for the garbage collector.

- Methods `+=` and `-=` on mutable sets are likely to be slightly more efficient than `+` and `-` on immutable sets, though not necessarily by much.

Overall, these disadvantages are likely to be minor compared to the benefit of simpler and safer data sharing and should not stop you from going the immutable route if that's what makes sense for your application. As always, there is no need to worry about minor differences in performance until profiling has established that they contribute to a bottleneck in your application.

Chapter 5

Pattern Matching and Algebraic Data Types

Most functional programming languages—as well as many of the hybrid languages that aspire to support functional programming—define a form of *pattern matching*. Pattern matching has many uses, from a simple switch-like construct to runtime type checking and casting, but it is most effective when applied to algebraic data types, which combine alternatives and aggregation.

5.1   Functional Switch

As a starting point, you can think of pattern matching as a form of functional `switch`. For instance, the earlier example using `if-then-else`

```scala
val verbosity = if arg == "-v" then 1 else if arg == "-vv" then 2 else 0
```

could be rewritten to use pattern matching instead:

```scala
val verbosity = arg match
    case "-v"  => 1
    case "-vv" => 2
    case _     => 0
```

Listing 5.1: Example of pattern matching used as a *switch* expression.

The whole `match-case` is an expression, used to set `verbosity`. Cases are considered in order, and the value of the whole pattern matching expression is the value associated with the first pattern that matches. The underscore represents a default case, which matches anything. There is no fall-through. The same expression can be associated with multiple patterns, as in `case "-v" | "--verbose" => 1`.

This is only the tip of the iceberg, though. Pattern-matching is much more than a simple switch expression and is used in more ways. For one thing, conditions—sometimes called *guards*—can be added to patterns:

── *Scala* ───

```scala
arg match
    case "--"                                    => ... // end of options
    case longOpt if longOpt.startsWith("--")     => ... // long option
    case shortOpt if shortOpt.startsWith("-")    => ... // short option
    case plain                                   => ... // plain argument
```

Listing 5.2: Example of pattern matching with guards.

Like the underscore, a simple variable name like **plain** matches anything. Adding a condition prevents a pattern from matching some values: **longOpt** by itself would match any string, but when you add the condition, it matches only strings that start with two dashes. The order is important. The third case matches everything that the second case matches, and thus has to come later. Both the second and third cases would match the string "--", which has to come first.

Pattern matching can also be used to perform runtime type testing and casting. This feature should not be abused, however, especially when subtype polymorphism can be used instead (see Section 15.6). However, it has its uses—for instance, when catching exceptions:

── *Scala* ───

```scala
try ...
catch
    case _: IOException           => // an I/O exception
    case e: IllegalStateException => // can refer to the exception, e.g., e.getMessage
    case _: Exception             => // some other exception
```

Listing 5.3: Example of pattern matching for type testing/casting.

Note how ordering again is important: The pattern **case _: Exception** would catch I/O and illegal state exceptions if it appeared at the top.

A functional switch with guards can be very useful, but to fully leverage the power of pattern matching, you need to apply it to composite types and types with alternatives. These types are sometimes referred to as *algebraic data types* (see the aside on sum and product types at the end of Section 5.5). The next few sections explore several common types of that nature.

5.2   Tuples

The simplest way to compose two types is to aggregate them into a pair. For instance, (**String, Int**) is Scala's type for pairs in which the first value is a string and the second value is an integer, like ("foo", 42) or ("bar", 0). This generalizes to *N*-tuples.

You can use pattern matching not only to "switch" between tuples—for instance, to select pairs in which the second value is zero—but also to extract values from the tuple:

```scala
                                                                  ──── Scala ────
val pair: (String, Int) = ("foo", 42)

pair match
    case (str, 0) => ... // no match because the number in pair is not zero
    case (str, n) => ... // str is the string "foo", n is the integer 42
```

Listing 5.4: Example of pattern matching to extract tuple elements.

If you only care about extracting the values, you can use a tuple pattern outside the `match` construct:

```scala
                                                                  ──── Scala ────
val (str, n) = pair // str is the string "foo", n is the integer 42
```

This is equivalent to

```scala
                                                                  ──── Scala ────
val str = pair(0)
val n   = pair(1)
```

Functional programming languages rely heavily on tuples as a mechanism to aggregate values. In an object-oriented language, you can use classes for this purpose. As a hybrid language, Scala implements tuples, but it also defines a notion of case classes, which you can often use to aggregate data. A noteworthy benefit of case classes is that they enable pattern matching.[1]

```scala
                                                                  ──── Scala ────
case class TempRecord(city: String, temperature: Int)

val rec = TempRecord("Phoenix", 122)

rec.city        // "Phoenix"
rec.temperature // 122

val TempRecord(name, temp) = rec // name is "Phoenix", temp is 122
```

By using a case class instead of a tuple, you can sometimes improve code legibility—`rec.city` instead of `rec(0)`—while keeping the convenience of pattern matching. In particular, you can define separate, distinct types that all contain the same type components, like a city and a temperature, or a label and a count, or a unit of time and a duration, instead of the more generic `(String, Int)`. Case classes are used for convenience in several of this book's case studies and illustrations.

---

[1]Case classes also differ from regular classes in a few other ways (they redefine equality and string representation, and their constructor arguments are implicitly public `val` variables), but they are mostly used in this book for the purpose of pattern matching.

5.3   Options

Tuples aggregate values but offer no choice: A pair is always made of two values. Other types are defined to take one of multiple forms as alternatives. Options are a simple and widely used type with two alternatives: An option can contain a value or it can be empty. Consider the following example:

```scala
val someNum: Option[Int] = Some(42)
val noNum: Option[Int]    = None
```

A value of type `Option[Int]`[2] represents either a single integer or nothing. You can use it as the return type of a function that is not guaranteed to produce a result, such as a search that may or may not find what it is looking for. Returning options is much preferable to using null for this purpose, a topic we will explore in Chapter 13.

You can use pattern matching on options:

```scala
optNum match
   case Some(x) => if x > 0 then x else 0
   case None    => 0
```

Listing 5.5: Example of pattern matching to both *switch* and *extract*.

In this example, `optNum` is an optional number, of type `Option[Int]`. If it contains a positive number, Listing 5.5 produces that number. Otherwise—if the option is empty or the number is not positive—it produces zero. In this example, pattern matching is powerful because it serves two purposes: It lets you decide whether an option is empty, and it is used to extract the value out of a non-empty option. You could achieve the same computation using a pattern with a condition:

```scala
optNum match
   case Some(x) if x > 0 => x
   case _               => 0
```

The underscore pattern handles any value that did not match the first pattern, in this case an option with a non-positive number or an empty option. Note that you can flip the patterns in the first variant, but not the second:

---

[2]Scala's `Option` type is called `Optional` in Java, and `Maybe` is other programming languages.

```scala
                                                                  ── Scala ──
optNum match
   case None    => 0
   case Some(x) => if x > 0 then x else 0
```

This code still works, but this next variant does not:

```scala
                                                                  ── Scala ──
// DON'T DO THIS!
optNum match
   case _              => 0
   case Some(x) if x > 0 => x
```

The underscore pattern matches anything, and the second pattern is unreachable.

5.4   Revisiting Functional Lists

Earlier, I introduced the notion of functional lists: Either a functional list is empty, or it consists of a head and a tail. Like options, the list type is based on an alternative: empty or non-empty. But like tuples, it also relies on aggregation: a head and a tail. This makes pattern matching ideal to process lists effectively. Using patterns, you can decide whether a list is empty, but you can also extract the head and tail of a non-empty list. In particular, pattern matching can be used to implement functions `head` and `tail` independently from the `head` and `tail` methods defined in the standard `List` type:

```scala
                                                                  ── Scala ──
def head[A](list: List[A]): A = list match
   case h :: _ => h
   case Nil    => throw NoSuchElementException("head(empty)")

def tail[A](list: List[A]): List[A] = list match
   case _ :: t => t
   case Nil    => throw NoSuchElementException("tail(empty)")
```

Listing 5.6: Reimplementing `head` and `tail` using pattern matching.

Observe how patterns are used to distinguish between empty and non-empty lists, and to capture the relevant part of a non-empty list, using an underscore for the part you wish to ignore.

Other list functions could be reimplemented using pattern matching—for instance, isEmpty:

```scala
def isEmpty[A](list: List[A]): Boolean = list match
  case Nil => true
  case _   => false

def isEmpty[A](list: List[A]): Boolean = list match
  case _ :: _ => false
  case _      => true
```

Listing 5.7: Reimplementing isEmpty using pattern matching.

The first variant uses Nil to match the empty list, and "_" to match every other—and therefore non-empty—list. The second variant matches non-empty lists first, using pattern "_ :: _", which matches any list with a head and a tail. The next pattern matches only the list without a head and tail—the empty list—and could have used Nil instead of "_" for clarity. Either approach is correct.

In the implementation of function isEmpty, patterns are used only to distinguish between empty and non-empty lists, while in head and tail they also extract a component from a non-empty list. Depending on your needs, you can match a non-empty list with any of the following patterns:

```scala
_ :: _              // nothing captured
head :: _           // capture head only
_ :: tail           // capture tail only
head :: tail        // capture head and tail
all @ head :: tail  // capture head, tail, and the entire list
all @ head :: _     // capture head and the entire list
all @ _ :: tail     // capture tail and the entire list
all @ _ :: _        // capture the entire list
```

Patterns can be nested arbitrarily. In particular, you can use "@" to capture a component of a composite type while breaking it into its own components at the same time. For instance, if an expression is a list of options of pairs, pattern matching can be applied to the list, and to an option inside the list, and to a pair inside an option, all within the same pattern:

```scala
List(Some(("foo", 42)), None) match
  case (head @ Some(str, n)) :: tail => <expr>
```

Inside expression <expr>, variables head, str, n, and tail denote the following values:

```
head is Some(("foo", 42))    : the first option in the list
str  is "foo"                : the first half of the pair in the first option
n    is 42                   : the second half of the pair in the first option
tail is List(None)           : the other options in the list
```

Finally, note that Scala defines additional list patterns for convenience. Instead of "x :: Nil", which matches a list with a single element, you can use the more readable pattern List(x). In a same way, a list of exactly three elements can be matched using List(x, y, z) instead of the awkward x :: y :: z :: Nil. Some of these more readable patterns are used in later code examples.

5.5 Trees

In this chapter, we have already applied pattern matching to several algebraic data types: tuples, options, and lists. Tuples are used to aggregate multiple types, options are an alternative between a type or nothing, and lists are defined both in terms of an alternative between empty and non-empty lists and as the aggregation of a head and a tail.

In addition to involving both alternatives and aggregation, the list type has the remarkable property of being defined inductively: Either a list is empty, or it consists of the aggregation of a value (the head) and another list (the tail). A data type like this is said to be recursive: Inside a (non-empty) list, there is a list. Trees are another classic recursive data type, frequently used in programming.

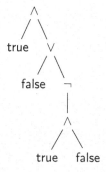

Figure 5.1 true ∧ (false ∨ ¬(true ∧ false)) as a tree.

As an illustration, consider trees that represent expressions. The Boolean expression true ∧ (false ∨ ¬(true ∧ false)) is represented as the tree from Figure 5.1. You can implement such a tree in Scala as an *enum* type:

```scala
                                                                    ── Scala ──
enum BoolExpr:
   case T
   case F
   case Not(e: BoolExpr)
   case And(e1: BoolExpr, e2: BoolExpr)
   case Or(e1: BoolExpr, e2: BoolExpr)
```

Listing 5.8: Boolean expressions as an algebraic data type.

As with lists, the tree type involves alternatives (five possibilities), aggregation (left and right operands of And and or), and recursion (Not, And, and Or are trees that contain subtrees). Using this type, the tree in Figure 5.1 becomes the following expression:

$$\texttt{And(T, Or(F, Not(And(T, F))))}$$

Trees can be processed very naturally using pattern matching to switch between alternatives and to extract subtrees. For instance, you can write a function that evaluates a tree to its truth value:

```scala
                                                                    ── Scala ──
def eval(expr: BoolExpr): Boolean =
   import BoolExpr.*
   expr match
      case T          => true
      case F          => false
      case Not(e)     => !eval(e)
      case And(e1, e2) => eval(e1) && eval(e2)
      case Or(e1, e2)  => eval(e1) || eval(e2)
```

Listing 5.9: Recursive evaluation of Boolean expressions using pattern matching.

Given the recursive nature of trees, it is not surprising that function eval is itself recursive. Recursion is the topic of Chapter 6.

Aside on Sum and Product Types

Explorations of types like the options, pairs, lists, and trees used in this chapter are often framed in terms of sum and product types. You do not need to know the names to effectively use these types, but a brief discussion of this terminology can help you better understand the algebraic nature of such types.

Consider two Scala types defined as follows:

```scala
                                                                    ── Scala ──
type Stooge = "Larry" | "Curly" | "Moe"
type Digit = 0 | 1 | 2 | 3 | 4 | 5 | 6 | 7 | 8 | 9
```

For the purpose of our discussion, types can be thought of as sets of values: The type `Boolean` contains two values, true and false; `Int` has 2^{32} possible values; and `String` has an infinite number of values. Here, we rely on two small types: `Stooge`, with three values, and `Digit`, with ten values.

Product types are used for aggregation. For instance, the pair type `(Stooge, Digit)` contains values that consist of one stooge and one digit:

```scala
————————————————————————————————————————— Scala ——
type StoogeAndDigit = (Stooge, Digit)
```

This type contains 30 values—`("Moe", 5)`, `("Larry", 1)`, etc.—which is the product of the number of stooges and the number of digits (hence the name). Instead of a pair, you might use a class to join a stooge and a digit in an object-oriented language. In the context of this note, all the types that aggregate one stooge with one digit are equivalent, and denoted as `Stooge` × `Digit`.

Types can be aggregated in arbitrary ways. For instance, the type `StoogeLink = (Stooge, Stooge, Boolean)`, denoted as `Stooge` × `Stooge` × `Boolean`, contains all 18 values that consist of two stooges and one Boolean.

Support for product types is almost universal in programming languages, whether through classes, records, or tuples. Functional languages, and many hybrid languages, also support sum types, which represent alternatives. A value that can be a stooge *or* a digit can be given a type `StoogeOrDigit`, defined as follows:

```scala
————————————————————————————————————————— Scala ——
enum StoogeOrDigit:
  case S(stooge: Stooge)
  case D(digit: Digit)
```

This type contains 13 values—`S("Larry")`, `S("Curly")`, `S("Moe")`, `D(0)`, `D(1)`, ..., `D(9)`—which is the sum of the number of stooges and the number of digits. The names `S` and `D` are irrelevant, and the type is denoted as `Stooge` + `Digit`. Note that sums can be built from types that are not disjoint sets:

```scala
————————————————————————————————————————— Scala ——
enum Number:
  case Zero
  case Pos(digit: Digit)
  case Neg(digit: Digit)
```

`Pos(3)` and `Neg(3)` are different values, and the `Number` type contains 21 values. The name `Zero` is no more relevant than the names `Pos` and `Neg`, and the type can be denoted as `Digit` + `Digit` + 1, where "1" represents the single-valued type that contains `Zero`.

Scala defines standard product types—all tuples are a subtype of `Product`—and sum types. For instance, `Option` defines a sum type as an alternative between a value or none. The type `Option[Stooge]` has four values: `Some("Moe")`, `Some("Larry")`, `Some("Curly")`, and `None`. We can denote it as `Stooge + 1`.

Given × and + thus (loosely) defined, algebraic transformations can be applied to types. For instance, `(Stooge+1) × Digit`—an optional stooge aggregated with a digit—can be implemented as the pair `(Option[Stooge], Digit)`. By distributing × over +, this type can be said to be equivalent to `(Stooge ×  Digit) + Digit`, a type that could be implemented in this way:

```scala
enum StoogeAndDigitOrDigit:
  case SD(stooge: Stooge, digit: Digit)
  case D(digit: Digit)
```

Conceptually, this type represents the same 40 values as type `(Option[Stooge], Digit)`. For instance, `(Some("Moe"), 5)` corresponds to `SD("Moe", 5)`, and `(None, 8)` is `D(8)`.

Finally, sums and products can be defined in a circular way, leading to recursive data types, like the type `BoolExpr` tree defined earlier, or a list of integers `IntList`, defined as `IntList = 1 + (Int × IntList)`, and implemented as follows:

```scala
enum IntList:
  case Nil
  case Cons(head: Int, tail: IntList)
```

5.6   Illustration: List Zipper

As a simple illustration of the power of pattern matching, this section implements a data type known as a *zipper*. This zipper is defined in terms of a pair of lists, making it possible to rely on various patterns in the code.

Consider the problem of maintaining a non-empty sequence of values with a cursor that points to the current element. You want to be able to move the cursor left or right, and to query or update the value under the cursor. A mutable implementation can simply store an index alongside an array of values. All the required operations can easily be achieved in constant time. The drawback of using a mutable type is that you may need defensive copies when passing values to and from functions (see our earlier discussion in Section 3.8). Even moving the cursor could require cloning the entire array.

What would be nice instead is an immutable implementation. A naive approach could store an index alongside a functional list. However, this would be inefficient. Recall that accessing an element at a specified index in a functional list is not a constant-time operation: It takes time proportional to the value of the index. Furthermore, to change a value at index n, you would have to discard n elements from the list, and allocate a new list of length n. For instance, if the index points to the first "a" in list [P,l,$\boxed{a}$,t,o], and you want to replace it with "u" to produce [P,l,$\boxed{u}$,t,o], you will need to create a new list [P,l,u]:

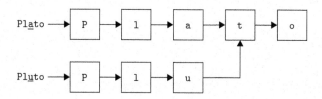

The zipper is a clever data structure that avoids this drawback. It is implemented as a pair of lists (*left*, *right*): The second list contains the elements right of the cursor; the first list contains the elements left of the cursor, but in *reverse order*. All the necessary operations—moving the cursor left or right, and querying and updating the element under the cursor—can then be implemented in constant time.

To help visualize zippers, consider again the list [P,l,$\boxed{a}$,t,o] with current element "a". It is represented as this zipper:

```scala
(List('l', 'P'), List('a', 't', 'o'))
```

Moving the cursor to the right produces the new zipper:

```scala
(List('a', 'l', 'P'), List('t', 'o'))
```

To implement zippers, first define a `Zipper` type as a pair of lists. A zipper value is constructed from a non-empty list of elements:

```scala
type Zipper[A] = (List[A], List[A])

def fromList[A](list: List[A]): Zipper[A] = (Nil, list)
```

Listing 5.10: List zipper definition and construction.

When you construct a zipper from a list, the cursor is in the leftmost position (no elements in the left list). A zipper always contains at least one value (the current element), and the right list in a pair is never empty (a proper implementation of `fromList` would reject an empty list argument with an exception).

The head of the right list is the element under the cursor. It can be queried and updated efficiently:

```scala
                                                                      Scala
def get[A](zipper: Zipper[A]): A = zipper match
  case (_, x :: _) => x

def set[A](zipper: Zipper[A], value: A): Zipper[A] = zipper match
  case (left, _ :: right) => (left, value :: right)
```

Listing 5.11: List zipper getting and setting.

Function `get` uses a pattern that matches pairs in which the second element is a non-empty list, with head `x`. This head is the value under the cursor and is returned. Since zippers are immutable, function `set` updates the value under the cursor by producing a new zipper. The pattern `_ :: right` matches a non-empty right list with an unspecified head. A new zipper is built by using a new right list with the `value` argument as its head. Thanks to data sharing in functional lists, both `set` and `get` are constant-time operations. Furthermore, the new zipper produced by function `set` also shares data with the zipper used as the argument—all of the first list and most of the second list.

To move the cursor to the left, you need function `moveLeft` to move the rightmost element left of the cursor from the first list to the second list. Because the elements left of the cursor are stored in reverse order, the element to move is the head of the first list, which needs to become the head of the second list: `x :: left` becomes `left`, and `right` becomes `x :: right`. In the preceding example, `(List('a','l','P'), List('t','o'))` becomes `(List('l','P'), List('a','t','o'))`. If the cursor is already in the leftmost position, the zipper is returned unchanged. This case is captured by the underscore pattern:

```scala
                                                                      Scala
def moveLeft[A](zipper: Zipper[A]): Zipper[A] = zipper match
  case (x :: left, right) => (left, x :: right)
  case _                  => zipper

def moveRight[A](zipper: Zipper[A]): Zipper[A] = zipper match
  case (left, x :: right) if right.nonEmpty => (x :: left, right)
  case _                                    => zipper
```

Listing 5.12: List zipper navigation.

Moving the cursor to the right is similar: Take the head of the second list and move it to the head of the first list. However, you also need to avoid moving the cursor past the rightmost element, since this would leave a zipper with no current value. The condition in the first pattern of function `moveRight` guarantees that the second list in the new zipper is non-empty. Both cursor movements are implemented as constant-time operations.

Instead of a condition, you could use the pattern "`_ :: _`" to ensure that `right` is non-empty:

```scala
                                                          ──── Scala ────
def moveRight[A](zipper: Zipper[A]): Zipper[A] = zipper match
  case (left, x :: (right @ _ :: _)) => (x :: left, right)
  case _                             => zipper
```

This also works but, unless you are programming in a language without pattern conditions (like SML), the variant with a condition is more readable.

Finally, a zipper can be turned back into a list if needed:

```scala
                                                          ──── Scala ────
def toList[A](zipper: Zipper[A]): List[A] = zipper match
  case (left, right) => left.reverse ::: right
```

Listing 5.13: Conversion from list zipper to list.

The left list, which stores elements left of the cursor in reverse order, is reversed back, and the elements right of the cursor are appended ("$:::$" is list concatenation in Scala). This is not a constant-time operation: It takes time proportional to the position of the cursor—the length of the first list.

Zippers can be designed for other types, such as trees, using a similar approach: One half of a pair represents the view at the cursor position, while the other half stores the steps used to bring the cursor there, in reverse order. A zipper on N-ary trees is implemented as a case study in Chapter 11.

5.7 Extractors

We have seen how pattern matching can be used to switch between alternatives and to extract components of a composite type. As a generalization, pattern matching can sometimes be used to decompose into parts a type that is not naturally composite.

As an example, consider the problem of extracting the alpha, red, green, and blue components from a color represented as a 32-bit ARGB integer. It can be implemented as follows:

```scala
                                                          ──── Scala ────
object ARGB:
  def unapply(argb: Int): (Int, Int, Int, Int) =
    var bits = argb
    val b = bits & 0xFF
    bits >>>= 8
    val g = bits & 0xFF
    bits >>>= 8
    val r = bits & 0xFF
```

```
val alpha = bits >>> 8
(alpha, r, g, b)
```

Listing 5.14: Example of an extractor (RGB values).

In Scala, the name **unapply** of the function plays a special role. With object ARGB in scope, you can now use pattern matching to split a number into its color elements:

```scala
———— Scala ————
val ARGB(a, r, g, b) = 0xABCDEF12
```

This sets variable a to 0xAB, variable r to 0xCD, etc.

Object ARGB is called an *extractor*. Many extractors are defined in the Scala standard library. For instance, you can use pattern matching to retrieve captured groups in regular expressions:[3]

```scala
———— Scala ————
val Phone: Regex = """(?:\+1\s)?([2-9]\d{2})[\s-]([2-9]\d{2})-?(\d{4})""".r

def formatNumber(str: String): Option[String] = str match
  case Phone(npa, nxx, number) => Some(s"($npa) $nxx-$number")
  case _                       => None

formatNumber("603 5551234")     // Some("(603) 555-1234")
formatNumber("+1 603-555-1234") // Some("(603) 555-1234")
formatNumber("6035551234")      // None
```

Listing 5.15: Example pattern matching on a regular expression.

5.8   Summary

- Pattern matching is a common feature of functional programming languages. In its simplest form, you can think of it as a powerful form of a `switch` expression. It can be used to test Boolean conditions, compare values to constants, or check runtime types.

- The real power of pattern matching, however, comes from being used to process algebraic data types. What characterizes these types is that they are defined in terms of alternatives (also called sums) and aggregations (also called products) of other types. Pattern matching can be used to switch between alternatives, and to extract components in aggregated types.

---

[3]In Scala, the r method creates a regular expression out of a string. Also, the s prefix enables interpolation in string literals: s"$x" is a string that contains the value of x.

- A number of algebraic data types are commonly used in functional programming. Some, like tuples and options, are very simple, yet versatile. Others, like lists and trees, are defined inductively and exhibit a recursive structure. Experienced functional programmers rely heavily on these types, and process them effectively using either pattern matching or higher-order functions (see Chapter 9).

- Pattern matching is especially handy when used on types that involve both an alternative and some aggregation, like functional lists: Patterns can be used to distinguish a non-empty list from an empty list, and to break a non-empty list into its head and tail.

- Some languages define a notion of extractors, which can be used to bring the power of pattern matching to non-composite types like integers and strings.

Chapter 6

Recursive Programming

Loops—the repetition of a code fragment—do not mesh well with functional programming's emphasis on pure functions, which gain nothing from being repeated. What is needed instead is a mechanism to nest expressions arbitrarily. This mechanism is recursion. Everything that can be computed with loops can be computed using recursion instead (and vice versa). Furthermore, algorithms that are naturally recursive benefit from an implementation that uses recursion directly, which tends to be simpler than the loop-based equivalents. This is especially true of computations that apply to recursive structures, such as lists and trees. Finally, tail recursive functions constitute a class of loop-like recursive functions that functional programming languages tend to implement directly as loops, for performance reasons.

6.1 The Need for Recursion

As mentioned earlier, loops are not well suited to functional programming, due to the central role given to immutability. Indeed, in the absence of side effects, there is no point in repeating a calculation—and that is exactly what loops are for. But you cannot simply ditch loops without having a replacement. Programs need to perform millions of operations without having millions of lines of code, so there has to be a way to "repeat" or "jump" (and no, we are not going to reintroduce GOTO).

Consider a simple imperative program as an illustration. It is based on a mutable collection type and uses an action that removes and processes one element from a non-empty collection:

```scala
// processes one element and removes it
def processOne[A](collection: MutableCollection[A]): Unit = ...
```

To process an entire collection, you simply use this action in a loop:

```scala
def processCollection[A](collection: MutableCollection[A]): Unit =
  while collection.nonEmpty do
    processOne(collection)
```

What would the processing of a collection look like in the functional world? First, you would replace the mutable collection with an immutable one. Then, since you cannot actually remove anything from an immutable collection, you would need to replace the action `processOne` with a function[1] that processes an element and returns a new collection with that element removed:

```scala
─────────────────────────────────────────────────── Scala ───
// processes one element, and returns a collection with this element removed
def processOne[A](collection: ImmutableCollection[A]): ImmutableCollection[A] = ...
```

So far, so good. Now, you need a way to use this function to process an entire collection, one element at a time. The same approach as before will not do: If `collection.nonEmpty` is true, `processOne(collection)` will not change that—the collection is immutable. Therefore, `collection.nonEmpty` will remain true, and the loop will never terminate. Can a loop be used at all? Yes, and this program would work:

```scala
─────────────────────────────────────────────────── Scala ───
def processCollection[A](collection: ImmutableCollection[A]): Unit =
  var remaining = collection
  while remaining.nonEmpty do
    remaining = processOne(remaining)
```

This gets the job done, but at the cost of reintroducing mutation through an assignment statement: Something in the body of the loop must have some side effect, and since `collection` cannot change, a mutable variable `remaining` is introduced. (The same approach was used in Section 3.6 to implement a mutable state in terms of an immutable data structure.) The loop-based solution works only because there is mutation. To achieve a fully immutable style—no `var`—you need to take a different route.

If a function `f` is free of side effects, the repetition `f(x); f(x); f(x)` is pointless. Think of code that executes `Math.sqrt(4.0); Math.sqrt(4.0); Math.sqrt(4.0)`. What is the point? Instead, the output of `f` must be used, typically as the input to further computing. Instead of loops, what you need is a mechanism that can arbitrarily nest function calls. This mechanism is recursion.

Let's go back to the problem of processing an entire immutable collection. A function needs to process one element from the collection and then process, in the same fashion, a new collection with that one element removed. In other words, you need to invoke `processOne` on the value produced by a previous call to `processOne`. Since `processCollection` is designed to invoke `processOne`, all you need to do is to call `processCollection` again on the output of `processOne`:

```scala
─────────────────────────────────────────────────── Scala ───
def processCollection[A](collection: ImmutableCollection[A]): Unit =
  if collection.nonEmpty then processCollection(processOne(collection))
```

Listing 6.1: Nesting function calls through recursion.

An initial call to `processCollection` processes the first element of a collection, and produces a new, reduced collection. This collection is then processed in the same way

---

[1]This function is not pure because processing an element must have some side effect. However, it has no side effect on the collection itself, which is all that matters for the purpose of this illustration.

through another call to function `processCollection`, and so on. The computation that processes the entire list is `processOne(processOne(processOne(...)))`, which is of the form `f(f(f(x)))`, not `f(x); f(x); f(x)`. No mutable variable is involved.

You can always replace code that uses loops and mutable variables with code that uses recursion and immutable variables instead. Function composition combined with recursion has the same expressive power as sequential composition combined with loops. Anything that can be computed using one of these approaches can be computed using the other.

6.2 Recursive Algorithms

In textbooks and tutorials, `factorial` is the most widely used example of a recursive function. Since no book that discusses recursive programming would be complete without it, here it is, in Scala:

Scala
```scala
def factorial(n: Int): Int = if n == 0 then 1 else n * factorial(n - 1)
```

Listing 6.2: Recursive implementation of `factorial`; contrast with Lis. 6.11.

This code is certainly elegant. It is shorter and uses fewer variables than a loop-based alternative. However, I do not believe it makes a very good motivation for the use of recursion. You can easily implement a factorial function with a loop, and the resulting code is likely to be more efficient. The same can be said of many other typical textbook illustrations of recursion, such as the greatest common divisor.[2] So, if you have seen the factorial example in the past, and it has left you unimpressed, no worries. This book contains dozens of examples of recursive functions, and ideally you will find later illustrations more persuasive.

The *Tower of Hanoi* is another classic teaching example, which is a more effective example than the factorial or greatest common divisor problem. It represents a puzzle, in which discs of assorted sizes are stacked on three pegs. Initially, all the discs are stacked on the leftmost peg, in decreasing order of size. The objective of the game is to move all the discs to the rightmost peg, using the middle peg for intermediate storage, and while adhering to the following rules:

- You can move only one disc at a time.
- Only the topmost discs can be moved.
- No disc can rest on top of a smaller disc.

Figure 6.1 shows the seven steps required to move a three-disc tower from left to right.

You can solve the Tower of Hanoi problem with a recursive algorithm: To move n discs from peg L to peg R using peg M, if $n > 0$, first move $n - 1$ discs from L to M

---

[2]Currently, the first three examples of recursive code on the Wikipedia page on *recursive programming* are factorial, greatest common divisor, and the Tower of Hanoi, which is discussed in this section.

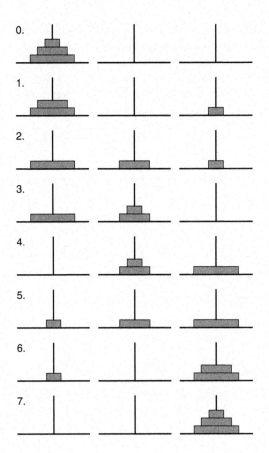

Figure 6.1 Tower of Hanoi problem.

using R; then move one disc from L to R; then move $n-1$ discs from M to R using L. If $n = 0$, there is nothing to do. This strategy can be translated into a recursive function that prints all the steps needed to move a given number of discs:

Scala

```scala
def hanoi[A](n: Int, from: A, middle: A, to: A): Unit =
  if n > 0 then
    hanoi(n - 1, from, to, middle)
    println(s"$from -> $to")
    hanoi(n - 1, middle, from, to)
```

Listing 6.3: Recursive solution to the Tower of Hanoi problem.

This function does nothing if $n = 0$. Otherwise, a first recursive call is used to move $n-1$ discs from the left peg to the middle peg, using the right peg as temporary storage. The effect of this call is to leave the nth disc free (position 3 in Figure 6.1). The print statement then moves this disc from left to right (position 4 in Figure 6.1). A second recursive call moves $n-1$ disc from their storage peg (middle) to the right peg, using the left peg as storage. When called as `hanoi(3, 'L', 'M', 'R')` this function produces the same sequence of steps as Figure 6.1:

```
L -> R
L -> M
R -> M
L -> R
M -> L
M -> R
L -> R
```

What makes the Tower of Hanoi a compelling example is that there is no straightforward loop-based equivalent that implements the same algorithm.[3] One reason for this is that function `hanoi` makes *two* recursive calls to itself, compared to the single call needed in the factorial or greatest common divisor examples.

6.3 Key Principles of Recursive Algorithms

The core idea behind recursive algorithms is to reduce a problem to one or more *smaller* instances of the *same* problem and to use the solutions to these subproblems to derive a solution to the original problem. The Tower of Hanoi function in Section 6.2 solves the problem of moving n discs by combining the solutions to two subproblems of moving $n - 1$ discs. Think of this strategy as a special case of the *divide and conquer* approach in which the subtasks are homologous with the original task.

When writing a recursive function, you need to pay attention to three major concerns:

- *At least one branch of the computation should not be recursive.* If the evaluation of your function always triggers a recursive call, the function keeps re-executing itself and cannot possibly terminate. In the Tower of Hanoi example, the case $n = 0$ does not require a recursive call.

---

[3]There are iterative solutions to the Tower of Hanoi that can be easily implemented in terms of loops, but their correctness is harder to justify, and even the simplest loop-based program is still more complex than the recursive function presented here.

Keep this principle in mind to help catch mistakes quickly. For instance, consider this incorrect attempt to define a function to extract the last element of a list:

```scala
                                                          ─── Scala ───
// DON'T DO THIS!
def last[A](list: List[A]): A = list match
   case Nil       => throw NoSuchElementException("last(empty)")
   case _ :: tail => last(tail)
```

Listing 6.4: Incorrect implementation of `last`; fixed in Lis. 6.10.

The algorithm is based on the idea that the empty list has no last element and that the last element of a non-empty list is the last element of its tail. However, the function cannot possibly work as written because it does not have a value-returning, non-recursive branch: The function either throws an exception or continues to run. Indeed, the intuition that the last element of a non-empty list is the last element of its tail is not valid on a list of size 1.

- *All the subproblems solved recursively must be smaller than the original problem in some way.* This is again necessary to guarantee termination. Common patterns include a list function applied to a shorter list; a number function applied to a smaller positive number (as in the case of `hanoi`); a tree function applied to a subtree; and so on.

As an illustration of a failure to adhere to this principle, consider this incorrect implementation of merge-sort (function `merge` is omitted):

```scala
                                                          ─── Scala ───
// DON'T DO THIS!
def mergeSort[A](list: List[A]): List[A] =
   if list.isEmpty then list
   else
      val (left, right) = list.splitAt(list.length / 2) // split in the middle
      merge(mergeSort(left), mergeSort(right))
```

Listing 6.5: Incorrect merge sort; fixed in Lis. 7.18.

Method `splitAt` splits a list as a given point: `List(A,B,C,D).splitAt(2)` is the pair `(List(A,B), List(C,D))`. This method is used to split a non-empty list into two halves. Each half is sorted recursively, and the two sorted halves are merged into a sorted list.

The issue here is that `mergeSort(right)` is not guaranteed to be a recursive call on a smaller list. If you split a list that contains exactly one element, you get two lists: One is empty, and the other is the original list unchanged. In the case of function `mergeSort`, this means that `right` could be the same as `list`, and the function is applied recursively to a sorting problem that is not smaller. This `mergeSort` function is incorrect: It does not terminate when called on a non-empty list.

When a problem has multiple parameters, it is sometimes enough that one of them, or a combination of them, becomes smaller. For example, a pair that consists of a positive number and a list can become smaller by the number getting smaller, the list getting shorter, or the sum of the number plus the length of the list getting smaller, among other ways.

Some cases are more complicated and necessitate more refined notions of "smaller." For instance, in this classic example (sometimes known as the *Ackermann function*),[4] the computation is guaranteed to terminate because the pair (x,y) decreases in lexicographic ordering: Either x decreases, or x stays unchanged and y decreases:

Scala

```scala
def a(x: BigInt, y: BigInt): BigInt = (x, y) match
  case (0, _) => y + 1
  case (_, 0) => a(x - 1, 1)
  case _      => a(x - 1, a(x, y - 1))
```

Listing 6.6: Ackermann function.

- *Your focus as a programmer should be on using the solutions to the smaller problems, not on how these smaller problems are themselves solved by the recursive calls.* This point is crucial and is key to effective recursive thinking. One common beginner's mistake is to try to unfold recursive calls to follow their computations. Except for the simplest functions, diving into the recursive calls quickly becomes intractable. (Try it on `hanoi`.) Instead, you must take the solutions to the smaller problems for granted—given to you by the "magic" of recursion—and focus on using these values to build a solution to the original problem.

6.4 Recursive Structures

As mentioned in Chapter 5, some algebraic data types present recursive structures, which can be handled quite naturally by recursive functions. Indeed, the processing of recursive structures is one of the major uses of recursive programming.

Trees are one of the most common recursive structures used in programming. Listing 5.9 used trees to represent expressions and a recursive function to evaluate a tree. As another example, consider binary trees. A non-empty binary tree consists of a root

---

[4] Although the function is guaranteed to terminate in theory, its complexity is huge, and its recursive evaluation will run out of stack space on most inputs. The Ackermann function was defined for the theoretical study of recursive functions and has no practical purpose.

value and two children, typically named left and right, which are themselves binary trees:[5]

```scala
enum BinTree[+A]:
  case Empty
  case Node(value: A, left: BinTree[A], right: BinTree[A])
```

On such a tree, you can compute the number of values recursively:

```scala
def size[A](tree: BinTree[A]): Int = tree match
  case Empty              => 0
  case Node(_, left, right) => 1 + size(left) + size(right)
```

Listing 6.7: Recursive implementation of `size` on binary trees.

The empty tree contains no value, and a non-empty tree contains as many values as in its combined children, plus one for the root. Many other computations on binary trees can proceed recursively, using the empty tree as a terminal, non-recursive case. Binary trees are the focus of a case study in Chapter 8.

Recursive structures are also sometimes defined in terms of mutually recursive types: Type A depends on type B, which depends on type A, for instance. This leads to code that uses mutually recursive functions, also called co-recursive functions. For instance, you can define N-ary trees, in which nodes have zero, one, or more children, in terms of two types: `Tree` and `Forest`. On the one hand, a forest is a list of non-empty trees; on the other hand, a non-empty tree consists of a root value and a forest of children:

```scala
enum Tree[+A]:
  case Empty
  case Node(value: A, trees: Forest[A])

type Forest[A] = List[Tree.Node[A]]
```

You can then calculate the size of a tree by relying on the size of its forest, and the size of a forest by relying on the sizes of its trees:

```scala
def treeSize[A](tree: Tree[A]): Int = tree match
  case Empty         => 0
  case Node(_, trees) => 1 + forestSize(trees)
```

---

[5]Ignore the "+" sign in front of type parameter A. Although necessary here, it is not relevant to our discussion. If curious, you can read about it in Section 15.8 on type variance.

```
def forestSize[A](forest: Forest[A]): Int = forest match
  case Nil          => 0
  case tree :: trees => treeSize(tree) + forestSize(trees)
```

Listing 6.8: Recursive implementation of `size` on N-ary trees.

These functions are mutually recursive: `treeSize` calls `forestSize`, and `forestSize` calls `treeSize`. N-ary trees are explored as a case study in Chapter 11.

6.5   Tail Recursion

Function invocation is typically implemented in terms of an execution stack. When you invoke a function, a new stack frame is allocated and pushed on the execution stack. The frame contains, among other things, the function's arguments and space for its local variables. It is popped from the stack when control returns from the call.

Recall that recursion was introduced as a mechanism that can nest function calls arbitrarily—it was used to replace a useless repetition `f(x); f(x); f(x)` with a more useful `f(f(f(x)))`. In the same way that loops can involve many repetitions, functions can involve many recursive calls. As a result, recursive code often leads to heavy usage of the execution stack. In particular, a deeply recursive function can fail to evaluate because it runs out of stack space.

Compilers of functional programming languages often optimize stack usage by focusing on *tail calls*. A tail call is a function call that takes place at the very end of another function, as in the following pattern:

```
                                                        ── pseudo code ──
function f(x,y,z) {
  <code>
  return g(t,u,v)
}
```

In this pattern, when control returns from the call to `g`, it will then immediately return from the call to `f`—function `f` has nothing to do after the call to `g`. In particular, by the time function `f` initiates its call to function `g`, its `x`, `y`, and `z` arguments are no longer needed (and neither are its local variables). They can be popped from the stack *before* branching into `g`, thus limiting stack growth—pop a frame, *then* push a frame. Furthermore, if the call is a recursive call (`f` and `g` are the same function), the whole stack frame can be reused by reassigning variables `x`, `y`, and `z` to have the values `t`, `u`, and `v`, and then branching back to the beginning of `f`. In that case, you can execute the computation as a loop, without using any stack at all.

Some functional languages may guarantee that some or all tail calls are optimized, while others might focus solely on tail *recursive* calls, and still others might leave the decision to specific compiler implementations. Hybrid languages, in which functions are implemented in terms of methods, tend to face a more challenging situation, since method invocation typically involves its own unique characteristics (see the discussion of dynamic dispatching in Section 15.7).

As an example, the current Scala compiler focuses on *tail recursive functions*—functions with a single recursive call, in tail position. It does not optimize other tail calls, including those inside mutually recursive functions. Furthermore, because functions are implemented as methods, and methods can be overridden, code that appears to be tail recursive may not be optimized. You can use a `tailrec` annotation to confirm that the optimization is indeed taking place: A function annotated with `tailrec` is guaranteed to be optimized by the compiler, or compilation will fail.

Aside on Optimized Bytecode for Tail Recursive Functions

As an experiment, consider the small class shown here, with a single recursive method:

Scala

```
class TailRecursionTest:
  def zero(x: Int): 0 = if x == 0 then 0 else zero(x - 1)
```

The useless method always returns zero (hence its name and return type). The bytecode generated for it by the Scala compiler looks something like this:

bytecode

```
public int zero(int);
  Code:
      0: iload 1
      1: iconst_0
      2: if_icmpne      9
      5: iconst_0
      6: goto          16
      9: aload 0
     10: iload 1
     11: iconst_1
     12: isub
     13: invokevirtual #16        // Method zero:(I)I
     16: ireturn
```

The details are unimportant. Line 2 is a comparison of variable x with 0. If x is non-zero, execution jumps to line 9. Lines 9–12 calculate x − 1, and line 13 invokes method `zero` again, on x − 1. No optimization is taking place. If the method is annotated with `tailrec`, compilation will fail.

What prevents the compiler from optimizing is the fact that method `zero` could be overridden in a class that extends `TailRecursionTest`. If overriding is disabled, by making `zero` a final method, for instance, the bytecode generated by the compiler changes:

```
                                                    ────── bytecode ──────
public final int zero(int);
  Code:
      0: aload 0
      1: astore 2
      2: iload 1
      3: istore 3
      4: iload 3
      5: iconst_0
      6: if_icmpne     13
      9: iconst_0
     10: goto          30
     13: aload 2
     14: astore        4
     16: iload 3
     17: iconst_1
     18: isub
     19: istore        5
     21: aload         4
     23: astore 2
     24: iload         5
     26: istore 3
     27: goto          31
     30: ireturn
     31: goto          4
     34: athrow
     35: athrow
```

Again, the details are unimportant, but the essential thing to notice is that the `invokevirtual` instruction is gone. Instead, we see `goto 4` on line 31: The recursive function is now implemented as a loop.

6.6   Examples of Tail Recursive Functions

The very first recursive function in this chapter—defined to process a collection of items in Listing 6.1—is tail recursive. Assuming it is not written as an overridable method, it will be compiled in Scala as a loop. As a more meaningful example, consider binary search in a sorted array. It can be implemented iteratively using a loop:

```scala
                                                              ───── Scala ─────
def search(sortedSeq: IndexedSeq[String], target: String): Option[Int] =
   var from = 0
   var to   = sortedSeq.length - 1
   while from <= to do
      val middle = (from + to) / 2
      sortedSeq(middle) match
         case midVal if target > midVal => from = middle + 1
         case midVal if target < midVal => to = middle - 1
         case _ /* found at middle */   => return Some(middle)
   end while
   None
```

This function works by searching a slice of the array between `from` and `to`, initialized to the entire array. Each loop iteration starts by looking at the value in the middle of the range, `midVal`. If the target is larger than the midpoint value, the function keeps looking in the upper part of the range, between `middle + 1` and `to`, using the fact that the sequence is sorted. If the target is less than the midpoint value, the function continues instead with the lower part of the range, between `from` and `middle - 1`. Otherwise, the value must be equal to the target, so the function returns the index at which it was found. Each new iteration of the loop performs a search in a smaller range. The search ends when the target value is found or the range becomes empty (`from > to`).

Instead of using a loop, you can implement these successive searches with recursive calls instead:

```scala
                                                              ───── Scala ─────
def search(sortedSeq: IndexedSeq[String], target: String): Option[Int] =
   @tailrec
   def doSearch(from: Int, to: Int): Option[Int] =
      if from > to then None
      else
         val middle = (from + to) / 2
         sortedSeq(middle) match
            case midVal if target > midVal => doSearch(middle + 1, to)
            case midVal if target < midVal => doSearch(from, middle - 1)
            case _ /* found at middle */   => Some(middle)

   doSearch(0, sortedSeq.length - 1)
```

Listing 6.9: Tail recursive implementation of binary search in a sorted sequence.

A helper function `doSearch` is defined to perform a search in a given range of indices. This function uses the same algorithm as before, but relies on recursive calls to continue the search in the upper or lower range.

Even though one uses a loop and the other uses recursion, these two implementations are fairly similar. Recursive calls to `doSearch` bring the computation back to the calculation of a new midpoint, just like the loop does. Indeed, function `doSearch` is tail recursive and is compiled in Scala as a loop. Thus, instead of invoking `doSearch` again, the recursive calls are implemented by updating a local variable—either `from` or `to`—and by jumping back to the beginning of the function, just like in the loop variant. After compilation, both implementations use bytecode that, for all practical purposes, is equivalent. Which one you decide to write is a matter of taste.

Sometimes, tail recursion happens quite naturally, without having to think too much about it, as in the binary search example. Function `last` from Listing 6.4, for instance, is tail recursive too. Of course, it is also incorrect, but that can be fixed without losing tail recursion:

```scala
                                                                          Scala
@tailrec
def last[A](list: List[A]): A = list match
  case Nil          => throw NoSuchElementException("last(empty)")
  case head :: tail => if tail.isEmpty then head else last(tail)
```

Listing 6.10: Correct tail recursive implementation of `last`; fixed from Lis. 6.4.

Sometimes, though, a function is not naturally tail recursive. For instance, the `factorial` function from Listing 6.2 is not tail recursive. The recursive call is not in a tail position: After control returns from it, the number still needs to be multiplied by `n` before a value is returned. If you need an optimized implementation that does not grow the execution stack, you can switch back to using a `while`-loop, if the programming language supports it. Otherwise, you need to rewrite the recursive function slightly differently. The standard trick consists of adding a second argument that serves as an accumulator for the value being calculated:

```scala
                                                                          Scala
def factorial(n: Int): Int =
  @tailrec
  def loop(m: Int, f: Int): Int = if m == 0 then f else loop(m - 1, m * f)

  loop(n, 1)
```

Listing 6.11: Tail recursive implementation of `factorial`; contrast with Lis. 6.2.

The second argument of function `loop` contains the part of the factorial already calculated, $\prod_{i=m+1}^{n} i$. The multiplication `m * f` takes place *before* the recursive call, which is now in tail position. Function `loop` is tail recursive, and is compiled as a loop. However, the elegance of the simple recursive implementation from Listing 6.2 is somewhat lost.

Functions that involve multiple recursive calls are never tail recursive—at most one recursive call can be in tail position. Can they be made tail recursive? Yes, but at the cost of introducing additional data structures. Consider, for instance, the case of function `size` on binary trees in Listing 6.7. This function makes two recursive calls, one on the left tree and one on the right tree. To trigger the tail recursion optimization, you might be tempted to employ the same trick used for function `factorial`:

```scala
                                                              ─── Scala ───
def size[A](tree: BinTree[A]): Int =
   def loop(tr: BinTree[A], sz: Int): Int = tr match
      case Empty              => sz
      case Node(_, left, right) => loop(right, loop(left, sz + 1))

   loop(tree, 0)
```

One recursive call to `loop` is now in tail position and could potentially be optimized, but the nested call `loop(left, ...)` still needs to use a stack frame: After controls returns from it, the `loop(right, ...)` call still needs to take place and still uses the current frame (to access local variable `right`).

A true tail recursive variant needs to make a single recursive call only. You can achieve this by introducing your own stack, as a list of trees:

```scala
                                                              ─── Scala ───
def size[A](tree: BinTree[A]): Int =
   @tailrec
   def sizeSum(list: List[BinTree[A]], sum: Int): Int = list match
      case Nil                          => sum
      case Empty :: trees               => sizeSum(trees, sum)
      case Node(_, left, right) :: trees => sizeSum(left :: right :: trees, sum + 1)

   sizeSum(List(tree), 0)
```

Listing 6.12: Tail recursive implementation of `size` on binary trees.

Function `sizeSum` computes the sum of the sizes of a list of trees. It is tail recursive. When an empty tree is found in the list, it contributes nothing to the sum. When a node is taken out of the list, the `sum` accumulator is incremented by one, and the node's children are added to the list of trees to be processed. The size of a tree is obtained by applying function `sizeSum` to a list that contains only this tree. In effect, the execution stack has been replaced with a regular list. As with `factorial`, tail recursion is achieved at the cost of a loss of elegance.

Seeking to replace general recursion with tail recursion involves trade-offs. While pushing and popping the execution stack is likely to be faster than list operations, stack space tends to be limited. By contrast, the added list in function `sizeSum` is allocated in heap memory alongside other objects. Heap memory is typically orders of magnitude larger than stack space.

Other approaches exist to optimize recursive calls and trade heap space for stack space. One notable technique, known as a *trampoline*, has been used to translate languages with tail-call optimization into languages without it. Trampolines are explored as a case study in Chapter 14.

6.7   Summary

- Loops are a programming language mechanism that implements repetition. A loop is only useful if its body implements some form of state change, either by mutating objects or by reassigning variables.

- Instead of mutation, a strict functional programming style relies on composition of pure functions, making loops useless. What is needed to replace loops is a mechanism that can arbitrarily nest function calls. Recursion is such a mechanism.

- Recursive functions are functions that trigger calls to themselves, either directly or via an intermediate function (possibly leading to mutual recursion). They can be used as an alternative to loops to structure programs.

- More importantly, recursive functions fit algorithms that recursively decompose a given problem into smaller problems of the same type. A recursive algorithm combines a strategy for using solutions to smaller instances of the same problem with one or more trivial (non-recursive) cases.

- Recursive functions must always include at least one trivial case that does not require recursion, and they must make sure that all recursive calls are applied to instances of the problem that are smaller—closer to one of the trivial cases. These two conditions are necessary to ensure that the function terminates.

- Recursive functions are well suited to processing recursive data types like trees and functional lists. Tasks on trees and lists can often be decomposed into similar tasks on subtrees and sublists, which are achieved recursively.

- Function calls that take place at the very end of another function—as in `return f(x)`—can sometimes be optimized to reduce usage of the execution stack. As a special case, a function that calls itself exactly once at the very end of its execution is said to be tail recursive. Tail recursive functions are commonly optimized in functional programming languages.

- When tail recursion is optimized by a compiler, it can safely be used to mimic repetition. Indeed, the code generated for an optimized tail recursive function will often be identical to code that is compiled from a loop.

Chapter 7

Recursion on Lists

Because functional lists are a recursive data structure—the tail of a non-empty list is a list—many list-processing functions nicely fit a recursive pattern in which recursion is applied to the tail of a list. This chapter uses this pattern to (re)implement several common list functions. The objective is twofold: It is both an exposure to standard list functions and a way to practice recursive thinking. Other patterns are also explored, in which recursion is applied to sublists other than the tail. Some performance considerations are discussed, such as the use of tail recursion or pure functions that rely internally on mutable structures.

NOTE

The Scala collection library implements many list operations as methods of its List type. In this chapter, several are reimplemented as functions for the purpose of our discussion of recursion and recursive algorithms. The code examples deliberately rely on previously defined functions instead of the corresponding standard methods—for instance, writing head(list) where list.head could be used—so the code is closer to what it could be in another programming language with functional lists. This approach is specific to this chapter. Later parts of the book use the corresponding List methods instead for convenience and readability.

7.1 Recursive Algorithms as Equalities

In Chapter 6, we implemented a function `last` to extract the last element of a list:

```scala
                                                                 ── Scala ──
def last[A](list: List[A]): A = list match
   case Nil          => throw NoSuchElementException("last(empty)")
   case head :: tail => if isEmpty(tail) then head else last(tail)
```

This function is based on the idea that, in general, the last element of a list is the last element of its tail. In other words, it relies on the following equality:

$$last(list) = last(tail(list))$$

Because empty lists have no last element, this equality holds only when neither `list` nor `tail(list)` is empty. These two special cases are handled non-recursively in function `last`—case `Nil` and `if isEmpty(tail)`—and the recursive call then simply follows the equality.

Every recursive algorithm is founded on such an equality. For instance, the size of a tree *equals* the sum of the sizes of the children, plus one; and the good old factorial implementation discussed earlier is based on the equality $n! = n \times (n-1)!$. To become fluent in recursive programming, you need to learn to identify these equalities.

A frequent list pattern involves calculating a function `f` on a list by using a single recursive call on the tail of the list:

$$f(\text{list}) = g(f(\text{tail}(\text{list})))$$

Your goal is to calculate `f(list)`, and you have the value `f(tail(list))` to work with. You get this value for free by the "magic" of recursion. Your job is to formulate and implement function `g`.

In the case of function `last`, `g` is the identity function, and `f(list)` is simply `f(tail(list))`. Many of the examples that follow rely on a function `g`, which may or may not be written explicitly. For instance, function `contains` in Listing 7.1, which searches for a target in a list, uses `g(x) = (head(list)==target) || x`. Function `length` in Listing 7.3, which calculates the length of a list, uses `g(x) = x + 1`.

Once you figure out the general equality, the recursive function usually follows straightforwardly. All you need is to take care of the special cases where the equality does not hold. They become the non-recursive cases of the computation, like short lists in function `last`, or zero in `factorial`. The equality itself defines the recursion. The next several sections illustrate this principle by looking at typical list calculations and by deriving for each a recursive function from an equality and one or more special cases.

7.2   Traversing Lists

Instead of traversing an entire list to reach its last element, you could have a specific target in mind and traverse a list until you find the element you are looking for. Function `contains` tests whether a target value is in a list: The target is in the list if it is at the head of the list or else if it is somewhere inside the tail. This suggests the following recursive equality:

`contains(list, target) = head(list) == target || contains(tail(list), target)`

The equality is ill defined for the empty list, which has neither head nor tail, and which needs to be treated as an easy special case (the empty list contains nothing):

```scala
————————————————————————————————————————————— Scala —————

@tailrec
def contains[A](list: List[A], target: A): Boolean =
    !isEmpty(list) && (head(list) == target || contains(tail(list), target))
```

Listing 7.1: Simple list lookup, using tail recursion; see also Lis. 7.2.

Note how the code practically reads itself: "A list contains a target if it is non-empty and either the first element of the list is the target, or the target is somewhere else in the list."[1] The function is tail recursive because the logical operator "||" uses shortcut evaluation in Scala (as in C or Java) and thus is equivalent to the following expression:

```
                                                            Scala
(if head(list) == target then true else contains(tail(list), target))
```

With "||" expanded as if-then-else, the tail recursion appears more clearly.

   Instead of relying on head and tail functions, you can use pattern matching:

```
                                                            Scala
@tailrec
def contains[A](list: List[A], target: A): Boolean = list match
   case Nil          => false
   case head :: tail => head == target || contains(tail, target)
```

Listing 7.2: Simple list lookup, using tail recursion and pattern matching.

In the remainder of this chapter—and throughout the book—code illustrations mostly follow this pattern-matching style, which I often find easier to read.

   The next example is a recursive function to calculate the length of a list. A non-empty list contains as many elements as its tail, plus one for the head of the list:

$$length(list) = 1 + length(tail(list))$$

After the empty list, of length zero, is handled as a special case, the implementation has the following form:

```
                                                            Scala
def length[A](list: List[A]): Int = list match
   case Nil        => 0
   case _ :: tail => 1 + length(tail)
```

Listing 7.3: List length, *not* tail recursive; contrast with Lis. 7.4.

A drawback of this implementation is that the function is not tail recursive. Its evaluation requires as many stack frames as there are values in the list and is likely to fail on large lists by running out of space.

   You can derive a tail recursive variant by applying the same transformation used to write a tail recursive **factorial** function: Add a second argument for the length, and update it before the recursive call. Helper function **addLength** adds the length of a list to a given accumulator. The length function is then implemented by using **addLength** to add the length of a list to zero:

---

[1]For this reason, functional programming is often said to be more *declarative* than imperative programming.

```scala
                                                                    Scala
def length[A](list: List[A]): Int =
   @tailrec
   def addLength(theList: List[A], len: Int): Int = theList match
      case Nil       => len
      case _ :: tail => addLength(tail, len + 1)

   addLength(list, 0)
```

Listing 7.4: List length, using tail recursion; contrast with Lis. 7.3.

Function `addLength` is tail recursive. The whole `length` function can now be compiled as a loop, which will avoid stack overflow issues.

7.3   Returning Lists

So far, we have considered only functions that extract information from a list: `last` returns an element, `contains` returns a Boolean value, and `length` returns an integer. Some functions, however, process lists by building and returning other lists.

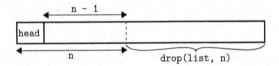

Figure 7.1 Recursive strategy for function drop.

As a first example, consider the standard function `drop`, which is used to remove the first n elements from a list: `drop(List(A,B,C,D), 2)` is `List(C,D)`. Its recursive equality follows from the fact that, to remove n elements from a list, you need to first remove the head of the list, and then remove $n - 1$ elements from the tail (Figure 7.1):

$$\text{drop(list, n) = drop(tail(list), n - 1)}$$

For the equality to be valid, the list needs to have a tail, and $n - 1$ cannot be a negative number, since negative numbers make no sense in this context. From this observation, two special cases follow, one for the empty list and one for $n = 0$:

```scala
                                                                    Scala
@tailrec
def drop[A](list: List[A], n: Int): List[A] =
   if n == 0 then list
   else list match
```

```
  case Nil      => Nil
  case _ :: tail => drop(tail, n - 1)
```

Listing 7.5: Recursive implementation of **drop** on lists; see also Lis. 7.6.

Function **drop** takes two arguments: a list and a number n of elements to drop. The special case $n = 0$ (no elements removed) is handled by returning the list unchanged. You can handle the other special case (empty list) in two different ways, depending on the desired semantics of removing elements from an empty list:

- There are no elements to remove in an empty list: *Throw an exception.*

- Whatever is removed, an empty list remains empty: *Return an empty list.*

Some programming languages, like ML, follow the first interpretation. The Scala standard library uses the second interpretation, which I also chose here. Function **drop** is tail recursive and does not incur stack space usage at runtime.

As an alternative to **if-then-else** followed by pattern matching, you can use pattern matching directly on both the number and the list by joining them as a pair:

```
                                                              ─ Scala ─
@tailrec
def drop[A](list: List[A], n: Int): List[A] = (list, n) match
  case (_, 0) | (Nil, _) => list
  case (_ :: tail, _)    => drop(tail, n - 1)
```

Listing 7.6: Recursive implementation of **drop** on lists; see also Lis. 7.5.

Pattern (_, 0) is the case $n = 0$, and pattern (Nil, _) is the empty list case. In both cases, the function returns the list unchanged.

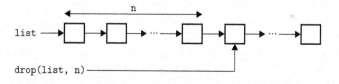

Figure 7.2 Data sharing between list and drop(list, n).

There is an important aspect of function **drop**—with either implementation—that needs to be emphasized: Even though the function returns a new list, it does not allocate any new list data in memory. The list that is returned shares all its storage with the argument list (Figure 7.2). Given that the function is tail recursive and does not create new data, it will be compiled into a loop that moves a pointer n times along a linked list until it reaches the desired position. As a consequence, you can use **drop** as a basis for the implementation of a function **getAt** that fetches an element at a specified index:

```
                                                                  Scala
def getAt[A](list: List[A], i: Int): A = drop(list, i) match
   case Nil         => throw NoSuchElementException("getAt(empty)")
   case value :: _ => value
```

Listing 7.7: Implementation of `getAt` on lists, using `drop`.

After i elements have been removed, the head of the remaining list, if any, is the element at position i in the original list (indexing is zero-based).

An easy mistake you want to avoid is to start using lists as if they were arrays with fast indexing.[2] Always remember that accessing the ith element of a functional list takes time proportional to i, as can be seen clearly from the implementation of functions `drop` and `getAt` in Listings 7.6 and 7.7.

7.4   Building Lists from the Execution Stack

You can think of `drop` as a generalization of the `tail` function: `drop(list, 1)` is almost[3] the same thing as `tail(list)`. Function `head` is similarly generalized into a function `take` that extracts the first n elements of a list. Function `take` is based on an equality similar to that of `drop`. That is, to take the first n elements from a list, take the head of the list, followed by $n - 1$ elements from the tail:

$$take(list, n) = head(list) :: take(tail(list), n - 1)$$

The corresponding code is straightforward:

```
                                                                  Scala
def take[A](list: List[A], n: Int): List[A] = (list, n) match
   case (_, 0) | (Nil, _) => Nil
   case (head :: tail, _) => head :: take(tail, n - 1)
```

Listing 7.8: Recursive implementation of `take`; contrast with Listings 7.21 to 7.23.

A key difference between functions `take` and `drop` is that in the case of `drop`, the input and output lists can share data in memory, but function `take` needs to allocate a new list to store the elements being extracted (Figure 7.3). Note also that, unlike `drop`,

[2]This is especially true in Scala, which uses the tempting syntax `list(i)` and `array(i)` to access the ith element of a list or an array.

[3]The only difference is that, given my choice of semantics, `drop(Nil, 1)` is the empty list, while `tail(Nil)` would throw an exception.

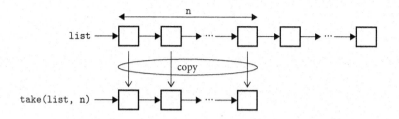

Figure 7.3 Data copying between `list` and `take(list, n)`.

function `take` is not tail recursive. It works by pushing the first n elements of the input list onto the execution stack, then building a list from them as the function calls return.

NOTE

Section 7.9 briefly discusses building lists with limited use of the execution stack, and possible scalable implementations of function `take` are discussed. However, many code examples throughout this book continue to build lists using the execution stack, as in Listing 7.8. My motivation for using this approach is to avoid unnecessary distractions and to keep code illustrations focused on the concepts at hand. In this section, which focuses on the equalities at the core of recursive algorithms, I am willing to sacrifice library-level performance and robustness for the benefit of code that draws more clearly from the corresponding equality. In the implementation of `take`, for instance, the code `head::take(tail, n - 1)` and the equality `head(list)::take(tail(list), n - 1)` are almost identical. Within the context of this book, it is not worth losing this clarity to improve the code's performance.

7.5 Recursion on Multiple/Nested Lists

Let us continue the illustration of recursion with several examples of recursive functions that involve multiple lists, including lists nested inside lists.

First, consider the case of a `concat` function that concatenates two lists (this functionality is available as a ":::" method in the standard Scala library):

```scala
val abc = List(A, B, C)
concat(abc, abc) // List(A, B, C, A, B, C); standard in Scala as abc ::: abc
```

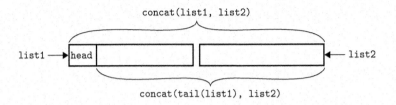

Figure 7.4 Recursive strategy for function `concat`.

As for the underlying equality, the concatenation of `list1` and `list2` produces, in general, a list that starts with the head of `list1` and continues with the concatenation of the tail of `list1` with `list2` (Figure 7.4):

concat(list1, list2) = head(list1) :: concat(tail(list1), list2)

For this equality to make sense, the first list needs to have a head and a tail (the second list can be empty). You handle the special case where the first list is empty by observing that the concatenation of an empty list and another list is the other list itself:

——————————————————————————————————————— *Scala* ———

```scala
def concat[A](list1: List[A], list2: List[A]): List[A] = list1 match
  case Nil            => list2
  case head1 :: tail1 => head1 :: concat(tail1, list2)
```

Listing 7.9: Recursive implementation of list concatenation.

Note how recursion proceeds on the first list only: The second list is unchanged in the recursive calls. This means that the computation time of a call to `concat` is proportional to the length of the first list independently from the size of the second list. In particular, you can append an element at the end of a list by concatenating a single-element list, but that takes time proportional to the length of the list.[4] The fact that the second list is short does not help in any way:

——————————————————————————————————————— *Scala* ———

```scala
def append[A](list: List[A], value: A): List[A] = concat(list, List(value))
```

Listing 7.10: Appending at the end of a list using concatenation.

Contrast this with prepending to a list, which you can achieve in constant time with a single call to ":::". This difference greatly impacts how you should implement algorithms expressed in terms of functional lists. Good performance is contingent on building lists by *prepending* instead of *appending*. In particular, *never* use a list as a first-in-first-out queue.

———————————————

[4]This is also true of Scala's standard methods ":::" (concatenation) and ":+" (append).

Lists can contain elements that are themselves lists. A list of lists can be flattened by repeated concatenation:

```scala
flatten(List(List(1, 2, 3), Nil, List(4, 5), List(6)))  // List(1, 2, 3, 4, 5, 6)
List(1, 2, 3) ::: Nil ::: List(4, 5) ::: List(6)         // List(1, 2, 3, 4, 5, 6)
```

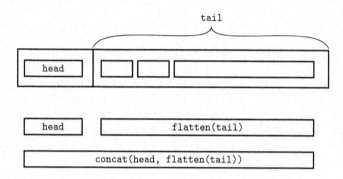

Figure 7.5 Recursive strategy for function `flatten`.

The list returned by function `flatten` begins with the elements of the first inner list and continues by concatenation with the result of flattening the tail (Figure 7.5):

$$\texttt{flatten(list) = concat(head(list), flatten(tail(list)))}$$

The actual implementation mimics the equality, adding only a special consideration for the empty list:

```scala
def flatten[A](list: List[List[A]]): List[A] = list match
  case Nil         => Nil
  case head :: tail => concat(head, flatten(tail))
```

Listing 7.11: Recursive implementation of list flattening.

Note the signature of the function, from `List[List[A]]` to `List[A]`, since it makes sense only for nested lists.

As a final example in this section, let us implement function `zip`, which traverses two lists simultaneously to build a list of pairs:

```scala
zip(List(A, B, C), List(1, 2, 3))  // List((A,1), (B,2), (C,3))
```

The intuition is straightforward:

```
zip(list1, list2) = (head(list1), head(list2)) :: zip(tail(list1), tail(list2))
```

The equality presumes that neither list is empty, and emptiness needs to be handled as a special case:

```scala
                                                          ─ Scala ─
def zip[A, B](list1: List[A], list2: List[B]): List[(A, B)] = (list1, list2) match
    case (Nil, _) | (_, Nil)          => Nil
    case (head1 :: tail1, head2 :: tail2) => (head1, head2) :: zip(tail1, tail2)
```

Listing 7.12: Recursive implementation of list zipping.

Function `zip` is parameterized by two types `A` and `B` to allow for two different types of list elements. In contrast to `concat`, function `zip` digs into both lists at the same time. It stops as soon as one of the lists is empty. As a result, if the two lists have unequal lengths, the remaining elements from the longer list are not included in the output.

7.6   Recursion on Sublists Other Than the Tail

Recursive functions on lists need smaller lists on which to apply recursion. So far in this chapter, the smaller lists have been the tails of one or more of the input lists. While this is a very common pattern, you can also process a list recursively using sublists that are not the tail of the list.

As an illustration, consider the problem of grouping list elements. Given a list and a positive number k, the objective is to produce a list of k-element lists:

```scala
                                                          ─ Scala ─
group(List(A, B, C, D, E), 2) // List(List(A,B), List(C,D), List(E))
```

All the inner lists have length k, except possibly the last list, which may contain fewer than k elements. The corresponding recursive equality is based on the following idea. First, use function `take` to take the first k elements of the main list—they form the first inner list. Then use function `drop` to remove these first k elements from the main list and process the remaining elements recursively:

```
group(list, k) = take(list, k) :: group(drop(list, k), k)
```

Functions `group`, `take`, and `drop` are all well defined on the empty list, leaving no special cases to consider:

```scala
// DON'T DO THIS!
def group[A](list: List[A], k: Int): List[List[A]] =
  take(list, k) :: group(drop(list, k), k)
```

Of course, as the comment indicates, this function is necessarily incorrect. It breaks one of the cardinal rules of recursive functions—namely, that a function must involve at least one case that is not recursive. As written, function **group** always calls itself and cannot possibly terminate. Even though **group**, **take**, and **drop** can be applied to an empty list, the inner lists of a grouping should never be empty, which means that a special treatment of the empty list is required after all.

Before we fix the **group** function, observe that its computation involves calling **take** and **drop** on the same list with the same number k. This is slightly inefficient because it requires traversing the first k elements of the list twice. Instead, you can use a single traversal to build both lists. This is the task of function **splitAt**:

```scala
def splitAt[A](list: List[A], n: Int): (List[A], List[A]) = (list, n) match
  case (_, 0) | (Nil, _) => (Nil, list)
  case (head :: tail, _) =>
    val (left, right) = splitAt(tail, n - 1)
    (head :: left, right)
```

Listing 7.13: Recursive implementation of list splitting.

This function uses the same recursive algorithms used in functions **take** and **drop** but combines them to construct both lists together as a pair. The expression **splitAt(L,k)** is always equivalent to **(take(L,k), drop(L,k))** but is implemented more efficiently. Using **splitAt**, and adding a case to avoid generating empty groups, you can implement a correct **group** function as follows:

```scala
def group[A](list: List[A], k: Int): List[List[A]] =
  if isEmpty(list) then Nil
  else
    val (first, more) = splitAt(list, k)
    first :: group(more, k)
```

Listing 7.14: Recursive implementation of list grouping.

7.7   Building Lists in Reverse Order

As mentioned in the discussion of function **append**, appending to a list takes time proportional to the length of the list, while prepending is a constant-time operation. This point is essential to keep in mind if you want to avoid writing list-based code that is grossly inefficient.

Consider the case of list reversal. To implement the function recursively, you could be tempted to use a recursive call to reverse the tail of a list and then append the head of the list at the end of the reversed tail:

$$\texttt{reverse(list) = append(reverse(tail(list)), head(list))}$$

While this equality is indeed valid on a non-empty list, using it results in an unacceptable **reverse** function:

```scala
// DON'T DO THIS!
def reverse[A](list: List[A]): List[A] = list match
  case Nil          => list
  case head :: tail => append(reverse(tail), head)
```

Although this function correctly produces a list in reverse order, it suffers from two major flaws. First, it is not tail recursive and will run out of stack space when applied to large lists. Second, and most importantly, its performance is unsatisfactory, even for those lists that fit in the execution stack.

If the list being reversed contains n elements, the length of **reverse(tail)** is $n - 1$, and the evaluation of **append** necessitates $n - 1$ operations. But inside the **reverse(tail)** computation, there is another call to **append** on a list with $n - 2$ elements; and inside the next nested computation is another call to **append** on a list of length $n - 3$; and so forth. Overall, $(n-1)+(n-2)+\cdots+1 = (n \times (n-1))/2$ operations are needed. As a result, the computing time of this **reverse** function is proportional to the *square* of the length of the list being reversed.

To avoid this, introduce a second list argument:

```scala
def reverse[A](list: List[A]): List[A] =
  @tailrec
  def addToStack(rem: List[A], rev: List[A]): List[A] = rem match
    case Nil           => rev
    case top :: bottom => addToStack(bottom, top :: rev)

  addToStack(list, Nil)
```

Listing 7.15: Linear, tail recursive implementation of list reversal.

This function proceeds by repeatedly adding the head of the list being reversed to the front of an accumulator list `rev`. You can think of it as peeling cards from a deck and putting them onto the table: In the end, the resulting deck of cards is the reverse of the original deck.

Contrary to the previous attempt, this implementation only uses "`::`" directly to build the resulting list, and is linear in complexity. As a simple experiment on the desktop computer used to typeset this book, it took approximately 75 milliseconds to reverse a list of 5000 numbers using the first implementation. This time decreased to 0.027 millisecond when the improved variant was used, a more than 1/2000 reduction. Incidentally, this implementation has also become tail recursive, and can handle lists of arbitrary length.

There may be situations where you are tempted to append to a list because prepending would not produce a list in the right order. Don't do it. Instead, build the list in the wrong order, efficiently, and then reverse it. For instance, to extract space-separated tokens from a stream of characters, it would feel natural to use `append` to add a character to the current token, then `append` again to add a token to a list of tokens. Instead, you can use a combination of prepending and reversing:

```scala
                                                              ─── Scala ───
def tokenize(stream: List[Char]): List[String] =
  def addToken(token: List[Char], tokens: List[String]): List[String] =
    if isEmpty(token) then tokens else reverse(token).mkString :: tokens

  @tailrec
  def loop(stream: List[Char], token: List[Char], tokens: List[String]): List[String]=
    stream match
      case w :: chars if w.isWhitespace => loop(chars, Nil, addToken(token, tokens))
      case c :: chars                   => loop(chars, c :: token, tokens)
      case Nil                          => addToken(token, tokens)

  reverse(loop(stream, Nil, Nil))
```

Listing 7.16: List building by prepending and reversing instead of appending.

Characters are processed one at a time in function `loop`. A non-whitespace character (`c`) is added to the current token, and the computation proceeds recursively. Upon encountering a whitespace character (`w`), the current token is added to a list of tokens, and a new token (`Nil`) is started. The last token, which is not necessarily followed by whitespace, is added at the end.

Note how characters are added to tokens using constant-time operation "`::`". As a result, tokens are built in reverse order. In function `addToken`, each token is reversed one time when it is added to the list. (The function skips empty tokens and uses standard method `mkString` to convert a list of characters into a string.) Similarly, tokens are added to a list of tokens using "`::`", and the list is reversed at the end. Since reversal was implemented in linear time, the entire tokenization time remains proportional to the lengths and number of tokens.

7.8   Illustration: Sorting

NOTE

Efficient sorting is typically not performed directly on lists. Instead, list values can be stored in a temporary array, the array sorted, and the list reconstructed. Furthermore, practical sorting functions should be parameterized by the type of the elements being sorted and the criterion used to order them. This section focuses on direct sorting of lists of integers because it offers a good illustration of recursive patterns. The resulting functions suffer from limitations and inefficiencies that would likely be unacceptable in production code.

Consider the problem of sorting a list of integers in increasing order. You can decompose a non-empty list into a head and a tail and apply recursion to sort the tail. You are then left with a single value (the head) and a sorted list (the sorted tail). All that is needed to complete the sorting function is to insert this value at the right place into the sorted list. This strategy results in a form of *insert-sort*:

```scala
def insertInSorted(x: Int, sorted: List[Int]): List[Int] = sorted match
  case Nil            => List(x)
  case min :: others =>
     if x < min then x :: sorted else min :: insertInSorted(x, others)

def insertSort(list: List[Int]): List[Int] = list match
  case Nil     => list
  case h :: t => insertInSorted(h, insertSort(t))
```

Listing 7.17: Insertion sort.

The sorting function uses a function `insertInSorted` to insert the head of a list into its sorted tail. In this auxiliary function, you insert an element x into an empty list by creating a one-element list `List(x)`. Otherwise, x is compared to the head of the sorted list, `min`, which is its smallest element. If x is smaller than the minimum, it is also smaller than all the other values and therefore belongs at the front of the list. Otherwise, the smallest value in the list is still `min`, and you need to insert x somewhere in the tail of the list, which is achieved through a recursive call.

Insert-sort is known to have poor performance—computation time proportional to the square of the length of the list—and better strategies have been devised based on splitting a list into two halves instead of a head and tail. There are two classic variants of this pattern, with which you are probably familiar:

- *Merge-sort*: Split a list in the middle, sort both halves recursively, then merge the two sorted lists into one.

- *Quick-sort*: Split a list into low and high values, sort both parts recursively, then concatenate the two sorted lists into one.

Merge-sort uses a simple strategy to split a list in two, but has more work to do to merge the lists after they have been sorted. Quick-sort relies on a more complicated splitting strategy, but once sorted, lists only need to be concatenated.

First, merge-sort:

```scala
def merge(sortedA: List[Int], sortedB: List[Int]): List[Int] = (sortedA, sortedB) match
  case (Nil, _)              => sortedB
  case (_, Nil)              => sortedA
  case (hA :: tA, hB :: tB) =>
    if hA <= hB then hA :: merge(tA, sortedB) else hB :: merge(sortedA, tB)

def mergeSort(list: List[Int]): List[Int] = list match
  case Nil | List(_) => list
  case _             =>
    val (left, right) = splitAt(list, length(list) / 2)
    merge(mergeSort(left), mergeSort(right))
```

Listing 7.18: Merge-sort; fixed from Lis. 6.5; see also Lis. 7.19.

The merging of sorted lists starts with two patterns to deal with empty lists—merging a list with an empty list results in the list itself. The last pattern then compares the heads of two non-empty lists. Whichever is smaller needs to come first in the merged list. Once this value is selected, the remainder of the two lists are merged recursively. With the merging function thus written, you implement the merge-sort by using functions `length` and `splitAt` to split a list in the middle.

An easy mistake would be to forget the case `List(_)` in the first pattern in `mergeSort`. As mentioned earlier, in the discussion of Listing 6.5, this would result in a non-terminating function. As a variant, you can apply pattern matching to the length of the list, which is needed for the split, and write the merge-sort function as follows:

```scala
def mergeSort(list: List[Int]): List[Int] = length(list) match
  case 0 | 1 => list
  case len   =>
    val (left, right) = splitAt(list, len / 2)
    merge(mergeSort(left), mergeSort(right))
```

Listing 7.19: Alternative implementation of merge-sort; see also Lis. 7.18.

Again, don't forget the case 1 for lists too short to be split.

To implement quick-sort, you need to split the list into low and high values. This is typically done by choosing one value, called the pivot, and splitting the list into values smaller than the pivot and values larger than the pivot. Function `splitPivot`, shown next, works by splitting the tail of a list into low and high values according to the pivot, and then adding the head of the list to the low or high part. With the splitting function implemented, a quick-sort function only has to split, sort recursively, and concatenate:

```scala
                                                              ───── Scala ─────
def splitPivot(pivot: Int, list: List[Int]): (List[Int], List[Int]) = list match
   case Nil    => (Nil, Nil)
   case h :: t =>
      val (low, high) = splitPivot(pivot, t)
      if h < pivot then (h :: low, high) else (low, h :: high)

def quickSort(list: List[Int]): List[Int] = list match
   case Nil            => list
   case pivot :: others =>
      val (low, high) = splitPivot(pivot, others)
      concat(quickSort(low), pivot :: quickSort(high))
```

Listing 7.20: Quick-sort with user-defined splitting; see also Lis. 10.1.

Merge-sort and quick-sort tend to outperform insert-sort: If the two lists to be sorted recursively have about the same size, sorting time is reduced from n^2 to $n \log_2(n)$, where n is the length of the list to be sorted. This equal size property of the split is guaranteed in merge-sort but not in quick-sort. Although quick-sort works well on average, it suffers from poor performance in extreme cases. For instance, if a list is already sorted, and you choose its head as the pivot, as in our example, quick-sort takes time proportional to the square of the length of the list.

The implementation of `splitPivot` shown here is not very good—it uses as much stack as there are values in the list. We could rewrite it as a tail recursive function, using accumulator variables for the low and high lists. However, there is an even better way to achieve the same functionality efficiently by using a higher-order function called `partition`. Higher-order functions are discussed in Chapters 9 and 10, and quick-sort is reimplemented in Listing 10.1.

7.9 Building Lists Efficiently

For clarity, several functions implemented in this chapter use the execution stack to build lists. If the sizes of the constructed lists are not known a priori, production code should instead rely on either tail recursion or loops. For instance, the implementation of function `take` from Listing 7.8 uses the stack to build a list. To make it tail recursive instead, you can add an accumulator argument:

```scala
                                                              ───── Scala ─────
def take[A](list: List[A], n: Int): List[A] =
   @tailrec
```

```
def takeAndAdd(list: List[A], n: Int, added: List[A]): List[A] = (list, n) match
   case (_, 0) | (Nil, _) => added
   case (head :: tail, _) => takeAndAdd(tail, n - 1, head :: added)

reverse(takeAndAdd(list, n, Nil))
```

Listing 7.21: Tail recursive implementation of <code>take</code>; contrast with Lis. 7.8.

Note how values are added to the accumulator using ":", not **append**, for performance reasons. As a result, function **takeAndAdd** accumulates the elements in reverse order, and the accumulated list is reversed before it is returned.

Another approach, which is frequently used in libraries, is to implement pure functions by using non-functional elements internally. You can implement **take** with an intermediate **ListBuffer**, a mutable accumulator designed to build immutable lists:

Scala

```
def take[A](list: List[A], n: Int): List[A] =
   @tailrec
   def takeAndAdd(list: List[A], n: Int, added: mutable.ListBuffer[A]): List[A] =
      (list, n) match
         case (_, 0) | (Nil, _) => added.result()
         case (head :: tail, _) => takeAndAdd(tail, n - 1, added += head)

   takeAndAdd(list, n, mutable.ListBuffer.empty[A])
```

Listing 7.22: Buffer-based implementation of <code>take</code>; contrast with Lis. 7.21.

To add elements to the accumulator, a list buffer is mutated by its method "+=". Once building is complete, method **result** is used to produce an immutable list from the mutable buffer, thus bringing us back into the realm of functional programming. Because the buffer supports a constant-time append operation, no reversal is needed at the end.

Finally, if your language supports it, you can always use loops instead of recursion to update the mutable buffer:

Scala

```
def take[A](list: List[A], n: Int): List[A] =
   val added = mutable.ListBuffer.empty[A]
   var elems = list
   var rem   = n
   while rem > 0 && elems.nonEmpty do
      added += head(elems)
      elems = tail(elems)
      rem -= 1
   added.result()
```

Listing 7.23: Loop-based implementation of <code>take</code>; contrast with Lis. 7.22.

After compilation, the last two variants of function `take` should be more or less equivalent. While Listings 7.22 and 7.23 are the "right" way to implement `take`, we will continue to rely mostly on "`::`" and immutable accumulators (or the execution stack) to build lists in Part I of this book. This is done for clarity. Using mutable builders, even hidden ones, would unnecessarily muddle the presentation of functional programming concepts.

7.10   Summary

- Behind every recursive function lies a recursive equality: The solution to a given problem *equals* a combination of solutions to smaller problems, solved recursively. Having these equalities in mind can help you design recursive algorithms correctly. This approach emphasizes the declarative side of functional programming by focusing attention on what the desired value *is*, instead of what the code must *do* to compute it.

- A recursive equality is often well defined only on a subset of input data. Values for which the equality does not hold need to be treated separately. They usually result in one or more non-recursive cases in a recursive function.

- Functional lists form a recursive data structure: A non-empty list consists of a head value, followed by another list (the tail). As such, lists are naturally amenable to recursive programming. Many operations can be implemented on lists as functions that perform a recursive call on the tail of the list. Recursion on one or more sublists other than the tail is possible as well.

- Some list functions end up being naturally tail recursive. Others may need to be rewritten from their natural form to achieve tail recursion. This rewrite usually involves including an accumulator as an additional argument to the function. There is often a trade-off between the simplicity of a recursive function in its natural form and the robustness of a tail recursive variant.

- Functions that need to build lists can sometimes rely on the execution stack to store list elements until the list is built. If, instead, tail recursion is needed, an accumulator should always build a list from the front, using a constant-time prepend operation. Building lists from the other end typically results in code that is quadratic in its runtime.

- If, as a consequence of building from the front, a list is constructed in reverse order, it can be reversed back after construction. List reversal takes time proportional to the length of the list. An additional reversal at the end is usually a better option than constructing a list in the right order if the cost of this construction is quadratic.

- In code designed to handle lists of arbitrary size, mutable buffers and/or re-assignable variables and loops can be used to build immutable lists. As long as mutation is restricted to local variables, the functions are still pure. It is not uncommon for functional code libraries to rely internally on such imperative constructs.

Chapter 8

Case Study: Binary Search Trees

Ordered mappings can be implemented as binary search trees. In this case study, trees are immutable, and values are added or removed by building new trees. Trees are recursive—the children of a tree are themselves trees—and most tree operations are implemented recursively. Binary search trees are only efficient to the extent that they are well balanced—not too deep in height. This case study refines the initial code to implement AVL trees, a classic self-balancing strategy.

8.1   Binary Search Trees

Binary search trees are a form of rooted trees sometimes used to implement mappings from keys to values. Key–value pairs are stored in the nodes of the tree. Each node has up to two children, the *left* child and the *right* child, which are themselves binary trees.

Binary search trees assume a total order on keys and maintain an invariant property: The key in any node is greater than all the keys in its left child, and less than all the keys in its right child. Using this property, you can search for a key k in a tree with the following algorithm: If k equals the key of the root, it is found, and the corresponding value can be retrieved; otherwise, if k is less than the key of the root, it is searched in the left tree, if any, using the same algorithm; otherwise, k is greater than the key of the root, and it is searched in the right tree, if any, using the same algorithm.

This algorithm is naturally recursive: A tree search proceeds by searching inside subtrees, recursively. A search ends either when it finds an equal key in a node (success) or when it reaches a point where a child is missing (failure). Many other tree operations are defined recursively, and to implement them is a good illustration of the recursive patterns discussed in earlier chapters.

The fundamental property of key lookup in a binary search tree is that you explore at most one of the children of any node. As a consequence, the worst-case time complexity of a search is bounded by the length of the longest branch in a tree, called the height of the tree. If a tree is well balanced, its height is no more than the binary logarithm of the number of nodes. This means that lookup in a balanced binary search tree that contains n keys takes time proportional to $\log_2(n)$.

Figure 8.1 depicts a binary search tree that contains the keys 6, 20, 32, 43, 51, 52, 57, 60, 71, 78, and 83. The values associated with the keys are omitted. As an illustration, to search for key 51, you would compare 51 to 57, follow the left branch, compare 51 to 43, follow the right branch, and find the node with the 51 key. A search for key 79 would

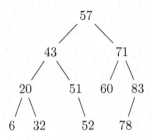

Figure 8.1 A binary search tree.

compare it to 57, 71, 83, and 78 before failing. The number of comparisons equals the length of the branch being followed.

8.2   Sets of Integers as Binary Search Trees

A proper implementation of mappings as binary search trees would define a tree type parameterized by the types of keys and values, and by some notion of ordering on the type used for keys. To keep the code clear, this case study does not use type or ordering parameterization: Keys are integers, compared by their natural order. Furthermore, all the apropos algorithms and implementing functions are centered on keys, not values—stored values are not relevant to the discussion of recursion. Accordingly, the code ignores values and stores only keys, thus implementing a set of keys instead of a mapping from keys to values.

Trees could be implemented as in earlier illustrations, following the same pattern as in Listings 5.8 and 6.7:

Scala

```scala
enum BinTree:
  case Empty
  case Node(key: Int, left: BinTree, right: BinTree)
```

Empty is the empty tree; non-empty trees consist of a Node that includes a key and two children. Missing subtrees are represented as empty trees. Given this type, you would then implement tree functions by using pattern matching. For instance, a function isEmpty can be written as follows:

```scala
                                                         ─── Scala ───
def isEmpty(tree: BinTree): Boolean = tree match
  case Empty          => true
  case Node(_, _, _) => false
```

This approach is well suited to a functional programming language. In a hybrid language, code is often easier to read when organized in terms of functional objects, as was done earlier for active–passive sets in Listing 4.4. The `BinTree` type is then implemented as an abstract class, which defines all the methods available on a tree, and `Empty` and `Node` are two subtypes for empty and non-empty trees, respectively:

```scala
                                                         ─── Scala ───
abstract class BinTree:
  def isEmpty: Boolean
  ... // all other tree functions, as abstract methods

case object Empty extends BinTree:
  def isEmpty = true
  ... // concrete methods for an empty tree

case class Node(key: Int, left: BinTree, right: BinTree) extends BinTree:
  def isEmpty = false
  ... // concrete methods for a non-empty tree
```

Instead of implementing functions of a tree argument, and using pattern matching on this argument, code is organized as methods of these two types: The `Empty` case of the function becomes a method in `Empty`; the `Node` case becomes a method in class `Node`. By using `case` classes, pattern matching remains available (as if the type was defined as an `enum`), and is used to implement rebalancing operations in Section 8.4.

NOTE

The `BinTree` class should be sealed to prevent subtypes other than `Node` and `Empty` from being added. Also, class `Node` and object `Empty` should be private to avoid the creation of nonsensical trees like `Node(1, Node(2, Empty, Empty), Empty)` (key 2 should be on the right, not the left, of root 1). On such ill-formed trees, most code behaves incorrectly (the search algorithm discussed earlier would fail to find key 2 in this tree). As important as they are when developing an actual library, these considerations are not relevant to the discussion of recursion that is the focus of this case study. For clarity, all classes and methods are left public throughout the chapter.

8.3   Implementation Without Rebalancing

The implementation of object `Empty` is straightforward:

```scala
                                                          ─── Scala ───
case object Empty extends BinTree:
   def isEmpty = true
   def contains(k: Int) = false

   def size = 0
   def height = 0

   def min = throw NoSuchElementException("Empty.min")
   def max = throw NoSuchElementException("Empty.max")

   def + (k: Int): BinTree = Node(k, Empty, Empty)
   def - (k: Int): BinTree = this

   def toList = List.empty
```

Listing 8.1: Empty binary search tree.

The empty tree contains nothing. In particular, it has no minimum and maximum values. Its size and depth are zero. Method "+" (insertion) adds a key into an empty tree by creating a single node that contains this key. Method "−" (deletion) returns the empty tree unchanged. The fact that trees are immutable is reflected in the signatures of methods "+" and "−", which produce a new tree.

The implementation of class `Node` is more interesting, due in particular to the use of recursion:

```scala
                                                          ─── Scala ───
case class Node(key: Int, left: BinTree, right: BinTree) extends BinTree:
   def isEmpty = false

   def size = 1 + left.size + right.size
   def height = 1 + (left.height max right.height)

   def min = if left.isEmpty then key else left.min
   def max = if right.isEmpty then key else right.max

   def contains(k: Int) =
      if k < key then left.contains(k)
```

```
    else if k > key then right.contains(k)
    else true
```

Listing 8.2: Querying methods on binary search trees.

Method `size` is implemented as in Listing 6.7, except that it uses `Empty` and `Node` methods instead of functions. Method `height` is almost the same, but since the height of a tree is the length of its longest branch, the heights of children are combined using `max` instead of "+". To find the smallest value in a tree, you only need to follow the leftmost branch: If a tree has no left child, its smallest value is its root; otherwise, it is the smallest value of the left child. Queries for the largest value are symmetric.[1]

Method `contains` follows the search algorithm outlined earlier. If the target of the search (`k`) is smaller than the key of the node (`key`), you search for it in the left child (it cannot possibly be in the right child). If the target is larger, you search for it in the right child. If it is neither smaller nor larger, it must be equal to the node key and therefore has been found. Recursion operates through a call to method `contains` on `left` or `right`. Note that these can be nodes (the search continues) or empty trees (terminal case).

The next method to implement is "+", used to insert a key into a tree:

```
                                                          Scala
def + (k: Int): Node =
  if k < key then Node(key, left + k, right)
  else if k > key then Node(key, left, right + k)
  else this
```

Listing 8.3: Key insertion in binary search trees.

The structure of this method is similar to that of the lookup method `contains`. If the key to be added, `k`, is less than the key of the node, it needs to be added inside the left child. The call `left + k` produces a new left child in which key `k` has been added. This new tree is combined with the existing right child, unchanged, to build a new node. Inserting a key greater than the key of the node works similarly on the right child. If the key to be added is already present, the tree is returned unchanged.

Adding a key to a tree is a functional operation in which no tree is modified. Its input is the tree before the insertion—`Node(key, left, right)`—and its output is a new tree after the insertion—for example, `Node(key, left + k, right)`. Note that the old tree and the new tree share data in memory: They refer to the same `right` tree.

---

[1]In Scala, no-argument methods can be implemented as fields: `def size = ...` could be replaced with `val size = ....` The memory footprint of nodes would increase, but `size` would become a constant-time operation. The same memory/speed trade-off is possible for `height`, `min`, or `max`. The self-balancing trees implemented in Section 8.4 rely heavily on height calculations and would benefit from making `height` a `val` instead of a `def`.

Indeed, with one tree being shared at each level of the recursion, the trees before and after insertion share all their nodes except for the one branch that is being traversed. This is a fundamental property of persistent data structures, which was discussed earlier in the context of functional lists in Section 3.7 (see, in particular, Figure 3.1).

If you are used to mutable types, beware of a common beginner mistake:

```scala
// DON'T DO THIS!
def + (k: Int): Node =
   if k < key then
      left + k
      Node(key, left, right)
   else if k > key then
      right + k
      Node(key, left, right)
   else this
```

Trying to implement method "+" like this is indicative of an imperative programming mindset, which assumes that `left + k` *modifies* the tree `left`. But `left + k` has no side effect. Instead, it builds a new tree, to be used in a larger expression. In this incorrect variant, the new tree is built but not used. Note also that `Node(key, left, right)` is the same thing as `this`, and that there is no value in constructing a node identical to an existing node.

As you are probably aware, key deletion in a tree tends to be trickier than key insertion. The difficulty stems from the fact that, after the root of a tree is removed, a new tree has to be built by somehow merging the left and right children, while maintaining the fundamental property of key ordering:

```scala
def - (k: Int): BinTree =
   if k < key then Node(key, left - k, right)
   else if k > key then Node(key, left, right - k)
   else if left.isEmpty then right
   else if right.isEmpty then left
   else
      val (minRight, othersRight) = right.minRemoved
      Node(minRight, left, othersRight)

def minRemoved: (Int, BinTree) =
   if left.isEmpty then (key, right)
   else
      val (min, othersLeft) = left.minRemoved
      (min, Node(key, othersLeft, right))
```

Listing 8.4: Key deletion in binary search trees.

Method "−" starts like method "+", by removing the target key k from either the left or the right child. However, the case k == key, which is trivial in the insertion method, is more challenging in the removal method. After removing the root of the tree, you are left with two separate child trees. If either child is empty, you can simply return the other tree, which contains all the keys in the set.

The complicated case is the final else: You are removing the root of a tree, and both the left and right children are non-empty. In that case, you need to extract a key from a child, and use it as the new root key. To maintain the ordering property of binary search trees, a common strategy is to focus on the smallest key of the right child (or, alternatively, the largest key of the left child). The smallest key of the right child is greater than all the keys in the left child (all the right child keys are). It is also smaller than all the other keys in the right child. Therefore, you can use this key as a new root, and use the remaining keys of the right child to create a new right child. This way, the new root is larger than all the keys in the left child and smaller than all the keys in the new right child.

Extracting this key is the task of method minRemoved, which returns a pair: the smallest key of a tree and the tree without this key. To remove key 57—the root—from the example tree in Figure 8.1, you apply minRemoved to the right child. This produces a pair (minRight, othersRight), where minRight is 60 and othersRight is the tree:

You then use minRight as the root of a new node whose right child is othersRight. The left child is unchanged. Figure 8.2 shows the resulting tree.

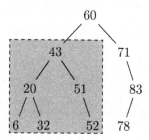

Figure 8.2 The binary search tree from Figure 8.1 after key 57 is removed.

To implement method minRemoved, you use a recursive approach similar to method min. The difference is that min only returns the minimum value, while minRemoved also builds a tree with the other values. If a node has no left child, then its root is the smallest key in the tree, and its right child is what is left of the tree once this key is removed. Otherwise, the smallest key in the tree is the smallest key in the left child, just as before. This left child, with the smallest key removed, becomes the new left child of the node. The key and right child of the node are unchanged.

If needed, you can build a list of all the keys in a tree. Because of the key ordering property of binary search trees, an in-order traversal—left child, then root, then right child—produces an ordered list of keys. A naive implementation is straightforward:

```
——————————————————————————————————————————— Scala ———
// DON'T DO THIS!

// in object Empty:
def toList = List.empty

// in class Node:
def toList = left.toList ::: key :: right.toList
```

Although this method does produce the right list, its performance suffers from the use of the list concatenation operator ":::", which takes time proportional to the length of the first operand (see the discussion of function `concat` from Listing 7.9). Keep in mind that, due to the recursive nature of method `toList`, this is not a one-time cost: The concatenation operator is used again within the calls `left.toList` and `right.toList`, and again in the recursive calls within these calls, and so on. To avoid this inefficiency, you can build the list in an accumulator argument instead:

```
——————————————————————————————————————————— Scala ———
// in class BinTree:
def toList: List[Int] = makeList(List.empty)
def makeList(list: List[Int]): List[Int]

// in object Empty:
def makeList(list: List[Int]) = list

// in class Node:
def makeList(list: List[Int]) = left.makeList(key :: right.makeList(list))
```

Listing 8.5: Conversion from binary search trees to sorted lists.

A helper method `makeList`, with an accumulator `list`, is added. In object `Empty`, which contains no key, the accumulator is returned unchanged. In class `Node`, a recursive call `right.makeList(list)` adds all the keys of the right child to the list. Then, the root of the node is added, using "::". Finally, another recursive call to `left.makeList` adds all the keys of the left child. Note how all the keys are added to the list using "::", and ":::" is never used.

When we used this technique earlier, in Section 7.9, it had the unfortunate consequence that a list was built in reverse order and had to be reversed once after building. In the case of binary search trees, you avoid this final reversal by traversing the tree from right to left. This way, the larger keys are added first, followed by the smaller keys.

Since keys are always added to the front of the list, you end up with a list in increasing order, as desired.

Finally, you can provide users with a tree-building function. (Recall that `Node` and `Empty` would not be public in an actual implementation.) The companion object defines methods `apply` and `fromSet` to build a tree directly from a set of keys:

```scala
                                                              ─── Scala ───
object BinTree:
  def empty: BinTree = Empty

  def fromSet(keys: Set[Int]): BinTree =
    def makeTree(list: List[Int]): BinTree =
      if list.isEmpty then Empty
      else
          val (left, mid :: right) = list.splitAt(list.length / 2)
          Node(mid, makeTree(left), makeTree(right))

    makeTree(keys.toList.sorted)
  end fromSet

  def apply(keys: Int*): BinTree = fromSet(keys.toSet)
```

Listing 8.6: Set conversion to balanced binary search trees, improved in Lis. 8.12.

Function `fromSet` works by first sorting the keys into a list. The middle value of the list is used as the root key of the tree. The two children are built recursively. The values left of the middle key make up the left child, and the values right of the middle key make up the right child. Because the list is sorted, the resulting tree satisfies the key ordering property of binary search trees. Furthermore, since the lengths of the left and right lists differ by at most one, you end up with a well-balanced tree. A function `apply` with variable-length arguments is added for convenience, so trees can be built directly from enumerated keys, as in `BinTree(4,5,1,3,2)`.

8.4 Self-Balancing Trees

Function `fromSet` in Listing 8.6 builds binary search trees that are well balanced. However, once you start to apply methods "+" and "–" on existing trees, the newly produced trees can become unbalanced. As an example of an extreme case, consider this alternative implementation of `fromSet`:

```scala
                                                              ─── Scala ───
// DON'T DO THIS
def fromSet(keys: Set[Int]): BinTree =
  var set = empty
  for key <- keys do set += key // i.e., set = set + key
  set
```

This function produces an extremely unbalanced tree if the input set of keys happens to be sorted. With this implementation, the expression `fromSet(BitSet(1,2,3,4,5))` produces the following tree:

On such a degenerate tree, method `contains` is linear in time, instead of logarithmic. What you want instead are methods "+" and "-" that always return balanced trees.

There are typically two notions of "balanced" used when discussing binary trees. One is based on the *size* of trees (number of keys), the other on their *heights* (number of nodes in the longest branch). A tree is balanced if every node has two children with (about) the same size/height. When implementing binary search trees, balancing strategies often focus on height, since the time performance of lookups depends on the length of branches. For the purpose of this case study, a tree is said to be balanced if all its nodes are such that the heights of their children differ by at most one. According to this definition, the tree depicted in Figure 8.1 is balanced. However, after key 57 is removed, the resulting tree in Figure 8.2 becomes unbalanced: Node 71 has an empty left child (height of zero) and a right child with a height of two.

Several strategies may be used to implement insertion and deletion operations that keep a tree balanced. One such approach is known as AVL trees, named after their inventors, Adelson-Velsky and Landis.[2] When applied to an AVL tree, insertion and deletion always produce a balanced tree. In the remainder of this chapter, the code from Section 8.3 is modified to implement AVL trees.

The strategy behind AVL trees is based on rebalancing a tree after an insertion or a deletion has made it unbalanced. This rebalancing is implemented in terms of tree rotations (Figure 8.3). A rotation maintains the key ordering property of binary search trees—$T_1 \ll k_1 \ll T_2 \ll k_2 \ll T_3$—and thus can be used to rebalance a tree. Left-to-right rotations are used to decrease the height of a left child tree and increase the height

---

[2]Many collections frameworks use a notion of *red-black trees* instead. Red-black trees implement a looser balancing notion in which the longest branch is guaranteed to be at most twice as long as the shortest branch. Insertion and deletion in red-black trees are slightly more efficient than in AVL trees, but the AVL trees are better balanced.

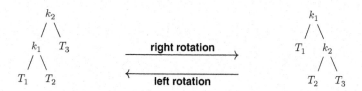

Figure 8.3 Tree rotations.

of a right child. Right-to-left rotations have the opposite effect. Pattern matching makes it straightforward to implement tree rotations in the `Node` class:

```scala
def rotateRight: Node = left match
  case Node(keyL, leftL, rightL) => Node(keyL, leftL, Node(key, rightL, right))

def rotateLeft: Node = right match
  case Node(keyR, leftR, rightR) => Node(keyR, Node(key, left, leftR), rightR)
```

Listing 8.7: Left and right rotations on binary search trees.

In `rotateRight`, k_1, k_2, T_1, T_2, and T_3 from Figure 8.3 are `keyL`, `key`, `leftL`, `rightL`, and `right`, respectively. There is no pattern for empty trees, which never need to be rotated.

Next, you introduce a method `imbalance` to detect imbalanced trees:

```scala
// in object Empty:
def imbalance = 0

// in class Node:
def imbalance = right.height - left.height
```

On balanced trees, this method returns a value that lies between -1 and 1 (included). When a key is added or removed, a tree's imbalance can reach -2 or 2. For instance, node 71 has imbalance 1 in the tree from Figure 8.1. After key 60 is removed, the imbalance becomes 2, an indicator that the tree needs to be rebalanced. When a tree has an imbalance of 2, you need to consider two cases:

- The right child is perfectly balanced or "right-heavy" (its own imbalance is 1). In that case, a single right-to-left rotation is enough to rebalance the tree:

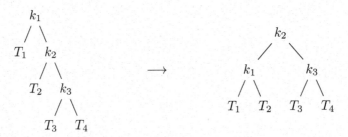

- The right child is "left-heavy" (its own imbalance is -1). In that case, two rotations are needed: first a left-to-right rotation of the right child, to get back to the previous case, and then a right-to-left rotation as before:

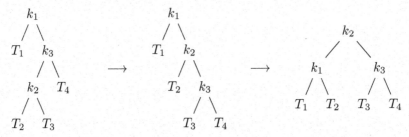

The case of a tree with a -2 imbalance is treated symmetrically. This strategy is implemented in a method `avl`, relying again on the power of pattern matching:

```scala
def avl: Node = imbalance match
  case -2 => left.imbalance match
    case 0 | -1 => rotateRight
    case 1       => Node(key, left.rotateLeft, right).rotateRight
  case 2 => right.imbalance match
    case 0 | 1       => rotateLeft
    case -1          => Node(key, left, right.rotateRight).rotateLeft
  case 0 | 1 | -1 => this
```

Listing 8.8: Rebalancing of binary search trees by rotations.

With the balancing method `avl` implemented, the insertion method is slightly modified to always produce balanced trees:

Scala

```
def + (k: Int): Node =
  if k < key then Node(key, left + k, right).avl
  else if k > key then Node(key, left, right + k).avl
  else this
```

Listing 8.9: Key insertion in self-balancing binary search trees.

The only change from before is that you apply method `avl` every time a new node is constructed. Subtrees `left + k` and `right + k` are built recursively using the same method "+", and thus are guaranteed to be balanced.

Deletion is similarly modified to make sure that all new trees are balanced. This requires changing both methods "−" and `minRemoved`:

Scala

```
def - (k: Int): BinTree =
  if k < key then Node(key, left - k, right).avl
  else if k > key then Node(key, left, right - k).avl
  else if left.isEmpty then right
  else if right.isEmpty then left
  else
    val (minRight, othersRight) = right.minRemoved
    Node(minRight, left, othersRight).avl

def minRemoved: (Int, BinTree) =
  if left.isEmpty then (key, right)
  else
    val (min, othersLeft) = left.minRemoved
    (min, Node(key, othersLeft, right).avl)
```

Listing 8.10: Key deletion in self-balancing binary search trees; see also Lis. 8.11.

Observe that removing a value from the right child can decrease its height by at most one. In other words, `othersRight.height` is equal to `right.height` or `right.height - 1`. So, if `right.height` is at least equal to `left.height`, the height of `left` and the height of `othersRight` differ at most by one. Therefore, in this case, `Node(minRight, left, othersRight)` is necessarily balanced, and the call to method `avl` is unnecessary. Conversely, if `left.height` is at least equal to `right.height`, you can build a balanced tree by removing the largest key in the left child instead of the smallest key in the right child. By always removing from the tallest tree, you reduce the number of rebalancing operations. This results in an improved implementation of method "-", in which the last call to `avl` is omitted:

```scala
def - (k: Int): BinTree =
  if k < key then Node(key, left - k, right).avl
  else if k > key then Node(key, left, right - k).avl
  else if left.isEmpty then right
  else if right.isEmpty then left
  else if left.height > right.height then
    val (maxLeft, othersLeft) = left.maxRemoved
    Node(maxLeft, othersLeft, right) // no call to avl needed
  else
    val (minRight, othersRight) = right.minRemoved
    Node(minRight, left, othersRight) // no call to avl needed
```

Listing 8.11: Key deletion in self-balancing binary search trees; see also Lis. 8.10.

Method `maxRemoved` is symmetrical to method `minRemoved` and is omitted.

To conclude this chapter, let us revisit function `fromSet` in Listing 8.6, which builds balanced trees from an existing set. Although the earlier implementation nicely illustrates list recursion and pattern matching, it will be inefficient on large sets because method `length` takes time proportional to the size of the list, and `splitAt` needs to allocate new lists (see the discussion of method `take` in Section 7.4). You could reimplement `fromSet` more efficiently by replacing the list with a sequence with fast indexing (typically backed by an array):

```scala
def fromSet(keys: Set[Int]): BinTree =
  val keySeq = keys.toIndexedSeq.sorted

  def makeTree(from: Int, to: Int): BinTree =
    if from > to then Empty
    else
      val mid = (from + to) / 2
      Node(keySeq(mid), makeTree(from, mid - 1), makeTree(mid + 1, to))

  makeTree(0, keySeq.length - 1)
```

Listing 8.12: Conversion from set to binary search trees, improved from Lis. 8.6.

The function follows the same algorithm as before, but does not explicitly create sublists. Instead, lists are represented as pairs of indices in a fixed sorted sequence. A helper function uses two integer arguments to represent a sublist from which to build a tree and relies on constant-time access to the middle element of the sequence. Function `makeTree` still uses non-tail recursion, but the depth of the recursion will not exceed the binary logarithm of the size of the set, which should be acceptable in practice.

8.5 Summary

Binary trees form a typical recursive structure on which recursive programming can be demonstrated. Many operations, such as lookups and insertions, are implemented in terms of applying the same operation to subtrees. Functional trees are defined in terms of a terminal case, the empty tree `Empty`, and a constructor `Node` that creates a new tree from two children and the contents of the root. This is reminiscent of functional lists, which are built from the empty list `Nil` and a `cons` operator "`::`". The fundamental difference is that a tree node can have two children, while a non-empty list has only one tail.

In languages that support pattern matching, trees can be processed by treating the empty tree as a special case, and deconstructing a non-empty tree into a node value and two children, in the same way a non-empty list is broken into its head and tail. Although tree operations could be implemented entirely in terms of functions using pattern matching, a functional–object-oriented style is often preferred in hybrid languages.

Functional trees cannot be mutated, and insertion and deletion operations produce new trees instead. However, many subtrees can be shared between the tree before and the tree after an insertion or deletion. This is again reminiscent of the data sharing already discussed in the context of lists.

Some tree operations, such as deletion, are more complex than their list counterparts. While removing the head of a list leaves a tail that is itself a list, the remaining children of a tree after the root is removed do not form a tree and need to somehow be merged.

Binary search trees extend binary trees by maintaining a key ordering property that can speed up lookups. This property needs to be preserved by all tree operations, including the merging of children after a tree root has been removed.

Binary search trees offer efficient lookup only to the extent that a tree is well balanced. While a balanced tree can easily be built from a list, further insertions and deletions can result in unbalanced trees. Algorithms have been devised for trees that remain balanced after every insertion and deletion. As an example, this case study extends basic binary search trees into self-balancing AVL trees. The implementation of rebalancing operations relies heavily on recursion and pattern matching.

Chapter 9

Higher-Order Functions

It is natural for a programming paradigm that centers on functions to treat them as first-class citizens. In functional programming, functions are values and can be stored in variables and passed as arguments. Functions that consume or produce other functions are said to be higher-order functions. Using higher-order functions, computations can be parameterized by other computations in powerful ways.

9.1 Functions as Values

Previous chapters have shown how pure functions from immutable values to immutable values can be used as building programming blocks, and how complex computations can be achieved by composing functions, including composing a function with itself through recursion. Although pure functions, immutability, and recursion are essential concepts, many would argue that the distinctive characteristic of a functional programming style is the use of functions as values.

To help motivate the benefits of functions as values, consider this first illustration. Suppose you need to search for a value in a list. You can implement such a lookup in a recursive function, similar to function **contains** from Chapter 7:

```
                                                              Scala
def find[A](list: List[A], target: A): Option[A] = list match
  case Nil     => None
  case h :: t => if h == target then Some(h) else find(t, target)
```

Listing 9.1: List lookup for a specific target.

This function checks whether the head of a non-empty list equals the target and, if not, keeps searching in the tail of the list. It returns an option to allow for cases where the target value is not found. You can use **find** to look for specific values in a list, like a list of temperatures:

```
                                                              Scala
val temps = List(88, 91, 78, 69, 100, 98, 70)
find(temps, 78) // Some(78)
find(temps, 79) // None
```

A limitation of this function, however, is that you can only search for a target if you already have a value equal to that target. For instance, you cannot search a list of temperatures for a value greater than 90. Of course, you can easily write another function for that:

```scala
def findGreaterThan90(list: List[Int]): Option[Int] = list match
   case Nil     => None
   case h :: t => if h > 90 then Some(h) else findGreaterThan90(t)

findGreaterThan90(temps) // Some(91)
```

But what if you need to search for a temperature greater than 80 instead? You can write another function, in which an integer argument replaces the hardcoded value 90:

```scala
def findGreaterThan(list: List[Int], bound: Int): Option[Int] = list match
   case Nil     => None
   case h :: t => if h > bound then Some(h) else findGreaterThan(t, bound)

findGreaterThan(temps, 80) // Some(88)
```

This is better, but the new function still cannot be used to search for a temperature *less* than 90, or for a string that ends with "a", or for a project with identity 12345.

You will notice that functions `find`, `findGreaterThan90`, and `findGreaterThan` are strikingly similar. The algorithm is the same in all three cases. The only part of the implementation that changes is the test in the `if-then-else`, which is `h == target` in the first function, `h > 90` in the next, and `h > bound` in the third.

It would be nice to write a generic function `find` parameterized by a search criterion. Criteria such as "to be greater than 90" or "to end with "a"" or "to have identity 12345" could then be used as arguments. To implement the `if-then-else` part of this function, you would apply the search criterion to the head of the list to produce a Boolean value. In other words, you need the search criterion to be a *function* from A to Boolean.

Such a function `find` can be written. It takes another function as an argument, named `test`:

```scala
def find[A](list: List[A], test: A => Boolean): Option[A] = list match
   case Nil     => None
   case h :: t => if test(h) then Some(h) else find(t, test)
```

Listing 9.2: Recursive implementation of higher-order function `find`.

The type of argument `test` is `A => Boolean`, which in Scala denotes functions from A to Boolean. As a function, `test` is applied to the head of the list `h` (of type A), and produces a value of type Boolean (used as the `if` condition).

You can use this new function `find` to search a list of temperatures for a value greater than 90 by first defining the "greater than 90" search criterion as a function:

```Scala
def greaterThan90(x: Int): Boolean = x > 90
find(temps, greaterThan90) // Some(91)
```

In this last expression, you do not invoke function `greaterThan90` on an integer argument. Instead, you use the function itself as an argument to `find`. To search for a project with identity 12345, simply define a different search criterion:

```Scala
def hasID12345(project: Project): Boolean = project.id == 12345L
find(projects, hasID12345) // project with identity 12345
```

Because it takes a function as an argument, `find` is said to be a *higher-order* function. Functional programming libraries define many standard higher-order functions, some of which are discussed in Chapter 10. In particular, a method `find` is already defined on Scala's `List` type. The two searches in the preceding examples can be written as follows:

```Scala
temps.find(greaterThan90)
projects.find(hasID12345)
```

From now on, code examples in this chapter use the standard method `find` instead of the earlier user-defined function.

Method `find` is a higher-order function because it takes another function as an argument. A function can also be higher-order by returning a value that is a function. For example, instead of implementing `greaterThan90`, you can define a function that builds a search criterion to look for temperatures greater than a given bound:

```Scala
def greaterThan(bound: Int): Int => Boolean =
    def greaterThanBound(x: Int): Boolean = x > bound
    greaterThanBound
```

Listing 9.3: Example of a function that returns a function; see also Lis. 9.4 and 9.5.

Function `greaterThan` works by first defining a function `greaterThanBound`. This function is not applied to anything but simply returned as a value. Note that `greaterThan` has return type `Int => Boolean`, which denotes functions from integers to Booleans. Given a lower bound `b`, the expression `greaterThan(b)` is a function, which tests whether an integer is greater than `b`. It can be used as an argument to higher-order method `find`:

```scala
──────────────────────────────────────────────── Scala ──
temps.find(greaterThan(90))
temps.find(greaterThan(80))
```

In a similar fashion, you can define a function to generate search criteria for projects:

```scala
──────────────────────────────────────────────── Scala ──
def hasID(identity: Long): Project => Boolean =
   def hasGivenID(project: Project): Boolean = project.id == identity
   hasGivenID

projects.find(hasID(12345L))
projects.find(hasID(54321L))
```

9.2   Currying

Functions that return other functions are common in functional programming, and many languages define a more convenient syntax for them:

```scala
──────────────────────────────────────────────── Scala ──
def greaterThan(bound: Int)(x: Int): Boolean = x > bound
def hasID(identity: Long)(project: Project): Boolean = project.id == identity
```

Listing 9.4: Example of higher-order functions defined through currying.

It might appear as if `greaterThan` is a function of two arguments, `bound` and `x`, but it is not. It is a function of a single argument, `bound`, which returns a function of type `Int => Boolean`, as before; `x` is actually an argument of the function being returned.

Functions written in this style are said to be *curried*.[1] A curried function is a function that consumes its first list of arguments, returns another function that uses the next argument list, and so on. You can read the definition of `greaterThan` as implementing a function that takes an integer argument `bound` and returns another function, which takes an integer argument `x` and returns the Boolean `x > bound`. In other words, the return value of `greaterThan` is the function that maps `x` to `x > bound`.

Functional programming languages rely heavily on currying. In particular, currying can be used as a device to implement all functions as single-argument functions, as in

---

[1]The concept is named after the logician Haskell Curry, and the words *curried* and *currying* are sometimes capitalized.

languages like Haskell and ML. For instance, we tend to think of addition as a function of two arguments:

```scala
                                                            ——— Scala ———
def plus(x: Int, y: Int): Int = x + y // a function of type (Int, Int) => Int
plus(5, 3)                            // 8
```

However, you can also think of it as a single-argument (higher-order) function:

```scala
                                                            ——— Scala ———
def plus(x: Int)(y: Int): Int = x + y // a function of type Int => (Int => Int)
plus(5)                               // a function of type Int => Int
plus(5)(3)                            // 8
```

Curried functions are so common in functional programming that the => that represents function types is typically assumed to be right-associative: Int => (Int => Int) is simply written Int => Int => Int. For example, the function

```scala
                                                            ——— Scala ———
def lengthBetween(low: Int)(high: Int)(str: String): Boolean =
    str.length >= low && str.length <= high
```

has type Int => Int => String => Boolean. You can use it to produce a Boolean, as in

```scala
                                                            ——— Scala ———
lengthBetween(1)(5)("foo") // true
```

but also to produce other functions:

```scala
                                                            ——— Scala ———
val lengthBetween1AndBound: Int => String => Boolean = lengthBetween(1)
val lengthBetween1and5: String => Boolean            = lengthBetween(1)(5)

lengthBetween1AndBound(5)("foo") // true
lengthBetween1and5("foo")        // true
```

Before closing this section on currying, we should consider a feature that is particular to Scala (although other languages use slightly different tricks for the same purpose).

In Scala, you can call a single-argument function on an expression delimited by curly braces without the need for additional parentheses. So, instead of writing

```scala
println({
    val two = 2
    two + two
}) // prints 4
```

you can simply write:

```scala
println {
    val two = 2
    two + two
} // prints 4
```

To use this syntax when multiple arguments are involved, you can rely on currying to adapt a multi-argument function into a single-argument function. For instance, the curried variant of function `plus` can be invoked as follows:

```scala
plus(5) {
    val two = 2
    two + 1
}
```

This is still value 8, as before.

Many functions and methods are curried in Scala for the sole purpose of benefiting from this syntax. The syntax is introduced here because we will encounter some example uses throughout the book, starting with the next section.

9.3 Function Literals

It would be inconvenient if, to use higher-order functions like `find`, you always had to separately define (and name) argument functions like `hasID12345` and `greaterThan90`. After all, when you call a function on a string or an integer, you don't need to define (and name) the values first. This is because programming languages define a syntax for strings and integer literals, like the `"foo"` and 42 that are sprinkled throughout this book's code illustrations. Similarly, functional programming languages, which rely heavily on higher-order functions, offer syntax for *function literals*, also called *anonymous functions*. The most common form of function literals is lambda expressions, which are often the first thing that comes to mind when you hear that a language has support for functional programming.

In Scala, the syntax for lambda expressions is (v1: T1, v2: T2, ...) => expr.[2] This defines a function with arguments v1, v2, ... that returns the value produced by expr. For instance, the following expression is a function, of type Int => Int, that adds 1 to an integer:

```scala
                                                             ── Scala ──
(x: Int) => x + 1
```

Function literals can be used to simplify calls to higher-order functions like find:

```scala
                                                             ── Scala ──
temps.find((temp: Int) => temp > 90)
projects.find((proj: Project) => proj.id == 12345L)
```

The Boolean functions "to be greater than 90" and "to have identity 12345" are implemented as lambda expressions, which are passed directly as arguments to method find.

You can also use function literals as return values of other functions. So, a third way to define functions greaterThan and hasID, besides using named local functions or currying, is as follows:

```scala
                                                             ── Scala ──
def greaterThan(bound: Int): Int => Boolean = (x: Int) => x > bound
def hasID(identity: Long): Project => Boolean = (p: Project) => p.id == identity
```

Listing 9.5: Example of higher-order functions defined using lambda expressions.

The expression (x: Int) => x > bound replaces the local function greaterThanBound from Listing 9.3.

Function literals have no name, and usually do not declare their return type. Compilers can sometimes infer the types of their arguments. You could omit argument types in all the examples written so far:

```scala
                                                             ── Scala ──
temps.find(temp => temp > 90)
projects.find(proj => proj.id == 12345L)

def greaterThan(bound: Int): Int => Boolean = x => x > bound
def hasID(identity: Long): Project => Boolean = p => p.id == identity
```

---

[2]Lambda expressions can also be parameterized by types, though this is a more advanced feature not used in this book. For instance, Listing 2.7 defines a function first of type (A, A) => A, parameterized by type A. It could be written as the lambda expression [A] => (p: (A, A)) => p(0).

Today, many programming languages have a syntax for function literals. The Scala expression `(temp: Int) => temp > 90` could be written in other languages as shown here:

```
(int temp) -> temp > 90                    // Java
(int temp) => temp > 90                    // C#
[](int temp) { return temp > 90; }         // C++
{ temp: Int -> temp > 90 }                 // Kotlin
fn temp: int => temp > 90                  // ML
fn temp -> temp > 90 end                   // Elixir
function (temp) { return temp > 90 }       // JavaScript
temp => temp > 90                          // also JavaScript
lambda { |temp| temp > 90 }                // Ruby
-> temp { temp > 90 }                      // also Ruby
(lambda (temp) (> temp 90))                // Lisp
(fn [temp] (> temp 90))                    // Clojure
lambda temp: temp > 90                     // Python
```

The argument (or arguments) of a lambda expression can be composite types. For example, assume you have a list of pairs (*date*, *temperature*), and you need to find a temperature greater than 90 in January, February, or March. You can use `find` with a lambda expression on pairs:

```
───────────────────────────────────────────────────── Scala ───────
val datedTemps: List[(LocalDate, Int)] = ...
datedTemps.find(dt => dt(0).getMonthValue <= 3 && dt(1) > 90)
```

The test checks that the first element of a pair (a date) is in the first three months of the year, and that the second element of the pair (a temperature) is greater than 90.

Languages that support pattern matching often let you use it within a lambda expression. In the preceding example, you can use pattern matching to extract the date and temperature from a pair, instead of `dt(0)` and `dt(1)`:

```
───────────────────────────────────────────────────── Scala ───────
datedTemps.find((date, temp) => date.getMonthValue <= 3 && temp > 90)
```

This is a lot more readable than the variant that uses `dt(0)` and `dt(1)`.

More complex patterns can be used. In Scala, a series of **case** patterns, enclosed in curly braces, also define an anonymous function. For instance, if a list contains temperatures with an optional date, and temperatures without a date are not eligible, you can search for a temperature greater than 90 in the first three months with the following code:[3]

---

[3]Here, I must admit that the Scala syntax can be confusing at first. As with code blocks, a call `f({...})` can omit extraneous parentheses, and be written as `f{...}`. This example becomes clearer once you understand that it is a call to a higher-order method on a function literal defined with pattern matching and that a pair of unnecessary parentheses have been dropped.

```scala
val optionalDatedTemps: List[(Option[LocalDate], Int)] = ...

optionalDatedTemps.find {
  case (Some(date), temp) => date.getMonthValue <= 3 && temp > 90
  case _                  => false
}
```
Scala

9.4 Functions Versus Methods

So far in this book, the words *function* and *method* have been used almost interchangeably. It is now time to discuss differences between the two. Methods are often defined as being functions associated with a target object: `x.m(y)`, which invokes method `m` on object `x` with argument `y`, is not much different from `f(x,y)`, which calls a function `f` on `x` and `y`. This way of differentiating methods from functions is premised on them being mechanisms used to encapsulate behaviors—blocks of code—which both methods and functions are.

However, the story somewhat changes once functions become values. A more meaningful difference between methods and functions in the context of this book is that functions are values in functional programming, while methods are not objects in object-oriented programming. In a hybrid language like Scala, functions *are* objects; methods are not. Instead of the function literal `(temp: Int) => temp > 90`, you could build a regular object explicitly. This object would implement the type `Function`:

```scala
object GreaterThan90 extends Function[Int, Boolean]:
  def apply(x: Int): Boolean = x > 90
```
Scala

The notation `Int => Boolean` is syntactic sugar for the type `Function[Int, Boolean]`. This type defines a method `apply`, which is invoked when the function is applied. The expression `temps.find(GreaterThan90)` could replace `temps.find(temp => temp > 90)` to perform the same computation.[4] `GreaterThan90` is an object—which defines a function—not a method. In contrast,

```scala
def greaterThan90(x: Int): Boolean = x > 90
```
Scala

defines a method `greaterThan90`, not a function.

But then, the plot thickens. We *did* write `temps.find(greaterThan90)` earlier to search a list of temperatures, as if `greaterThan90` were an object, which it is not. This is possible because the language implements bridges between methods and functions. In

---

[4]In JVM languages, anonymous functions are often compiled through a separate mechanism but, as a function, object `GreaterThan90` is conceptually equivalent to the earlier lambda expression.

Section 2.5, we discussed extension methods, a mechanism to make a function appear as a method. Here, what we need is a conversion in the opposite direction so that we can use a method as a function.

The fancy name for this is η-*conversion*. In λ-calculus, it states the equivalence between f and $\lambda x. f\, x$. In plainer terms, you can think of it as an equivalence between `greaterThan90` and `x => greaterThan90(x)`. As units of computation, both perform the same task of asserting whether an integer is greater than 90. Given that the argument of `find` must have type `Int => Boolean`, and `greaterThan90` is a method from `Int` to `Boolean`, the intent of the expression `temps.find(greaterThan90)` is pretty clear, and the compiler is able to insert the necessary η-conversion.

Other languages offer similar bridges to create a function out of a method, sometimes by relying on a more explicit syntax. In Java, for instance, a lambda expression `x -> target.method(x)` can be replaced with a method reference `target::method`. Kotlin uses a similar syntax.

9.5   Single-Abstract-Method Interfaces

In hybrid languages, functions are objects, and lambda expressions are used as a convenient way to create such objects. Indeed, the lambda expression syntax is so handy that many languages let you use it to create instances of types other than functions.

A single-abstract-method (SAM) interface is an interface that contains exactly one abstract method. In Scala, for instance, the type `Function[A,B]` (or, equivalently, `A => B`) is a SAM interface with a single abstract method `apply`. We have used lambda expressions in code illustrations to create instances of `Function[A,B]`, but it turns out that all SAM types can be instantiated using lambda expressions, even types that are not related to `Function`:

```
                                                    ─ Scala ─
abstract class Formatter:
   def format(str: String): String
   def println(any: Any): Unit = Predef.println(format(any.toString))
```

Class `Formatter` defines only one abstract method `format` and is therefore a SAM interface. It can be implemented using lambda expressions:

```
                                                    ─ Scala ─
val f: Formatter = str => str.toUpperCase
f.println(someValue)
```

Note how method `println` is called on object `f`, which was defined as a lambda expression. This is possible only because `f` was declared with type `Formatter`; the expression `(str => str.toUpperCase).println("foo")` would make no sense.

Many Java interfaces can be implemented as lambdas, even though they predate Java's syntax for lambda expressions and have little to do with functional programming:

```scala
                                                                 ─ Scala ─
val absComp: Comparator[Int] = (x, y) => x.abs.compareTo(y.abs)

val stream: IntStream = ...
val loggingStream: IntStream = stream.onClose(() => logger.info("closing stream"))
```

Comparator is a Java 2 SAM interface with an abstract method compare. Stream method onClose uses a single argument of type Runnable, a Java 1 SAM interface with an abstract method run. Both Comparator and Runnable can be implemented as lambda expressions.

9.6   Partial Application

In addition to lambda expressions, currying, and η-conversion, partial application is yet another mechanism used to create function values. In Scala, it takes the form of an underscore used in place of a part of an expression. This produces a function that, when applied, replaces the underscore with its argument in the given expression. For instance, the following code searches for a temperature greater than 90 (in Fahrenheit) in a list of Celsius temperatures:

```scala
                                                                 ─ Scala ─
celsiusTemps.find(temp => temp * 1.8 + 32 > 90)
```

Instead of a lambda expression, you can build the desired function argument by replacing temp with an underscore in the expression temp * 1.8 + 32 > 90:

```scala
                                                                 ─ Scala ─
celsiusTemps.find(_ * 1.8 + 32 > 90)
```

The expression _ * 1.8 + 32 > 90 represents a Boolean function that maps temp to temp * 1.8 + 32 > 90, just like the function defined by the lambda expression temp => temp * 1.8 + 32 > 90. Searches written earlier using lambda expressions can use partial application instead:

```scala
                                                                 ─ Scala ─
temps.find(_ > 90)
projects.find(_.id == 12345L)
```

Partial application is generalized to multi-argument functions by using several underscores in the same expression. For instance, _ * 1.8 + 32 > _ is a two-argument function that compares a Celsius temperature to a Fahrenheit bound, and `_.id == _` is a function that takes a project and an identity and checks whether the project has the given identity.[5]

Partial application can easily be abused. Code is often easier to read with lambda expressions that name (and sometimes type) their arguments. Compared to the shorter `_.id == 12345L`, the longer expression `project => project.id == 12345L` makes it clearer that projects are being searched, and `(project, id) => project.id == id` is a lot easier to read than `_.id == _`.

Aside on Scoping

After a variable is introduced in a program, the variable's name is bound to that variable's value. The part of the program where this binding exists is called the *scope* of the declaration. Scoping rules vary from programming language to programming language. The state of affairs is somewhat simpler than it used to be because almost all languages rely on *static* (or *lexical*) scoping. Only a few languages continue to offer a form of *dynamic* (or *late binding*) scoping. However, many popular languages implement their static scoping rules differently, so caution is still warranted.

The following Scala program involves multiple scopes:

Scala

```
var str: String = ""

def f(x: Int): Int =
  if x > 0 then
    val str: Int = x - 1
    str + 1
  else
    val x: String = str.toUpperCase
    x.length
```

The outermost scope defines a variable `str`, of type `String`. The body of function `f` creates its own scope, in which a variable `x`, of type `Int`, is defined (the argument to the function). The block of code that constitutes the **then** part of the conditional has its own scope in which a new variable `str`, of type `Int`, is declared. Similarly, the **else** block defines a new variable `x`, of type `String`, in its own scope. Variables do not exist outside their scopes: Outside function `f`, variable `str` is the string defined on the first line, and there is no variable named `x`.

The variables `str` and `x` declared in the inner scopes *shadow* the variables with the same names from the outer scopes. Java forbids such shadowing and

---

[5]Be careful, because details vary from language to language. For instance, while "`_ + _`" is a two-argument adding function in Scala, `it + it` is a single-argument doubling function in Kotlin. In Elixir, `&(&1 + &2)` is the two-argument adding function, and `&(&1 + &1)` is the single-argument doubling function.

forces you to pick different names for the variables declared inside the **then** and **else** blocks.

While it is often the case that every block of code defines its own scope, not all languages adhere to this rule. JavaScript and Python, for instance, introduce a new scope for the body of a function, but *not* for the **then** and **else** branches of a conditional, or the body of a loop. This can be confusing when you are used to the more mainstream scoping rules. As an illustration, consider the following Python program:

——— Python ———

```python
x = 1

def f():
    x = 2
    if x > 0:
        x = 3
        y = 4
    print(x) # prints 3
    print(y) # prints 4

f()
print(x) # prints 1
print(y) # error: name 'y' is not defined
```

The body of function **f** defines its own scope, but the block of code inside **if** does not. Instead, x=3 is an assignment to the variable x declared in the scope of the function (initialized with 2), and y=4 introduces a variable y inside that same scope. In particular, this variable y continues to exist after the **if** statement and has value 4. The **print(x)** statement inside function **f** prints the value of the variable x in the scope of the function, which is 3, while the **print(x)** statement outside function **f** prints the value of the variable x in the outermost scope, which is 1. The final **print(y)** statement triggers an error, since no y variable has been declared outside the scope of the function. The behavior would be the same in JavaScript. Contrast this with Scala:

——— Scala ———

```scala
var x = 1

def f() =
    var x = 2
    if x > 0 then
        var x = 3
        var y = 4
    println(x) // prints 2
    println(y) // rejected at compile-time
```

```
f()
println(x) // prints 1
println(y) // rejected at compile-time
```

Most languages now use static scoping, with variations as to which programming language constructs introduce a new scope. Dynamic scoping, in contrast, is error-prone and has become less popular. It was used in the original Lisp and remains available as an option in modern variants of that language. It is also used in some scripting languages, most notably Perl and various Bourne Shell implementations.

As an illustration, this Scala program follows static scoping rules:

```
                                                                    Scala
var x = 1

def f() =
  x += 1
  println(x) // prints 2

def g() =
  var x = 10
  f()

g()
println(x) // prints 2
```

Function g defines a local variable x, then invokes f. The variable x used inside function f, however, is the one declared on the first line of the program, which is the one in scope where function f is defined. The local variable with the same name defined inside function g plays no part. The behavior would be the same for an equivalent program written in Java, Kotlin, C, or any one of a multitude of languages that use static scoping.

Contrast this with the following Bash implementation:

```
                                                                    Bash
x=1

f() {
```

```
  (( x++ ))
  printf "%d\n" $x # prints 11
}

g() {
  local x=10
  f
}

g
printf "%d\n" $x # prints 1
```

In Bash, the variable x used inside function f is not the variable in scope where f is defined, but the variable in scope where function f is invoked. This variable, equal to 10, is incremented to 11. The variable x declared at the beginning of the program was never modified.

Dynamic scoping can be used to override a global variable with a local variable, thus changing the behavior of a function. This is sometimes useful, and a similar behavior can be achieved in Scala through implicit arguments. For instance, by reusing the Formatter type from Section 9.5, a function can be defined to print an object with the default formatter in scope:

—————————————————————————————————— *Scala* ———

```
def printFormatted(any: Any)(using formatter: Formatter): Unit =
  formatter.println(any)

printFormatted("foo") // uses the default formatter in scope (there must be one)
```

Within a function—or any block of code that introduces its own scope—a different formatter can be specified:

—————————————————————————————————— *Scala* ———

```
given UpperCaseFormatter: Formatter = str => str.toUpperCase

printFormatted("foo") // prints "FOO"
```

This technique brings back some of the flexibility of dynamic scoping but is much safer: Function printFormatted is explicit in the fact that it allows a locally defined formatter to impact its behavior.

The code examples in this book do not rely much on implicit arguments, except on occasion in Part II. In particular, Scala tends to use implicit arguments to specify the thread pool on which to execute concurrent activities.

9.7   Closures

Recall our first implementation of function `greaterThan`, in Listing 9.3:

```scala
def greaterThan(bound: Int): Int => Boolean =
   def greaterThanBound(x: Int): Boolean = x > bound
   greaterThanBound
```

You can apply `greaterThan` to different values to produce different functions. For example, `greaterThan(5)` is a function that tests if a number is greater than 5, while `greaterThan(100)` is a function that tests if a number is greater than 100:

```scala
val gt5    = greaterThan(5)
val gt100 = greaterThan(100)

gt5(90)   // true
gt100(90) // false
```

The question to ponder is this: In the `gt5(90)` computation, which compares 90 to 5, where does the value 5 come from? A 5 was pushed on the execution stack as local variable `bound` for the call `greaterThan(5)`, but this call has been completed, and the value removed from the stack. In fact, another call has already taken place with local variable `bound` equal to 100. Still, `gt5(90)` compares to 5, not to 100. Somehow, the value 5 of variable `bound` was captured during the call `greaterThan(5)`, and is now stored as part of function `gt5`.

The terminology surrounding this phenomenon is somewhat ambiguous, but most sources define *closures* to be functions associated with captured data.[6] When a function, like `greaterThanBound`, uses variables in its body other than its arguments—here, `bound`—these variables must be captured to create a function value.

Closures are sometimes used in functional programming languages as a way to add state to a function. For instance, a function can be "memoized" (a form of caching) by storing the inputs and outputs of previous computations:

```scala
def memo[A, B](f: A => B): A => B =
   val store = mutable.Map.empty[A, B]

   def g(x: A): B =
      store.get(x) match
         case Some(y) => y
```

---

[6]The term *closure* is sometimes used to refer to the data only, or to the capturing phenomenon itself. The word *closure* comes from the fact that, in λ-calculus, a function like `greaterThanBound` is represented by an *open* term that contains a free variable `bound`, and that needs to be *closed* to represent an actual function.

```
      case None =>
        val y = f(x)
        store(x) = y
        y

  g
```

Listing 9.6: Memoization using closures; see also Lis. 12.2.

Function `memo` is a higher-order function. Its argument `f` is a function of type `A => B`. Its output is another function, g, of the same type. Function g is functionally equivalent to `f`—it computes the same thing—but stores every computed value into a map. When called on some input `x`, function g first looks up the map to see if value `f(x)` has already been calculated and if so, returns it. Otherwise, `f(x)` is computed, using function `f`, and stored in the map before being returned. You apply `memo` to a function to produce a memoized version of that function:

```scala
val memoLength: String => Int = memo(str => str.length)

memoLength("foo") // invokes "foo".length and returns 3
memoLength("foo") // returns 3, without invoking method length
```

Function `memoLength` is a function from strings to integers, like `str => str.length`. It calculates the length of a string and stores it. The first time you call `memoLength("foo")`, the function invokes method `length` on string `"foo"`, stores 3, and returns 3. If you call `memoLength("foo")` again, value 3 is returned directly, without invoking method `length` of strings. Another invocation `memo(str => str.length)` would create a new closure with its own `store` map.

What is captured by a closure is a lexical environment. This environment contains function arguments, local variables, and fields of an enclosing class, if any:

```scala
def logging[A, B](name: String)(f: A => B): A => B =
  var count  = 0
  val logger = Logger.getLogger("my.package")

  def g(x: A): B =
    count += 1
    logger.info(s"calling $name ($count) with $x")
    val y = f(x)
    logger.info(s"$name($x)=$y")
    y

  g
```

Listing 9.7: Example of a function writing in its closure.

Like `memo`, function `logging` takes a function of type `A => B` as its argument and produces another function of the same type. The returned function is functionally equivalent to the input function, but it adds logging information, including the input and output of each call and the number of invocations:

```scala
val lenLog: String => Int = logging("length")(str => str.length)

lenLog("foo")
// INFO: calling length (1) with foo
// INFO: length(foo)=3

lenLog("bar")
// INFO: calling length (2) with bar
// INFO: length(bar)=3
```

For this to work, the returned closure g needs to maintain references to arguments `name` and `f`, as well as to local variables `count` and `logger`.

Note that variable `count` is modified when the closure is called. Writing into closures can be a powerful mechanism, but it is also fraught with risks:

```scala
// DON'T DO THIS!
val multipliers = Array.ofDim[Int => Int](10)

var n = 0
while n < 10 do
    multipliers(n) = x => x * n
    n += 1
```

This code attempts to create an array of multiplying functions: It fills the array with functions of type `Int => Int` defined as `x => x * n`. The idea is that `multipliers(i)` should then be `x => x * i`, a function that multiplies its argument by `i`. However, as written, the implementation does not work:

```scala
val m3 = multipliers(3)
m3(100) // 1000, not 300
```

All the functions stored in the array close over variable `n` *and share it*. Since `n` is equal to 10 at the end of the loop, all the functions in the array multiply their argument by 10 (at least, until `n` is modified). Some languages, including Java, emphasize safety over flexibility and do not allow local variables captured in closures to be written.

As with other forms of implicit references (e.g., inner classes), you need to be aware of closures to avoid tricky bugs caused by unintended sharing. This is especially true when closing over mutable data. As always, emphasizing immutability tends to result in safer code.

9.8 Inversion of Control

You may sometimes see higher-order functions being discussed within the broader notion of inversion of control. When using higher-order functions, control flow moves from the caller into the callee, which uses function arguments as callbacks into the caller.

To search a list of temperatures for a value greater than 90, you can use the recursive function findGreaterThan90 defined earlier in this chapter, or the loop-based equivalent:

```scala
def findGreaterThan90(list: List[Int]): Option[Int] =
  var rem = list
  while rem.nonEmpty do
    if rem.head > 90 then return Some(rem.head) else rem = rem.tail
  None
```

Whether you use recursion or a loop, the list is queried for its values (head and tail), but the flow of control remains within function findGreaterThan90. If instead you use the expression temps.find(greaterThan90), you no longer query the list for its values. Function find is now responsible for the flow of control—and may use recursion or a loop, depending on its own implementation. It makes callbacks to your code, namely the test function greaterThan90.

This shift of control flow from application code into library code is one of the reasons functional programming feels more abstract and declarative compared to imperative programming. However, once higher-order functions are well understood, they become convenient abstractions that can improve productivity and reduce the need for debugging. By using a method like find, you not only save the time it takes to write the three or four lines needed to implement the loop, but more importantly, eliminate the risk of getting it wrong.

9.9 Summary

- A defining characteristic of functional programming is the use of functions as values. Functions can be stored in data structures, passed as arguments to other functions, or returned as values by other functions. Functions that take functions as arguments or return functions as values are said to be higher-order functions.

- Passing functions as arguments to other functions makes it possible to parameterize a higher-order function by the behavior of its function arguments—for example, a searching method parameterized by a search criterion.

- To facilitate the implementation and usage of higher-order functions, many programming languages offer a syntax for function literals, which are expressions that evaluate to function values. This can take different forms, but a very common syntax is that of a lambda expression, which defines an anonymous function in terms of its arguments and return value.

- A curried function consumes its first argument (or argument list) and returns another function that will use the remaining arguments (or argument lists). By currying, a function that uses a list of multiple arguments can be transformed into a function that uses multiple lists of fewer arguments. This facilitates partial application to some but not all of the original arguments.

- In hybrid languages that combine object-oriented and functional programming, function values tend to appear as objects, and a function is applied by invoking a method of the object. Functions and methods are thus conceptually different: Functions are objects, which contain methods. Note that both methods and functions can be higher-order.

- Hybrid languages define syntax to bridge methods and functions, specifically to build a function value out of code defined in a method. One example is method reference: `obj::method` represents the function `x -> obj.method(x)` in Java. Another is implicit η-conversion: `obj.method` is transformed by the Scala compiler into `x => obj.method(x)` based on context.

- Partial application is another convenience mechanism used to generate functions. It relies on placeholders—for example, "`_`" in Scala, `it` in Kotlin—that make a function out of an arbitrary expression and can be thought of as a generalization of currying.

- The syntax used to implement function literals—lambda expressions, method references, partial application, etc.—can often be used in hybrid languages to create instances of SAM interfaces, which are interfaces and abstract classes with a single abstract method. This results in frequent use of lambda expressions as a replacement for more verbose mechanisms, such as anonymous classes, independently from functional programming patterns.

- When a function value is produced from code in a function or method that refers to variables other than its arguments, the compiler needs to construct a closure. The closure associates the function being created with a lexical environment that captures those variables. This is necessary for a function value to be usable outside its defining context.

- Programming with higher-order functions often involves a form of inversion of control. Control flow is embedded into a higher-order function, which then uses arguments as callbacks into the caller's code. It is an effective programming style once mastered, but the resulting code is more abstract and can require some adjustment for programmers used to imperative programming.

Chapter 10
Standard Higher-Order Functions

Functional programming libraries typically define a common collection of higher-order functions that implement a core set of patterns. Developers can also implement their own higher-order functions to provide users with these standard patterns. Of particular interest are `filter`, `map`, and `flatMap`, which have deep theoretical underpinnings and are supported with a dedicated syntax in some languages. Most code examples in this chapter focus on lists and options for simplicity, but higher-order functions are typically available on many other types.

10.1 Functions with Predicate Arguments

The theme of higher-order functions was motivated in Chapter 9 using a function `find`, which takes as an argument a test function and searches for an element that satisfies the test. The functional argument of `find` is a Boolean function, also called a predicate. This section explores other standard higher-order functions that use a predicate argument. As was done for `find`, functions are discussed in terms of the corresponding methods available in Scala.

Function `find` searches for an element that satisfies a Boolean test and returns it as an option. Sometimes, you only need to know whether such an element exists, without getting the element itself. Function `exists` does just that:

```scala
val temps = List(88, 91, 78, 69, 100, 98, 70)

temps.exists(_ > 90)  // true
temps.exists(_ > 100) // false
```

Function `exists` corresponds to the existential quantifier in logic ($\exists$). The dual universal quantifier ($\forall$) is available as a function `forall`:

```scala
temps.forall(temp => 32 <= temp && temp <= 100) // true
```

Keep in mind that on an empty structure, `exists` is always false and `forall` is always true:

```scala
Some("foo").exists(_.endsWith("o")) // true
Some("foo").forall(_.endsWith("o")) // true
Some("bar").exists(_.endsWith("o")) // false
Some("bar").forall(_.endsWith("o")) // false

None.exists((proj: Project) => proj.id == 12345L) // false
None.forall((proj: Project) => proj.id == 12345L) // true   <- BE CAREFUL HERE!
```

The last case is the one most likely to trip up a careless developer.

Functions `exists` and `forall` only tell you if some or all the elements have the desired property. In scenarios that require knowing more precisely how many values satisfy a condition, you can rely on function `count` instead:

```scala
temps.count(_ > 90) // 3
```

If the list `temps` represents temperatures over time, you can use `count` to calculate how many times the temperature increased:

```scala
val ups = temps.sliding(2).count(pair => pair(1) > pair(0)) // 2
```

The expression `temps.sliding(2)` produces a sliding window of two successive temperatures: 88 and 91, 91 and 78, 78 and 69, etc. Value `ups` counts how many of those pairs have a second number larger than the first, which is two (88 to 91 and 69 to 100).

When the number of values that satisfy a given property is not enough information and you need the values themselves, use `filter`:

```scala
temps.filter(_ > 75) // List(88, 91, 78, 100, 98)
```

Scala also has a method `filterNot` that reverses its test. To separate values with and without a desired property, use `partition` to produce both collections, usually in a more efficient single traversal than a call to `filter` followed by a call to `filterNot`:

```scala
temps.filterNot(_ > 75) // List(69, 70)
temps.partition(_ > 75) // (List(88, 91, 78, 100, 98), List(69, 70))
```

The previous implementation of quick-sort in Listing 7.20 can be simplified by replacing the user-defined function `splitPivot` with a call to `partition`:

```scala
                                                          ── Scala ──
def quickSort(list: List[Int]): List[Int] = list match
  case Nil                => list
  case pivot :: others =>
    val (low, high) = others.partition(_ < pivot)
    quickSort(low) ::: pivot :: quickSort(high)
```

Listing 10.1: Quick-sort, using `partition`.

In the same vein, `takeWhile` and `dropWhile` are another pair of higher-order functions that use a predicate. They are similar to, but different from, `filter` and `filterNot`:

```scala
                                                          ── Scala ──
temps.takeWhile(_ > 75) // List(88, 91, 78)
temps.dropWhile(_ > 75) // List(69, 100, 98, 70)
```

Function `takeWhile` takes elements from the front of the list, as long as they satisfy the test. The function stops as soon as it encounters one element that does not pass the test (or the list has been exhausted). When testing whether temperatures are greater than 75, `takeWhile` produces 88, 91, and 78. It stops when it encounters 69. Contrast this with the behavior of `filter`, which skips value 69, but continues with 100 and 98. Like `drop` (see Listing 7.6), `dropWhile` does not need to allocate a new list in memory. Accordingly, you could implement an efficient `find` using `dropWhile`:

```scala
                                                          ── Scala ──
def find[A](list: List[A], test: A => Boolean): Option[A] =
  list.dropWhile(!test(_)).headOption
```

Listing 10.2: Implementation of `find` using `dropWhile`.

The list returned by `dropWhile` starts with the first element that satisfies the test or is empty if no such element is found. Function `headOption` returns the head of a list as an option and handles the empty list by returning `None`.

In the same way that `partition` combines `filter` and `filterNot`, function `span` can be used when you need the outputs of both `takeWhile` and `dropWhile` on the same predicate. For instance, to build a list in which the first temperature not greater than 75 has been replaced with zero, you can use the following expression:

```scala
                                                          ── Scala ──
temps.span(_ > 75) match
  case (all, Nil) => all
  case (left, _ :: right) => left ::: 0 :: right
```

Recall that `temps` is the list [88,91,78,69,100,98,70]. The list `left` is the same list that would be returned by `takeWhile(_ > 75)`: [88,91,78]. The second list is as if obtained with `dropWhile(_ > 75)` and starts with 69. Its tail, list `right`, is [100,98,70]. Overall, the code produces the list [88,91,78,0,100,98,70]. If all the values in temps were larger than 75, the first pattern would produce a complete list unchanged (all == temps).

10.2   map and foreach

All the higher-order functions discussed in Section 10.1 use a predicate argument. Other standard higher-order functions use non-Boolean functions as arguments. Functions map and foreach take a function with an arbitrary return type and apply it to all the elements in a structure. The difference between the two is that map produces a structure with the results of applying the function, while foreach applies the function for the purpose of side effects and ignores return values.

For instance, you can convert a list of Fahrenheit temperatures to Celsius values using map:

```scala
temps.map(temp => ((temp - 32) / 1.8f).round) // List(31, 33, 26, 21, 38, 37, 21)
```

The return type of the function being applied determines the type of the elements in the collection that is returned:

```scala
temps.map(temp => if temp > 72 then "high" else "low")
// List("high", "high", "high", "low", "high", "high", "low")

temps.map(temp => (72, temp - 72))
// List((72,16), (72,19), (72,6), (72,-3), (72,28), (72,26), (72,-2))
```

The strings and pairs in this example are returned as a list because temps is a list. If instead the temperatures were stored in an array, temps.map would produce an array. A method map is available on many types in Scala:

```scala
Set(0.12, 0.35, 0.6).map(1.0 - _) // Set(0.88, 0.65, 0.4)
Some("foo").map(_.toUpperCase)     // Some("FOO")
```

Because some collections make no sense for some types, map may return a structure of a different type:

```scala
"foo".map(_.toInt)              // IndexedSeq(102, 111, 111)
BitSet(12, 35, 60).map(_ / 100.0) // SortedSet(0.12, 0.35, 0.6)
```

A string is a sequence of characters, but a sequence of integers is no longer a string, and a different type of (indexed) sequence must be used. Similarly, a bit-set makes sense only for integers, and a different type of (sorted) set must be chosen to contain floating-point numbers.

If you want to apply a function for side-effect purposes, and the values it returns are irrelevant, use `foreach` instead of `map`:

```Scala
val out: DataOutputStream = ...
temps.foreach(temp => out.writeInt(temp))
```

Function `foreach` applies the given function to all the elements in a structure, just like `map`. The difference is that `foreach` does not return anything—its return type is `Unit`. Note that `temps.map(temp => out.writeInt(temp))` would write all the temperatures to the output stream but would also produce a list of *unit* values—returned by method `writeInt`, which is `void` in Java—one per temperature written. This list is useless but, short of a compiler optimization, would have to be created and garbage collected.

You can also use `foreach` to apply functions that return meaningful values, but the values are still ignored:

```Scala
val writer: Writer = ...
temps.foreach(temp => writer.append(temp.toString).append('\n'))
```

Even though method **append** returns the writer itself, the call to `foreach` returns *unit*. Using `map` instead of `foreach` would produce a useless list of references to the writer.

10.3 flatMap

Function `flatMap` is a variation of `map` that "flattens" the values being produced:

```Scala
List(1, 2, 3).map(x => List(x, x, x))
// List(List(1, 1, 1), List(2, 2, 2), List(3, 3, 3))

List(1, 2, 3).flatMap(x => List(x, x, x))
// List(1, 1, 1, 2, 2, 2, 3, 3, 3)
```

What `flatMap` does is easy to understand. What can be harder to grasp is how useful this behavior can be. With experience, you will come to realize that `flatMap` is probably the most powerful and most useful of the standard higher-order functions. Function `flatMap` is a fundamental operation. In particular, by using one-to-one and one-to-zero mappings, you can express `map` and `filter` in terms of `flatMap`:

```
                                                              ── Scala ──
def map[A, B](list: List[A], f: A => B): List[B] = list.flatMap(x => List(f(x)))

def filter[A](list: List[A], test: A => Boolean): List[A] =
  list.flatMap(x => if test(x) then List(x) else List.empty)
```

Listing 10.3: Using `flatMap` to implement `map` and `filter`.

To emphasize the benefits of `flatMap`, consider this simple illustration. An application needs to parse a request to extract user information, retrieve a user account, and apply an operation to the account. You can implement these stages using functions with the following signatures:

```
                                                              ── Scala ──
def parseRequest(request: Request): User = ...
def getAccount(user: User): Account = ...
def applyOperation(account: Account, op: Operation): Int = ...
```

The functions can then be composed to combine the three stages:

```
                                                              ── Scala ──
applyOperation(getAccount(parseRequest(request)), op)
```

Suppose now that each stage is not guaranteed to succeed: It is possible that a request cannot be parsed, an account is not found, or an operation is unsuccessful. To handle these contingencies, you modify each function to return an option, and use `None` to represent a failure:

```
                                                              ── Scala ──
def parseRequest(request: Request): Option[User] = ...
def getAccount(user: User): Option[Account] = ...
def applyOperation(account: Account, op: Operation): Option[Int] = ...
```

The problem now is to combine these three functions to parse a request, retrieve an account, and apply an operation. The expression

        applyOperation(getAccount(parseRequest(request)), op)

no longer works because each stage may return `None`, which prevents the computation from continuing. You could use pattern matching to test options for emptiness and extract contents into local variables:

```
                                                              ── Scala ──
parseRequest(request) match
  case None => None
  case Some(user) =>
```

```
        getAccount(user) match
          case None            => None
          case Some(account) => applyOperation(account, op)
```

Listing 10.4: Processing options through pattern matching; contrast with Lis. 10.5.

This works but is definitely not as nice as the earlier function composition.

As an alternative, `map` can be used to apply a function to the value inside an option, if any:

—— *Scala* ——

```
Some(42).map((x: Int) => x + 1) // Some(43)
None.map((x: Int) => x + 1)     // None
```

You could use `map` to retrieve an account from a user (if any), then again to apply an operation to the account (if any):

—— *Scala* ——

```
// DON'T DO THIS!
parseRequest(request)
   .map(user => getAccount(user).map(account => applyOperation(account, op)))
```

This approach is inadequate for several reasons. First, the type of this expression is `Option[Option[Option[Int]]]`. In other words, if the last stage produces a value v, the expression returns it as `Some(Some(Some(v)))`, which is obviously far from ideal. Furthermore, if a computation stage fails, the expression results in somewhat confusing values. If the request cannot be parsed, the expression is `None`. If, however, the request can be parsed but no account is found, it is `Some(None)`, which is another way of not having a value. If an account is found but the operation fails, the expression is `Some(Some(None))`, yet another expression without a meaningful value.

All this can be avoided by replacing `map` with `flatMap`. When you apply a function with an optional result to an optional input, `flatMap` flattens the "option of option" into a simple option:

—— *Scala* ——

```
parseRequest(request)
   .flatMap(user => getAccount(user))
   .flatMap(account => applyOperation(account, op))
```

Listing 10.5: Example of using `flatMap` in a pipeline; see also Lis. 10.9.

This expression has type `Option[Int]`. It is `Some(v)` if an operation output v is produced and `None` if any stage of the computation is unsuccessful.

Some scenarios require more careful error handling—for instance, by triggering fall-back computations. For those, you can still rely on `flatMap`, but use it on other types like `Either` and `Try`, in addition to `Option`. Functional error handling is the topic of Chapter 13.

In the code example, `flatMap` is used to apply transformations that might fail to outputs of previous computations, which might also have failed. You can use a similar strategy to transform asynchronous computations using transformations that can themselves be asynchronous by using `flatMap` to avoid nesting futures. This will be explored in Part II of the book (contrast Listing 10.5 with Listing 26.9, for instance).

Another area where `flatMap` is handy is reactive programming organized in terms of streams of events. While `map` is limited to a one-to-one mapping, `flatMap` is not. In particular, when an event is processed, it can be entirely consumed (triggering no further events), or it can trigger exactly one event, or it can trigger multiple events. By using `flatMap` instead of `map`, you avoid nesting streams of events, in the same way you avoid nesting options when dealing with missing values, or nesting futures when dealing with asynchronous computations (see Listing 27.9 for an illustration).

Indeed, `flatMap` is such a fundamental operation that it has its own underlying theory (*monads*), and Scala defines convenient syntax to organize `flatMap`-based computations (see Section 10.9).

Aside on Functors and Monads

More than five minutes of browsing on the topic of functional programming is likely to bring you in contact with two intimidating words: *functor* and *monad*. These terms have their origin in category theory. The simplest definitions are as follows: A functor is a structure that implements `map`, and a monad is a structure that implements `flatMap`.

Technically, the `map` and `flatMap` functions need to satisfy a few properties for functors and monads to qualify as such. These properties are generic for all functors and all monads, and are expressed here in terms of a functor F and a monad M. Think of `F[A]` and `M[A]` as types like `List[A]` or `Option[A]`. For F to be a functor, the `map` method on `F[A]` must have the following signature:

Scala
```scala
def map[B](f: A => B): F[B] = ...
```

It must also satisfy the two following properties on every `struct` of type `F[A]`:

Scala
```scala
struct == struct.map(identity)
// or equivalently: struct == struct.map(x => x)
struct.map(f).map(g) == struct.map(f andThen g)
// or equivalently: struct.map(f).map(g) == struct.map(x => g(f(x)))
```

The first property states that mapping the identity function has no effect. The second property requires that `map` preserves function composition: Mapping `f` and then g produces the same value as mapping a single function that applies f and then g. When implementing a map function on your own structure, strive to maintain these properties. As a mental exercise, you can check that the map functions used in the book's code illustrations all satisfy these conditions.

Monads can be defined in terms of a function unit and a method flatMap. The unit function has type A => M[A] and is used to build a monad—for example, from x to List(x) or from x to Some(x). Method flatMap on M[A] has the following signature:

```scala
def flatMap[B](f: A => M[B]): M[B] = ...
```

Monads have their own conditions to satisfy. First, the unit function maintains two properties with respect to flatMap:

```scala
struct.flatMap(unit) == struct
unit(x).flatMap(f) == f(x)
```

The first property states that "flat-mapping" unit does nothing (as mapping the identity does nothing). The second property corresponds to the fundamental intuition behind flatMap: Function unit places x into a container, and flatMap(f) applies f to the contents of the container (see Section 10.9). Finally, flatMap must satisfy a form of composition similar to map:

```scala
struct.flatMap(f).flatMap(g) == struct.flatMap(x => f(x).flatMap(g))
```

As mentioned earlier, map can be implemented in terms of flatMap (Listing 10.3). Indeed, a monad M[A] is also a functor, in which map is defined as follows:

```scala
def map[B](f: A => B): M[B] = flatMap(x => unit(f(x)))
```

There is a lot more to functors and monads than is covered in this short note. Indeed, entire books have been dedicated to the subject. You are likely to see functors and monads (and other similar abstractions) explicitly in genuine functional programming languages (like Haskell) and libraries (like Scala's Cats). Even if you intend to stay away from those, keep in mind that the various map and flatMap functions you encounter share some fundamental properties and lead to similar programming patterns.

10.4   fold and reduce

As mentioned earlier, iterations are not a good fit for functional programming, and recursion is instead needed to arbitrarily nest function composition. When processing a collection, a family of higher-order functions exists that is specifically designed to implement the necessary nesting of function calls, without additional need for loops or recursion. Internally, these higher-order functions might be implemented using iteration or recursion.

As an illustration, let `abc` be a list that contains values A, B, and C, in that order. Then, `abc.foldLeft(X)(f)` is equivalent to the expression `f(f(f(X,A),B),C)`. The given function `f` is used to combine an initial value X with the first element of the list: `f(X,A)`. This new value is then combined with the next element in the list, still using `f`: `f(f(X,A),B)`. The computation proceeds in this fashion on the entire list, and the value produced by the final invocation of `f` is returned. When using `foldLeft`, elements are processed from left to right. A similar function `foldRight` processes the elements from right to left instead: `abc.foldRight(X)(f)` is `f(A,f(B,f(C,X)))`. Unordered collections, like sets, tend to offer a single function `fold`, which does not specify the order in which the elements are processed and thus typically requires that you use it with an argument function that is symmetric and associative.

You can use fold variants to replace computations that would otherwise be done iteratively or recursively:

Scala

```scala
def calculate(numbers: List[Int]): Double =
  var acc = 10.0
  for x <- numbers do acc = 3.0 * acc + x + 1.0
  acc

def calculate(numbers: List[Int]): Double =
  @tailrec
  def loop(nums: List[Int], acc: Double): Double = nums match
    case Nil => acc
    case x :: r => loop(r, 3.0 * acc + x + 1.0)
  loop(numbers, 10.0)

def calculate(numbers: List[Int]): Double =
  numbers.foldLeft(10.0)((acc, x) => 3.0 * acc + x + 1.0)
```

Listing 10.6: Example of iteration, recursion, and fold for the same computation.

In Listing 10.6, all three `calculate` functions perform the same computation: one iteratively, one with a tail recursive function, and one using `foldLeft`. In each vari-

ant, a current value `acc` is combined with a list element `x` through the expression
`3.0 * acc + x + 1.0`.

Folding functions are versatile, and you can use them to implement many collection-processing computations. For example:

```scala
def sum(list: List[Int]): Int = list.foldLeft(0)(_ + _)

def product(list: List[Int]): Int = list.foldLeft(1)(_ * _)

def reverse[A](list: List[A]): List[A] = list.foldLeft(List.empty[A])((1, x) => x :: 1)

def filter[A](list: List[A], test: A => Boolean): List[A] =
  list.foldRight(List.empty[A])((x, 1) => if test(x) then x :: 1 else 1)
```

Listing 10.7: `sum`, `product`, `reverse`, and `filter` implemented using fold.

Functional libraries often implement a simplified version of `fold` named `reduce`. The difference with `fold` is that `reduce` uses an element from the collection as the starting point of the computation. If abc is the list A, B, C as before, `abc.reduceLeft(f)` is `f(f(A,B),C)`. The `sum` and `product` functions in Listing 10.7 can be written in terms of `reduce`:

```scala
def sum(list: List[Int]): Int     = list.reduce(_ + _)
def product(list: List[Int]): Int = list.reduce(_ * _)
```

Note that `reduce` is not defined on empty collections and is limited to a return type that is the same as (or a supertype of) the collection's elements. To reduce elements into a value of a different type, you can sometimes apply `map` to first convert types, and then `reduce`. Assume, for instance, a text file with one number per line and a task that consists of adding the logarithms of all the absolute values of the numbers, ignoring zeros. You can implement that with a combination of `map`, `filter`, and `reduce`:

```scala
lines.map(_.toDouble.abs).filter(_ != 0.0).map(math.log).reduce(_ + _)
```

This expression uses `map` to change strings into non-negative numbers, then `filter` to ignore zeros, `map` again to apply the logarithm function, and finally `reduce` to calculate the sum. A drawback of this approach is that it requires the creation of three intermediate lists, one with all the absolute values (the output of the first `map`), one with the zeros removed (the output of `filter`), and one with all the logarithms (the output of the second `map`). This could lead to performance issues if the file is large.

As an alternative, you can use `foldLeft` to perform the same computation without the need for additional lists—arguably, at the cost of a minor loss in readability:[1]

―― *Scala* ――

```scala
lines.foldLeft(0.0) { (sum, line) =>
    val x = line.toDouble.abs
    if x != 0.0 then sum + math.log(x) else sum
}
```

The folded function leaves the accumulator unchanged when processing a zero. Otherwise, the logarithm of the absolute value is added to the accumulator, thus achieving the same result as the `filter/map/reduce` combination. Note how, in this last example, the argument function is more elaborate than before and benefits from the fact that `foldLeft` is defined using currying.

10.5   iterate, tabulate, and unfold

While functions of the fold family reduce a collection of values into a single element, other higher-order functions work in the reverse direction and are used to build collections. The simplest of these is `tabulate`, whose argument is a function on integer inputs: `List.tabulate(n)(f)` is the list `[f(0), f(1), f(2), ..., f(n-1)]`.

―― *Scala* ――

```scala
List.tabulate(5)(i => "X" * i) // List("", "X", "XX", "XXX", "XXXX")
```

By contrast, `iterate` is given an initial value and a function that can be reapplied on its own output (its input and output types are the same): `List.iterate(X,n)(f)` consists of n values `[X, f(X), f(f(X)), f(f(f(X))), ...]`, where each value is obtained by applying function `f` to the previous value.

―― *Scala* ――

```scala
List.iterate("", 5)(str => str + "X") // List("", "X", "XX", "XXX", "XXXX")
```

Finally, function `unfold` works as a kind of reverse fold. You give it an initial state and a function that, from a state, produces a value and the next state, if any. Applied to a state `s`, this function produces a pair `(fVal(s), fNext(s))` with the next value and the next state. The function can then be applied to `fNext(s)` to produce another value `fVal(fNext(s))` and a next state `fNext(fNext(s))`, and so forth, thus producing the sequence of values `[fVal(X), fVal(fNext(X)), fVal(fNext(fNext(X))), ...]`, given

―――――――――――――――――――――――――――――――――――――――

[1] A more readable alternative can be obtained through lazy evaluation; see Section 12.6.

an initial value X. The argument function produces an option, and the computation terminates when it returns None:

```scala
List.unfold("XXXX")(str => if str.isEmpty then None else Some((str, str.tail)))
// List("XXXX", "XXX", "XX", "X")
```

10.6   sortWith, sortBy, maxBy, and minBy

To sort sequences, you need to have a way to compare elements. In Java, for instance, subtypes of the Comparable interface implement an ordering, and sequences of these types can be sorted using the java.util.Collections.sort method. Alternatively, the method can take an explicit Comparator argument to sort values that are not naturally comparable (or to override a default ordering). Scala offers a similar method sorted, which takes an optional argument of type Ordering, much like Java's Comparator.

In this section, we want to focus on higher-order alternatives to method sorted. First is sortWith, which takes a comparison function, instead of a comparator object:

```scala
temps.sortWith(_ < _) // List(69, 70, 78, 88, 91, 98, 100)
temps.sortWith(_ > _) // List(100, 98, 91, 88, 78, 70, 69)
```

You could use sortWith to sort a list of strings by length:

```scala
val strings: List[String] = ...

strings.sortWith(_.length < _.length)
```

A better alternative in this scenario is to use sortBy. This function takes as its argument a function that maps the elements to be sorted to arbitrary ordered values:

```scala
strings.sortBy(_.length)
```

In the preceding expression, strings are also sorted in increasing order of their lengths. This is achieved by mapping strings to their lengths, and then relying on the default ordering of integers. Note that the result is a list of strings, not a list of integers (as strings.map(_.length).sorted would be). If 2D points are represented as pairs, you can use sortBy to sort them in increasing order of Euclidean distance to origin:

```scala
                                                               ─── Scala ───
val points: List[(Double, Double)] = ...

points.sortBy((x, y) => x * x + y * y)
```

Again, the result is a list of points, not a list of distances.

Similar to `sortBy` are the functions `minBy` and `maxBy`:

```scala
                                                               ─── Scala ───
val temps: List[Int] = ...
val datedTemps: List[(LocalDate, Int)] = ...

temps.max       // highest temperature
datedTemps.max // highest temperature on the last date
```

Note that the second expression needs to compare pairs. The default behavior, in Scala, is to compare them in lexicographic order—that is, according to the first component, or the second component if the first components are equal. As a result, `datedTemps.max` finds the last (highest) date, and within this date, the highest temperature. To retrieve the highest temperature overall, ignoring dates, use `maxBy`:

```scala
                                                               ─── Scala ───
datedTemps.maxBy((_, temp) => temp) // highest temperature overall
```

To get the highest temperature overall, but pick its earliest date if it occurs multiple times, is a little more complicated:

```scala
                                                               ─── Scala ───
val byTemp: Ordering[(LocalDate, Int)] = Ordering.by((_, temp) => temp)
val byDate: Ordering[(LocalDate, Int)] = Ordering.by((date, _) => date)

datedTemps.max(byTemp.orElse(byDate.reverse))
```

Note the use of a higher-order function `by` to build ordering objects, which are then combined to sort dated temperatures according to temperatures first, and for equal temperatures, by reverse order of dates.

10.7 groupBy and groupMap

The last standard higher-order function discussed in this chapter is `groupBy`, also commonly found in functional libraries (and even in Java as `Collectors.groupingBy`). As its name indicates, this function is used to form groups of elements from a collection.

Like `sortBy` and `maxBy`, it takes a mapping function as its argument and groups together all the elements that map to the same value:

```scala
List(2, 5, 4, 10, 7, 1, 20).groupBy(n => n % 2)
```

This expression maps even numbers to 0 and odd numbers to 1, resulting in an expression of type `Map[Int,List[Int]]` with two keys:

```
0 -> List(2, 4, 10, 20)
1 -> List(5, 7, 1)
```

You can group dated temperatures by date:

```scala
val tempsOn = datedTemps.groupBy((date, _) => date)
```

Value `tempsOn` has type `Map[LocalDate, List[(LocalDate, Int)]]`; the expression `tempsOn(someDate)` produces the list of all (dated) temperatures for the given date.[2] Alternatively, dated temperatures can be grouped by temperatures:

```scala
val daysWith = datedTemps.groupBy((_, temp) => temp)
```

Then, `daysWith(temp)` is a list of dates (and temperatures) with a temperature of `temp`.

Given that all the pairs in `tempsOn(d)` have the same date `d`, and all the pairs in `daysWith(t)` have the same temperature `t`, you can reduce pairs to their relevant component via a suitable application of higher-order function `map`:

```scala
datedTemps.groupBy((d, _) => d).map((d, list) => (d, list.map((_, t) => t)))
```

This expression is a little hard to parse, but the first call to `map` is used to transform each list of dated temperatures into a list of plain temperatures; the second `map` is the transformation of a dated temperature into an integer. If you are lucky, your language offers `groupMap`, which combines `groupBy` and `map` into a single function:

```scala
datedTemps.groupMap((d, _) => d)((_, t) => t) // of type Map[LocalDate, List[Int]]
```

Function `groupMap` takes two mapping functions as arguments (in curried style), one for grouping (as in `groupBy`) and one for transforming (as in `map`).

---

[2]If there are no temperatures recorded on that date, the lookup in the map will fail with an exception. This can be avoided by using the map method `withDefaultValue` to create a map that returns an empty list instead.

10.8   Implementing Standard Higher-Order Functions

You can implement your own higher-order functions on user-defined structures. When it makes sense, you can choose to implement functions that mimic standard behavior such as `foreach` or `map`. As an illustration, we could extend the tree-based set implemented in Chapter 8 with higher-order methods `exists`, `foreach`, and `fold`:

```scala
case object Empty extends BinTree:
  def exists(test: Int => Boolean): Boolean = false
  def foreach[U](f: Int => U): Unit = ()
  def fold[A](init: A)(f: (A, Int) => A): A = init
  ...

case class Node(key: Int, left: BinTree, right: BinTree) extends BinTree:
  def exists(test: Int => Boolean): Boolean =
    test(key) || left.exists(test) || right.exists(test)

  def foreach[U](f: Int => U): Unit =
    left.foreach(f)
    f(key)
    right.foreach(f)

  def fold[A](init: A)(f: (A, Int) => A): A =
    right.fold(f(left.fold(init)(f), key))(f)
  ...
```

Listing 10.8: Extending binary search trees with `exists`, `foreach`, and `fold`.

Method `exists` is false on an empty tree. On a node, it checks the node's key with the given predicate and continues checking each subtree if the key does not satisfy the test. Method `foreach` does nothing on an empty tree. On a node, it applies the argument function to all the values of the left tree, then on the node's key, and finally on all the values of the right tree. Given the ordering property of binary search trees, this in-order traversal guarantees that the function is applied to all values in increasing order. In the same way, method `fold` starts by folding the left tree, uses the resulting value to apply the argument function to the node's key, and finishes by folding the right tree, thus guaranteeing that tree values are processed in increasing order. (See also Chapter 14 for an example of user-defined `map` and `flatMap` implementations.)

10.9   foreach, map, flatMap, and for-Comprehensions

A useful way to think of functions `foreach`, `map`, and `flatMap` is that they implement a mechanism that acts inside a container. Think of a structure as a "box" and of these higher-order functions as ways to act on the contents of the box without opening it. In Listing 10.5, for instance, parsing a request produces a box that (possibly) contains a user. Function `flatMap` is used to process this user, if any, and returns a box that (possibly) contains an account, which is itself processed with another use of `flatMap`.

This pattern is common enough—functional programming is all about transforming values through functions—that languages sometimes define a special syntax for it. In Scala, it is called `for`-comprehension. You could write the request parsing example as follows:[3]

```scala
for
   user    <- parseRequest(request)
   account <- getAccount(user)
   result  <- applyOperation(account, op)
yield result
```

Listing 10.9: Rewritten pipeline from Lis. 10.5 using `for`-comprehension.

This code is transformed by the compiler into an expression that uses `flatMap`, equivalent to Listing 10.5. Both `for-do` and `for-yield` are syntactic sugar for a combination of calls to higher-order functions. For instance,

```scala
for load <- loads yield load.reduced
```

was used in Chapter 3 to create a list of updated load objects. It is compiled into

```scala
loads.map(load => load.reduced)
```

---

[3]The choice of `for` as a keyword is somewhat unfortunate. It suggests a loop of some sort, but in many cases, no such loop is needed. Here, `for` is used to process the contents of an option, and no loop is involved. In Chapter 26, `for` is applied to a future, again without a loop.

Similarly,

```scala
for load <- loads do load.reduce()
```

was used to update a list of mutable objects. It is compiled into

```scala
loads.foreach(load => load.reduce())
```

When `for-do` and `for-yield` use conditions, a filtering step is inserted by the compiler. The expression

```scala
for load <- loads if load.weight != 0 yield load.reduced
```

is compiled into[4]

```scala
loads.withFilter(load => load.weight != 0).map(load => load.reduced)
```

Listing 10.8 added a method `foreach` to binary trees. As a result, you can now process trees using `for-do`:

```scala
val tree: BinTree = ...

for x <- tree do println(x) // prints all the values in the tree, in order
```

The `for-do` expression is compiled into `tree.foreach(println)`.

Many libraries implement `foreach`, `map`, `flatMap`, and `filter` functions, but few programming languages define a `for`-comprehension syntax identical to Scala's. Some constructs, though, are similar, like Python's list comprehensions. The Python code

```python
[round((temp - 32) / 1.8) for temp in temps if temp > 75]
```

corresponds to the following Scala code:

```scala
for temp <- temps if temp > 75 yield ((temp - 32) / 1.8f).round
```

---

[4] Method `withFilter` is semantically equivalent to `filter`, but uses a form of delayed evaluation to avoid the creation of an intermediate list (see the discussion of views and lazy evaluation in Section 12.9).

In Java, which has higher-order functions only, you need to use `filter` and `map` directly:

```Java
IntStream temps = ...
temps.filter(temp -> temp > 75).map(temp -> Math.round((temp - 32) / 1.8f))
```

NOTE

Given my intent to prepare developers for a variety of languages, I often use higher-order functions in code examples instead of `for-do` or `for-yield`, especially outside of case studies. This is a choice I made for pedagogical reasons, to better emphasize the similarities of patterns across languages, but it tends to result in Scala code that is not always idiomatic. Readers with Scala experience will forgive me.

10.10 Summary

- The functions presented in this chapter form a core set of higher-order functions commonly found in functional libraries. They are often available on many types, such as streams and collections, but also options and futures.

- Several functions use a predicate—a Boolean function—as their argument. They are used to find, count, filter, or assert the existence of elements that satisfy this predicate.

- Function `map` is used to apply an arbitrary transformation to elements within a structure and produces a new structure that contains the transformed values. If an operation is applied to elements for the purpose of side effects only, and no resulting structure is needed, function `foreach` can be used instead of `map`.

- Function `flatMap` is similar to `map` but takes care of "flattening" nested structures, like lists of lists or options of options. This function is powerful and can be used to apply a computation with optional output to an optional input (to avoid an option of option), or to handle an event that triggers a new stream of events (to avoid a stream of stream), or to asynchronously transform a value that is itself calculated asynchronously (to avoid a future of future).

- Fundamentally, `foreach`, `map`, `flatMap`, and `filter` (or `withFilter`) are used to transform the contents of a structure (e.g., list, option, future) from outside the structure. This common pattern is sometimes supported by syntax at the language level, like Scala's `for`-comprehension or Python's list comprehension.

- Folding functions are used to reduce the elements of a structure into a single value using a combining operator. Many computations that would process the elements of a collection iteratively can be implemented in terms of a folding function.

- Conversely, higher-order functions can be used to generate a collection of elements. Functions `iterate` and `unfold`, for instance, rely on an initial seed and the repeated application of a function to generate a sequence of values.

- Calculations such as minimum, maximum, and sorting, which require element comparison, need to be parameterized by the criterion used to compare values. Higher-order variants often use a comparison function (e.g., `sortWith`) or a mapping into an existing ordered type (e.g., `sortBy`, `maxBy`).

- As an alternative to a comparison criterion for sorting or for minimum/maximum calculation, a grouping criterion is sometimes used to collect related elements (e.g., `groupBy`).

- Many other higher-order functions exist beside this fundamental core group. For instance, the `Observable` class of the RxJava reactive library has more than a hundred higher-order methods, some of which deal with error handling, threading, or real time, in addition to the core functional transformations discussed in this chapter.

Chapter 11

Case Study: File Systems as Trees

The contents of a file system can be represented as a tree: The children of a directory are its files and subdirectories. In contrast to the binary search trees of Chapter 8, nodes in a file system can have more than two children, making the tree N-ary. A navigable file system extends a file system by maintaining a current position that can be moved up and down the tree. It is implemented functionally as a zipper. Trees form a recursive data structure in which a node contains a list of trees. Recursion is combined with higher-order list methods to build and traverse trees and zippers.

11.1 Design Overview

Our previous case study discussed a possible implementation of binary search trees, in which internal nodes have one or two children. Trees can be generalized to allow nodes to contain any number of children. Such trees are often referred to as N-ary (as opposed to binary) or *general* trees.

In this case study, an N-ary tree is used to represent a file system: Non-empty directories are internal nodes, and files (and empty directories) are leaves. Directories can contain any number of subdirectories and files. Directories and files are identified by their names. Directories contain a list of children (subdirectories and files). Files contain arbitrary information (size, permissions, timestamps, etc.), which is omitted here for the sake of simplicity.

As a design choice, the trees implemented in this chapter maintain a single list of children within each directory—as opposed to two separate lists, one for files and one for subdirectories. As a result, files and directories share a common supertype, called `Node`, resulting in the following Scala definitions:[1]

```scala                                                        Scala
trait Node:
    ...

final class Dir(val name: String, nodes: List[Node]) extends Node:
    ...

final class File(val name: String) extends Node:
    ...
```

---

[1] As was the case in Chapter 8 with binary trees, the code in this chapter omits all visibility modifiers for clarity. An actual implementation would leave many elements non-public, including the `Node` trait.

The list of nodes in a directory should never contain two nodes with the same name. The order of nodes in a list is irrelevant: Directories that contain the same files and sub-directories in different orders are considered equivalent. Trees are immutable: Adding or removing files and directories is achieved via functions that produce a new tree.

11.2   A Node-Searching Helper Function

Several tree operations need to update a directory's list of children. This requires finding a node by name in a list, removing it, and possibly replacing it with a new node. The following helper method is defined for this purpose:

```scala
// inside class Dir
def removeByName(name: String): Option[(Node, List[Node])] =
  nodes.partition(_.name == name) match
    case (Nil, _)            => None
    case (List(found), others) => Some((found, others))
```

Higher-order method `partition` is used to partition a list of nodes between those that have a given name (there is at most one) and those that have a different name. If there is no node with the given name, the function returns `None`. Otherwise, it returns a pair with the node that was extracted and a list of remaining nodes. As an example, if you look for name B in a list of nodes that contains directories/files A, B, C, and D, the method returns the pair: (B, [A,C,D]).

11.3   String Representation

Both files and directories define a `toString` method that returns their name. To help distinguish between files and directories, a trailing slash is added to directory names:

```scala
// inside class Dir
override def toString = name + "/"

// inside class File
override def toString = name
```

Directories also define a method `ls` that lists their contents by name, and a method `lsFiles` that only lists the names of files, ignoring subdirectories. You can implement ls by using the higher-order method **map** to produce a list of strings from a list of nodes. For **lsFiles**, you use **flatMap** to keep the names of files and skip subdirectories:[2]

```scala
// inside class Dir
def ls: List[String] = nodes.map(_.toString)

def lsFiles: List[String] = nodes.flatMap {
   case file: File => List(file.toString)
   case _ => Nil
}
```

In addition to **ls** and **lsFiles**, you may want to build a string that represents the entire contents of the directory, including subdirectories. To emphasize the tree structure, file and directory names are indented according to their depth.[3] Figure 11.1 shows a file system tree and its string representation.

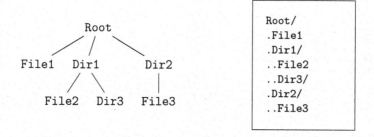

Figure 11.1 A file system tree and its string representation.

To implement this method efficiently, you can create a string builder and use recursion to add lines to it, one line for each file and directory in the tree. To achieve indentation, each line starts with a prefix that consists of a repetition of a separator (the separator is a single dot in Figure 11.1). A method **mkString** allocates a string builder and an empty prefix and delegates the recursion to another method, also named **mkString**, whose responsibility is to add lines to the builder:

```scala
// inside trait Node
def mkString(sep: String): String = mkString(sep, StringBuilder(), "").result()
def mkString(sep: String, builder: StringBuilder, prefix: String): StringBuilder
```

---

[2]Method **flatMap** is used here to combine filtering (keep files, ignore directories) and mapping (transform files into their names). Alternatively, **lsFiles** could be written in terms of **filter** and **map**.

[3]This is similar to the **tree** command often found on Unix systems.

The implementation of this second `mkString` method is straightforward inside class `File`. You simply add to the builder a line that consists of the prefix followed by the file name and a newline:

```scala
// inside class File
def mkString(sep: String, builder: StringBuilder, prefix: String): StringBuilder =
  builder ++= prefix ++= name += '\n'
```

Inside the `Dir` class, the method starts by adding a line for the directory itself. It then proceeds by adding all the nodes (files and subdirectories) inside the directory. This is achieved recursively by calling `mkString` on all the nodes, using a longer prefix and the same string builder. You can perform these recursive calls by applying higher-order method `foreach` on the list of nodes:

```scala
// inside class Dir
def mkString(sep: String, builder: StringBuilder, prefix: String): StringBuilder =
  builder ++= prefix ++= name ++= "/\n"
  val newPrefix = prefix + sep
  nodes.foreach(_.mkString(sep, builder, newPrefix))
  builder
```

Listing 11.1: Example of using `foreach` with a mutable string builder.

Method `mkString` mixes higher-order functions and recursion: The action applied by `foreach` invokes `mkString`, which uses `foreach` to invoke `mkString`, and so on. This is a consequence of the fact that a node contains a list (hence the use of higher-order functions) of nodes (hence the use of recursion). You will notice how this pattern is used again in other tree functions in this chapter.

As mentioned earlier, method `foreach` makes sense only when the function being applied has a side effect. Here, the side effect comes from modifying a mutable string builder. Tree users, however, would call only the first `mkString` method—the only one public in an actual implementation. From their standpoint, the function is pure and produces a string from a tree, without any observable side effects.

11.4   Building Trees

The constructor of the `Dir` class makes it possible to build invalid directories that contain multiple nodes with the same name. In practice, this constructor would not be public. Instead, you would provide public methods to create empty directories and to add files and subdirectories to an existing directory.

Inside the companion object of the `Dir` class, you can define a function that creates an empty directory:

```scala
                                                               ─── Scala ───
def apply(name: String): Dir = Dir(name, List.empty)
```

Then, you define methods `mkFile` and `mkDir` inside class `Dir` to add contents to an existing directory. These methods take in a path as a list of names. They travel down this path inside the tree and create a file or a directory at the end of the path. As a design decision, I choose to create missing directories along the path. However, if a file exists where a directory is needed, no further travel on the path is possible and creation fails.

To avoid code duplication, `mkFile` and `mkDir` rely on the same method `mkPath`. In addition to a path, this method takes an optional file name. It always creates the path—and thus can be used to implement `mkDir`—and optionally creates a file at the end of the path, so as to implement `mkFile`:

```scala
                                                               ─── Scala ───
// inside class Dir
def mkPath(path: List[String], filename: Option[String]): Dir = path match
  case Nil =>
    filename match
      case None => this
      case Some(name) =>
        if nodes.exists(_.name == name) then
          throw FileSystemException(name, "cannot create file: node exists")
        else Dir(this.name, File(name) :: nodes)

  case dirname :: more =>
    removeByName(dirname) match
      case None => Dir(this.name, Dir(dirname).mkPath(more, filename) :: nodes)
      case Some((node, otherNodes)) =>
        Dir(this.name, node.mkPath(more, filename) :: otherNodes)
```

Listing 11.2: Example of node insertion in a general tree.

The first case, `Nil`, corresponds to reaching the end of the path, where a file might be added. If no file name is supplied, return the tree `this` as is. Otherwise, use higher-order method `exists` to check whether a node already exists with the given name. If so, the file cannot be created—throw an exception. Otherwise, replace `this` with a new directory, using the same name, but with a new file added at the front of the list of nodes.

The second case deals with the general path traversal. Take the first name in the path, `dirname`, and use helper method `removeByName` to extract the current node by that name, if it exists. If no such node is found (case `None`), create a subdirectory (`Dir(dirname)`), add the remainder of the path (`more`) to it, and add this new directory to the front of the current list of nodes. If instead the name corresponds to an existing node (case `Some`), add the remainder of the path to it: `node` becomes `node.mkPath(more, filename)` and is reinserted in the list of children.

You need to think functionally to follow this code. Trees are immutable, and node modification is achieved by replacing nodes with new nodes to create new trees. For instance, when adding a file, node `this`—which is `Dir(this.name, nodes)`—is replaced with a new tree `Dir(this.name, File(name) :: nodes)`. In the same way, you add a new subdirectory by first creating it as `(Dir(dirname).mkPath(more, filename))`— call it `newDir`—and by replacing the current tree `Dir(this.name, nodes)` with a new tree `Dir(this.name, newDir :: nodes)`.

When an existing node needs to change, you remove it from the current list of children—`nodes` becomes `otherNodes`—and replace it with a new node—`node` becomes `node.mkPath(more, filename)`. In that case, the new node is inserted at the front of the list instead of where the original node was. This is for performance reasons: List insertion away from the head is costly. Furthermore, in the common case where a newly created file or directory is used immediately, this strategy makes it more easily reachable with the next operation, since a list of nodes is always traversed from the front.

The recursive call `node.mkPath(more, filename)` may call `mkPath` on a directory node, thus continuing the traversal/construction, or on a file node, in which case the path being followed does not exist and cannot be created because its creation would require replacing an existing file with a directory with the same name. Accordingly, method `mkPath` in class `File` simply throws an exception:

```scala
// inside class File
def mkPath(path: List[String], filename: Option[String]) =
  throw FileSystemException(name, "cannot create dir: file exists")
```

Once method `mkPath` is defined, you can implement the public methods `mkFile` and `mkDir` in terms of it:

```scala
// inside class Dir
def mkDir(name: String, names: String*): Dir = mkPath(name :: names.toList, None)

def mkFile(name: String, names: String*): Dir =
  val allNames = name :: names.toList
  mkPath(allNames.init, Some(allNames.last))
```

Both methods use variable-length arguments and require at least one name to operate. In the case of `mkDir`, all the names are directories, and the path to be added is `name :: names.toList`. In `mkFile`, the last name is the file to add. The path of directories starts with `name`, followed by all the strings in `names`, except the last: This is `allNames.init` (`init` returns all the elements of a list, except the last). As an illustration, the file system from Figure 11.1 can now be created with the following expression:

```scala
                                                                    ─ Scala ─
Dir("Root")
  .mkFile("Dir2", "File3")
  .mkDir("Dir1", "Dir3")
  .mkFile("Dir1", "File2")
  .mkFile("File1")
```

You can remove files and directories from a tree by following a similar strategy. Method `rmPath` follows a path to its last element and removes it from the tree, whether it is a file or a directory. A first difference with `mkPath` is that, instead of creating missing directories, `rmPath` can stop traversing a branch as soon as a directory is missing (nothing to remove). Another difference is that you need to stop following the path one level above the last element so you can remove this element from the list of nodes of its parent. In other words, you remove a node by replacing `Dir(name, list)` with `Dir(name, shorterList)`, not by replacing `this` with "nothing." This results in a recursion that ends with a single-element list instead of an empty list:

```scala
                                                                    ─ Scala ─
// inside class Dir
def rmPath(path: List[String]): Dir = path match
  case nodename :: more =>
    removeByName(nodename) match
      case None => this
      case Some((node, otherNodes)) =>
        if more.isEmpty then Dir(this.name, otherNodes)
        else Dir(this.name, node.rmPath(more) :: otherNodes)

def rm(name: String, names: String*): Dir = rmPath(name :: names.toList)
```

Listing 11.3: Example of node removal in a general tree.

First, split the path, which is never empty, into its first name (`nodename`) and the remainder of the path (`more`). Use helper method `removeByName` to extract an existing node by that name, if any. If no node is found, there is nothing to delete from the tree, so return `this`. If a node is found and is the last path element (`more.isEmpty`), remove it from the list of nodes. Otherwise, proceed recursively with the rest of the path (`node.rmPath(more)`) to create a replacement node. In that case, you know that `more` is not empty, and therefore that `rmPath` is not applied to an empty list.

As before, a path that encounters an existing file cannot proceed. However, there is no actual node to remove in this case—the path denotes a non-exiting file or directory—and method `rmPath` in class `File` just leaves the file unchanged instead of throwing an exception:

─── *Scala* ───

```
// inside class File
def rmPath(path: List[String]) = this
```

11.5   Querying

Section 11.4 focused on building and modifying trees that represent file systems. Once a tree is built, you can define additional methods to query it. Because directories are implemented in terms of a list of nodes, many querying methods can rely on standard higher-order functions on lists. For instance, you can calculate the total number of files and directories in a system by folding:

─── *Scala* ───

```
// inside class Dir
def fileCount: Int = nodes.foldLeft(0)(_ + _.fileCount)
def dirCount: Int  = nodes.foldLeft(1)(_ + _.dirCount)

// inside class File
def fileCount: Int = 1
def dirCount: Int  = 0
```

Listing 11.4: Example of using `fold` to count nodes in a general tree.

In a directory, the total number of files is obtained by folding the list of nodes with a function that adds the number of files of each node to an accumulator, initially 0. In a file, the total number of files is 1—the file itself. The total number of directories is calculated using a similar approach, except that folding a directory starts with 1—the directory itself—and files are counted as 0 instead of 1.

You can also define your own higher-order methods on file systems for easier querying. For instance, `fileExists` and `dirExists` are used to assert the existence of files or directories that satisfy a given criterion:[4]

─── *Scala* ───

```
// inside class Dir
def fileExists(test: File => Boolean): Boolean =
    nodes.exists(_.fileExists(test))

def dirExists(test: Dir => Boolean): Boolean =
    test(this) || nodes.exists(_.dirExists(test))
```

---

[4] A `nodeExists` method is also possible but would imply that type `Node` is public. The code presented in this chapter is predicated on the assumption that the `Node` trait remains private.

```
// inside class File
def fileExists(test: File => Boolean): Boolean = test(this)
def dirExists(test: Dir => Boolean): Boolean   = false
```

Listing 11.5: Example of implementing `exists` on a general tree.

Method `fileExists` takes a Boolean function as an argument and returns true if at least one file in the tree satisfies the test function. This, in turn, is true if there exists a node in which such a file exists. Thus, you implement `fileExists` on a directory by relying on the method `exists` of lists to check all the nodes and, on each node, on the method `fileExists` itself, recursively. On a file, `fileExists` simply applies the test to the file.

Method `dirExists` is implemented similarly. It takes a Boolean function that operates on directories instead of files and applies it first to the current directory (`test(this)`) before trying the nodes by using `exists` as before. On a file, this method always returns false.

By leveraging recursion and the `exists` method of lists, only two lines each are needed to implement `fileExists` and `dirExists` on trees. In the same manner, you can implement tree folding functions that combine recursion with list method `foldLeft` (or `foldRight`, since the order of nodes in a directory is irrelevant):

```scala
                                                              ─── Scala ───
// inside class Dir
def fileFold[A](init: A)(f: (A, File) => A): A =
  nodes.foldLeft(init)((acc, node) => node.fileFold(acc)(f))

def dirFold[A](init: A)(f: (A, Dir) => A): A =
  nodes.foldLeft(f(init, this))((acc, node) => node.dirFold(acc)(f))

// inside class File
def fileFold[A](init: A)(f: (A, File) => A): A = f(init, this)
def dirFold[A](init: A)(f: (A, Dir) => A): A = init
```

Listing 11.6: Example of implementing `fold` on a general tree.

You fold a directory by folding all its children nodes, one by one. When you fold a file processing function, the folding of children starts with `init`, but when you fold a directory processing function, it starts with `f(init, this)` to first process the current directory before traversing the children. (The same principle is behind the 0 and 1 of `fileCount` and `dirCount` in Listing 11.4.) On nodes that are files, `fileFold` applies the given function `f` to the file, while `dirFold` leaves the folding accumulator unchanged.

Methods `fileFold` and `dirFold` are powerful and can be used to implement various file system queries. For instance, if `fileCount` and `dirCount` had not already been implemented as methods of class `Dir`, you could write them in terms of `fileFold` and `dirFold` instead:

```scala
                                                              ── Scala ──
def fileCount(dir: Dir): Int = dir.fileFold(0)((acc, _) => acc + 1)
def dirCount(dir: Dir): Int = dir.dirFold(0)((acc, _) => acc + 1)
```

You can also use `fileFold` to find the longest file name in a tree:[5]

```scala
                                                              ── Scala ──
def longestFilename(dir: Dir): String = dir.fileFold("") { (longest, file) =>
   if file.name.length > longest.length then file.name else longest
}
```

Likewise, you can use `dirFold` to build a list of all the file names in a file system:

```scala
                                                              ── Scala ──
def allFileNames(dir: Dir): List[String] =
   dir.dirFold(List.empty[String])((list, subdir) => subdir.lsFiles ::: list)
```

Be careful, however: Folding functions are not well suited to implementing searches because they always traverse the entire tree,[6] even after an element has been found. For instance, this implementation of a `fileFind` method is undesirable:

```scala
                                                              ── Scala ──
// DON'T DO THIS!

// inside class Dir
def fileFind(test: File => Boolean): Option[File] =
   fileFold(Option.empty[File]) { (found, file) =>
      found.orElse(if test(file) then Some(file) else None)
   }
```

The drawback of this method is that it continues to traverse the tree after a suitable file has been found.[7]

To make `fileFind` stop once a file has been found, while keeping a functional programming style, is not completely straightforward. Given that we implemented `fileExists` by using `exists` on a list and `fileFold` by using `foldLeft` on a list, you might be tempted to implement `fileFind` by using `find` on a list. The problem is that applying `find` to a list of subtrees will produce a tree (if any) in which the desired file can be found, but not the file itself. You would need to search this tree again, using `fileFind`, to extract the file:

---

[5]The body of the function could also be written as `Seq(file.name, longest).maxBy(_.length)`.

[6]Short of throwing an exception. Throwing (and catching) an exception is sometimes used as a technique to prematurely terminate a folding computation.

[7]Even though all the files are visited, this implementation stops applying the test function after a file has been found. This is because, when `orElse` is applied to a non-empty option, the expression used as its argument is not evaluated. This phenomenon is known as *lazy* or *delayed* evaluation, and is explored in Chapter 12.

```scala
——————————————————————————————————— Scala ———
// DON'T DO THIS!

// inside class Dir
def fileFind(test: File => Boolean): Option[File] =
  nodes.find(_.fileExists(test)).map(_.fileFind(test).get)
```

This implementation uses `find` to search for a node that contains the desired file. If found, `map` is invoked on the option to apply `fileFind` on this node to get the actual file. This is undesirable because the node inside the option has already been searched for the file and indeed contains it (the call to `fileFind` is guaranteed to succeed, hence the use of `get` to get the actual file). The node is thus searched twice and, because of the recursive nature of `findFile`, inner nodes end up being searched multiple times (the deeper the node, the more times it is searched).

Instead of using `find` to locate a subtree that contains a suitable file, a better strategy is to extract the desired file from each subtree by using the method `map` of lists. The expression `nodes.map(_.fileFind(test))` has type `List[Option[File]]` and contains an acceptable file (if any) for each subtree. Method `find` can then be used to find a non-empty option from the list. The expression `nodes.map(_.fileFind(test)).find(_.nonEmpty)` produces the desired file, but as an `Option[Option[File]]`, which can be flattened:

```scala
——————————————————————————————————— Scala ———
// DON'T DO THIS!

// inside class Dir
def fileFind(test: File => Boolean): Option[File] =
  nodes.map(_.fileFind(test)).find(_.nonEmpty).flatten
```

The problem with this approach is that `map` will process the entire list of nodes no matter what, and all the nodes inside a directory are searched, even after a file has been found. The standard technique to avoid this issue is to introduce a form of lazy evaluation:

```scala
——————————————————————————————————— Scala ———
// OK, but can be improved

// inside class Dir
def fileFind(test: File => Boolean): Option[File] =
  nodes.view.map(_.fileFind(test)).find(_.nonEmpty).flatten
```

By calling higher-order method `map` on `nodes.view` instead of `nodes`, you prevent nodes from being explored after a file has been found. Lazy evaluation is discussed in detail in Chapter 12. For now, it is enough to know that the implementation in the example stops when the first file is found (or traverses the entire tree if no file can be found).

You can replace the `map`/`flatten` combination with a call to `flatMap` to produce all the files unwrapped instead of being inside options. In the end, the desired implementations of `fileFind` and `dirFind` are as follows:[8]

```scala
// inside class Dir
def fileFind(test: File => Boolean): Option[File] =
  nodes.view.flatMap(_.fileFind(test)).headOption

def dirFind(test: Dir => Boolean): Option[Dir] =
  if test(this) then Some(this) else nodes.view.flatMap(_.dirFind(test)).headOption

// inside class File
def fileFind(test: File => Boolean): Option[File] =
  if test(this) then Some(this) else None

def dirFind(test: Dir => Boolean): Option[Dir] = None
```

Listing 11.7: Example of implementing `find` on a general tree.

The expression `nodes.view.flatMap(_.fileFind(test))` produces a (lazily evaluated) collection of files that satisfies the given test, one for each subtree. Invoking `headOption` forces the view to be evaluated until either a file is found or the view has been exhausted without producing a file.

11.6   Navigation

A last set of methods in classes `Dir` and `File` deal with navigation inside a file system. You can define a method `cd` to enter subdirectories, which mimics the Unix command by the same name:

```scala
// inside class Dir
def cdPath(path: List[String]): Dir = path match
  case Nil => this
  case dirname :: more =>
    nodes
        .find(_.name == dirname)
        .getOrElse(throw FileSystemException(dirname, "cannot change: no such dir"))
        .cdPath(more)
```

---

[8]Instead of `if test(this) then Some(this) else None`, the body of `fileFind` in class `File` could be written `Some(this).filter(test)`. There are other places in the code where `filter` could also be applied to options. Although this would illustrate the use of higher-order method `filter`, some code readability might be lost. I chose to stick with `if-then-else` for clarity.

```
def cd(name: String, names: String*): Dir = cdPath(name :: names.toList)

// inside class File
def cdPath(path: List[String]): Dir =
   throw FileSystemException(name, "cannot change: not a directory")
```

As was done earlier with `mkFile`, `mkDir`, and `rm`, method `cd` is implemented in terms of a helper method `cdPath` that traverses a list of directories, specified by name. If the list of names is empty, return the current directory. Otherwise, use `find` to find a subdirectory with the specified name, if any. Using `getOrElse`, extract the directory from the resulting option or throw an exception if the option is empty. The remainder of the path is then applied to the subdirectory, recursively. If, at any point, the path encounters a file instead of a directory, an exception is thrown.

11.7 Tree Zipper

Method `cd` can be used to go down a tree. How about going back up? It is crucial to realize that the problem is not to somehow keep references to enclosing trees as they are traversed. The reason is that trees are immutable, and adding or removing files or subdirectories produces a new tree. After such a modification, going back to a tree that contains a subtree as it was *before the modifications* does not make sense. What you need to implement are methods `up` and `down` so that the following code produces the same file system as the one in Figure 11.1:

```scala
                                                              Scala
Dir("Root").nav
   .mkDir("Dir2")
   .down("Dir2")
   .mkFile("File3")
   .up
   .mkDir("Dir1")
   .down("Dir1")
   .mkDir("Dir3")
   .mkFile("File2")
   .up
   .mkFile("File1")
   .dir
```

Notice that the first call to method `up`, for instance, cannot simply go back to the tree on which `down("Dir2")` was invoked, because this tree does not contain `File3`. In other words, `up` does not necessarily bring you back to a previous tree, but also needs, in some cases, to create a new tree.

A viable approach is to modify the tree type into a zipper. Section 5.6 implemented a zipper to navigate lists leftward and rightward. The same idea can be used to move up and down a tree.[9] Zippers are immutable. A tree zipper combines a subtree with the sequence of steps that led to that subtree. Those steps can be reapplied, in reverse order, to go up. In contrast to returning to an existing tree, applying a step builds a new tree, which contains updated subtrees that reflect modifications to the file system. In the preceding code, the call to `nav` changes the type of the file system from a tree to a tree zipper, which implements navigation via its `up` and `down` methods. The final call to `dir` brings you back to a regular tree.

To go down a subdirectory, you create a step that contains the name of the parent directory, as well as a list of all the other nodes in that directory. For instance, going down into `Dir1` in the file system from Figure 11.1 returns the subtree rooted at `Dir1` but also creates a step that contains the name `Root` and a list of subtrees other than `Dir1`:

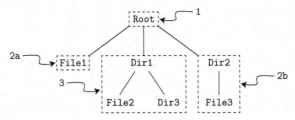

You can see that from the subtree (labeled 3), the step name (labeled 1), and the step trees (labeled 2a and 2b), the previous tree can be reconstructed to go up. If the subtree has been changed—that is, replaced with a different tree—going up by reassembling will produce a different tree (same 1 and 2 parts, but a different subtree 3).

The zipper is implemented in a class `DirNav`:

```scala
final class DirNav (val dir: Dir, steps: List[(String, List[Node])]):
    ...
```

A zipper consists of a current directory (`dir`) and a list of down steps that led to it (`steps`). Each step is a pair that contains the name of the parent node as a `String`, and a list of the siblings of the current directory, of type `List[Node]`. The list of steps is empty when the current directory is the root of the file system.

The zipper implements two methods `up` and `down`. To move down to a subdirectory, method `down` produces the same subdirectory as the earlier `cd` method, but adds a step to the list of steps so the downward move can be reversed by method `up` to go back up:

___

[9]This section considers only up and down movements. A more complex zipper can be written to move left and right among siblings.

```scala
                                                               ─── Scala ───
// inside class DirNav
def down(dirname: String): DirNav =
  dir.removeByName(dirname) match
    case None =>
      throw FileSystemException(dirname, "cannot change: no such directory")
    case Some((file: File, _)) =>
      throw FileSystemException(dirname, "cannot change: not a directory")
    case Some((subdir: Dir, otherNodes)) =>
      DirNav(subdir, (dir.name, otherNodes) :: steps)

def up: DirNav = steps match
  case Nil                   => this
  case (name, nodes) :: more => DirNav(Dir(name, dir :: nodes), more)
```

Listing 11.8: Navigation methods in a tree zipper (1).

To go down, search the target subdirectory by name and remove it from the list of nodes. If it is not found, or if a file is found by that name instead, throw an exception. Otherwise, if the subdirectory exists (`subdir`), create a zipper with it by adding a new step. This step contains the name of the parent directory (`dir.name`) and all the siblings of `subdir` (`otherNodes`). The new step is added at the front of the list of steps, which is used like a stack. To go back up, method `up` pops the first step from the stack and uses its name and list of nodes to construct a new tree `Dir(name, dir :: nodes)`, which is wrapped in a zipper with the remaining steps.

For convenience, you can also implement a method to go down multiple times and a method to go back to the root of the tree:

```scala
                                                               ─── Scala ───
// inside class DirNav
def down(dirname1: String, dirname2: String, dirnames: String*): DirNav =
  (dirname1 :: dirname2 :: dirnames.toList).foldLeft(this)(_.down(_))

@tailrec
def top: DirNav = if steps.isEmpty then this else up.top
```

Listing 11.9: Navigation methods in a tree zipper (2).

To go down a path made of multiple subdirectories, you use `foldLeft` with the current directory as the initial value to invoke the single-name variant of method `down` on all the names in the path, one by one. To move all the way to the top, method `top` repeatedly applies `up` until the root of the tree is reached.

All the other methods of class `DirNav` are implemented by forwarding calls to the corresponding method in class `Dir`, except that creation methods (adding and removing files and subdirectories) need to return a navigable directory instead of a plain directory:

Scala

```scala
// inside class DirNav
override def toString = dir.toString

def mkFile(name: String, names: String*): DirNav =
  DirNav(dir.mkFile(name, names*), steps)

def mkDir(name: String, names: String*): DirNav =
  DirNav(dir.mkDir(name, names*), steps)

def rm(name: String, names: String*): DirNav =
  DirNav(dir.rm(name, names*), steps)

export dir.{
  mkString, ls, lsFiles,
  dirCount, dirExists, dirFold, dirFind, fileCount, fileExists, fileFold, fileFind
}
```

Finally, a method `nav` is added to class `Dir` to make a plain directory navigable:

Scala

```scala
// inside class Dir
def nav: DirNav = DirNav(this, List.empty)
```

11.8 Summary

In this chapter, a file system is represented as a tree of files and directories. The contents of a directory are stored as a list of nodes, and the higher-order methods of lists are used to process these nodes effectively. The tree also defines its own higher-order methods. They are implemented recursively, and recursive calls on subdirectories are performed using the higher-order methods of lists on a directory's contents. Finally, trees are extended into zippers to become navigable, with methods to go down a subdirectory and back up to the parent directory. In all (including the many footnotes), this file system case study uses and/or reimplements standard higher-order methods `exists`, `find`, `flatMap`, `foldLeft`, `foreach`, `filter`, `map`, `maxBy`, and `partition`.

Chapter 12

Lazy Evaluation

By using functions as values, it becomes possible to replace data with a function that computes this data. With this approach, the evaluation of arguments can be delayed until they are needed, making it possible to pass unevaluated code to methods and functions. Combined with syntactic help from the language, it becomes possible to define additional control structures from within a programming language, leading potentially to the definition of an internal domain-specific language. Functions can also be stored within data structures to delay the evaluation of parts of that structure. Streams are a classic functional programming structure that implements lazily evaluated sequences. Besides unevaluated arguments and lazy data structures, lazy evaluation can take a few other forms, such as views that delay the evaluation of higher-order functions and mechanisms for the lazy initialization of variables.

12.1 Delayed Evaluation of Arguments

We have seen that higher-order functions can take in arguments that are themselves functions. By replacing an explicit argument, such as a string, with a function that computes this argument, you can delay the computation of the string until its value is needed.

Functions sometimes go this route for performance reasons. For instance, the `Logger` type from `java.util.logging` defines a method `info` to log a message at the `INFO` level:

```Scala
val logger: Logger = ...

logger.info(s"incoming request from ${ip.getHostName} (${ip.getHostAddress})")
```

A drawback of this method is that the string argument is always built, even when logging at the `INFO` level is disabled. In this example, if logging is set at the `WARNING` level, a potentially costly hostname lookup still takes place to create a string that is immediately discarded.

Java 8 introduced a second `info` method to the `Logger` class. It replaces the string argument with a function that returns a string:

```Scala
logger.info(() => s"incoming request from ${ip.getHostName} (${ip.getHostAddress})")
```

You can invoke this `info` method just as easily as the previous one by using a lambda expression for the function argument. The preceding expression does not perform a hostname lookup. A lookup will happen only within the logger and only if logging has been set to a level that includes `INFO` messages.

You can define your own methods that use function arguments to replace explicit values that may not be needed. For instance, the Java `Properties` class defines a method for property lookup with a second argument that specifies a default value if a key is not found:

```scala
val properties: Properties = System.getProperties

properties.getProperty("hostname", "unknown")
```

This is sufficient when the default value is a constant, like `"unknown"`. However, if calculating the default value is expensive, this computation is wasted if a property key is already associated with a value. There is no `getProperty` method that takes a function as its second argument. However, you can easily add one as as an extension by relying on a single-argument `getProperty` method that returns null when a key is not found:

```scala
extension (properties: Properties)
   def getProperty(key: String, fallback: () => String): String =
      val prop = properties.getProperty(key)
      if prop ne null then prop else fallback()
```

The default value is specified as a fallback function, which is invoked only if the property is not found. With this extension in scope, you can write

```scala
properties.getProperty("hostname", () => InetAddress.getLocalHost.getHostName)
```

without incurring any additional cost if the `hostname` property is already defined.

12.2 By-Name Arguments

In any programming language with higher-order functions—which includes all functional programming languages—you can achieve delayed evaluation of arguments by replacing values with functions that produce those values. Those no-argument functions, used to delay evaluation, are sometimes called *thunks*. If your language has support for lambda expressions, they are usually the most convenient way to generate thunks.

Some languages offer an additional mechanism in the form of *by-name* argument passing. For instance, this produces a list of pseudo-random numbers:

```scala
                                                          ── Scala ──
val rand = Random(42)
List.fill(5)(rand.nextInt(100)) // List(30, 63, 48, 84, 70)
```

If you are coming from languages like Java or C, this may look surprising. Indeed, method `fill` from `java.util.Collections` behaves differently:

```java
                                                           ── Java ──
List<Integer> numbers = ...
Collections.fill(numbers, rand.nextInt(100)); // sets the list to 30, 30, 30, 30, ...
```

In the Java variant, the expression `rand.nextInt(100)` produces the value 30, and the list is filled with this value. In the Scala code, however, `fill` behaves as if the thunk `() => rand.nextInt(100)` had been passed as its argument. This is because the argument to Scala's `fill` is passed by name, unevaluated. You could implement your own `fill` function as follows:

```scala
                                                          ── Scala ──
def fill[A](len: Int)(value: => A): List[A] =
    val buffer = List.newBuilder[A]
    var i = 0
    while i < len do
        buffer += value
        i += 1
    buffer.result()
```

Listing 12.1: Reimplementing `List.fill`.

The "magic" comes from adding an arrow in front of the type of the argument—`value: => A` instead of `value: A`—which triggers by-name argument passing. Without the arrow, the `fill` function would behave as in Java, filling the list with a repetition of the same value. But because the argument is passed by name instead, the expression `rand.nextInt(100)` is reevaluated with each iteration of the `while`-loop, resulting in different numbers. By-name arguments implement a form of *lazy* evaluation, by contrast to regular argument passing, which is sometimes referred to as *eager* evaluation. They can enhance code readability by avoiding the explicit creation of thunks.

Many functions and methods in the Scala standard library use by-name arguments. For instance, the `Option` type defines methods `orElse` and `getOrElse` to replace an empty option with an alternative. They are defined in the `Option` class as follows:

─── *Scala* ──────

```scala
// inside class Option:
def orElse[B >: A](alternative: => Option[B]): Option[B] =
  if isEmpty then alternative else this


def getOrElse[B >: A](default: => B): B =
  if isEmpty then default else this.get
```

The `alternative` and `default` arguments are passed by name and are evaluated only if the option is empty.

The `getProperty` extension could rely on `getOrElse` for its implementation:

─── *Scala* ──────

```scala
def getProperty(key: String, fallback: () => String): String =
  Option(properties.getProperty(key)).getOrElse(fallback())
```

The predefined function `Option` wraps values inside options, mapping null to `None`. (For an illustration of `orElse` in a branching algorithm, see Section 12.11.)

Similar to `orElse` and `getOrElse`, mutable maps have `getOrElseUpdate(k,v)`, a method that retrieves the value associated with key `k` or, if the key is not present, updates the map with a new pair `(k,v)`. The argument `v` is passed by name: If the key is present, `v` is not needed and will not be evaluated. You can use `getOrElseUpdate` to simplify the implementation of the higher-order function `memo` from Listing 9.6:

─── *Scala* ──────

```scala
def memo[A, B](f: A => B): A => B =
  val store = mutable.Map.empty[A, B]
  x => store.getOrElseUpdate(x, f(x))
```

Listing 12.2: Memoization uisng a by-name argument, improved from Lis. 9.6.

As before, the function starts with a lookup in the map. If `x` is found in the map, `getOrElseUpdate` does not evaluate its second argument. Only if the key is not found will function `f` be called on `x`.

12.3   Control Abstraction

The `fill` function embeds a `while`-loop; `getOrElseUpdate` embeds a conditional. Many of the higher-order functions discussed in Chapter 10 also implement a form of control abstraction: Somewhere in the implementation of `map`, `filter`, and `find`, there is a loop—or a recursive function—that performs the necessary iteration. Using delayed evaluation, various forms of flow control—such as loops, conditional, and exception handling—can be abstracted away in user-defined, higher-order constructs.

Consider, for instance, Java's try-with-resources, used to ensure that resources are released at the end of a computation:

```java
                                                             ─── Java ───
<A> void writeToFile(Path file, Iterable<A> values) throws IOException {
  try (var out = new ObjectOutputStream(Files.newOutputStream(file))) {
    for (var item : values) out.writeObject(item);
  }
}
```

This function writes a collection of objects into a file. The `try` construct guarantees that the file is closed after writing, even in the presence of exceptions. You can write a similar method in Scala:

```scala
                                                             ─── Scala ───
def writeToFile[A](file: Path, values: Iterable[A]): Unit =
  Using.resource(ObjectOutputStream(Files.newOutputStream(file))) { out =>
    for item <- values do out.writeObject(item)
  }
```

A key difference, however, is that Java's try-with-resources is a construct of the language, while Scala's `Using.resource` is a regular function, defined in the standard library. In its simplest form, you could implement it yourself as follows:

```scala
                                                             ─── Scala ───
def resource[R <: AutoCloseable, A](res: R)(use: R => A): A =
  try use(res) finally res.close()
```

Function `resource` is curried and higher-order. It is parameterized by the type of the resource, R, which must be a subtype of Java's `AutoCloseable`,[1] and by the type A of the value produced from the resource, using a given function `use`. The implementation invokes this function `use` within a `try-finally` construct to guarantee that the resource is closed: `resource(r)(f)` is the value `f(r)`, and `r` is closed after `f` is applied.

Function `resource` needs to tie the given resource to the code that uses it, so it makes sense to pass the code as a function of the resource. When no such tie is necessary, the code to execute becomes a no-argument function, which you can replace with a by-name value. The result is a control abstraction that hides the fact that an argument is actually a function. For instance, you can write a construct that calculates the duration of the execution of an arbitrary code fragment:

```scala
                                                             ─── Scala ───
def timeOf[U](code: => U): Double =
  val startTime = System.nanoTime()
  code
  val endTime = System.nanoTime()
  (endTime - startTime) / 1E9
```

Listing 12.3: Control abstraction example: function `timeOf`.

---

[1]Operator "`<:`" is used in Scala to specify a type bound. It is discussed in Section 15.9.

This function takes a by-name argument, keeps track of the amount of time needed to evaluate it, and returns the duration in seconds. You can use it without explicitly creating a thunk function:

```scala
val seconds: Double = timeOf {
    InetAddress.getLocalHost.getHostName // or any code for which you want the duration
}
```

The popular Scala library `Scalactic` defines a `times` construct, used as follows:

```scala
3 times {
    println("Beetlejuice!")
}
```

Although `times` looks like a keyword and a language construct, it is actually defined as a regular function. You could implement it as an extension method:

```scala
extension (count: Int)
    infix def times[U](code: => U): Unit =
        var n = count
        while n > 0 do
            code
            n -= 1
```

Listing 12.4: Control abstraction example: function `times`.

This method is defined as an extension so it can be called on regular integers. It uses a by-name argument for the code to be repeated: The code is passed unevaluated, and is evaluated by the `times` method as many times as needed.

As a more elaborate example, let's define a new looping construct `repeat-until`:

```scala
class Repeat[U](code: => U):
    infix def until(test: => Boolean): Unit =
        code
        while !test do code

def repeat[U](code: => U) = Repeat(code)
```

Listing 12.5: Control abstraction example: `repeat-until`.

Class `Repeat` uses a by-name argument in its constructor. The constructor produces an object that implements the repetition in its `until` method, using a termination test that is also passed by name. You can use this new construct as follows:

```scala                                                           Scala
var n = 3
repeat {
  println("Beetlejuice!")
  n -= 1
} until (n == 0)
```

In this example, `println("Beetlejuice!"); n -= 1` is passed (unevaluated) to the function `repeat`, then to the constructor of class `Repeat`. Finally, method `until` is invoked on the resulting object, with the (unevaluated) argument `n == 0`.

12.4   Internal Domain-Specific Languages

As the earlier examples show, clever use of by-name arguments can produce abstractions that look very much like programming language constructs. You can apply this technique to define domain-specific languages (DSL), which are small languages, often used for modeling or architecting in a specific domain. Instead of being implemented as a stand-alone language, an *internal* DSL is embedded into a general-purpose programming language like Scala. For instance, the testing framework `Scalatest` defines a DSL for writing unit tests:[2]

```scala                                                           Scala
class ExampleSpec extends AnyFlatSpec with should.Matchers:

  "A Stack" should "pop values in last-in-first-out order" in {
    val stack = Stack[Int]()
    stack.push(1)
    stack.push(2)
    stack.pop() should be (2)
    stack.pop() should be (1)
  }

  it should "throw NoSuchElementException if an empty stack is popped" in {
    val emptyStack = Stack[Int]()
    a [NoSuchElementException] should be thrownBy {
      emptyStack.pop()
    }
  }
```

Methods and objects are carefully named `it`, `should`, `in`, `a`, `be`, and `thrownBy` so that testing code flows naturally, and suitable error messages are produced when a test fails.

---

[2]This example is taken quasi-verbatim from the `Scalatest` website.

12.5   Streams as Lazily Evaluated Lists

Consider a scenario in which data, somehow produced by a component of an application, is being searched for specific values by another component. A possible design could rely on a searching method with the following signature:

```scala
def searchData(data: List[Data]): Option[Data] = ...
```

A drawback of this approach is that the entire list of data has to be produced before it can be searched, possibly resulting in situations where the list is large and only the first few elements are needed for the search. As an alternative, you could use a lazily evaluated argument:

```scala
def searchData(data: => List[Data]): Option[Data] = ...
```

But that does not help at all, because the entire list still has to be evaluated before the search starts. What you want instead is to delay the evaluation of each list element. You could do it with thunks:

```scala
def searchData(data: List[() => Data]): Option[Data] = ...
```

However, this is far from ideal because all the thunks need to be created before the search starts. With this approach, you may not have to produce all the actual data, but you still need to create as many thunk functions as there are potential pieces of data.

What you really want is to avoid creating anything beyond the data elements needed for the search to complete. In Scala, you achieve this with a searching method with the following signature:

```scala
def searchData(data: LazyList[Data]): Option[Data] = ...
```

LazyList is a type of linear sequence—like a list—in which elements are lazily evaluated. Such sequences are often called *streams*. Scala streams are immutable. They are also memoized:[3] Once computed, each element is stored in the stream.

You can often use streams like regular lists. For instance, to search for the first piece of data with a value greater than 10, you can define a tail recursive function:

---

[3]This means that mutation actually occurs within streams, to replace unevaluated elements with actual values. As a sequence, though, streams are conceptually immutable and a stream always represents the same sequence.

```scala
                                                                  ── Scala ──
def searchData(data: LazyList[Data]): Option[Data] =
  if data.isEmpty then None
  else if data.head.value > 10 then Some(data.head)
  else searchData(data.tail)
```

Except for the method's signature, this code is identical to a variant that uses lists. Note that, due to memoization, the head of the stream is evaluated only once, even though `data.head` is used twice in the code. Furthermore, if this first piece of data has a value greater than 10, no other stream element is evaluated.

   LazyList supports pattern matching, and you can also write the recursive searching function as follows:

```scala
                                                                  ── Scala ──
def searchData(data: LazyList[Data]): Option[Data] = data match
  case LazyList()  => None
  case head #:: tail => if head.value > 10 then Some(head) else searchData(tail)
```

This implementation is similar to pattern matching and recursion on lists. The only differences are the empty stream pattern—LazyList() instead of Nil—and the "cons" operator—named "#::" on streams instead of "::" on lists. For this simple searching task, though, your best strategy is to rely on the standard higher-order methods defined on the LazyList type:

```scala
                                                                  ── Scala ──
def searchData(data: LazyList[Data]): Option[Data] = data.find(_.value > 10)
```

   Usually, list-creating code can be easily modified to produce streams instead. For instance, the `hanoi` function, written in Chapter 6 to illustrate recursion, simply prints each move as a string. To display moves graphically, it could be inconvenient to incorporate graphics code directly inside the solving function. Instead, you can separate the creation of moves from their display by having a solving function create a list of moves and a displaying function consume it:

```scala
                                                                  ── Scala ──
def hanoi[A](n: Int, from: A, mid: A, to: A): List[(A, A)] =
  if n == 0 then List.empty
  else hanoi(n - 1, from, to, mid) ::: (from, to) :: hanoi(n - 1, mid, from, to)
```

Listing 12.6: Tower of Hanoi moves as a list; contrast with Lis. 12.7.

Instead of printing them, this function returns the moves as a list of pairs (from, to). If you want a stream instead of a list, the necessary changes to the code are trivial:

```scala
                                                        ─────── Scala ───────
def hanoi[A](n: Int, from: A, mid: A, to: A): LazyList[(A, A)] =
  if n == 0 then LazyList.empty
  else hanoi(n - 1, from, to, mid) #::: (from, to) #:: hanoi(n - 1, mid, from, to)
```

Listing 12.7: Tower of Hanoi moves as a stream.

This function looks almost the same, but it does not compute any actual move. It returns a stream, and moves will be created on demand when the stream is queried:

```scala
                                                        ─────── Scala ───────
val allMoves     = hanoi(100, 'L', 'M', 'R')
val oneMove      = allMoves(999) // ('M', 'L')
val anotherMove  = allMoves(49)  // ('L', 'R')
```

Note that `allMoves` is a stream of $2^{100} - 1$ elements, a number on the order of 10^{30}. Obviously, such a collection would not fit in memory with a list-based implementation. The computation of `oneMove` triggers the evaluation of the first 1000 elements of the stream. The evaluation of `anotherMove` does not involve any additional calculation: The 50th move, already in the stream, is retrieved.

12.6   Streams as Pipelines

Because they are lazily evaluated, streams are a great structure for pipelined transformations. Consider, for instance, the problem of searching a file for long words. Function `longWords(lines, min)` takes in a list of lines and a minimum word length. It proceeds by splitting the lines into words, removing characters that are not letters, and selecting all the words with a length at least equal to the specified minimum. You can do this functionally with the following code:

```scala
                                                        ─────── Scala ───────
def clean(str: String): String = str.filter(_.isLetter) // remove non-letters

def longWords(lines: List[String], min: Int): List[String] =
  lines
    .flatMap(_.split(' '))
    .map(clean)
    .filter(_.length >= min)
```

Since the function's first argument is a list of lines, and each line is a list of words, `flatMap` is used to avoid nested lists. Words are then cleaned, and only the long words are included in the final result.

This code produces the desired output, but suffers from a minor inefficiency: Each stage of the computation produces a list—first a list of words, then a list of clean words, and finally the desired list of long words. These intermediate lists have to be allocated in memory, then garbage-collected, which is not free.

In Section 10.4, we discussed a possible approach to avoid this problem: Replace a pipeline of higher-order functions with a single fold. You might recall that this change did not improve code readability. In the case of longWords, it is even worse:

```scala
                                                                          Scala
def longWords(lines: List[String], min: Int): List[String] =
  lines.foldRight(List.empty[String]) { (line, words) =>
    line.split(' ').foldRight(words) { (word, moreWords) =>
      val cleanWord = clean(word)
      if cleanWord.length >= min then cleanWord :: moreWords else moreWords
    }
  }
```

Don't bother trying to understand this function. It is here to show you that the problem can indeed be solved by using foldRight, but the resulting code is difficult to read—certainly much harder than the flatMap/map/filter variant.

A better strategy that avoids the intermediate lists is to keep using flatMap, map, and filter, but on streams instead of lists:

```scala
                                                                          Scala
def longWords(lines: List[String], min: Int): List[String] =
  lines.to(LazyList)
    .flatMap(_.split(' '))
    .map(clean)
    .filter(_.length >= min)
    .toList
```

The initial list of lines is converted into a stream. Because streams are lazily evaluated, calls to flatMap, map, and filter do not trigger any computation, and in particular, do not create intermediate lists. The final call to toList forces an evaluation of the last stream and produces the desired list without allocating any intermediate list.

This approach is particularly popular in Java, where the Stream class implements all the necessary higher-order methods but collections like List do not. You would write the longWords function in Java as follows:

```java
                                                                          Java
List<String> longWords(List<String> lines, int min) {
  return lines.stream()
      .flatMap(line -> line.replace(' ', '\n').lines())
      .map(word -> clean(word))
      .filter(word -> word.length() >= min)
      .toList();
}
```

12.7   Streams as Infinite Data Structures

Function `hanoi` from Listing 12.7 builds its resulting stream by using "`#::`" and "`#:::`". These operations are implemented lazily and can build a stream without triggering the evaluation of their stream arguments. In particular, they can be used to define streams that are conceptually infinite:

```scala
def countUp(n: Int): LazyList[Int] = n #:: countUp(n + 1)

val naturals = countUp(0) // 0, 1, 2, 3, ...
```

At first sight, function `countUp` makes no sense. It seems to violate one of the principles of a good recursive function—namely, to terminate, a function should always define at least one non-recursive branch. Here, `countUp` always invokes `countUp`. Indeed, if you write this function using lists, it will never terminate. On streams, however, the definition is valid. It produces a never-ending stream of numbers. Of course, any attempt to evaluate the entire stream—for example, `naturals.toList`—would result in a non-terminating computation.

You can sometimes use infinite streams to replace mutable data with values of a more functional flavor. For instance, a (mutable) pseudo-random number generator can be replaced with an infinite stream of pseudo-random numbers:

```scala
def randomNumbers: LazyList[Float] = Random.nextFloat() #:: randomNumbers
```

Infinite streams are often created using generative higher-order functions. For example, the `naturals` and `randomNumbers` streams can be created in this way:

```scala
val naturals      = LazyList.iterate(0)(_ + 1)
val randomNumbers = LazyList.continually(Random.nextFloat())
```

12.8   Iterators

The "$3n + 1$" problem defines the following sequence: If a natural number n is even, its successor is $n \div 2$; otherwise, it is $3n + 1$. This sequence, sometimes known as the Collatz sequence, is conjectured to always reach 1 eventually, for any starting natural number. For instance, if you start with 27, the sequence produces 111 numbers before reaching 1 for the first time (and then continues forever as 4, 2, 1, 4, 2, 1, ...):

```
27 82 41 124 62 31 94 47 142 71 214 107 322 161 484 242 121 364 182 91 274 137
412 206 103 310 155 466 233 700 350 175 526 263 790 395 1186 593 1780 890 445
1336 668 334 167 502 251 754 377 1132 566 283 850 425 1276 638 319 958 479 1438
719 2158 1079 3238 1619 4858 2429 7288 3644 1822 911 2734 1367 4102 2051 6154
3077 9232 4616 2308 1154 577 1732 866 433 1300 650 325 976 488 244 122 61 184
92 46 23 70 35 106 53 160 80 40 20 10 5 16 8 4 2 1
```

You can write a function to calculate the number of steps needed to reach 1. An imperative implementation could be:

―― *Scala* ――

```scala
def collatz(start: BigInt): Int =
  var count = 0
  var n     = start
  while n != 1 do
    n = if n % 2 == 0 then n / 2 else 3 * n + 1
    count += 1
  count

collatz(27) // 111
collatz(BigInt("9927745071052606638932498077818326168220161436501347309332270")) // 2632
```

Listing 12.8: Imperative implementation of the $3n + 1$ sequence.

What is the functional equivalent of this iterative program? At first glance, it could be expressed as the length of the actual sequence of numbers:

―― *Scala* ――

```scala
// DON'T DO THIS!
def collatz(start: BigInt): Int =
  LazyList
    .iterate(start)(n => if n % 2 == 0 then n / 2 else 3 * n + 1)
    .takeWhile(_ != 1)
    .length
```

This implementation builds the sequence explicitly, as an infinite stream, then uses `takeWhile` to look for the first occurrence of the number 1. The length of the sequence from the starting number to 1 is the desired output of the function.

Although it produces the correct output for the two previous examples, this function is inefficient and would actually fail on larger numbers. The reason is that the entire list of numbers is allocated in memory—2632 numbers in the second test—before calculating the length. Fortunately, there is an easy fix: Replace the lazy list with an iterator. Scala's `Iterator` type implements many standard higher-order methods, including `iterate` and `takeWhile`:

```scala
                                                              ─── Scala ───
def collatz(start: BigInt): Int =
  Iterator
    .iterate(start)(n => if n % 2 == 0 then n / 2 else 3 * n + 1)
    .takeWhile(_ != 1)
    .length
```

Listing 12.9: Functional implementation of the $3n + 1$ sequence.

This variant does not allocate any explicit sequence in memory. Its performance is comparable to that of the iterative version.

When you use pipelined computations, it is often beneficial—and usually straightforward—to stack transformations on a type that is lazily evaluated, such as streams or iterators. Some iterators are easy enough to build directly, as with the collatz function. Others can be trickier, and you can sometimes use streams as an intermediate stage.

For instance, it is not easy to write an iterator that produces the Tower of Hanoi moves.[4] Instead, you can use the stream-based hanoi function from Listing 12.7 to create a stream and then derive an iterator from the stream:

```scala
                                                              ─── Scala ───
def hanoiIterator[A](n: Int, from: A, mid: A, to: A): Iterator[(A, A)] =
  hanoi(n, from, mid, to).iterator

val moves = hanoiIterator(100, 'L', 'M', 'R')
```

Value moves is an iterator, which can be used to retrieve the moves one by one, with no actual sequence of moves expanded in memory. The iterator method is correctly implemented in the LazyList class to not keep a reference to the head of the stream, thus avoiding memory leaks.

As a last example of introducing laziness via iterators, consider the problem of searching text files for lines that match a given criterion. First, consider the (unwieldy) imperative implementation:

```scala
                                                              ─── Scala ───
def read(file: Path): List[String] = ...

def searchFiles(files: List[Path], lineTest: String => Boolean): Option[String] =
  val fileArray = files.toIndexedSeq
  var fileIndex = 0
  while fileIndex < fileArray.length do
    val lineArray = read(fileArray(fileIndex)).toIndexedSeq
    var lineIndex = 0
```

---

[4] At least while using the recursive algorithm of the hanoi function. There exists an alternative, non-recursive algorithm, from which deriving an iterator is actually straightforward.

```
      while lineIndex < lineArray.length do
        val line = lineArray(lineIndex)
        if lineTest(line) then return Some(line)
        lineIndex += 1
      end while
      fileIndex += 1
  end while
  None
```

A function **read** is used to load the contents of a file into an array of lines. An outer loop traverses all the files. For each file, an inner loop examines all the lines, until a suitable line is found, in any file.

The functional equivalent is remarkably simpler. First, you use **flatMap** to flatten all the files into a single sequence of lines, on which you apply **find** to search for the desired line:

Scala
```
// DON'T DO THIS!
def searchFiles(files: List[Path], lineTest: String => Boolean): Option[String] =
  files.flatMap(read).find(lineTest)
```

This implementation looks nice, but it actually opens and reads all the files, no matter what. By contrast, the imperative program opens files only until a suitable line is found; the remaining files are left untouched. To achieve this in a functional programming style, use lazy evaluation:

Scala
```
def searchFiles(files: List[Path], lineTest: String => Boolean): Option[String] =
  files.iterator.flatMap(read).find(lineTest)
```

The call to method **flatMap** on an iterator produces an iterator; no files are open. Method **find** searches this iterator by opening the files one by one, until a line is found. The function now performs the same computation as the imperative program.

12.9   Lists, Streams, Iterators, and Views

Streams bring laziness to lists. However, because streams are memoized, they turn into regular lists as their elements are evaluated. This can result in wasted memory. For instance, passing a stream of Tower of Hanoi moves to a display function is dangerous: As moves are displayed, the stream grows and could eventually fill the entire memory. Instead, you can use a display function that consumes an iterator of moves, like the one defined earlier.

The main difficulty of working with iterators, however, is that most methods are destructive, including higher-order methods:

```scala
                                                              Scala
val iter1 = List(1, 2, 3).iterator
iter1.find(_ > 1) // Some(2)
iter1.next()      // invalid call

val iter2 = List(1, 2, 3).iterator
iter2.map(_ + 1) // a new iterator
iter2.next()      // invalid call
```

A call to `find` invalidates the iterator. You cannot invoke any method on the iterator
after that. Similarly, after you use method `map`, you need to rely on the new iterator that
is returned; the old iterator on which `map` was applied is no longer invalid.

In consequence, iterators are well suited to pipelined computations, such as in functions `collatz` and `searchFiles`. For other uses, you should exercise extreme caution. If
you want to avoid wasted memory due to memoization but need something that is more
reusable than an iterator, other types are sometimes available. In Scala, for instance,
views behave like non-memoized streams, without the drawbacks of iterators.[5]

Let's illustrate the differences between lists, streams, and views with a simple
example. Assume a function `times10` that multiplies its input by 10, but also prints
`multiplying` on the terminal each time it is invoked—to keep track of which operations
are performed lazily. First, consider the case of plain lists:

```scala
                                                              Scala
val list = List(1, 2, 3).map(times10)
println(list)
println(list.head)
println(list.last)
println(list.head)
```

This produces the following output, as expected:

```
multiplying
multiplying
multiplying
List(10, 20, 30)
10
30
10
```

The call to method `map` eagerly applies function `times10` on all the list elements before
the list is even displayed. As the list is queried, there is no further computation.

---

[5]The details vary from language to language. For instance, Java's `Stream` type is not memoized,
defines many methods that consume the stream, and is closer to Scala's `Iterator` than Scala's `LazyList`.

If you use streams, the output is different:

```scala                                                    Scala
val stream = LazyList(1, 2, 3).map(times10)
println(stream)
println(stream.head)
println(stream.last)
println(stream.head)
```

```
LazyList(<not computed>)
multiplying
10
multiplying
multiplying
30
10
```

The stream is displayed first as not yet computed. Function `times10` is not called at all when method `map` is invoked. When the first element of the stream is needed, a single call to `times10` takes place and value 10 is printed. Querying the last value of the stream triggers an evaluation of all its remaining elements, resulting in two calls to `times10` before 30 is displayed. After that, if the head of the stream is queried again, no further computation takes place, due to memoization.

Views behave differently from streams:

```scala                                                    Scala
val view = List(1, 2, 3).view.map(times10)
println(view)
println(view.head)
println(view.last)
println(view.head)
```

```
SeqView(<not computed>)
multiplying
10
multiplying
multiplying
multiplying
30
multiplying
10
```

As with streams, the call to `map` does not invoke `times10` at all, and the view is first displayed unevaluated. Displaying the first element triggers one call to `times10`. Displaying the last element triggers *three* calls to `times10`—instead of two with streams—as the head of the view is reevaluated (no memoization). For the same reason, displaying the head one more time requires another call to function `times10`.

12.10   Delayed Evaluation of Fields and Local Variables

We have seen several forms of "laziness" in this chapter (and I hope you are not getting tired). There is one more that I wish to discuss, and with which you may already be familiar: lazy initialization. This technique is used when object creation is expensive—because, for instance, it requires network access or the processing of large data—but the object may never be needed. A typical pattern is as follows:

```scala
class SomeClass:
   private var theValue: ExpensiveType = null
   def value: ExpensiveType =
      if theValue eq null then theValue = ExpensiveType.create()
      theValue
```

Users retrieve the object via the method `value`. The first time this method is called, the object is created and stored in field `theValue`. Further calls simply return the stored object. If method `value` is never called, the object is never created.

Some languages define mechanisms that facilitate the implementation of this pattern. In Scala, for instance, you can declare a `val` field to be `lazy`:

```scala
class SomeClass:
   lazy val value: ExpensiveType = ExpensiveType.create()
```

This will trigger a single evaluation of `ExpensiveType.create` the first time `value` is accessed, if any. If the field is never used, the object is not created. One way you can think of it is that a `lazy val` behaves like a one-value stream—delayed evaluation and memoization.[6]

Although it is less common, lazy initialization can also be applied to local variables. Consider, for instance, the `hanoi` function from Listing 12.7, rewritten here to introduce two local variables `before` and `after`:

```scala
def hanoi[A](n: Int, from: A, mid: A, to: A): LazyList[(A, A)] =
   if n == 0 then LazyList.empty
   else
```

---

[6] As an added benefit, `lazy val` is thread-safe: Even if multiple threads access `value` at the same time, the expensive object is guaranteed to be created only once. This is notoriously not true of the previous variant. If you don't need it, this thread-safety can be turned off for increased performance.

```scala
    lazy val before = hanoi(n - 1, from, to, mid)
    lazy val after  = hanoi(n - 1, mid, from, to)
    before #::: (from, to) #:: after
```

Without `lazy`, the streams `before` and `after` would be fully evaluated before "`#:::`" and "`#::`" can work their magic, and laziness would be entirely lost.

12.11 Illustration: Subset-Sum

Subset-sum is a classic problem of theoretical computer science. It can be defined as follows: Given a multiset of integers, find a subset that adds up to a given target. (A multiset is a set with possible repetitions, which is represented in this section as a list, and referred to simply as a set.) Some problems have one or more solutions, while others have none. For instance, given the set of numbers -1, 3, -6, -6, 11, 7, and 3, target 18 is reachable ($11 + 7 = 18$) but target 19 is not.

Subset-sum is known to be NP-complete. However, you can solve it using a simple (but inefficient) divide-and-conquer approach. To reach a target T, pick an element x from the set and try to reach $T - x$ with the remaining numbers. If this can be done, you add x to the set that does it to make a set that adds up to T. If $T - x$ cannot be reached, then x cannot be used. The only possibility left is to try to reach all of T with the remaining numbers.

This algorithm is naturally recursive: Subset-sum is solved in terms of two subset-sum problems on a smaller set, one that tries to reach $T - x$ and one that tries to reach T. A key difference from some of the recursive algorithms discussed earlier, such as the Tower of Hanoi, quick-sort, and merge-sort, is that you may not need to solve both subproblems: If the first recursive computation succeeds, there is no need for the other one. You can write a recursive function to solve subset-sum:

Scala

```scala
def findSum(target: Int, numbers: List[Int]): Option[List[Int]] =
  if target == 0 then Some(List.empty) // target is zero: trivial solution
  else
    numbers match
      case Nil => None // target is non-zero and set is empty: no solution
      case first :: others =>
        (findSum(target - first, others).map(first :: _) // first rec call succeeds
          orElse findSum(target, others)) // otherwise, try second rec call
```

Listing 12.10: Recursive implementation of subset-sum; see also Lis. 12.11.

To deal with problems that have no solution, the function returns an option. Variable `target` corresponds to T in the preceding algorithm, and `first` is x. The first recursive call—`findSum(target - first, others)`—tries to solve the $T - x$ problem. If it succeeds, `map` is used to add `first` to the list inside the option. If the first recursive call does not produce a list, a second call—`findSum(target, others)`—tries to solve the problem without using `first`. It is important that the second recursive call only takes place if the first one fails to produce a solution. This behavior is guaranteed here by the fact that the argument to `orElse` is passed by name and is evaluated only if the first option is empty.

As a side note, notice that the implementation is simplified by the fact that lists are immutable. In particular, even though the recursive calls are conceptually digging into the list of numbers, the same list `others` is used as an argument in both recursive calls. If lists were mutated, you would need to "undo" changes from the first computation before reusing the list in a second call.

Subset-sum problems may have multiple solutions. For instance, 18 can also be reached as $3 - 6 + 11 + 7 + 3 = 18$ using the numbers from the example set. To compute all the solutions, you can modify `findSum` to always make the second recursive call, even if the first call succeeds:

```scala
def findAllSums(target: Int, numbers: List[Int]): Set[List[Int]] =
  if target == 0 then Set(List.empty)
  else
    numbers match
      case Nil => Set.empty
      case first :: others =>
        (findAllSums(target - first, others).map(first :: _)
          union findAllSums(target, others))
```

Listing 12.11: All the solutions to subset-sum; contrast with Lis. 12.10 and 12.12.

The differences between `findSum` and `findAllSums` are minimal. Options are replaced with sets, and `orElse` is replaced with `union`. Contrary to `orElse`, method `union` always evaluates both of its arguments.

Given how similar they are, is there a way to avoid having to write both functions? If you have all the solutions to a problem, you can always pick one, so you could be tempted to implement `findSum` in terms of `findAllSums`:

```scala
// DON'T DO THIS!
def findSum(target: Int, numbers: List[Int]): Option[List[Int]] =
  findAllSums(target, numbers).headOption
```

The problem with this approach is that `findSum` now calculates all the solutions even though it needs only one. By contrast, the function in Listing 12.10 stops once a solution has been found. This can be remedied by writing a lazily evaluated variant of `findAllSums`:

```scala
def lazyFindAllSums(target: Int, numbers: List[Int]): LazyList[List[Int]] =
  if target == 0 then LazyList(List.empty)
  else
```

```
numbers match
  case Nil => LazyList.empty
  case first :: others =>
    lazyFindAllSums(target - first, others).map(first :: _)
      #::: lazyFindAllSums(target, others)
```

Listing 12.12: The solutions to subset-sum derived lazily; contrast with Lis. 12.11.

Again, the required changes to the code are minimal. Sets are replaced with streams, and `union` is replaced with "`#:::`", which brings back lazy evaluation. You can then use this function as the basis for various subset-sum functions:

─── *Scala* ───

```scala
def findSum(target: Int, numbers: List[Int]): Option[List[Int]] =
  lazyFindAllSums(target, numbers).headOption

def findAllSums(target: Int, numbers: List[Int]): Set[List[Int]] =
  lazyFindAllSums(target, numbers.sorted).toSet

def findShortestSum(target: Int, numbers: List[Int]): Option[List[Int]] =
  lazyFindAllSums(target, numbers).minByOption(_.length)
```

This `findSum` function evaluates only the first element of the stream, and stops computing as soon as one solution is found, as in Listing 12.10. In `findAllSums`, the call to `toSet` forces the evaluation of the entire stream to compute all the solutions.[7] Function `findShortest` also computes the entire stream to find a solution of minimal length. It relies on `minByOption`—a variant of `minBy` that does not fail on an empty collection—to compare solutions by their length.

12.12 Summary

- In languages that support higher-order functions, you can replace explicit arguments with functions that compute them, thus delaying evaluation of an argument until its value is needed. In particular, if the value of an argument is never needed, it may never be computed.

- Some programming languages add syntax so arguments can be passed unevaluated without explicitly creating a function—typically, the function is created by the compiler and hidden from the user. For a while, functional programming languages, such as Miranda and Haskell, even experimented with the idea of passing all arguments unevaluated.

- Unevaluated arguments can sometimes be used to create abstractions that embed reusable patterns and resemble standard programming language constructs.

─────────────────────────────

[7]The list of numbers is sorted beforehand so that solutions are always produced as sorted lists of numbers. Otherwise, the set could contain "duplicates"—`List(3,7)` and `List(7,3)`, for instance.

Such constructs can be designed to form an internal domain-specific programming language—a kind of mini-language within a language.

- Streams are sequences that are lazily evaluated and (typically) memoized. Their values are computed only when (and if) needed and, if the stream is memoized, stored for later retrieval.

- Streams are well suited to pipelined transformation of data. Being lazily evaluated, they do not require allocation of a separate data structure for each stage of a pipeline.

- Streams can also be used to implement sequences that are conceptually infinite, as long as there is never an attempt to evaluate the entire sequence. Infinite streams can often replace mutable objects, such as iterators and stateful generators, with a more functional alternative.

- Because of memoization, streams involve a risk of leakage as they grow in memory. Languages may define non-memoized variants that introduce only laziness. They are sometimes called views (but also iterators or even streams, which can be confusing).

- In addition to delayed arguments and lazily evaluated data structures, languages may support lazy initialization of fields and local variables. This can be used to delay costly evaluation of code until a value is first used, possibly avoiding an entire computation if a value is never used.

Chapter 13

Handling Failures

Functional programming is centered on the use of values, produced and consumed by functions. It is therefore natural, when programming functionally, to treat failures as special values instead of using exceptions. A few standard types are commonly used to represent failures, most notably `Option`, `Try` (also called `Result`), and `Either`. These types can be manipulated by higher-order functions to process valid values and to propagate errors or to recover from them. This approach to error handling is particularly well suited to pipelined computations in which catching exceptions is unwieldy because of higher-order functions that embed their own control flow.

13.1 Exceptions and Special Values

A component of a software application that faces unexpected circumstances is often unable to fully react to them, typically because the data and logic needed to address the situation are only present in another component. Failure information then needs to be propagated elsewhere in the system where the problem can be properly handled.

One way is to use "special" values that represent failures, but this is notoriously error-prone. A famous and most widely used special value is null. It is also the source of innumerable bugs. Another common error value is -1, used to represent a missing integer. In Section 5.3, I briefly mentioned that using options is preferable to relying on null. This chapter develops this argument and introduces other types, beside options, suitable for error handling.

In languages that support them, you can use exceptions as alternatives to special values. A major benefit of exceptions is that there is no risk of using them as if they were valid outputs, like null or -1. The danger of exceptions, however, is that they can disrupt an application in major ways when they are not handled, up to forcing an abrupt termination.

To contrast these various approaches, consider the following illustration. A function searches for a given element in a list, and returns, as an index, the position at which it is found. It has the following signature:

Scala

```scala
def search[A](values: List[A], target: A): Int = ... // returns -1 when not found
```

This function needs to return an integer, even when a target is not found in the list. A common convention—used, for instance, by Scala's `indexWhere` function—is to return -1 as a special value to represent a failed search.

195

Suppose now that you use this **search** function to extract from a list all the values between two given targets:

```scala
// DON'T DO THIS!
def between[A](values: List[A], from: A, to: A): List[A] =
  val i = search(values, from)
  val j = search(values, to)
  values.slice(i min j, (i max j) + 1)
```

As long as both targets are found in the list, this is fine:

```scala
val words = List("one", "two", "three", "four")

between(words, "two", "four") // List("two", "three", "four")
between(words, "four", "two") // List("two", "three", "four")
```

But if either target is missing, the function falls apart:

```scala
between(words, "two", "five")  // List("one", "two")
between(words, "ten", "four")  // List("one", "two", "three", "four")
```

No error is reported, but the outputs make no sense. Of course, the problem is that the implementation of function **between** is missing code to check that the targets were indeed found in the list. However, you get no help from the compiler to let you know that something is missing. A special value like −1, which can potentially be used as an actual value, is particularly dangerous. In some languages, −1 is actually a valid index, which refers to the last element of a sequence.

Another value frequently used to represent failures is null:[1]

```scala
def search[A](values: List[A], target: A): Integer = ... // returns null when not found
```

The null value cannot be used as a number, and the same implementation of **between** does not produce nonsensical values when a target is not found:

```scala
between(words, "two", "four")  // List("two", "three", "four")
between(words, "four", "two")  // List("two", "three", "four")
between(words, "two", "five")  // throws NullPointerException
between(words, "ten", "four")  // throws NullPointerException
```

---

[1] The return type is changed from **Int** to **Integer** because type **Int** does not contain null in Scala.

This is a mixed blessing. On the one hand, the risk of continuing the computation with an incorrect list is eliminated. On the other hand, the exception, if it is not handled, has the potential to cause a lot of damage—for instance, by stopping a server entirely instead of only failing one transaction.

Instead of using special values, function **search** could rely on an exception to indicate that an element is missing:

```scala
// throws NoSuchElementException when not found
def search[A](values: List[A], target: A): Int = ...
```

But there is still nothing that forces function **between** to handle the exception. An implementation without checks for missing targets now throws `NoSuchElementException` instead of `NullPointerException`, with the same potential for widespread damage.[2]

13.2   Using Option

Options are a primary mechanism to deal with computations that may not produce a value. We have already discussed options in the context of searching functions like `find` (Section 9.1) and `findSum` (Section 12.11). Indeed, our own binary search function in Listing 6.9 uses an option to return an index.

Instead of returning −1 or null, `search` could produce a value of type `Option[Int]`, and use `None` to indicate that a search was unsuccessful:

```scala
def search[A](values: List[A], target: A): Option[Int] = ...
```

The benefit of this definition is that the previous implementation of function **between**, which is missing error-handling code, can no longer be compiled. Instead, you need to handle failed searches explicitly:

```scala
def between[A](values: List[A], from: A, to: A): List[A] =
  (search(values, from), search(values, to)) match
    case (Some(i), Some(j)) => values.slice(i min j, (i max j) + 1)
    case _                   => List.empty
```

---

[2]Java uses the notion of a *checked* exception, which forces the calling code to either handle an exception or declare it explicitly as being rethrown. The mechanism is intended to prevent developers from ignoring possible exceptions, but it is unwieldy, especially when using lambda expressions. It would not help in this illustration because you may prefer to ignore the exception if you know for sure that the targets are in the list. Indeed, `NoSuchElementException` is an unchecked exception in Java. I am not aware of another language today that uses checked exceptions.

The failure case could be handled in any way. Here, the chosen semantics is to return an empty list.

13.3 Using Try

Using options can go a long way toward handling errors without exceptions while avoiding the dangers of using special values within the same type. Options, however, are completely silent as to the cause of failure. When you need more information regarding the nature of an error, you can instead use a `Try` type (also called `Result` in some languages). It is a type with two alternatives, like `Option`. The first alternative, `Success(value)`, represents a usable value, similar to `Some(value)`. The second alternative, `Failure(error)`, represents an error and can be used to provide more information than options do with `None`.

As an example, the list searched by function `between` could come from a file, and reading that file may fail for a number of reasons: The file is not found, the file is empty, the permissions do not allow reading, and so on. A `readFile` function that returns an option would hide the cause of the failure entirely. Alternatively, you can define `readFile` to return a `Try`:

```scala
def readFile(file: Path): Try[List[String]] = ...
```

Like `Option`, the `Try` type supports higher-order methods. You can use `map` to feed the list of strings, if any, to function `between`. On `Try`, function `map` transforms a valid value; failures are left unchanged:

```scala
readFile(wordFile).map(between(_, "two", "three")) // Success(List("two", "three"))
readFile(notFound).map(between(_, "two", "three")) // Failure(...)
```

These two expressions have type `Try[List[String]]`. If file `wordFile` contains the sequence of words used earlier, the first expression is a success value. If file `notFound` does not exist, the second expression is the failure returned by `readFile`, is unchanged by `map`, and contains the relevant `NoSuchFileException`.

In Section 10.3, we saw how `flatMap` can be used to transform optional values with computations that themselves produce options. The same is true of `Try`:

```scala
def compute(list: List[String]): Int = ...
def computeOrFail(list: List[String]): Try[Int] = ...

readFile(...).map(compute)            // of type Try[Int]
readFile(...).flatMap(computeOrFail)  // of type Try[Int]
```

If reading the file has failed, both expressions produce a failed value with the exception that caused `readFile` to fail. If the file can be read, the first expression is a success. The second expression can still be a success or a failure, depending on what is returned by `computeOrFail`.

If you prefer to ignore the cause of a failure, you can change a `Try` type into an option:

```scala
readFile(...).toOption // of type Option[List[String]]
```

The `Try` type is heavily used in concurrent programming to carry exceptions from one thread to another (several examples are provided in Part II). Contrast this use of a future in Java:

```java
future.whenComplete((value, error) -> {
  if (error == null) ... // use value
  else ... // handle error
});
```

with the same program in Scala:

```scala
future.onComplete {
    case Success(value) => ... // use value
    case Failure(error) => ... // handle error
}
```

Using `Try` is cleaner and safer than dealing with a pair (`value`,`error`) of which one element is always null.

13.4   Using Either

The `Try` type is very much dedicated to handling failures, unlike `Option`, which you can use for other purposes as well. Another standard, general-purpose type with two alternatives, `Either`, is also sometimes used in error handling.

While `Option` is a value or nothing and `Try` is a value or an exception, `Either` is a value or another value, possibly of a different type. A value of type `Either[A,B]` is either a `Left[A]` or a `Right[B]`. Conceptually, you can think of `Option[A]` as `Either[None.type,A]`, and of `Try[A]` as `Either[Throwable,A]`. It is customary to use `Right` to represent the successful path and `Left` for an alternative. Accordingly, methods like `contains`, `map`, and `filter` work on the inside of the right part.[3]

---

[3]This can be changed via a `left` method: `either.left.map(...)` will transform the left part of the `either` value.

You can define a `readFile` function that returns the contents of a file as a list or an error message if the file cannot be read:

```scala
                                                              ─── Scala ───
def readFile(file: Path): Either[String, List[String]] = ...
```

You can then use the return value through `map` and `flatMap` as you would with `Option` or `Try`:

```scala
                                                              ─── Scala ───
readFile(wordFile).map(between(_, "two", "three")) // Right(List("two", "three"))
readFile(notFound).map(between(_, "two", "three")) // Left("not found: ...")
```

The `Either` type is versatile. If the left part of an `Either` value is an exception, you can use `toTry` to change the `Either` into a `Try`. You can also ignore the left part entirely with `toOption`. Conversely, an option can be turned into a value of type `Either` by specifying an additional left or right part, which, in Scala, is lazily evaluated:

```scala
                                                              ─── Scala ───
Some(42).toRight("no number") // Right(42)
None.toRight("no number")     // Left("no number")
```

You can also use `fold` to extract the contents of a value of type `Either[A,B]` into a value of type `C` by providing two functions, one for the left, of type `A => C`, and one for the right, of type `B => C`:

```scala
                                                              ─── Scala ───
def mkString(stringOrNumber: Either[String, Int]): String =
   stringOrNumber.fold(identity, n => if n < 0 then s"($n)" else s"$n")

mkString(Right(-42))        // "(-42)"
mkString(Left("no number")) // "no number"
```

When you need to return a special value of the same type as a regular value—say, an error message in a string function—you can use `Either` with the same type on the left and right. For instance, Java's library function `binarySearch` searches a sorted array. If the element is found, the corresponding index is returned. Otherwise, the function returns a negative number n such that $-n - 1$ is the index where the element would be if it were in the array. This way, you can easily access the element just before or just after the missing element.

To eliminate the risk of using this negative value as an index, you could make `binarySearch` return a value of type `Either[Int,Int]`, using `Right` when the element is found and `Left` to return useful information when it is not found. For a given number x, the values `Left(x)` and `Right(x)` are distinct, and the calling code can handle them in different ways.

13.5 Higher-Order Functions and Pipelines

In addition to the issue of code that leaves out necessary handling, exceptions present another difficulty in a functional programming style: higher-order functions. Throwing and catching exceptions is a form of flow of control: By throwing an exception, you "jump" to code that can handle the situation. Higher-order functions, in contrast, tend to embed their own control flow and cannot afford to see it being disrupted by exceptions.

As an illustration, consider files of city names and Fahrenheit temperatures formatted as follows:

```
Austin: 101
Chicago: 88
Big Spring: 92
```

An application needs to read locations and temperatures from a file, focus on temperatures recorded in Texas, convert the Fahrenheit temperatures to Celsius, and produce a list of strings formatted like the input file. You can implement it as a pipeline of higher-order functions:

```scala
@throws[IOException]
def readFile(file: Path): List[String] = ...

@throws[ParseException] @throws[NumberFormatException]
def parse(line: String): (String, Int) = ...

@throws[NoSuchElementException]
def stateOf(city: String): String = ...

def convert(input: Path): List[String] =
  readFile(input).view
    .map(parse)
    .filter((city, _) => stateOf(city) == "TX")
    .map((city, temp) => (city, ((temp - 32) / 1.8f).round))
    .map((city, temp) => s"$city: $temp")
    .toList
```

Listing 13.1: Pipeline example with no handling of failures; contrast with Lis. 13.2.

You use `map` to parse lines into pairs, `filter` to eliminate cities outside of Texas, `map` again to convert the temperatures to Celsius, and `map` one more time to generate the final strings. The bracketing pair `view`/`toList` is not strictly necessary but is used to avoid the creation of intermediate lists. On the sample file, function `convert` produces the list `["Austin: 38", "Big Spring: 33"]`.

A number of things can go wrong in this computation: A file cannot be read, a city is not found in the database, or a line cannot be parsed into a city name and a number.

For each of these situations, an exception is thrown. If it is not handled, any exception terminates the entire pipeline. As an alternative, you might prefer to flag incorrect lines, skip unknown cities, or replace missing temperatures with a default value. The problem is that handling exceptions within the pipeline is not easy. Functions `map` and `filter` implement generic behaviors, and you cannot tell them to skip or replace a value when an exception happens without modifying the functions used as their arguments.

What you need are variants of `readFile`, `parse`, and `stateOf` that, instead of throwing exceptions, return special values, for which you can use types like `Option`, `Try`, and `Either`. As an exercise, let's modify Listing 13.1 so that the possible failures mentioned earlier are handled as follows:

- I/O errors while reading the input file are forwarded to the user.

- Lines that cannot be parsed as a name and a temperature are left unchanged but enclosed in square brackets.

- Cities outside Texas or unknown to function `stateOf` are ignored.

- Temperatures that cannot be parsed as integer values are replaced with the word `"unknown"`.

Functions `readFile`, `stateOf`, and `parse` are modified to not use exceptions, and the pipeline then relies on `Option`, `Try`, and `Either` methods to perform the desired error handling:

```scala
def readFile(file: Path): Try[List[String]] = ...

def parse(line: String): Either[String, (String, Option[Int])] = ...

def stateOf(city: String): Option[String] = ...

def convert(input: Path): Try[List[String]] =
  readFile(input).map { lines =>
    lines.view
      .map(parse)
      .filter(_.forall((city, _) => stateOf(city).contains("TX")))
      .map { badLineOrPair =>
        badLineOrPair
          .map((city, temp) => (city, temp.map(t => ((t - 32) / 1.8f).round)))
          .fold(
            line => s"[$line]",
            (city, temp) => s"""$city: ${temp.getOrElse("unknown")}"""
          )
      }
      .toList
  }
```

Listing 13.2: Pipeline example with failure handling; contrast with Lis. 13.1.

Let's unpack this. Function `readFile` returns a `Try` that contains either a list of lines or an I/O exception. Function `parse` return an `Either` value. It produces a pair when a line can be parsed (right) or leaves the line unchanged (left). Each pair contains the name of a city and a temperature, but the temperature is wrapped in an option to handle strings that cannot be converted to integer values. Finally, function `stateOf` maps cities to states but uses options to deal with cities that are not in the database.

The very first thing `convert` does is apply `map` to the `Try` value returned by `readFile`. If it is an exception, `map` leaves it unchanged, and `convert` returns a `Failure` value with the I/O exception. Otherwise, we have a list of lines to work with: Make it lazy with `view`, and apply `parse` to each line using `map`. Function `filter` is then applied to what is now a list of `Either` values. Each value is either a line that could not be parsed or a pair with a city name and an optional temperature. These values are tested using `forall`, which is true on any `Left` value but applies a test on `Right` values.[4] Thus, unparsed lines are left as they are, but pairs are potentially eliminated. The test that is used to eliminate them invokes `stateOf` on the city name and checks that the option being returned contains the string `"TX"`. This test is false on `None` (unknown cities) and on options with a string other than `"TX"` (cities outside of Texas).

The next stage of the pipeline uses `map` to transform each remaining `Either` value (variable `badLineOrPair` in the code). The first transformation converts Fahrenheit temperatures to Celsius. Unparsed lines are again left unchanged because `map` only transforms `Right` values. The conversion itself is achieved by using `map` on an option that contains the temperature. The second and final transformation creates a string from each `Either` value by adding square brackets to an unparsed line or by formatting a city name with a temperature. The temperature, now in Celsius, is extracted from its option, with `getOrElse` being used to replace missing temperatures with the string `"unknown"`.

This variant of `convert` produces the same output as before on the sample file. On a file with defects such as:

```
Austin: hot
Chicago: 88
Big
Spring: 92
```

it produces the list `["Austin: unknown", "[Big]"]`. `Chicago` is eliminated for being out of Texas, and `Spring` for not being in the database.

Note that, in this programming style, errors tend to propagate down the pipeline in the form of an empty `Option`, a failed `Try`, or a left `Either` value. By contrast, a thrown exception would go up to the top of the pipeline, unhandled by the higher-order functions above it and ignoring all the stages below it.

Compared to its previous version, the updated code for function `convert` may look complicated, especially if you are new to functional programming, but error handling is rarely easy. Alternative approaches, without `Option`, `Try`, `Either`, and their higher-order methods, are unlikely to be simpler.

---

[4]This line is tricky: `filter` is applied to a sequence, `forall` to a value of type `Either`, and `contains` to an option.

13.6 Summary

- Functions can deal with failure by returning special values. However, choosing these values within the same return type—null for an object, -1 for an integer—is error-prone. It makes it too easy for code on the calling site to forget to check for those values. Null values, in particular, have notoriously been abused as a cheap form of error reporting.

- To produce error values, functional programs often rely on specific types, usually in the form of alternatives. The simplest of those types is `Option`, which can represent either a value or the absence of a value. When more failure-related information is needed, other types can be used, including `Try` (which stores an exception) and `Either` (which contains a substitute value).

- These types tend to be supported by higher-order functions that allow computations to keep progressing in the presence of failures. Higher-order functions are used to transform a valid value, to propagate an error, or to recover from an error, without explicit error checking.

- In general, exceptions are not well suited to a functional programming style. They deviate from the core principle of value-returning functions and often disrupt control flow embedded in higher-order functions.

Chapter 14

Case Study: Trampolines

The Scala compiler optimizes (most) tail recursive functions and generates code that implements them as loops. Other languages, like Java, do no such thing. Even in Scala, tail-calls outside tail recursive functions are not optimized. This case study implements trampolines, a classic strategy used for tail-call optimization. It shows how trampolines can be used to implement tail recursive calls without growing the execution stack, even in Java. The strategy is then refined to handle non-tail-calls.

14.1 Tail-Call Optimization

Recall our earlier discussion of tail recursive functions in Section 6.5. Some compilers, including Scala's, optimize the implementation of functions that make a single recursive call as their very last operation:[1]

```scala
                                                          ─── Scala ───
@tailrec
def zero(x: Int): Int = if x == 0 then 0 else zero(x - 1)

zero(1_000_000) // 0
```

Function `zero` is implemented as a loop and can handle large input values.

The current Scala compiler, however, does not optimize all tail-calls. In particular, tail-calls in mutually recursive functions grow the execution stack:

```scala
                                                          ─── Scala ───
def isEven(n: Int): Boolean = if n == 0 then true else isOdd(n - 1)
def isOdd(n: Int): Boolean  = if n == 0 then false else isEven(n - 1)

isEven(42)      // true
isOdd(42)       // false
isEven(1_000_000) // throws StackOverflowError
```

Listing 14.1: Example of non-optimized tail-calls; contrast with Lis. 14.3.

---

[1]Throughout the chapter, integer arguments are assumed to be non-negative in all illustrations.

Even though the call to `isOdd` is the very last expression inside function `isEven` (and vice versa), no optimization takes place and a call to `isEven` on a large enough number causes a stack overflow.

14.2   Trampolines for Tail-Calls

Trampolines[2] were mentioned briefly at the end of Chapter 6 as a possible technique to optimize tail-calls. You can implement trampolines in terms of thunks, the no-argument functions already discussed in the context of lazy evaluation. The central idea is to replace a function call with a thunk that delays this call. When evaluated, this thunk produces another thunk that contains the next function call, and so on. This chain of thunks is lazily built and requires little memory. Furthermore, the thunks can be evaluated one by one in a tail recursive function (or in a loop), irrespective of stack size limitations.

Trampolines can be implemented as a type `Computation`, parameterized by the return type of the computation. As in earlier case studies, access modifiers are omitted, and all classes in this chapter are left public:[3]

```scala
trait Computation[A]:
  @tailrec
  final def result: A = this match
    case Done(value) => value
    case Call(thunk) => thunk().result


case class Done[A](value: A)                      extends Computation[A]
case class Call[A](thunk: () => Computation[A]) extends Computation[A]
```

Listing 14.2: Trampoline for tail-call optimization in Scala.

A computation takes two forms: `Done` represents a completed computation with a final value, and `Call` represents an ongoing computation as an unevaluated thunk. Method `result` evaluates a computation by running all the thunks, one by one. It is tail recursive and optimized by the Scala compiler into a loop.

---

[2]The name *trampoline* comes from the fact that an execution "bounces" from computation to computation instead of relying on nested function calls. Trampolines can be described in terms of continuations, but continuations are not covered in this book, and introducing trampolines and continuations together in this case study would be confusing. Instead, in this chapter, trampolines are viewed as a form of delayed evaluation.

[3]The `Computation` trait should be sealed to prevent subtypes other than `Done` and `Call` from being added.

Two add-ons can be defined for a nicer syntax (and, from this point on, are assumed to be in scope):

```scala
implicit def done[A](value: A): Computation[A]        = Done(value)
def call[A](comp: => Computation[A]): Computation[A] = Call(() => comp)
```

The `done` function wraps a value inside an instance of the `Done` class to create a completed computation. It is defined as an implicit function, so the conversion can be automatically triggered by the compiler, based on type analysis. Function `call` uses a by-name argument (see Section 12.2) to hide the thunk from the trampoline user.

With these in place, you can rewrite the even–odd example as follows:

```scala
def isEven(n: Int): Computation[Boolean] = if n == 0 then true else call(isOdd(n - 1))
def isOdd(n: Int): Computation[Boolean] = if n == 0 then false else call(isEven(n - 1))

isEven(1_000_000).result // true
```

Listing 14.3: Optimized tail-calls, using a trampoline; contrast with Lis. 14.1.

When evaluated, the expression `isEven(1_000_000)` creates a computation object `Call(() => isOdd(999_999))` and stops there. The actual computation is triggered by the call to `result` and, as mentioned earlier, is executed as a loop. It does not grow the execution stack at all. In effect, the execution stack has been replaced with a lazily evaluated sequence of thunks. Without the add-ons, the two functions would not look as nice. You would have to write `isEven` in this way:

```scala
def isEven(n: Int): Computation[Boolean] =
  if n == 0 then Done(true) else Call(() => isOdd(n - 1))
```

14.3 Tail-Call Optimization in Java

In the previous section, trampolines were evaluated using a tail recursive function, which the Scala compiler implements as a loop. You could also write a loop yourself. This makes trampolines a suitable technique to bring tail-call optimization to a language that does not support it in any form. Trampolines have been used to compile functional languages, which tend to support tail-call optimization, into languages that do not, like C.

As an illustration, let's reimplement the trampoline in Java, a language with no
tail-call optimization at all (yet):[4]

```java
interface Computation<A> {
  A result();

  static <T> Computation<T> done(T value) {
    return new Done<>(value);
  }

  static <T> Computation<T> call(Supplier<Computation<T>> thunk) {
    return new Call<>(thunk);
  }
}

record Done<A>(A value) implements Computation<A> {
  public A result() {
    return value;
  }
}

record Call<A>(Supplier<Computation<A>> thunk) implements Computation<A> {
  public A result() {
    Computation<A> calc = this;
    while (calc instanceof Call<A> call)
      calc = call.thunk().get();
    return calc.result();
  }
}
```

Listing 14.4: Trampoline for tail-call optimization in Java.

The approach is the same as Listing 14.2. The Java type `Supplier<T>` corresponds to
a function with no argument and return type `T`. To help build trampolines, two helper
functions, `done` and `call`, are defined as before. Because Java does not support any
tail recursion optimization, the evaluation of the trampoline in method `result` uses a
regular `while`-loop. It performs the same computation as the Scala variant.

The even–odd example can now be rewritten in Java:

```java
Computation<Boolean> isEven(int n) {
  if (n == 0) return done(true);
  else return call(() -> isOdd(n - 1));
}
```

---

[4]Record classes are used for code compactness and increased similarity with Scala.

```
Computation<Boolean> isOdd(int n) {
  if (n == 0) return done(false);
  else return call(() -> isEven(n - 1));
}

isEven(1_000_000).result() // true
```

Listing 14.5: Optimized tail-calls, using a trampoline, Java variant.

The main differences from the Scala variant are that you need to invoke function **done** explicitly (instead of relying on an implicit conversion in Scala), and you must use a lambda expression as the argument for function `call` (instead of a by-name argument in Scala).

14.4   Dealing with Non-Tail-Calls

The trampolines implemented in Listings 14.2 and 14.4 can only deal with tail-calls. Can anything be done to handle non-tail-calls, and thus tackle general recursion with no need to grow the execution stack? If a call is not in tail position, you need a way to use the value produced by the call in the continuing code. The key idea is to use map (and flatMap) as a mechanism to transform the result of a function call according to some additional computation. This section extends the `Computation` type with map and flatMap methods to handle non-tail-calls.

Consider first a non-tail recursive `factorial` function as an illustration:

Scala
```
def factorial(n: Int): BigInt = if n == 0 then BigInt(1) else factorial(n - 1) * n

factorial(1_000_000) // throws StackOverflowError
```

This function is not tail recursive because a computation—a multiplication by n—needs to take place *after* the recursive call. For this, you need to keep n on the execution stack while computing `factorial(n - 1)`, and the stack grows. For large enough inputs, the function fails with a `StackOverflowError`.

If the `Computation` type from Listing 14.2 is used, the recursive call `factorial(n - 1)` produces a value of type `Computation[BigInt]`. What you need then is to multiply the (yet to be computed) `BigInt` inside this computation by n to produce another `Computation[BigInt]`. This suggests regarding a computation as one of those "boxes" from our earlier discussion of `map` in Section 10.9. Indeed, the computation that calculates the factorial of n is `factorial(n - 1).map(x => x * n)`. So, what we need is to add a `map` method to the `Computation` type. It could be implemented naively as follows:

```scala
// DON'T DO THIS!
trait Computation[A]:
   @tailrec
   final def result: A = this match
      case Done(value) => value
      case Call(thunk) => thunk().result

   def map[B](function: A => B): Computation[B]

case class Done[A](value: A) extends Computation[A]:
   def map[B](f: A => B): Computation[B] = Done(f(value))

case class Call[A](thunk: () => Computation[A]) extends Computation[A]:
   def map[B](f: A => B): Computation[B] = Call(() => Done(f(thunk().result)))
```

Invoking `map(f)` on a `Done` object simply applies `f` to the value inside. On a `Call` object, `map` produces a new computation that will apply `f` to the result of the current computation.

The problem with this approach is that the execution stack grows when you compute the result of a computation. If `c2 = c1.map(f)`, then the evaluation of `c2.result` involves computing `f(c1.result).result`. In other words, before the tail-call to `result`—which is still optimized as a loop—the execution reenters `result` to apply `f`. If you evaluate a long enough chain of calls to `map`, you will still run out of stack space.

To avoid this, the implementation of `Computation` needs to be refined. The remainder of this section focuses on the implementation of `flatMap` instead of `map`. The reason is that `flatMap` is needed to handle functions with multiple recursive calls, and `map` can always be derived from `flatMap`.

NOTE

The implementation developed here follows a strategy defined by Rúnar Óli Bjarnason in his article "Stackless Scala with Free Monads." The same strategy is implemented, more robustly, in the standard Scala library as `scala.util.control.TailCalls`.

The implementation of `Computation` just given runs into problems because the `map` method in class `Call` uses `result` to generate a suitable input for function `f`. This can be avoided by delaying the creation of the computation that uses `f` until you are inside the implementation of `result`. There, you can deal with chained calls to `flatMap` explicitly, in ways that avoid growing the execution stack:

```scala
                                                        ─── Scala ───
trait Computation[A]:
  @tailrec
  final def result: A = this match
    case Done(value) => value
    case Call(thunk) => thunk().result
    case FlatMap(f, arg) => arg match
        case Done(v)        => f(v).result
        case Call(thunk)    => thunk().flatMap(f).result
        case FlatMap(g, arg2) => arg2.flatMap(x => g(x).flatMap(f)).result

  def flatMap[B](f: A => Computation[B]): Computation[B] = FlatMap(f, this)

  def map[B](f: A => B): Computation[B] = flatMap(x => Done(f(x)))

case class Done[A](value: A)                     extends Computation[A]
case class Call[A](thunk: () => Computation[A]) extends Computation[A]

case class FlatMap[A, B](f: A => Computation[B], arg: Computation[A])
  extends Computation[B]
```

Listing 14.6: Trampoline extended with `map` and `flatMap`.

Listing 14.6 introduces a third class, `FlatMap`. Invocations of `flatMap` do nothing but create an instance of this class.

The implementation of `result` is trickier. You can deal with the first two cases, `Done` and `Call`, as before. However, when you need to evaluate an instance `FlatMap(f,arg)`, you need special handling for the case where `arg` is itself a `FlatMap` to deal with chains of calls to `flatMap`. The evaluation of `FlatMap(f,arg)`, which is `arg.flatMap(f)`, proceeds according to the nature of `arg`:

- `Done(v).flatMap(f)` is `f(v)`.

- `Call(thunk).flatMap(f)` evaluates to `thunk().flatMap(f)`, which is processed recursively.

- The last case represents chained calls to `flatMap`. The expression to evaluate is `FlatMap(g, arg2).flatMap(f)`, which is `arg2.flatMap(g).flatMap(f)`. It is replaced with the equivalent expression `arg2.flatMap(x => g(x).flatMap(f))`,[5] which reduces a two-`flatMap` chain to a single `flatMap` and is evaluated recursively. This avoids any nested invocation of `result`, which was the source of our troubles in the previous implementation.

Once `flatMap` is implemented, `map` can be written in terms of it: `comp.map(f)` is equivalent to `comp.flatMap(x => Done(f(x)))`. With this implementation of

---

[5]This equivalence is one of the fundamental properties of `flatMap`, discussed in an aside on monads at the end of Section 10.3.

Computation in place, you can use `map` to handle the non-tail recursive call inside the `factorial` function:

```scala
def factorial(n: Int): Computation[BigInt] =
  if n == 0 then BigInt(1) else call(factorial(n - 1)).map(_ * n)

factorial(1_000_000).result // a number with 5,565,709 digits
```

Listing 14.7: Non-tail recursive `factorial`, as a trampoline; see also Lis. 14.10.

The `factorial` function makes a single recursive call, for which `map` is sufficient. When a function makes multiple recursive calls, they can be combined with `flatMap`. For instance, you can rewrite our earlier function `size` on binary trees in terms of a trampoline:

```scala
def size[A](tree: BinTree[A]): Computation[Int] = tree match
  case Empty => 0
  case Node(_, left, right) =>
    call(size(left)).flatMap(ls => call(size(right)).map(rs => 1 + ls + rs))
```

Listing 14.8: Non-tail recursive `size` on trees, as a trampoline; see also Lis. 14.10.

The first recursive call, `size(left)`, produces the size of the left child as a value `ls`. This value is transformed using `flatMap` instead of `map` because the function being applied in the transformation produces a `Computation[Int]`, not an `Int`. This computation is obtained by recursively calling `size(right)` to get a right size `rs`, then by transforming `rs` into `1 + ls + rs`, using `map`.

Function `hanoi` from Listing 12.6 can be similarly trampolined:

```scala
def hanoi[A](n: Int, from: A, middle: A, to: A): Computation[List[(A, A)]] =
  if n == 0 then List.empty
  else
    val call1 = call(hanoi(n - 1, from, to, middle))
    val call2 = call(hanoi(n - 1, middle, from, to))
    call1.flatMap(moves1 => call2.map(moves2 => moves1 ::: (from, to) :: moves2))
```

Listing 14.9: Non-tail recursive `hanoi`, as a trampoline; see also Lis. 14.10.

Recall from Section 10.9 that Scala's `for-yield` construct is transformed at compile time into suitable calls to higher-order methods. Instead of using `flatMap` directly, you can write functions `factorial`, `size`, and `hanoi` very nicely as follows:

```scala ─── Scala ───
def factorial(n: Int): Computation[BigInt] =
  if n == 0 then BigInt(1) else for f <- call(factorial(n - 1)) yield f * n

def size[A](tree: BinTree[A]): Computation[Int] = tree match
  case Empty => 0
  case Node(_, left, right) =>
    for
      ls <- call(size(left))
      rs <- call(size(right))
    yield 1 + ls + rs

def hanoi[A](n: Int, from: A, middle: A, to: A): Computation[List[(A, A)]] =
  if n == 0 then List.empty
  else
    for
      moves1 <- call(hanoi(n - 1, from, to, middle))
      moves2 <- call(hanoi(n - 1, middle, from, to))
    yield moves1 ::: (from, to) :: moves2
```

Listing 14.10: `For-yield` on trampolines; contrast with Lis. 14.7 to 14.9.

These functions are compiled into the same `map` and `flatMap` combinations used earlier.

14.5 Summary

The idea of using thunks to delay argument evaluation, which was explored in Chapter 12, can also be used to delay the evaluation of recursive tail-calls, a technique sometimes known as a trampoline. Each call is represented as a thunk, and the execution stack is replaced with a lazily built series of thunks, which requires very little memory. These thunks can be evaluated one by one using a loop (or a tail recursive function in a language that optimizes it into a loop). When a recursive call is not in tail position, its value is used for further computation after the call. To maintain lazy evaluation, the computation that uses this value needs to be embedded into the trampoline as a transformation using either `map` (for a regular function call, using the execution stack) or `flatMap` (for a transformation that requires further recursive calls). The implementation of `flatMap` is delicate because it must ensure that the evaluation of long chains of calls proceeds without growing the execution stack. Once method `flatMap` is implemented efficiently, `map` can be derived from it.

A Brief Interlude

Chapter 15

Types (and Related Concepts)

Much of the power—but also much of the learning curve—associated with modern languages like Scala or Rust—or newer incarnations of earlier languages, like Java—revolves around types. As an interlude between our exploration of functional and concurrent programming language features, this chapter discusses several type-related concepts from a developer's perspective—no type theory here. Readers are likely to be familiar with common features, such as static and dynamic type checking, abstract data types, subtyping, and polymorphism, but maybe less comfortable with others—for example, type inference, type variance, type bounds, and type classes—that not all programming languages support.

15.1 Typing Strategies

It is a major understatement to observe that different programming languages tend to treat types differently. To thoroughly discuss every type-related concept would take as much space as all the other chapters in the book combined, even without getting into implementation issues, like type inference algorithms. This is not the intent of this interlude. Rather, the aim here is to briefly introduce a few basic ideas that will help you navigate the programming languages landscape and transition to new languages.

Although type theory is rigorously based on sound mathematical foundations, less formal, user-focused discussions of types are often more vague and ambiguous. The difficulty is caused in part by the lack of agreement on the precise meaning of routine terminology. For instance, type systems are often discussed in terms of *dynamic* versus *static*, and of *strong* versus *weak*. What is meant by that is actually far from clear. Some authors regard the dichotomies static/dynamic and strong/weak as equivalent, while others treat them as orthogonal. Furthermore, while the differences between static and dynamic type checking are mostly agreed upon, there is no such agreement as to the exact meaning of strong and weak in the context of types. This is not a debate that I care to enter: Enough key ideas can be introduced through code examples without having to settle the question of terminology first.

For the most part, static typing refers to type checking—and type inference—performed by the compiler as part of its analysis of the source code. Dynamic type checks, in contrast, are performed at runtime, using additional code generated by the compiler.

As an illustration, consider the case of Scala—statically typed—and Python—dynamically typed. Assume that a `Book` class has been defined and includes a `title` attribute.

An application creates a list of books and displays their titles but, by mistake, a number is inserted in the list of books:

```scala
                                                        ─ Scala ─
val books: List[Book] = List(book1, book2, 42) // rejected by the compiler
for book <- books do println(book.title)
```

The code is rejected by the Scala compiler:

```
Found:    (42 : Int)
Required: Book
```

The error message is clear: The number 42, of type `Int`, cannot be part of a list of books.

If the compiler is left to infer the type of the list,

```scala
                                                        ─ Scala ─
val books = List(book1, book2, 42)
for book <- books do println(book.title) // rejected by the compiler
```

the error is different:

```
value title is not a member of Matchable
```

You want to put `book1`, `book2`, and 42 inside the same list, and the compiler is trying to please you. It compiles the first line by inferring variable `books` to be of type `List[Matchable]` because `Matchable` is the narrowest type that fits both integers and books (see Section 15.5). Compilation then fails on the second line because not all values of type `Matchable` define a `title` attribute. (`Matchable` is a very broad type: Strings, lists, and options are all "matchable" and don't have a title.)

In both scenarios—type declared or type inferred—the programmer's mistake halts compilation and must be dealt with before the program can be executed. Contrast these compile-time errors with the behavior of a Python program:

```python
                                                        ─ Python ─
books = [book1, book2, 42]
for book in books:
    print(book.title)
```

You can compile and run this code, but the execution fails with the following error:

```
AttributeError: 'int' object has no attribute 'title'
```

This behavior is noteworthy in two ways:

- Compilation is successful, and code is being generated. Parts of the program do run. The program even displays the titles of `book1` and `book2` before failing. The error takes place at runtime. If the faulty code resides in a branch of the program that is not executed, the mistake remains undetected.

- The error is not so much about number 42 having the wrong type—not being a book—but more that it is missing a `title` attribute—somewhat like in the second Scala program. This suggests that the runtime system would be satisfied with a non-book value, as long as it has a title (see the discussion of structural typing in Section 15.6).

The difference between static and dynamic typing is pretty clear: One checks types (mostly) at compile time; the other (mostly) at runtime. The distinction between strong and weak typing, however, is less clear. It usually revolves around how strict or loose a compiler is with types, but unequivocally placing a language in the "strong" or "weak" camp can be hard. For instance, many consider Python to be a strongly—albeit dynamically—typed language. However, consider this valid Python code:

```
                                                              ─── Python ───
book_or_string = book
... # use variable book_or_string as a book
book_or_string = "Le Comte de Monte-Cristo"
... # use variable book_or_string as a string
```

The Scala equivalent does not work:

```
                                                              ─── Scala ───
var bookOrString = book
bookOrString = "Le Comte de Monte-Cristo" // rejected by the compiler
... // use variable bookOrString as a book
```

In Scala, variable `bookOrString` is given type `Book` by the compiler, and the second assignment is rejected. Python, by contrast, does not assign a type to variable `book_or_string`, and allows it to be assigned with values of different types at different times. Accordingly, you could argue that Scala's typing is stronger than Python's.

However, if `price` is defined as a number, the expression

$$book.title + ": " + price$$

is accepted by Scala, but rejected by Python:

```
TypeError: can only concatenate str (not "float") to str
```

In this instance, Python is the fussier language, refusing to append a number to a string. So, it is not necessarily the case that a language is always stronger, or always weaker. Furthermore, what's acceptable varies not only from language to language, but also over time. As of today, the variant

$$\text{price + ": " + book.title}$$

is rejected by Python, triggers a deprecation warning in Scala, and is perfectly fine in Java. Before concluding that Python is more strongly typed than Scala—itself more strongly typed than Java—consider a different scenario:

```
——————————————————————————————————————————————— Python ———
if book.pagecount:
    print(book.title)
```

In this program, the number of pages in a book—ostensibly an integer—is being used as a Boolean value in a test. This works in Python, but would trigger a type error in both Scala and Java.

You might argue that using numbers in tests is convenient—**pagecount** in the preceding test stands for **pagecount != 0**—but being loose with the Boolean type can also be dangerous. Consider first this Java program:

```
———————————————————————————————————————————————— Java ———
Set<Book> books = ... // a set of books

if (books.add(book))
    added += 1;
```

Method **add** returns true if an element is actually added (that is, if it was not already in the set). As a result, this code correctly counts added books. However, don't write the same thing in Python:

```
——————————————————————————————————————————————— Python ———
books = ... # a set of books

# DON'T DO THIS!
if books.add(book):
    added += 1
```

The **add** method in Python is "void": It returns **None**,[1] and **None** evaluates to false in a Boolean test. Python's type checking does not catch the mistake—the program can be executed, but variable **added** is not incremented.

---

[1] This is Python's **None**, not the **None** of options in Scala. Python's **None** is closer to Scala's *unit*.

To further muddy the discussion, languages can also define backdoors to their own type system, inviting weakness where the language is strong. The Python function

```
───────────────────────────────────────────────── Python ───
def print_title(book):
    print(book.title)
```

displays book titles but can also be called on an integer, in which case it will fail from not finding a suitable `title` attribute (as described earlier). To better handle the mistake, the function can be rewritten to test the type of its argument explicitly:

```
───────────────────────────────────────────────── Python ───
def print_title(book):
    if isinstance(book, Book):
        print(book.title)
    else:
        raise TypeError("not a book")
```

This added code is not needed in Scala, since the compiler can be trusted to check that the argument has the desired type. However, you can still write an equivalent to the Python function:

```
───────────────────────────────────────────────── Scala ───
// DON'T DO THIS!
def printTitle(item: Any) =
    if item.isInstanceOf[Book] then
        val book = item.asInstanceOf[Book]
        println(book.title)
    else throw IllegalArgumentException("not a book")
```

Type checking by the compiler is bypassed, and replaced with a form of dynamic checking at runtime, thus weakening the overall type safety of the language.

Methods like `isInstanceOf/asInstanceOf` constitute a backdoor to the type system. They are sometimes necessary, but should not be abused. Some languages have no such loopholes. For example, the runtime type checking and casting used in function `printTitle` is not possible in—more static? more strongly typed?—languages like SML or Haskell.

Although compilers can sometimes use type information to improve performance, the main motivation for types is to help programmers catch—and fix—mistakes. From a developer's standpoint, a useful type system is one that contributes to this goal, whether it does so by being "strong" or by being "static."

Three characteristics of types often matter more to you as a programmer than the static/dynamic or strong/weak opposition. First, typing utility is determined by how safe types are—that is, how effective they are at catching mistakes before these mistakes trigger runtime bugs. Second, convenience is contingent on how flexible a type system is: A flexible type system does not get in the way of the developer's design. And third is simplicity: Some type systems are easier to understand, while others are more complex.

Of safety, flexibility, and simplicity, a programming language typically favors two at the expense of the third. How languages handle type variance, discussed in Section 15.8, is a perfect example. A language could make all data structures covariant; it would be simple and flexible, but unsafe. Or it can have them all be invariant, which is simple and safe, but lacks flexibility. Or it can define mechanisms for users to specify variance through annotations, which is safe and flexible, but more complex. In the case of variance, older languages (Java, C++) have favored simplicity and rigidity, but more modern languages (C#, Scala, Kotlin) have improved flexibility at the cost of increased complexity. The remainder of this chapter discusses several concepts that contribute to type safety, flexibility, and complexity.

15.2 Types as Sets

One simple way you can look at types is to think of them as sets of values.[2] The type `String`, for instance, is the set of all string values, and the type `Int`, the set of all (32-bit) integers. In terms of sets, `"foo"` $\in$ `String` and $42 \in$ `Int`.[3] If a program declares variable `x` to have type `S`, then $x \in S$ should be true at all times during the execution of the program; otherwise, the type system is unsound. Similarly, if a function `f` specifies that its argument is of type `T`, a call `f(x)` is only valid if $x \in T$. Most importantly, if type `S` is a subtype of `T`, then $S \subseteq T$. Subtypes are discussed in Section 15.6.

As sets, types can be combined using standard set union and set intersection. Type `S | T` is the union of types `S` and `T`—in other words, the set of values that belong to `S` or to `T`. Type `S & T` is the intersection of types `S` and `T`. As an example, type `Book & Serializable` contains those book objects that can be serialized.

Some types are very small sets. For instance, Scala defines a type `42` that contains only the integer 42, and a type `"foo"` that contains only the string `"foo"`. Type `Unit` also has a single element, value *unit*—denoted as "()"—and type Null contains only null. Type `Boolean` contains just two values, and so does type `0 | 1`. This function flips 0 into 1 and 1 into 0, and can be invoked on only these two values:

```Scala
def flip(x: 0 | 1): 0 | 1 = if x == 0 then 1 else 0
```

Smaller types are more precise and convey more information. The `List(1,2,3)` value is in type `List[Int]`, but also in types `Seq[Int]`, `List[Any]`, and `Any`. Type `List[Int]` is the most informative: `Seq[Int]` includes non-list sequences, `List[Any]` includes lists of non-integer values, and `Any` includes objects that are not lists at all.

---

[2]Some languages, including Scala, also define *kinds* as sets of types. For instance, `List` is a kind that contains the types `List[String]` and `List[Int]`, among others. This chapter does not cover kinds.

[3] "$x \in S$" denotes the fact that value x is an element of set S. "$S \subseteq T$" means that S is a subset of T: All the elements of S are also in T.

In Scala, every variable x defines a small type x.type that contains only x—the singleton {x} in terms of sets. For instance, the function

```scala
                                                                — Scala —
def doSomethingWithBook(book: Book): book.type = ...
```

does something with a book before returning it. Using Book as the return type would allow the function to return a different book, possibly a copy of the input. The very specific type book.type guarantees that the function returns the same book object used as input.

This approach is often used in "builder" classes to chain method calls. For instance, you can define a buffer with an append method:

```scala
                                                                — Scala —
class Buffer[A]:
    def append(value: A): Buffer[A] = ...
    ...

// used as:
val buffer = Buffer[String]()
buffer.append("foo").append("bar");
```

The intent is for method append to add an element to the buffer and to return the buffer itself so further operations can be applied. However, the Buffer[A] return type allows an implementation to return a different buffer. You can use a more specific type to make it clear that the buffer itself if being returned:

```scala
                                                                — Scala —
class Buffer[A]:
    def append(value: A): this.type = ...
    ...
```

Finally, some languages define a type Nothing that contains no value—the empty set. In Scala, for instance, the empty list, Nil, has type List[Nothing]. A function that specifies Nothing as its return type, such as Nil.head, cannot possibly return a value, since type Nothing is empty. All it can do is keep running forever or throw an exception. Because the empty set is a subset of every set, Nothing is a subtype of every type.

15.3   Types as Services

Another way you can look at types is to focus on how typed values can be used. In this view, a type is a collection of operations, or services, that you can utilize. A book is an object with a title, an author, and a page count. You can create a Book type to specify which operations are available on a book. In object-oriented languages, this is often done by defining a class (or a trait/interface):

```scala
case class Book(title: String, author: String, pageCount: Int)
```

This defines a `Book` type with three functionalities: title, author, and page count. This class implements books as simple records[4] of two strings and an integer, but of course other implementations are possible:

```scala
class Book(pages: Seq[String]):
  def title: String   = pages(0)
  def author: String  = pages(1)
  def pageCount: Int   = pages.length
```

In this variant, a book is implemented as a sequence of pages, with the assumption that the first page is the title and the second page is the author. The implementation has changed, but the type is the same as before. You can also define a `Book` type independently from how books are implemented:

```scala
trait Book:
  def title: String
  def author: String
  def pageCount: Int
```

The functionalities offered by the `Book` type are specified, but not implemented.

When viewed as collections of services, undesirable types are not so much large sets—like `Any`—but rather interfaces that fail to include necessary information, or, contrariwise, bloated interfaces with too many methods, or even interfaces that leak irrelevant implementation-specific details.

15.4   Abstract Data Types

These two views—sets and services—form the basis of a formal definition of types known as *abstract data types* (ADT). An abstract data type is defined as a set of values, together with operations on those values.[5] The behavior of these operations is specified, but no implementation is given (hence the name *abstract*).

---

[4]In Scala, the constructor arguments of a case class are all available as public services. This chapter uses case classes for the sake of compactness, but regular classes could be used instead.

[5]Similarly, in mathematics, sets are augmented with laws, which are obeyed by their elements, to become algebraic structures, like groups and fields. The sets of integers, for instance, must satisfy laws that state $x + y = y + x$, $x + (y + z) = (x + y) + z$, $x + 0 = x$, and $x + (-x) = 0$, for all x, y, and z, making it an abelian group.

ADTs use various mechanisms to define their operations, but a common approach is to specify semantics as a set of axioms. As an example, consider functional lists, introduced in Section 3.7 and used throughout Part I of the book. You can define a functional list as an ADT by specifying axioms like these, for every value x and every list L (empty denotes the empty list):

$$\text{head}(\text{cons}(x, L)) = x$$
$$\text{tail}(\text{cons}(x, L)) = L$$
$$\text{length}(\text{empty}) = 0$$
$$\text{length}(\text{cons}(x, L)) = \text{length}(L) + 1$$

The first axiom states that if you prepend x in front of a list L, using cons, the head of the new list is x. The second axiom says that prepending x in front of list L, then taking the tail of the new list, gives you back list L. The last two axioms define the length of a list, recursively. From these axioms, you can then derive other list properties:

$$\text{head}(\text{tail}(\text{cons}(y, \text{cons}(x, L)))) = \text{head}(\text{cons}(x, L)) = x$$

This derivation shows that if you prepend x and y in front of a list—in that order—and then take the tail of the resulting list, its head is x. This list ADT corresponds to an abstract class in Scala:

```scala
                                                        Scala
abstract class ListADT[A]:
   type List[A]
   val empty: List[A]
   def cons(x: A, list: List[A]): List[A]
   def head(list: List[A]): A
   def tail(list: List[A]): List[A]
   def length(list: List[A]): Int
```

The Scala class is only an approximation of the ADT. It does not specify the behavior of list operations, as defined by the ADT's axioms. Such semantics are typically expressed outside the type system through comments and other forms of documentation.

15.5   Type Inference

Throughout this book, the code examples rely on the capabilities of Scala—and occasionally of other languages—to infer the types of variables or the return types of methods and functions. The details of the type inference algorithms used by a compiler are typically not known by a programmer and might even change as a language evolves. Nevertheless, it is helpful for developers to understand one prevailing principle underlying all type inference strategies: When inferring a type, compilers tend to calculate the smallest set—typically a least upper bound—that satisfies a given series of constraints.

For instance, the expression

```scala
if x > 0 then List(1, 2, 3) else List.empty
```

is given type `List[Int]` by the compiler, while

```scala
if x > 0 then List(1, 2, 3) else Vector(1, 2, 3)
```

is given type `Seq[Int]`, because both `List` and `Vector` are subtypes of `Seq`. In contrast,

```scala
if x > 0 then List(1, 2, 3) else "123"
```

is given type `AnyRef`—the common type of all objects in Scala—because there is no smaller type that contains both `List[Int]` and `String`. Similarly, the expression

```scala
List(Some(42), Some(31))
```

is given type `List[Some[Int]]`, while

```scala
List(Some(42), None)
```

is given the larger type `List[Option[Int]]`, which can also accommodate value `None`.

Strictly speaking, the types inferred by the compiler are not always the absolute smallest sets given the constraints. Instead, user intent is taken into account. For instance,

```scala
var n = 0
```

infers type `Int` for variable n, not type 0. Similarly, given the definitions

```scala
val book1, book2: Book = ...
val books = List(book1, book2)
```

variable books is given type `List[Book]`, not `List[book1.type | book2.type]`.

Sometimes, what constitutes the "best" inferred type is not obvious. Given the expression

```scala
List(book1, book2, "book")
```

type `List[book1.type | book2.type | "book"]` is unlikely to be what you want. However, the choice between `List[Book | String]` or `List[AnyRef]` is more debatable—the current Scala compiler infers `List[AnyRef]`.

In their effort to please, compilers can infer complicated types:

```scala
val v = if x > 0 then List(1, 2, 3) else Set(4)
```

With the current Scala compiler, variable v is given the following type:

```scala
scala.collection.immutable.Iterable[Int] & (Int => Int | Boolean) & Equals
```

Recall that "&" is type intersection. So, variable v is assigned three types. First it is an iterable, immutable collection of integers, which both `List[Int]` and `Set[Int]` are. But lists and set are also functions: `List[A]` is a subtype of `Int => A`, and `Set[A]` is a subtype of `A => Boolean`. Therefore, the expression can also be seen as a function of type `Int => Int | Boolean`. Finally, both `List` and `Set` support equality comparison, which is not the case of all iterables and functions—hence the type `Equals`.

Thanks to this complex type, you can use v as an iterable collection:

```scala
v.iterator.next() // 1 or 4, of type Int
```

or as a function:

```scala
v(1) // 2 or false, of type Int | Boolean
```

It also supports equality:

```scala
v == List(1, 2, 3) || v == Set(4) // true
```

Sometimes, the type being inferred cannot even be expressed in the programming language:

```java
                                                                    Java
var task = new Runnable() {
  public int result;

  public void run() {
    result = 42;
  }
};

task.run();
int r = task.result; // 42
```

Variable `task` is defined using `var`, without an explicit type. The type inferred by the Java compiler is not `Runnable`—for which `task.result` on the last line would be rejected—but a form of `Runnable` that also defines a public field `result`. This type cannot be expressed within the Java language.[6]

When a compiler makes a decision that does not suit your needs, you can sometimes specify a desired type explicitly, as long as you choose a type that contains the value. For instance, this code cannot be compiled:

```scala
                                                                    Scala
var books = List.empty
books ::= book1 // rejected by the compiler
```

The intent is for `books` to start as an empty list, to which books can then be added. However, the compiler infers type `List[Nothing]` for variable `books` and refuses to reassign it with a list of books. Instead, you can express your intent with an explicit type declaration:

```scala
                                                                    Scala
var books: List[Book] = List.empty
books ::= book1 // adds book1 to the list
```

The variants `var books = List.empty[Book]` (an explicit type parameter to function `empty`) and `var books = List.empty: List[Book]` (a type ascription on value `List.empty`) would also work. Similarly,

```scala
                                                                    Scala
var solution = None
if solutionIsFound then solution = Some(value) // rejected by the compiler
```

---

[6]It can be expressed in Scala as `Runnable { def result: Int }`.

does not work because variable `solution` is given type `None.type` by the compiler. Instead, you can specify a type explicitly, using, for instance, `Option.empty[...]`. Note that, because compilers tend to infer types as small as possible, the point of an explicit type declaration is always to widen a type to a larger set, not to specify a smaller type.[7]

15.6 Subtypes

Thinking of types in terms of sets helps us understand the notion of subtype. If types are sets, subtypes are basically subsets. If a type `S` is a subtype of a type `T`, all the values in type `S` are also in type `T` and therefore implement (at least) the functionalities defined by type `T`. When type `S` is a subtype of `T`, type `T` is called a supertype of `S`. Like subsets, subtyping is a transitive relation: If `S` is a subtype of `T`, and `T` is a subtype of `U`, then `S` is a subtype of `U`.

As an illustration, the `Book` type can be part of a type hierarchy:

```scala
trait Publication:
  def title: String
  def pageCount: Int

case class Book(title: String, author: String, pageCount: Int)  extends Publication
case class Magazine(title: String, number: Int, pageCount: Int) extends Publication
```

Type `Publication` has two functionalities, `title` and `pageCount`. Types `Book` and `Magazine` are both subtypes of `Publication`. They are therefore subsets: Every book is a publication and every magazine is a publication. As a consequence, books and magazines must implement the publication functionalities: `title` and `pageCount`. In addition to these, books have an author (but magazines do not), and magazines have a number (but books do not). Types `Book` and `Magazine` are not related to each other: `Book` is not a subtype of `Magazine`, and `Magazine` is not a subtype of `Book`.

The most fundamental property of subtypes is that their values can be substituted for values of a supertype. Thinking again in terms of sets, they *are* values of the supertype. This is sometimes referred to as the *Liskov substitution principle* or as *behavioral subtyping*. For instance, you can define a function to print the title of a publication:

```scala
def printTitle(publication: Publication): Unit = println(publication.title)
```

Because types `Book` and `Magazine` are subtypes of `Publication`, a book or a magazine is guaranteed to have a title and can be used as argument to function `printTitle`. This is enforced by the type system at the programming language level:

---

[7]In Scala, a type declaration can also trigger an implicit conversion: `String` is not a subtype of `Seq[Char]`, but you can still write `val chars: Seq[Char] = "a string"`.

```scala
                                                    ─── Scala ───
// rejected by the compiler
case class Book(author: String, pageCount: Int) extends Publication
```

This definition is rejected by the Scala compiler because values of this `Book` type have no title, and therefore cannot be part of the set of publications.

As an alternative, you can define books without titles by taking them out of the `Publication` type. Then, of course, these books cannot be used as arguments of type `Publication`:

```scala
                                                    ─── Scala ───
case class Book(author: String, pageCount: Int) // OK
val book: Book = ...
printTitle(book) // rejected by the compiler
```

Semantically, however, there is nothing in a programming language that forces a value of a subtype to behave like a value of the supertype—you can implement method `title` in class `Book` to do anything, as long as it returns a string. If a value of type `S` cannot meaningfully be used in code that expects a value of type `T`, then type `S` should *not* be a subtype of type `T`, and you must be careful not to introduce such a subtyping relationship inadvertently (see the aside on composition and inheritance).

The discussion of subtypes so far in this section refers to *nominal subtyping*: A type `S` is a subtype of a supertype `T` because the definition of `S` refers to `T` explicitly—by name. Some programming languages use a different notion, known as *structural subtyping* or *duck typing*.[8] As an illustration, you can define a type `Book` with all the characteristics of a publication, but which is not a subtype of type `Publication`:

```scala
                                                    ─── Scala ───
case class Book(title: String, author: String, pageCount: Int)
```

An instance of this type is not a `Publication` and cannot be used as an argument to function `printTitles`, even though it does have a `title` method that returns a string.

Contrast this with a language like Python, which uses structural subtyping:

```python
                                                    ─── Python ───
def print_title(book):
    print(book.title)

book = Book(title="Le Comte de Monte-Cristo", author="Alexandre Dumas", pagecount=1476)

print_title(book) # prints "Le Comte de Monte-Cristo"
```

---

[8]Named after the saying that if something looks like a duck, quacks like a duck, and walks like a duck, it is probably a duck, even if you call it something else.

Function `print_title` does not specify a type for its `book` argument. You can use it successfully on any object that defines a suitable `title` method:

```
──────────────────────────────────────────── Python ──
magazine = Magazine(title="Life", number=123, pagecount=45)
print_title(magazine) # prints "Life"
```

This approach to typing increases flexibility: As long as an object defines a `title` method, it can be used as an argument to function `print_title`. This helps a programmer deal with classes defined independently from function `print_title`, including those that predate the function. Of course, flexibility is not without risk:

```
──────────────────────────────────────────── Python ──
person = Noble(name="Edmond Dantès", title="Comte de Monte-Cristo")
print_title(person) # prints "Comte de Monte-Cristo"
```

The `person` object can also be passed to function `print_title` because it happens to have a `title` method, entirely unrelated to publications. Languages with nominal subtyping can sometimes achieve the same flexibility in a more controlled way by using type classes, which are discussed in Section 15.10.

Aside on Composition and Inheritance

The Liskov substitution principle is the main reason composition is often preferable to inheritance. Consider, for instance, a type `T` with three services:

```
──────────────────────────────────────────── Scala ──
class T:
    def service1: Int          = ...
    def service2(str: String): Int = ...
    def service3(n: Int): String   = ...
```

Assume that a type `S` is needed that keeps `service1` unchanged, modifies the behavior of `service3`, and adds a new `service4`, but does not support `service2`. You could define `S` using inheritance:

```
──────────────────────────────────────────── Scala ──
class S extends T:
    override def service3(n: Int): String = super.service3(n + service1)
    def service4: Double = ...
```

In that case, a value of type `S` can be used wherever a value of type `T` is expected, including in places that invoke `service2`, which type `S` is not supposed to implement. Now suppose composition is used:

```scala                                                              Scala
class S:
    private val underlying: T = ...
    export underlying.service1

    def service3(n: Int): String = underlying.service3(n + service1)
    def service4: Double = ...
```

Type S is now independent from type T, and attempts to use an S value where a T value is expected are rejected at compile time. There is no `service2` in type S and therefore no risk of it being invoked by mistake. Using `export`, method `service1` is available in type S and is forwarded unchanged to the underlying T instance. By contrast, method `service3` uses the underlying instance explicitly to modify the behavior of the method by the same name defined in class T.

15.7 Polymorphism

Polymorphism is defined in the *Oxford Dictionary* as "the condition of occurring in several different forms." The idea behind polymorphism in programming languages is to have a service exist in multiple forms, depending on the types of its arguments. Polymorphism itself exists in different forms (!), and languages typically implement some or all of three variants.

First is the notion of *ad hoc polymorphism*, implemented by overloading method or function names:

```scala                                                              Scala
def displayBook(book: Book)      = println(s"${book.title} by ${book.author}")
def displayMagazine(mag: Magazine) = println(s"${mag.title} (${mag.pageCount} pages)")
```

Here, two distinct services are implemented, one for books and one for magazines. The services use different names, and books should use the `displayBook` function while magazines use the `displayMagazine` function. However, languages that support ad hoc polymorphism can offer both services under the same name:

```scala                                                              Scala
def display(book: Book)    = println(s"${book.title} by ${book.author}")
def display(mag: Magazine) = println(s"${mag.title} (${mag.pageCount} pages)")
```

Listing 15.1: Example of ad hoc polymorphism.

You can think of function `display` as two services accessed uniformly, or as a single service that takes a different form for books and for magazines—a polymorphic service.

A second type of polymorphism is *parametric polymorphism*, which relies on functions and methods parameterized by one or more types, like generics in Java or templates in C++:

```scala
                                                          ─── Scala ───
def withHash[T](value: T): (T, Int) = (value, value.##)
```

Listing 15.2: Example of parametric polymorphism.

This function combines a value with its hash code, as a pair. It is parameterized by a type T and is polymorphic in the sense that it exists in multiple forms, one for each possible type argument. This single parameterized function represents a collection of type-specific functions—for instance:

```scala
                                                          ─── Scala ───
def bookWithHash(book: Book): (Book, Int)              = (book, book.##)
def magazineWithHash(magazine: Magazine): (Magazine, Int) = (magazine, magazine.##)
```

Instead of defining multiple functions, you invoke the same `withHash` on books and magazines to obtain values of type (Book,Int) or (Magazine,Int) as necessary:

```scala
                                                          ─── Scala ───
val hashedBook: (Book, Int)          = withHash(book)
val hashedMagazine: (Magazine, Int) = withHash(magazine)
```

The third and most interesting kind of polymorphism is *subtype polymorphism*. It is based on the idea that a service in a type can have multiple forms, one for each subtype. For instance, you can define a function to print the titles of a list of publications:

```scala
                                                          ─── Scala ───
def printTitles(pubs: List[Publication]) = for pub <- pubs do println(pub.title)
```

Listing 15.3: Example of subtype polymorphism; see also Lis. 15.4.

A list of publications may contain books or magazines. When a book is processed, method `title` from the Book class is invoked, and when a magazine is processed, method `title` from the magazine class is invoked. In other words, the code fragment `pub.title` takes multiple forms, depending on the type of the object inside variable `pub`.

You may know this phenomenon under the name *dynamic dispatch* or *dynamic binding* or *late binding*. These terms all reflect the fact that which code is executed by `pub.title` is not decided at compile time, but dynamically at runtime, once the type of the object inside `pub` is known. Compilers typically rely on a structure called *Virtual Method Table* to store references to different implementations of a given method, and subtype polymorphism is sometimes known as using *virtual methods*.

In languages like Java and Scala, the power of subtype polymorphism derives from the fact that a method invocation `x.m(y)` can execute different implementations of method m based on the runtime type of x. Some languages, such as C# and some Lisp variants, implement *multiple dispatch* to dynamically choose which method to invoke based on arguments other than the target—deciding on an implementation of method m using the types of both x and y in the preceding example. Because Scala supports only single dispatch polymorphism, the following code cannot be compiled, even with both display functions from Listing 15.1 defined:

```scala
// rejected by the compiler
def displayCollection(pubs: List[Publication]) = for pub <- pubs do display(pub)
```

The call display(pub) is resolved at compile time. It fails because there is no display function defined for an argument of type Publication, even though at runtime, pub will be of type Book or Magazine, for which such a function exists.

Of course, you could query types at runtime within the program to select a suitable function:

```scala
// DON'T DO THIS!
def displayCollection(pubs: List[Publication]) =
    for pub <- pubs do
        pub match
            case book: Book        => display(book)
            case magazine: Magazine => display(magazine)
```

The main drawbacks of this approach are its verbosity and rigidity. Not only do all existing subtypes need to be enumerated explicitly, but a later addition of a new subtype will call for an update everywhere this pattern is used. For instance, if you create a new subtype of Publication, say Report, and displayCollection is called on a list that contains reports, it will fail with a MatchError exception because the pattern-matching code has no case to handle reports.

Instead, you should design your code to leverage subtype polymorphism. In the case of displayCollection, this means replacing the display functions of Listing 15.1 with a display method invoked on a target of type Publication:

```scala
trait Publication:
    def title: String
    def pageCount: Int
    def display(): Unit

case class Book(title: String, author: String, pageCount: Int) extends Publication:
    def display() = println(s"$title by $author")
```

```
case class Magazine(title: String, number: Int, pageCount: Int) extends Publication:
  def display() = println(s"$title ($pageCount pages)")

def displayCollection(pubs: List[Publication]) = for pub <- pubs do pub.display()
```

Listing 15.4: Using subtype polymorphism to process a heterogeneous collection.

The implementation of `displayCollection` is simpler and, more importantly, does not need to be updated after a new type of publication is introduced:

——————————————————————————————— *Scala* —

```
case class Report(title: String, pageCount: Int) extends Publication:
  def display() = println(s"Report: $title")

displayCollection(List(book, magazine, report)) // OK
```

Heavy use of explicit runtime type testing and casting—including through pattern matching—is often a sign of a flawed design that should be modified to rely instead on subtype polymorphism.

15.8   Type Variance

The concept of behavioral subtyping discussed earlier gives rise to an interesting problem. I introduce the issue first in Java because, on this topic, Java is simpler to work with than more recent languages like C#, Scala, and Kotlin. The Java version of Listing 15.3 is shown here:

——————————————————————————————— *Java* —

```
import java.util.List;

void printTitles(List<Publication> pubs) {
  for (Publication pub : pubs) System.out.println(pub.title());
}
```

The type `List` refers here to Java's `List` interface. As before, `printTitles` relies on subtype polymorphism, and invokes the `title` method that corresponds to the runtime type of object `pub`. You can call it on a mixed list of books and magazines:

——————————————————————————————— *Java* —

```
List<Publication> pubs = List.of(book, magazine);
printTitles(pubs); // prints both titles
```

However, you cannot call this `printTitles` function on a List<Book> value:

```Java
List<Book> books = List.of(book1, book2);
printTitles(books); // rejected by the compiler
```

The Java compiler rejects the call with an error:

```
java: incompatible types:
  java.util.List<Book> cannot be converted to java.util.List<Publication>
```

In other words, in Java, List<Book> is not a subtype of List<Publication>, even though Book *is* a subtype of Publication.

To understand why, consider a variant of `printTitles` that prints titles *and* adds a magazine to the list:

```Java
void printTitlesAndAddMagazine(List<Publication> pubs) {
  for (Publication pub : pubs) System.out.println(pub.title());
  pubs.add(new Magazine(...));
}
```

If the Java compiler lets you call `printTitles` on a List<Book> value, it must also let you call `printTitlesAndAddMagazine` on that same value—both functions have the same signature, and an argument that is valid for one must be valid for the other. But the compiler cannot allow a call to `printTitlesAndAddMagazine` on a List<Book> value because this would cause a magazine to be added to a list of books, which is unsound type-wise, since type Magazine is not a subtype of type Book. Type List<Book> is not a subtype of type List<Publication> because it does not adhere to the substitution principle: It does not support all the functionalities of the supertype. In particular, a magazine can be added to a List<Publication> but not to a List<Book>.

The situation is different in Scala. You can apply function `printTitles` from Listing 15.3 to a List[Book] value:

```Scala
def printTitles(pubs: List[Publication]) = for pub <- pubs do println(pub.title)

val books: List[Book] = List(book1, book2)
printTitles(books) // prints both titles
```

How come? If such a call is unsound in Java, why is it allowed in Scala? The key difference is that Scala lists are immutable: You cannot write a Scala equivalent of the

Java `printTitlesAndAddMagazine` function.[9] Indeed, Scala's mutable types face the same difficulty encountered in Java:

```scala
def printTitles(pubs: Array[Publication]) = for pub <- pubs do println(pub.title)

val books: Array[Book] = Array(book1, book2)
printTitles(books) // rejected by the compiler
```

A magazine could be inserted into an `Array[Publication]` value but not into an `Array[Book]` value, and thus the compiler is justified in rejecting the call: `Array[Book]` is not a subtype of `Array[Publication]`.

In Scala, `List` is said to be *covariant*: If S is a subtype of T, and C is covariant, then `C[S]` is a subtype of `C[T]`. By contrast, Java's lists and Scala's arrays are *non-variant* (also called *invariant*): If C is non-variant, any subtyping relationship between types S and T is not carried over to `C[S]` and `C[T]`.

In Java, all data structures are non-variant—except arrays, as discussed later. In Scala, mutable structures are non-variant, but most immutable structures are covariant. Variance is specified when defining a type, using annotations. For instance, arrays are defined as

```scala
class Array[A] extends ...
```

while lists use

```scala
class List[+A] extends ...
```

The relevant difference here is between `[A]`, which specifies non-variance, and `[+A]`, which indicates covariance. Many immutable types in Scala use a covariant annotation:

```scala
class Tuple2[+T1, +T2] ...
class Option[+A] ...
class Vector[+A] ...
class HashMap[K, +V] ... // inside package immutable
class HashMap[K, V] ...  // inside package mutable
class LazyList[+A] ...
```

---

[9]If a magazine is "added" to a list of books, as in `magazine :: books`, a new list of type `List[Publication]` is created.

Accordingly, in Scala, `Option[Book]` is a subtype of `Option[Publication]`, and `LazyList[Magazine]` is a subtype of `LazyList[Publication]`. In contrast, in Java, `Optional<Book>` is not a subtype of `Optional<Publication>`, and `Stream<Magazine>` is not a subtype of `Stream<Publication>`.

In languages that support variance annotations, you can define your own covariant types:

```scala
                                                                    Scala
class Ref[+A](contents: A):
  private var count = 0

  def get(): A =
    count += 1
    contents

  def accessCount: Int = count

  def reset(): Unit = count = 0
```

Listing 15.5: Example of a user-defined covariant type.

Class `Ref` implements a wrapper that keeps track of how many times a value is accessed. Thanks to the variance annotation, `Ref[Book]` is a subtype of `Ref[Publication]`. Note that instances of class `Ref` are mutable—both methods `get` and `reset` can modify the state of the object. However, the contents of a reference cannot be changed. An attempt to change `contents` into a `var` and to add a setter method are rejected by the compiler:

```scala
                                                                    Scala
// rejected by the compiler
class Ref[+A](private var contents: A):
  private var count = 0

  def set(value: A): Unit =
    contents = value
    count = 0
  ...
```

Methods in class `Ref[+A]` can return values of type `A`, but any method that declares an argument of type `A`—like method `set`—will be rejected. If you want a resettable reference, you will need to declare it as `class Ref[A]` and make it non-variant.

Covariance has a dual concept called *contravariance*: If `C` is contravariant and `S` is a subtype of `T`, then `C[T]` is a subtype of `C[S]`. The contravariance annotation in Scala is a minus sign:

```scala
                                                                      ─── Scala ───
class TrashCan[-A](log: Logger):
  def trash(x: A): Unit = log.info(s"trashing: $x")
```

Listing 15.6: Example of a user-defined contravariant type.

Because of the contravariance annotation, `TrashCan[Publication]` is a subtype of `TrashCan[Book]`. This makes sense: An object of type `TrashCan[Publication]` can trash any type of publication, including books, and thus implements the functionality of a `TrashCan[Book]` value.

Constraints on contravariant types mimic those of covariant types: Inside class `TrashCan[-A]`, you can use type `A` for method arguments, but not for return values. Covariance and contravariance constraints are reflected in the choice some languages made for their variance annotations. In C# and `Kotlin`, for instance, the covariance annotation is named `out`, and the contravariance annotation is named `in` (instead of "+" and "-" in Scala).

The main use of contravariance—in some languages, the only use, as in Rust and SML—is within function types. One-argument functions are defined in Scala as follows:

```scala
                                                                      ─── Scala ───
trait Function1[-A, +B] extends ...
```

This is the type of functions with a single argument of type `A` and a return value of type `B`—also denoted `A => B`. If `S` is a subtype of `T`, type `A => S` is a subtype of `A => T`. By returning a value of type `S`, a function of type `A => S` does indeed implement the functionality of a function of type `A => T`: It consumes a value of type `A` and produces a value of type `T`—because of type `S`. But because of contravariance in the input side, type `T => B` is also a subtype of type `S => B`, by the same argument used for class `TrashCan`—type `TrashCan` is basically `A => Unit`. Functions of multiple arguments follow the same pattern:

```scala
                                                                      ─── Scala ───
trait Function2[-T1, -T2, +R] extends ...
trait Function3[-T1, -T2, -T3, +R] extends ...
...
```

In a functional programming style, where functions are used as arguments to higher-order functions, you sometimes need to decide whether a function is a subtype of another function. Figure 15.1 shows that type `Publication => Magazine` is a subtype of `Book => Publication` because `Publication` is a supertype of `Book`—and functions are contravariant in their input type—and because `Magazine` is a subtype of `Publication`—

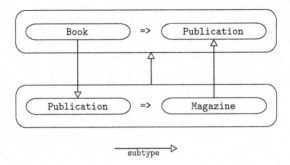

Figure 15.1 Subtype relationship of two functions.

and functions are covariant in their output type. Indeed, if you have a higher-order function defined as

```
                                                          — Scala —
def higherOrder(f: Book => Publication) = ...
```

you can safely call it on an argument of type `Publication => Magazine`. As a function, this argument can be applied to values of type `Book` (it can be applied to any publication type) and will produce values of type `Publication` (specifically, magazines), so it is consistent with the type requirements of argument `f`.

Peculiarities might arise when variance is considered. Here are two examples. First, immutable sets in Scala are non-variant. The reason is that `Set[A]` is a subtype of `A => Boolean`. The data structure view calls for covariance, but the function type would require contravariance.

Second, while all other data structures are non-variant in Java, arrays are covariant. This design choice predates the introduction of generics and was necessary to improve flexibility. For instance, you can define a sorting function with signature `Object[]` and apply it to a `String[]` value—`String[]` is a subtype of `Object[]`. Since arrays are mutable, however, this covariance leads to type unsoundness:

```
                                                          — Java —
void printTitlesAndAddMagazine(Publication[] pubs) {
  for (Publication pub : pubs) System.out.println(pub.title());
  pubs[0] = new Magazine(...);
}

Book[] books = new Book[]{book1, book2};
printTitlesAndAddMagazine(books); // throws ArrayStoreException
```

The type system allows the invocation of function `printTitlesAndAddMagazine` on an array of books, but an attempt to insert a magazine into the array results in a runtime exception. The situation is the same in C#, where arrays are also covariant and may trigger an `ArrayTypeMismatchException`. Arrays are non-variant in Scala and Kotlin.

15.9   Type Bounds

Many types cannot be made covariant or contravariant, including most mutable collections. Still, you can improve flexibility by specifying variance requirements in the code that uses these types. You can do this through *type bounds*, sometimes also referred to as *use-site variance annotations*.

For instance, the definition of `printTitles`

```scala
                                                            ———— Scala ————
def printTitles(pubs: Set[Publication]): Unit = for pub <- pubs do println(pub.title)
```

is too restrictive because `Set`, whether mutable or immutable, is non-variant in Scala. You cannot invoke this function on a `Set[Book]`, for instance. But you can rewrite `printTitles` in a way that leaves the set element type unspecified—it can be `Book` or `Magazine`—as long as it is a subtype of `Publication`. You do this with a type bound:

```scala
                                                            ———— Scala ————
def printTitles[A <: Publication](pubs: Set[A]): Unit =
    for pub <- pubs do println(pub.title)
```

Listing 15.7: Example of an upper type bound for use-site variance.

The function is now parameterized by a type `A`, and its argument is of type `Set[A]`. Type `A`, however, cannot just be any type: It must be type `Publication` or a subtype of `Publication`. The Scala type operator "`<:`" specifies such a constraint: `S <: T` means that `S` is a subtype of `T`, or type `T` itself. You can also define `printTitles` by using a wildcard instead of naming type `A`:

```scala
                                                            ———— Scala ————
def printTitles(pubs: Set[? <: Publication]): Unit =
    for pub <- pubs do println(pub.title)
```

The last two variants of `printTitles` can be called on a value of type `Set[Book]`, or `Set[Magazine]`, or `Set[Publication]`.

The use of an explicit name `A` for the unknown type is usually preferred because it helps with type inference. For instance, the current Scala compiler rejects the first implementation of (useless) function `f` shown here but accepts the second:[10]

```scala
                                                            ———— Scala ————
def f(pubs: Set[? <: Publication])     = pubs += pubs.head // cannot be compiled
def f[A <: Publication](pubs: Set[A]) = pubs += pubs.head // OK
```

---

[10]The `Set` type is always non-variant in Scala. Some examples in this section use a mutable set, which defines a method "`+=`". Other examples leave the mutability of the set unspecified.

You can use "<:" to specify an upper bound, meaning that you require a type variable to be a subtype of another type. You can use the opposite operator ">:" to specify a lower bound, requiring a type variable to be a supertype of another type:

```scala
def addMagazine[A >: Magazine](pubs: Set[A]): Unit = pubs += Magazine(...)
```

Listing 15.8: Example of a lower type bound for use-site variance.

Function `addMagazine` adds a magazine to a mutable set, requiring type `A` to be a supertype of `Magazine`. The function is flexible, and you can call it on values of type `Set[Magazine]`, `Set[Publication]`, or `Set[AnyRef]`.

When you use type bounds, you face constraints similar to what we saw earlier with covariant and contravariant types. For instance, these functions are rejected by the compiler:

```scala
def printTitlesAndAddMagazine[A <: Publication](pubs: Set[A]): Unit =
   for pub <- pubs do println(pub.title)
   pubs += Magazine(...) // rejected by the compiler

def printTitlesAndAddMagazine[A >: Magazine](pubs: Set[A]): Unit =
   for pub <- pubs do println(pub.title) // rejected by the compiler
   pubs += Magazine(...)
```

The first function is rejected because it attempts to add a magazine to a `Set[A]` value, but all you know is that type `A` is a subtype of `Publication`. There is no guarantee that type `A` is a supertype of type `Magazine`—it could be `Book`, for instance. The second function fails because it tries to invoke a `title` method on a value of type `A`, but `A` is only known to be a supertype of `Magazine`, not necessarily a subtype of `Publication`—type `A` could be `AnyRef`, for instance. To make it work, `printTitlesAndAddMagazine` needs `A` to be both a subtype of `Publication` *and* a supertype of `Magazine`. You implement it by specifying both a lower bound and an upper bound:

```scala
def printTitlesAndAddMagazine[A >: Magazine <: Publication](pubs: Set[A]): Unit =
   for pub <- pubs do println(pub.title)
   pubs += Magazine(...)
```

Listing 15.9: Example of a type parameter with both lower and upper bounds.

In more complex scenarios, you can combine type bounds with type intersections to specify multiple upper or lower bounds:

```scala
────────────────────────────────────────────────────────── Scala ──
def printTitlesInOrder[A <: Publication & Ordered[A]](pubs: Set[A]): Unit =
  for pub <- SortedSet.from(pubs) do println(pub.title)
```

Listing 15.10: Example of a combined upper type bound; contrast with Lis. 15.14.

Publications can be gathered in a sorted set because type A is known to be an ordered type, in addition to being a subtype of Publication.

Most of the functions used as illustrations in this section can be written in Java:

```java
──────────────────────────────────────────────────────────── Java ──
<A extends Publication> void printTitles(Set<A> pubs) {
  for (Publication pub : pubs) System.out.println(pub.title());
}

void addMagazine(Set<? super Magazine> pubs) {
  pubs.add(new Magazine(...));
}

<A extends Publication & Comparable<A>> void printTitlesInOrder(Set<A> pubs) {
  for (Publication pub : new TreeSet<>(pubs)) System.out.println(pub.title());
}
```

Java uses S extends T and ? extends T to express upper bounds and ? super T to express lower bounds. Java has no S super T syntax, making it necessary to use a wildcard in the definition of function addMagazine. As of this writing, lower bounds and upper bounds cannot be combined in Java, preventing you from writing an equivalent to function printTitlesAndAddMagazine from Listing 15.9.

When designing libraries that depend on non-variant types, it is good practice to rely on type bounds for increased flexibility. Consider, for instance, a function that executes tasks in parallel and returns a list of their outputs.[11] Tasks are specified as no-argument functions:

```java
──────────────────────────────────────────────────────────── Java ──
public <A> List<A> runInParallel(List<Function0<A>> tasks) {...}
```

Because lists are non-variant in Java, a limitation of runInParallel is that it cannot be invoked on a value of type List<T> where T is a subtype of Function0<Book>. For instance, suppose BookPublisher is a book-generating function:

```java
──────────────────────────────────────────────────────────── Java ──
class BookPublisher implements Function0<Book> { ... }
```

---

[11]See the case study in Chapter 24 for a possible implementation strategy.

You cannot invoke `runInParallel` on a List<BookPublisher>. Adding a type bound can make the function more flexible:

```Java
public <A> List<A> runInParallel(List<? extends Function0<A>> tasks) {...}
```

You can now call this function on a List<BookPublisher>. However, it then returns a value of type List<Book> specifically:

```Java
List<BookPublisher> bookPublishers = ...
List<Book> books = runInParallel(bookPublishers); // OK
List<Publication> pubs = runInParallel(bookPublishers); // rejected by the compiler
```

For the last line to work, type `A` would have to be `Publication`. But `BookPublisher` is a subtype of `Function0<Book>`, *not* a subtype of `Function0<Publication>`, and function types are not covariant in Java: `Function0<Book>` is not a subtype of `Function0<Publication>`.

You can further improve the `runInParallel` function by using a second type bound, inside the function type:

```Java
public <A> List<A> runInParallel(List<? extends Function0<? extends A>> tasks) {...}
```

Listing 15.11: Using type bounds on non-variant types for increased flexibility.

This second bound makes it possible to call `runInParallel(bookPublishers)` and have the return value be of type List<Publication> because `BookPublisher` *is* a subtype of `Function0<? extends Publication>`. You can define a similar function in Scala:[12]

```Scala
def runInParallel[A](tasks: List[() => A]): List[A] = ...

val bookPublishers: List[BookPublisher] = ...
val pubs: List[Publication] = runInParallel(bookPublishers) // OK
```

The definition is simpler and needs no type bounds because, in Scala, lists are covariant and functions are also covariant in their return type. Type `A` can be `Publication` because `BookPublisher` is a subtype of `() => Book`, and `() => Book` is a subtype of `() => Publication`.

---

[12]An even more flexible function would use *kinds* (higher-order types) so a list is returned from a list, a set from a set, etc.

15.10   Type Classes

Earlier, a distinction was made between nominal subtyping, which is typically used in statically typed languages, and structural subtyping, which is less safe but more flexible and popular in dynamically typed languages. At times, programmers who would otherwise benefit from static typing decide they cannot use a particular language because they need more flexibility. Before you run to Python or JavaScript because you absolutely need structural subtyping, be aware that some statically typed languages offer mechanisms that achieve much of the same flexibility, possibly in a safer way.

As an illustration, imagine that a class `Report` predates the definition of type `Publication`:

```scala
case class Report(title: String, number: Int) // does not refer to Publication
```

Even though reports have titles, you cannot use a function `printTitle` defined as

```scala
def printTitle(pub: Publication): Unit = println(pub.title)
```

to display the title of a report because `Report` is not a subtype of `Publication`.

As we have seen, this is not an issue in languages that rely on structural subtyping (*duck typing*): In these languages, a call is valid as long as the runtime argument has a `title` method, no matter its nominal type. Although Scala uses nominal subtyping at its core, the language lets you define structural types as well:

```scala
type Titled = { def title: String }

def printTitle(doc: Titled): Unit = println(doc.title)
```

Listing 15.12: Example of a structural type in Scala.

Type `Titled` represents objects that have a string-valued `title` method. You can use this `printTitles` function on anything with a title, including a report:

```scala
val report = Report("Count to count: from Monte-Cristo to Mathias Sandorf", 123)
printTitle(report) // prints "Count to count: from Monte-Cristo to Mathias Sandorf"
```

Of course, this increased flexibility comes with the same risks discussed in Section 15.6 in the context of Python:[13]

```scala
─────────────────────────────────────────────── Scala ───
val person = Noble(name = "Edmond Dantès", title = "Comte de Monte-Cristo")
printTitle(person) // prints "Comte de Monte-Cristo"
```

There is a better alternative to structural subtyping, one that has its origins in the world of functional programming: *type classes*. This concept appears complicated at first glance, but it is quite powerful and used extensively in functional programming libraries.

As with structural typing, the starting point is to define a type of values with a title:

```scala
──────────────────────────────────────────────── Scala ───
trait Titled[A]:
    def titleOf(document: A): String
```

`Titled` represents a type class, the class of all types that have a title. You can then use an object of type `Title[A]` to display the title of a value of type `A`:

```scala
──────────────────────────────────────────────── Scala ───
def printTitle[A](doc: A, titledEvidence: Titled[A]): Unit =
    println(titledEvidence.titleOf(doc))
```

Function `printTitle` takes a second argument as evidence that type `A` is "titled." You can apply `printTitle` on reports, as long as an object of type `Titled[Report]` is available:

```scala
──────────────────────────────────────────────── Scala ───
object ReportsAreTitled extends Titled[Report]:
    def titleOf(report: Report): String = report.title

printTitle(report, ReportsAreTitled) // prints the string returned by report.title
```

Note that you can create an evidence value like `ReportsAreTitled` for any existing type, including one that predates function `printTitle`. In Scala, the evidence that a type belongs to a type class is typically passed implicitly using a *context bound*:

```scala
──────────────────────────────────────────────── Scala ───
def printTitle[A : Titled](doc: A): Unit =
    val titledEvidence = summon[Titled[A]]
    println(titledEvidence.titleOf(doc))
```

The syntax `A : Titled` indicates that you must pass an implicit value of type `Titled[A]` to function `printTitle`, in addition to the document doc. This value can be retrieved

---

[13]Additionally, the default implementation of this mechanism in Scala uses Java reflection, with a non-negligible runtime performance cost.

with the **summon** function. Once a value similar to object **ReportsAreTitled** is made implicitly available, you can display report titles without mentioning the evidence:

Scala
```scala
given Titled[Report] with
   def titleOf(report: Report): String = report.title

printTitle(report) // prints the string returned by report.title
```

If you define "given" values of type **Titled[Book]** and **Titled[Magazine]**, you can display book and magazine titles as well.

For convenience, you can add an **apply** method to retrieve the implicit argument more easily:

Scala
```scala
object Titled:
   def apply[A : Titled]: Titled[A] = summon[Titled[A]]
```

You can also add an extension so "titled" values have a **title** method:

Scala
```scala
extension [A : Titled](document: A) def title: String = Titled[A].titleOf(document)
```

Let's put all these elements together in a typical application of type classes:

Scala
```scala
// define a Titled type class, with convenience methods
trait Titled[A]:
   def titleOf(document: A): String

object Titled:
   def apply[A : Titled]: Titled[A] = summon[Titled[A]]

extension [A : Titled](document: A) def title: String = Titled[A].titleOf(document)

// use the type class in methods and classes, e.g.:
def printTitle[A : Titled](document: A): Unit = println(document.title)

// make books, magazines, and reports members of the type class:
given Titled[Report]   = _.title
given Titled[Book]     = _.title
given Titled[Magazine] = _.title

printTitle(report)   // OK
printTitle(book)     // OK
printTitle(magazine) // OK
```

Listing 15.13: Example of polymorphism through a type class.

A shorted syntax `_.title` is used to define given values. Since `Titled` is a SAM interface, you can use a function to define a `Titled` object and thus rely on partial application or lambda expressions.

When you define type classes, you rely on ad hoc polymorphism—various `titleOf` methods with distinct signatures—instead of subtype polymorphism—the same `title` method implemented differently in separate subtypes. This improves flexibility because existing types can easily be added to a type class without modification: The necessary code, like method `titleOf`, resides outside the type.

For instance, this definition of method `printTitlesInOrder` is preferable to that of Listing 15.10, which uses a `Publication & Ordered[A]` bound:

```
                                                                    Scala
def printTitlesInOrder[A <: Publication : Ordering](pubs: Set[A]): Unit =
   for pub <- SortedSet.from(pubs) do println(pub.title)
```

Listing 15.14: Example of combining type bounds and type classes for flexibility.

This variant of the function is more flexible because you can use it on any publication type A for which an `Ordering[A]` value is defined, including publication types that are not subtypes of `Ordered`. For instance, thanks to implicit conversions from the standard library, `printTitlesInOrder` can now be called on publications that extend Java's `Comparable` interface.

There are several benefits to using type classes instead of structural types. First, an attempt to print the title of a noble person is now rejected:

```
no implicit argument of type Titled[Noble] was found for an implicit parameter
   of method printTitle
```

Second, you can use `printTitles` on documents that conceptually have a title but define no `title` method. You simply need to create a suitable evidence object:

```
                                                                    Scala
case class Memo(header: String)
val memo = Memo("Famous Counts")

given Titled[Memo] = _.header

printTitle(memo) // prints "Famous Counts"
```

Even though memos have headers instead of titles, you can call `printTitle` on memos.

Third, values and methods can be associated with each type class:

```
                                                                    Scala
trait Titled[A]:
   def titleOf(document: A): String
   def logger: Logger = Logger.getAnonymousLogger
```

```
given Titled[Book] with
  def titleOf(book: Book) = book.title
  override def logger      = Logger.getLogger("book_logger")
```

This type class associates a logger with each titled type, so book-related activities, for instance, are logged separately from other publications. This is something you cannot do with plain subtype polymorphism. (See also the case of `zero` and `fromInt` in the next example.)

In Scala, type classes are used extensively in the design of libraries. The standard library defines several type classes like `Ordered` (used earlier), `Numeric` (numbers with addition and multiplication), and `Fractional` (a subclass of `Numeric` with division). As a final illustration, consider a function that averages a list of numbers:

```
                                                          ─── Scala ───
def average(numbers: Seq[Double]): Double =
  if numbers.isEmpty then 0.0 else numbers.sum / numbers.length.toDouble
```

This function returns zero if the sequence of numbers is empty. Otherwise, it divides the sum of all the numbers by the length of the sequence to compute the average. You can generalize this function to any type `A` that supports arithmetic operations:

```
                                                          ─── Scala ───
def average[A : Fractional](numbers: Seq[A]): A =
  if numbers.isEmpty then Fractional[A].zero
  else Fractional[A].div(numbers.sum, Fractional[A].fromInt(numbers.length))
```

A `Fractional[A]` evidence value is used to fetch a zero, a division operation, and a conversion from `Int` to `A`. It is also used, implicitly, by method `sum` to add all the numbers.

You can use a few well-chosen `import` statements to improve code legibility. In Listing 15.15, `infixFractionalOps` is similar to the extension `title` in Listing 15.13:

```
                                                          ─── Scala ───
def average[A : Fractional](numbers: Seq[A]): A =
  val evidence = Fractional[A]
  import evidence.{ fromInt, zero }
  import math.Fractional.Implicits.infixFractionalOps

  if numbers.isEmpty then zero else numbers.sum / fromInt(numbers.length)
```

Listing 15.15: An averaging function based on a type class.

You can use this `average` function on double values, as well as other `Fractional` types, like `BigDecimal`:[14]

---

[14]To create the `decimals` list, a standard implicit conversion is triggered that converts 1.2 and 2.4 into `BigDecimal` values.

```scala
                                                                  ─ Scala ─
val doubles: List[Double]      = List(1.2, 2.4)
val decimals: List[BigDecimal] = List(1.2, 2.4)


average(doubles)                // 1.7999999999999998, as a Double
average(List.empty[Double])     // 0.0, as a Double
average(decimals)               // 1.8, as a BigDecimal
average(List.empty[BigDecimal]) // 0, as a BigDecimal
```

Note that even if `Double` and `BigDecimal` implemented a common numerical type—say, `Number`—you could not rely on subtype polymorphism to implement the `average` function because there would be no way to obtain a value `zero` and a function `fromInt` for a given subtype `A`.

15.11 Summary

- Typing strategies vary from programming language to programming language. They are often compared in terms of static (compile time) versus dynamic (run-time), and/or strong (fussier) versus weak (looser). The terminology is somewhat ambiguous and not universally agreed upon.

- A more important characteristic of type systems is that they vary in terms of safety (how effective they are at catching mistakes), flexibility (the degree to which they enable rather than prevent a preferred design), and simplicity (how easy they are to understand and exercise). Languages typically favor two of these attributes at the expense of the third.

- One possible view of types is that they are sets of values. Some sets, such as `String` and `List[Int]`, are large. Others, such as `Unit` and `Boolean`, are small. If a variable has a given type, its value always belongs to the corresponding set. The smaller the type, the more valuable this information will be.

- The dual view seeks to identify types with the services—for example, methods and attributes—that they define. When defining a type as an interface in an object-oriented language, for instance, the focus is not so much on the set of values this interface can contain, but rather on the operations that can be applied to these values.

- Abstract data types (ADTs) are a formal model of types that is based on the dual view of sets and operations. ADTs define the semantics of all the operations available on a type, typically in the form of axioms. Programming language types are only an approximation of ADTs, as they usually specify the signatures of their operations, but not their semantics.

- In addition to explicit type declarations in the source code, many programming languages rely on inference algorithms to calculate types that have not been specified. An overarching principle of type inference is to calculate the smallest type—typically a least upper bound—that fits the constraints expressed in a program. Occasionally, an inferred type might be too narrow for a programmer's purpose and needs to be widened using an explicit declaration or a type ascription. (Cases where an inferred type is too broad and needs to be narrowed are possible, but much more unusual.)

- When types are viewed as sets, subtyping corresponds to a subset relationship: S (as a type) is a subtype of T if S (as a set) is a subset of T. Accordingly, all the values in subtype S are also in supertype T and implement (at least) the same functionalities. Subtypes satisfy a substitution property: Values of a subtype can be used wherever values of a supertype are expected.

- Some programming languages use a notion of nominal subtyping, by which subtypes are linked to their supertypes by name. Other languages use structural subtyping, in which a subtype only needs to implement the functionalities of the supertype and does not need to refer to the supertype explicitly. Structural subtyping tends to be more flexible but less safe: Semantically independent values that happen to share a method name can become related by a subtyping relationship that was not intended.

- Polymorphism relies on the idea of a single service that takes several forms. Programming languages typically implement some or all of three kinds of polymorphism: ad hoc (separate methods or functions by the same name), parametric (methods or functions parameterized by one or more types), and subtype (methods implemented differently in different subtypes).

- A heterogeneous collection of values from different subtypes of a common supertype can often be processed uniformly using subtype polymorphism. The resulting code is concise, robust, and flexible. In particular, it requires no modification if new subtypes of the supertype are created at a later time.

- A parameterized type may either preserve a subtyping relationship of its type parameter (covariance), reverse it (contravariance), or ignore it (non-variance, also called invariance). In other words, when S is a subtype of T, it is possible that C[S] is a subtype of C[T] (C is covariant), C[T] is a subtype of C[S] (C is contravariant), or there is no subtype relationship between C[S] and C[T] (C is non-variant).

- Support for type variance varies from one programming language to another. Some languages implement fixed rules—for instance, all types except arrays are non-variant in Java. Others offer mechanisms for user-defined variance—for instance, C#, Scala, and Kotlin use similar variance annotations.

- Typically, immutable data structures can safely be made covariant, while mutable structures are only type-safe when they are non-variant. In languages that support functional programming, function types are often covariant in their output types and contravariant in their input type. For simplicity, languages may deliberately introduce type unsoundness by making some mutable structures covariant, as is the case with arrays in Java and C#.

- To increase flexibility, code that uses non-variant types can rely on type bounds—also called use-site variance annotations—instead of specifying exact types. An upper bound is used to constrain a type argument to be a subtype of another type; a lower bound is used to require it to be a supertype of another type.

- Ad hoc and parametric polymorphism are sometimes packaged into the notion of type class, especially in languages that have no support for subtype polymorphism. Type classes can be used to uniformly access services on values of different types, even when those services are not related by a common supertype. In particular, types developed independently from a function that uses a type class can be adapted and used as arguments to this function.

Part II

Concurrent Programming

Chapter 16

Concepts of Concurrent Programming

Part I started with the observation that there is no single definition of functional programming. Unfortunately, there is no universally agreed-upon definition of concurrent programming either, and defining concurrent programming is at least as difficult a task as defining functional programming was in Part I of the book. The issue is similar: The terminology is ambiguous, and different people choose to emphasize different aspects. Nevertheless, from the indisputable premise that concurrent programs do not execute in a purely sequential manner, several key concepts of concurrent programming emerge, including synchronicity, atomicity, threads, synchronization, and nondeterminism.

16.1   Non-sequential Programs

A possible starting point is to think of concurrent programs as programs that are not sequential. A sequential program executes its instructions, one at a time, from beginning to end. Most programmers learned how to program by first writing sequential programs. A "main" function starts with its first programming statement and continues through conditional, loops, and function calls, until it executes its very last statement, then terminates.

Can a program execution not be sequential? A common answer is that a program may involve multiple threads of execution. Each thread executes the program sequentially, but several threads do it at the same time. Another answer is that a program stops being sequential by having some of its parts executed out of order, due to the presence of asynchronous operations. Quite often, asynchronous operations involve threads, and threads are used mostly through asynchronous operations, so both answers coincide. However, asynchronous code need not be multithreaded, and threads do not necessarily make code asynchronous.

As an illustration, consider the following program:

```
                                                          pseudocode
println('A')
println('B')
println('C')
```

This program is sequential and prints A, B, and C, in that order. You can break sequentiality by letting the second print statement execute out of order. In Scala, it could be written as follows:

```scala
                                                         ─── Scala ───
println('A')
Future(println('B'))
println('C')
```

The second print statement is scheduled to be executed out of order, and the program output is no longer guaranteed to be A followed by B followed by C. Out-of-order execution can also be triggered in other languages like Kotlin:

```kotlin
                                                         ─── Kotlin ───
println('A')
launch { println('B') }
println('C')
```

or JavaScript:

```javascript
                                                         ─── JavaScript ───
console.log('A');
Promise.resolve().then(() => console.log('B'));
console.log('C');
```

In the initial pseudocode, `println('B')` is a synchronous call: It takes place here and now, within the current run, between the printing of A and the printing of C. By contrast, the Scala line `Future(println('B'))`, the Kotlin line `launch { println('B') }`, and the JavaScript line `Promise.resolve().then(() => console.log('B'))` have the similar effect of invoking the printing of B asynchronously, not here and/or not now, out of the current flow of operations.

As a noncomputing analogy, if I order a sandwich and stand at the counter while the sandwich is being prepared in front of me, that's synchronous. If instead I place my order, get a number, and don't wait for the sandwich to be ready before leaving the counter, that's asynchronous.[1]

So, the three programs just shown are no longer sequential. Are they concurrent? The JavaScript program uses a single thread and guarantees that B will be printed after A and C, in an ACB order. The printing of B is not happening "now," but in a way it is still happening "here," within the same thread of execution. Given that the program is single-threaded, and that the ACB order is guaranteed, you can even argue that the execution is still sequential, only in a different order.

---

[1]In this case, it is also multithreaded, unless I'm being asked to make the sandwich myself when I come back to the counter to pick it up.

Is concurrency, then, tied to the use of multiple threads? Depending on how they are configured, the example Scala and Kotlin programs may or may not rely on an additional thread to execute the printing of B. Can the same program be concurrent or not, depending on external configuration? Even if we assume that the Scala and Kotlin programs are configured to use multiple threads when `Future` or `launch` is invoked, does that necessarily make them concurrent? Consider these variants:

```scala
                                                          —————— Scala ——————
println('A')
Await.ready(Future(println('B')), Duration.Inf)
println('C')
```

```kotlin
                                                          —————— Kotlin ——————
println('A')
launch { println('B') }.join()
println('C')
```

Because of added synchronization, these programs, even when they use multiple threads, will print A, B, and C sequentially, in the ABC order. You could say that the printing of B is not taking place "here," in the current thread of execution, but it is still happening "now," between A and C. Does this make the programs sequential, or are they still concurrent? Are there multithreaded sequential programs?[2] Furthermore, even in the earlier, non-synchronized versions of the programs, A, B, and C are bound to be printed in *some* order, one at a time, sequentially. It's not as if two letters could end up on top of each other, or even on the same line. So, what is concurrent in these nominally non-sequential programs?

Let's modify the Scala program to use a slow printing function:

```scala
                                                          —————— Scala ——————
def slowPrint(x: Any) =
   var n = BigInt("1000000000")
   while n > 0 do n -= 1
   println(x)

slowPrint('A')
Future(slowPrint('B'))
slowPrint('C')
```

Printing each letter now takes time because it requires counting down from a large number using big integers. Using a single-threaded configuration, on the multicore computer

---

[2]You might argue that these last two examples are silly and artificial (they are). But more realistic illustrations exist. For instance, the code that handles incoming messages in actors (Section 27.5) is typically executed sequentially by multiple threads, one at a time.

used for typesetting this book, the program takes 7.6 seconds to complete and prints the
letters in the ACB order, like the JavaScript program. With a multithreaded configuration, the running time is reduced to 5.2 seconds, about two-thirds of the single-threaded
time. This is because the slow printing of B and the slow printing of C are now running
concurrently, inside two separate threads of execution. The time is reduced from

$$(\text{printing of A}) + (\text{printing of B}) + (\text{printing of C})$$

to

$$(\text{printing of A}) + \max((\text{printing of B}) + (\text{printing of C}))$$

Two of the computer's cores perform the slow countdown at the same time, in parallel,
even if the actual printing of the two letters on the terminal still happens sequentially,
B before C or C before B. In other words, there is concurrency at the level of two cores
executing big integer operations, but printing on a shared terminal remains sequential
(as it should), even when multiple threads are involved.

NOTE

At this point, you may expect the obligatory discussion of concurrency versus parallelism to take
place. In books and Internet blogs, this is often considered to be a fundamental point to be addressed
early on. I disagree. As definitive as the many explanations aim to be, they tend to be inconsistent
with one another. If you corner me, as students have, and insist that I make a distinction, my
view—inspired by the Association for Computing Machinery (ACM) *Computer Science Curricula
2013*—is that parallelism is the concurrency I want (for speed!), and concurrency is the parallelism
I need to deal with (all those things happening at the same time in my program). However, my
argument here is that it doesn't matter much. By and large, you face the same programming challenges whether you attribute them to parallelism or to concurrency. For the purposes of this book,
it is enough to stick with basic dictionary definitions and to think of parallelism and concurrency as
synonymous, both representing the idea of several actions taking place at (about) the same time.
In the following chapters, I use both terms interchangeably.

16.2   Concurrent Programming Concepts

The code snippets from Section 16.1 did not lead to a clear definition of what concurrency is, but they can still be used to illustrate several fundamental concepts of
concurrent programming, explored in the following chapters.

- *Asynchronicity* is what triggers out-of-order execution. Concurrent programs
  involve asynchronous operations, which deviate from the simpler, sequential programs all developers are familiar with: `println('B')` prints B synchronously;
  `Future(println('B'))` does it asynchronously, whether it introduces parallelism
  or not. When writing concurrent programs, you need to take into consideration

actions that do not happen "here" and "now," but instead elsewhere (another thread) or later, or both.

- *Threads of execution*, or *threads* for short, are a common source of concurrency in programs, but they are not the only one: Processes tend to run concurrently as well, and external events such as user clicks or incoming server connections also introduce concurrency. Furthermore, programmers often handle concurrency at non-thread levels—for instance, in terms of tasks, or futures, or actors, or coroutines.

- *Atomicity* defines elementary program units, the "parts" that can be executed out of order, or "at the same time." In the examples in Section 16.1, for instance, decrementing a `BigInt` by one is an atomic operation, but counting down from 1,000,000,000 to zero is not. Similarly, a letter is printed on the terminal, or it is not; it cannot be "partially printed." In contrast, printing multiple letters is not necessarily atomic. The single-threaded JavaScript program guarantees that the A and C lines form an atomic unit, with no possible B in between, while the Scala and Kotlin programs—when configured to use multiple threads—do not. As a programmer, you must be aware of what needs to be atomic in your program and of the atomicity guarantees of the languages and libraries with which you are programming.

- *Synchronization* is often needed to coordinate concurrent activities. You can use *synchronizers*, such as locks and semaphores, to reduce the concurrency of a program to a level that does not jeopardize the program's correctness. When synchronizers are misused—as I did earlier with Scala's `Await` and Kotlin's `join`—they can turn a concurrent program into a sequential one, or even prevent the program from running at all (see the discussion of deadlocks in Section 22.3).

- *Nondeterminism* is a natural consequence of concurrency and is the bane of concurrent programming. The most salient difference between the JavaScript program, on the one hand, and the Scala and Kotlin programs, on the other hand—when configured to be multithreaded, without additional synchronization—is that the former can produce the three letters in only one possible sequence, ACB, while the others may produce different sequences in different runs. The impact of such nondeterministic behaviors on testing and debugging is momentous.

16.3 Summary

There is no need to delve into a philosophical discussion of what constitutes concurrent programming to introduce several of the core concepts that underlie many programming language constructs, such as threads of executions, asynchronous calls, atomic actions, synchronization, and nondeterminism. The art of concurrent programming is to write programs that properly balance multiple facets of concurrency: Too many threads (or not enough) may impact performance; not enough synchronization (or too much) may impact correctness; atomicity is key to reasoning about concurrent systems, but non-determinism makes such reasoning difficult; and so on. The following chapters explore these intertwined concepts of concurrent programming through code illustrations in Scala, Java, and Kotlin.

NOTE

All of the code examples in this book rely on a JVM implementation of the languages. Although most examples from Part I would behave similarly on a different implementation—both Scala and Kotlin define an alternative, JavaScript-based implementation—this is less true of the code illustrations in Part II. Multithreading typically involves a close interaction with the operating system (OS). Threads, in particular, are often managed by the OS as lightweight processes. In the remainder of the book, the discussion of concurrent programming is predicated on a standard JVM running on a Unix system. Some comments and explanations would need to be adjusted if code is compiled and executed on a different platform, such as Android.

Chapter 17

Threads and Nondeterminism

Sequential programs have a single thread of execution. Programs can be made concurrent by creating additional threads so that multiple threads execute a program in parallel. How threads access hardware computing resources is typically orchestrated by a scheduler—often in the operating system—which is not under a programmer's control. As a result, and in the absence of additional synchronization, the exact order in which multiple threads jointly execute their instructions is unpredictable. Consequently, multithreaded programs tend to exhibit nondeterministic behavior. This nondeterminism vastly complicates testing and debugging.

17.1 Threads of Execution

A thread of execution—or *thread*, for short—represents the execution of a series of instructions. Programs often start with a single thread[1] and terminate when this thread is finished. The program

```scala
                                                              ── Scala ──
import tinyscalautils.text.{ println, threadTimeDemoMode }

println("START")
println("END")
```

produces an output of the following form:

```
main at XX:XX:14.216: START
main at XX:XX:14.217: END
```

This program relies on a `println` function that is defined to add thread and timing information to the message being displayed.[2] Here, a thread called "main," created and started by the JVM, executes both statements in sequence, within a few milliseconds, at which point the program ends and the JVM terminates.

To create additional threads (besides `main`), Java defines a `Thread` class, and JVM languages rely on Java's mechanisms for thread creation. You instantiate the `Thread`

---

[1]More precisely, user code is executed within a single thread of execution. Typically, a JVM uses additional threads for garbage collection, just-in-time compilation, and other operations.

[2]In the following chapters, many code examples use this modified `println` function—or its `printf` variant—without importing it explicitly.

class by passing to its constructor an argument of type `Runnable`, an interface with a single method `run`. When started, the newly created thread executes this `run` method, then terminates:

```scala
println("START")

class LetterPrinter(letter: Char) extends Runnable:
    def run(): Unit = println(letter)

val tA = Thread(LetterPrinter('A'))
val tB = Thread(LetterPrinter('B'))
val tC = Thread(LetterPrinter('C'))

tA.start()
tB.start()
tC.start()

println("END")
```

Listing 17.1: Example of a multithreaded program.

This program defines a runnable class `LetterPrinter`, and instantiates it three times to create three threads, `tA`, `tB`, and `tC`, which are then started. The program produces an output of the form:

```
main at XX:XX:42.767: START
Thread-0 at XX:XX:42.789: A
Thread-2 at XX:XX:42.789: C
Thread-1 at XX:XX:42.789: B
main at XX:XX:42.789: END
```

The `START` and `END` messages are printed by the main thread, as before. Letters A, B, and C are printed by three different threads, named `Thread-0`, `Thread-1`, and `Thread-2`, respectively. When you invoke `start` on `tA`, `tB`, and `tC`, you effectively introduce parallelism in the system. After the three new threads are started, there are four running threads in the program—main, `Thread-0`, `Thread-1`, and `Thread-2`—and all the printing statements (A, B, C, and END) happen together at about the same time.

It is good practice to name threads as they are created. This makes it easier to read logs and thread dumps (see Section 22.4). To name them, you could create the three threads `tA`, `tB`, and `tC` as shown here:

```scala
val tA = Thread(LetterPrinter('A'), "printerA")
val tB = Thread(LetterPrinter('B'), "printerB")
val tC = Thread(LetterPrinter('C'), "printerC")
```

17.2   Creating Threads Using Lambda Expressions

Section 9.5 discussed the implementation of single-abstract-method (SAM) interfaces using lambda expressions. Since `Runnable` is a SAM interface, you can use lambda expressions to generate threads. Threads `tA`, `tB`, and `tC` could be created without class `LetterPrinter`:

```scala
val tA = Thread(() => println('A'), "printerA")
val tB = Thread(() => println('B'), "printerB")
val tC = Thread(() => println('C'), "printerC")
```

Listing 17.2: Example of creating threads using lambda expressions.

Java's lambda expressions and method references can be used as well:

```java
void printB() {
  println('B');
}

var tA = new Thread(() -> println('A'), "printerA");
var tB = new Thread(this::printB, "printerB");
```

17.3   Nondeterminism of Multithreaded Programs

Let's modify the program from Listing 17.1 to name its threads and run it three times in succession. You might observe outputs such as these:

```
main at XX:XX:30.563: START
printerC at XX:XX:30.585: C
printerA at XX:XX:30.585: A
printerB at XX:XX:30.585: B
main at XX:XX:30.585: END
```

```
main at XX:XX:51.482: START
printerA at XX:XX:51.505: A
printerB at XX:XX:51.505: B
main at XX:XX:51.505: END
printerC at XX:XX:51.505: C
```

```
main at XX:XX:38.261: START
main at XX:XX:38.283: END
printerB at XX:XX:38.283: B
printerA at XX:XX:38.283: A
printerC at XX:XX:38.283: C
```

Of particular interest is the fact that the three letters are printed in CAB order in the first run, but in ABC and BAC order in the next two. This is an illustration of the non-determinism of multithreaded programs.

When the `start` method is called on a `Thread` object, the runtime needs to create an actual thread—often a lightweight process managed by the OS—and schedule it for execution. How the runtime schedules threads is not under a programmer's control. A scheduler allocates runtime quorums to threads in ways that are unknown at the level of an application. When I ran the demo program, my computer reported 2985 active threads—most of them outside the JVM—sharing eight processor cores. All the running threads are constantly swapped in and out of execution at times you don't know and can't choose. As a consequence, you cannot know exactly when your threads execute their instructions and for how long before they are suspended by the OS to let other threads run. The exact order in which the letters are printed by the example program is unpredictable and typically varies from run to run.

Notice also that in the last two runs, the main thread terminates before the printing is complete. After the main thread invokes `start` on another thread, it continues its own run, and the runnable target is executed later, inside a separate thread. Because there are other active threads, the JVM keeps running after the main thread is finished. It stops only after all the threads are terminated.[3]

17.4   Thread Termination

Once started, a thread keeps running until the end of the `run` method specified in its runnable task. For a thread to terminate, the `run` method must be completed, either normally or abruptly through an exception. There is no way to forcibly terminate a thread from another thread. Instead, you need to signal a thread that it should end its run, giving it a chance to clean up resources and shared data before terminating. Keep in mind, however, that a thread that chooses to ignore such signals will keep running, possibly preventing termination of the JVM.

---

[3] Java also has a notion of *daemon* threads that do not prevent JVM termination, but they are seldom used.

A common strategy for graceful termination is as follows:

```scala
                                                          ──── Scala ────
object task extends Runnable:
   @volatile private var continue = true

   def terminate() = continue = false

   def run() =
      while continue do
         // perform task
      end while
      // cleanup
end task

val runner = Thread(task, "Runner")
runner.start()
// other code while runner is running
task.terminate()
```

Listing 17.3: Requesting thread termination using a volatile flag.

The **runner** thread keeps executing code from its task while regularly checking a flag, named **continue** here. Thread termination is requested by setting this flag to false.

This pattern for thread termination is adequate as long as there is no danger of the thread getting "stuck" somewhere in the loop, unable to test the termination flag. This can happen because of synchronization (e.g., a thread blocked on a lock or some other synchronizer) or I/O (e.g., a thread blocked reading data from an empty socket). Dealing with termination in the presence of blocking operations can be quite tricky and is a topic left for a more advanced discussion.

Variable **continue** must be made *volatile* because it is shared among threads without any form of synchronization (see Section 22.5 on the Java Memory Model). Volatile variables are an advanced concept that you can safely ignore until you decide to dive more deeply into concurrent programming. A termination flag like **continue** is the most common use of a volatile variable outside advanced programming patterns.

The call **task.terminate()** is a request for termination, but the thread running the task will continue to run until (and unless) it checks the **continue** flag, executes its cleanup code, and completes the **run** method, at which point the task can be considered done and its state usable by the main thread. There is a frequent need for a thread to wait until another thread is finished—for instance, a supervisor thread waiting for a worker thread to complete its task. You can use thread method **join** for this purpose.

Listing 17.1 can be modified to make the main thread pause until the three printing threads are finished:

```scala
...

tA.join()
tB.join()
tC.join()

println("END")
```

Listing 17.4: Waiting for thread termination without a timeout; see also Lis. 17.5.

With the added calls to `join`, the main thread will not reach its final print statement until the other three threads are terminated, thus guaranteeing that the END message appears last—the A, B, and C messages can still appear in any order. Some of the nondeterminism of the program execution is thus reduced by the use of additional inter-thread synchronization, a topic that is discussed in more detail in Chapter 22.

A variant of `join` is also available with a timeout. You must use it in conjunction with `isAlive`:

```scala
runner.join(500) // timeout in milliseconds
if runner.isAlive then
    // handle timeout case
else
    // runner is terminated
```

Listing 17.5: Waiting for thread termination with a timeout.

The invocation `runner.join(500)` blocks the calling thread until thread **runner** terminates or 500 milliseconds has elapsed, whichever comes first.

Method `join` is often used to implement a pattern, known as *fork-join* or *scatter-gather*, in which a thread creates several worker threads, starts them on their tasks (scatter), and waits for their termination to assemble the results (gather). Variations of this fundamental pattern are explored in later sections, notably when waiting on tasks instead of threads in Section 22.2 and when scheduling a gathering of results without waiting for task completion in Chapters 26 and 27.

17.5   Testing and Debugging Multithreaded Programs

Testing and debugging of multithreaded programs is notoriously difficult. This difficulty stems mainly from nondeterministic behavior. Many runs of an incorrect program can perform satisfactorily, and you may have to repeat a test thousands (or millions) of times to trigger an incorrect behavior. This situation creates a double headache for developers:

- *Testing:* You can test a program successfully a million times, only to have it fail on the next run of the tests—or even in production—because of an unfortunate timing of the executions of threads. It can even be that the circumstances needed for such an unfortunate timing exist only in the environment in which the application is deployed, perhaps due to specific data (which impact running times) or the presence of other activities running on the same hardware.

- *Debugging:* After you observe a failure (in testing or in production), it can be difficult to reproduce it: The next execution of the exact same run may now appear to be working. This complicates debugging tremendously. Even when you can reproduce a failure, it is often the case that the faulty scenario involves high levels of concurrency (e.g., hundreds of threads), which makes it very difficult to track bugs. Even worse, any step you apply in the debugging process (breakpoints, logging, etc.) impacts the synchronization and the timing of threads and can make the bug undetectable (see the aside on "Heisenbugs" at the end of Section 18.3).

While there is no silver bullet for testing and debugging multithreaded programs, it helps to keep a few basic principles in mind:

- *Avoid premature optimization.* This advice is usually valid for single-threaded code, but in the case of multithreaded programs, it is even more important that you start with safe, straightforward strategies that are easy to understand. This will make it less challenging to reason about, maintain, and modify code. One thing to keep in mind is that concurrent programs are harder to test than sequential programs, and you cannot rely as much on a safety net of tests to catch breaking changes.

- *Maximize concurrency when testing.* It is not enough to try "reasonable" scenarios when testing a concurrent application. Bugs are likely to be triggered by unusual or even extreme timing—for instance, due to tasks that are uncommonly short or uncommonly long. To generate a broad variety of interleaving of actions, you should strive to test programs with high levels of concurrency. It is not uncommon for a test to run successfully with a dozen threads and to start failing when a hundred threads are used.[4] It is equally important to make sure that larger thread counts do, in fact, increase concurrency. A common mistake is to introduce an artificial bottleneck (e.g., a logging data structure, a pseudo-random generator) that serializes operations and prevents threads from running as concurrently as they should.

The `Thread` class defines a static method `yield`,[5] which is, according to its documentation, "a hint to the scheduler that the current thread is willing to yield

---

[4]This does not mean that the program is correct with a dozen threads and incorrect with a hundred, but only that the fault is easier to trigger and observe with a hundred threads.

[5]This method has nothing to do with Scala's for-yield construct. However, because `yield` is a keyword in Scala, the `Thread.yield` method needs to be invoked as `Thread.'yield'()`.

its current use of a processor." While testing, you can insert calls to `yield` in a program in an attempt to increase the number of ways actions are interleaved in a run. (Section 18.3 on atomicity discusses examples of suitable uses of `yield`.) Because threads can always be suspended at any time by the scheduler, using `yield` does not produce scenarios that were not already possible, and therefore added calls to `yield` should never cause a fault in a correct program.

- *Name threads and log fine-grain activities.* It is hard enough to cause an incorrect concurrent program to fail using tests. It is even harder to figure out the sequence of steps that caused the failure, especially when many threads are involved. Detailed logging information—which unfortunately grows with the number of threads—is often necessary to pinpoint a synchronization mistake. When logging, you can access information on the thread that is executing a code fragment by using the Java static method `Thread.currentThread`.

- *Complement testing with static analysis tools.* Static analysis techniques can be applied at the design, source code, or compiled code level, and many such techniques are primarily focused on concurrency issues. Because they do not rely on the nondeterministic occurrence of a particular series of runtime steps, they can often discover bugs that have escaped other forms of testing. (See the aside on model checking at the end of Section 23.4.)

17.6   Summary

- By default, many programs are single-threaded. Concurrency/parallelism is introduced by creating additional threads of execution. Threads can then run concurrently within the same program and interact with each others.

- JVM languages rely on Java's `Thread` class to create threads. An instance of this class is a regular object, with methods and fields. However, when its `start` method is invoked, a new (real) thread of execution is created. This thread is typically implemented as a lightweight process of the operating system, but could also be handled directly by a JVM.

- The behavior of a new thread is specified by an object with a no-argument `run` method, which contains the code to be executed by the thread. This object can often be implemented as a function, using a lambda expression syntax.

- Threads terminate when they reach the end of their code, either normally or abruptly through an exception. Threads can wait for the termination of other threads via a method `join`, which is often used by a supervisor thread to wait for completion of worker threads. A JVM terminates when all its application threads are finished.

- Threads need to share computing resources with other computer activities, including threads from other processes outside the JVM. A scheduling mechanism, typically part of the operating system, is in charge of allocating computing time to all the threads. Threads are thus suspended—to let other threads run—and later resumed in ways that are not under the control of the application. This unpredictable scheduling of threads tends to make multithreaded programs nondeterministic: The same program, on the same input, can exhibit different behaviors in successive runs.

- Nondeterminism often makes testing and debugging of multithreaded programs very tricky. A given test may succeed or fail unpredictably, and faulty scenarios can be hard to reproduce when debugging. Bugs that are exhibited only rarely and in the presence of many threads can be very hard to track.

Chapter 18

Atomicity and Locking

During the execution by a thread of a compound operation that consists of multiple steps, other threads can observe and interfere with the state of an application as it exists between these steps. By contrast, an atomic operation consists of a single step, with no possibility of disruption during that step. Locking is a mechanism that can be used to make a compound operation by a thread appear atomic to other threads, thereby preventing them from interfering during its execution in ways that would be detrimental to correctness. Different systems define their own locking mechanisms. In particular, Java defines a basic form of locks that can be used with any JVM language.

18.1 Atomicity

Chapter 17 discussed a program in which three threads shared a terminal to output the letters A, B, and C. The three letters could appear in different orders from run to run, and this nondeterminism was due to the unpredictable scheduling of threads.

Consider this variant in which, instead of sharing a terminal, two threads (in addition to main) share an integer value:[1]

```scala
// DON'T DO THIS!
var shared = 0

def add(n: Int): Unit = n times (shared += 1)

val t1 = Thread(() => add(5), "T1")
val t2 = Thread(() => add(5), "T2")

t1.start(); t2.start()
t1.join(); t2.join()

println(shared)
```

Listing 18.1: Multiple threads share an integer unsafely.

---

[1] Function `times` is used to repeat code n times. It was defined in Listing 12.4.

Two threads are started by the main thread. Each thread increments a shared integer five times. The main thread waits for completion of all the increment operations and then prints the value of the shared integer.

On its first run, the program's output was

```
main at XX:XX:19.251: 10
```

In my experiment, the output was similar on the next run and, using a loop to repeat execution, in the next 3189 runs. The 3190th run, however, produced this output:

```
main at XX:XX:26.180: 7
```

The remaining 96,810 runs all produced the value 10. In other words, two threads performing five increments each increase the value of a shared integer by 10 most of the time, but not always.

Looking at the bytecode[2] resulting from the compilation of **shared += 1** can be informative:

```
                                                                ─ bytecode ─

0: aload 1
1: getfield      #92                   // Field scala/runtime/IntRef.elem:I
4: iconst_1
5: iadd
6: istore 2
7: aload 1
8: iload 2
9: putfield      #92                   // Field scala/runtime/IntRef.elem:I
```

Field 92 corresponds to variable **shared** in Listing 18.1. The bytecode shows that the field is read from memory (**getfield**), incremented by one (**iconst_1/iadd**), and the new value stored in memory (**putfield**).

When threads T1 and T2 execute this code concurrently, the scenario depicted in Figure 18.1 is possible. In this scenario, T2 reads the same value of **shared** read by T1 (say, 3), also increments it to 4 (as T1 did), and writes 4 back into **shared**. After both threads have completed their execution of **shared += 1**, the value has changed from 3 to 4, and an increment has been lost. Because of overlapping read/write sequences by separate threads during a run, you can end up with a final value of **shared** that is less than 10, like the value 7 observed in the 3190th run.

This example illustrates that incrementing an integer variable is not an atomic operation. It is implemented using multiple instructions—at least reading, incrementing, and writing back—and those steps can end up being interleaved among multiple threads in arbitrary ways.

---

[2]Of course, the bytecode could be different with another compiler and is often recompiled into machine code by the JVM's just-in-time compilers anyway. Nonetheless, looking at it helps emphasize the non-atomicity of an integer increment.

shared=3

Thread T1	Thread T2
aload 1	
getfield #92 ⟶ 3	
iconst_1	
iadd	aload 1
istore 2	getfield #92 ⟶ 3
aload 1	iconst_1
iload 2	iadd
putfield #92 ⟵ 4	istore 2
	aload 1
	iload 2
	putfield #92 ⟵ 4

shared=4

Figure 18.1 Possible interleaving of two increment operations.

18.2 Non-atomic Operations

If something as basic as incrementing an integer is not atomic, very few functions and methods can be expected to run atomically when executed by multiple threads. This has important consequences for the multithreaded behavior of code designed with a single thread in mind: Simply put, it doesn't work.

For instance, you can modify the previous program to share a Java list instead of an integer:

Scala

```scala
// DON'T DO THIS!
val shared = ArrayList[String]()

def addStrings(n: Int, str: String): Unit = n times shared.add(str)

val t1 = Thread(() => addStrings(5, "T1"), "T1")
val t2 = Thread(() => addStrings(5, "T2"), "T2")

t1.start(); t2.start()
t1.join(); t2.join()

println(shared.size)
```

Listing 18.2: Multiple threads share a list unsafely; fixed in Lis. 18.5.

As before, some runs display a size of 10 for the list at the end, while others finish with fewer than ten elements. If you think about it, somewhere in the implementation of `ArrayList`, an index needs to be incremented to fill the next slot in the array. Since integer increments are not atomic and can produce incorrect values in a multithreaded context, it is not surprising that multiple threads calling method `add` at the same time can overwrite each other, resulting in lost values.

If you run the program enough times, it will also exhibit another interesting behavior. The 6,402,829th run in my experiment produced an exception in thread `T1`:

```
Exception in thread "T1" java.lang.ArrayIndexOutOfBoundsException:
  Index 3 out of bounds for length 0
    at java.base/java.util.ArrayList.add(ArrayList.java:455)
  ...
```

An examination of the source code of the class `ArrayList` used in the test suggests an explanation. Lists are created using an empty array with zero capacity. When a first element is added to a list, this array is replaced with a newly allocated array (with a capacity of 10). In the failed run shown here, thread `T2` created this new array and used it to insert three values into the list. Because class `ArrayList` does not include any mechanism for synchronization, thread `T1` then tried to insert its first value (4th list element, at index 3) into the previous array, with zero capacity.

Functions typically consist of multiple statements, and most statements consist of even more elementary instructions at the machine code level. These can be interleaved in arbitrary ways by independent threads. As a result, code that was not designed to handle such interleaving is likely to break when instances are shared among threads. In particular, and with very few exceptions (`Random` is one), most classes in `java.util` are not safe for multithreaded use without synchronization. If you improperly share instances of classes such as `HashMap` and `PriorityQueue` between threads, they will exhibit unpredictable behavior similar to what was demonstrated using `ArrayList`.

Note that the programs being tested in this experiment were designed to fail, and they still can appear to behave correctly in thousands of successive runs. In these programs, threads interact in unrealistic ways, modifying shared data as often as possible, which increases the chances for an undesirable interaction. In an actual application, threads will perform independent work and only occasionally access a shared data structure at the same time. Failures will be more infrequent and harder to produce but still potentially devastating.

18.3 Atomic Operations and Non-atomic Composition

Some operations are guaranteed to be atomic. For instance, reading or writing a primitive `int` on the JVM is atomic: A thread will never see "half" an integer, or a mixture of bits from two separate integers. As we have seen, however, code that combines multiple atomic operations—such as reading and then writing to implement an increment—is not atomic by default.

As an illustration, consider the problem of assigning a unique rank to users as they register for a service: The first user gets rank 1, the next user rank 2, and so on. You can implement registration by incrementing a `userCount` value with each incoming user. However, if you want it to work correctly when a service is shared among threads, you cannot write the increment as `userCount += 1`, which is not atomic. Instead, you would need to rely on a different type, one that implements an atomic increment. Java defines a class `AtomicInteger` for this purpose:

```scala
                                                                    Scala
private val userCount = AtomicInteger(0)

// DON'T DO THIS!
def getRank(): Int =
   userCount.increment()
   userCount.get
```

A single atomic integer is created and initialized with zero. The `getRank` function increments this integer using a method `increment`, which is designed to be safe when called by multiple threads. This way, all the registrations are guaranteed to be recorded—no lost increments as occurred earlier—and after ten users register, the value of `userCount` will be 10.

However, the program is still incorrect. It does not satisfy the desired property that all users are assigned unique ranks. A scenario is possible in which two users, say the third and fourth, register at about the same time. Both threads execute `userCount.increment()`, which brings the counter value to 3, then to 4. Both threads then execute `userCount.get`, which returns the value 4 for both, and both users end up with identical ranks (Figure 18.2).

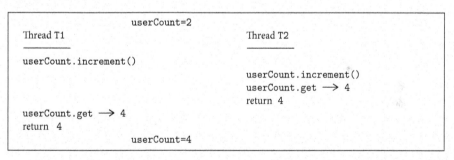

Figure 18.2 Possible interleaving of two non-atomic compound actions.

The increment that took multiple steps with a regular integer has become atomic, but in `getRank`, incrementing *and* getting the incremented value are still two separate steps. Indeed, Java's class `AtomicInteger` does not define an `increment` method; I added it only for the purposes of this illustration. Instead, the class defines a method `incrementAndGet`, which first increments the integer, then returns the incremented value, all in one atomic step. This is exactly what you need to implement `getRank`:

```scala
                                                              ──────── Scala ───

private val userCount = AtomicInteger(0)

def getRank(): Int = userCount.incrementAndGet()
```

Listing 18.3: Using an `AtomicInteger` to generate unique values.

Consider now this variant of the problem in which only the first five users are allowed to register. Registration success or failure is indicated by returning an option:

```scala
                                                              ──────── Scala ───

// DON'T DO THIS!
def getRank(): Option[Int] =
  if userCount.get < 5 then Some(userCount.incrementAndGet()) else None
```

Listing 18.4: Example of non-atomic check-then-act; fixed in Lis. 18.7.

This variant is incorrect. The use of `incrementAndGet` guarantees that ranks will be unique. However, this code makes it possible for more than five users to register. A possible scenario is depicted in Figure 18.3. The failure is caused by two threads checking the condition `userCount.get < 5` at the same time. The issue here is the non-atomicity of the test and the action that follows it, which still take two steps: one to check that a value is less than five, then another to increment it and return the incremented value. Class `AtomicInteger` does not define a method that executes the whole computation—check, increment, and get—in one atomic step.[3]

```
                            userCount=4
Thread T1                                   Thread T2
─────────                                   ─────────

userCount.get < 5 ──→ true

                                            userCount.get < 5 ──→ true
                                            userCount.incrementAndGet() ──→ 5
                                            return Some(5)

userCount.incrementAndGet() ──→ 6
return Some(6)
                            userCount=6
```

Figure 18.3 Possible interleaving of two non-atomic check-then-act.

Non-atomic check-then-act is a common source of concurrency bugs. You should always think carefully when you write a conditional in a multithreaded program. With practice, it becomes second nature to start thinking about threads switched out of execution right after an `if`, before the `then` or `else` code.

You can show that the two flawed `getRank` implementations are incorrect by writing a test in which multiple threads call the function at the same time. The test succeeds

---

[3] `AtomicInteger` does define a method that can be used to check the current value and then modify it in a single atomic step. It is reserved for advanced usage, and is illustrated in Chapter 27.

sometimes, but sometimes fails. It fails when the atomic integer is accessed by another thread between `increment` and `get` (first example), or between `if` and `then` (the second example). You can make these failures more likely by inserting calls to `Thread.yield` (see Section 17.5) in the code of function `getRank`:

```scala
def getRank(): Int =
   userCount.increment()
   Thread.`yield`()
   userCount.get()

def getRank(): Option[Int] =
   if userCount.get() < 5 then
      Thread.`yield`()
      Some(userCount.incrementAndGet())
   else None
```

With added calls to `Thread.yield`, the test fails much more frequently. By contrast, adding calls to `Thread.yield` in a correct program should never break it. It is often a good testing strategy to insert such calls in places where a thread losing control of the CPU is thought to potentially be unsafe; correct code should continue to behave correctly.

Aside: Example of a Heisenbug

Consider this modified version of Listing 18.2:

```scala
val shared = ArrayList[String]()

def addStrings(n: Int, str: String): Unit =
   var added = 0
   while added < n do
      if shared.size >= 2 * added then
         shared.add(str)
         added += 1

val t1 = Thread(() => addStrings(5, "T1"), "T1")
val t2 = Thread(() => addStrings(5, "T2"), "T2")

t1.start(); t2.start()
t1.join(); t2.join()

println(shared.size)
```

In this variant, each thread checks that it is not too far ahead of the other thread before adding a value into the shared list. A thread adds a new item to the list only if the list is at least twice as long as the number of items already added by that thread. When run on my computer, this program prints nothing and keeps running.

In an attempt to help debug the problem, you can log the value of variable `added` using a simple print statement:

Scala

```
...
while added < n do
    println(added)
    if shared.size >= 2 * added then
...
```

Remarkably, this modified program does terminate, with the expected output:

```
T1 at XX:XX:28.543: 0
T2 at XX:XX:28.543: 0
T1 at XX:XX:28.543: 1
T2 at XX:XX:28.543: 1
T1 at XX:XX:28.544: 2
T2 at XX:XX:28.544: 2
T1 at XX:XX:28.544: 3
T2 at XX:XX:28.544: 3
T2 at XX:XX:28.544: 4
T1 at XX:XX:28.544: 4
main at XX:XX:28.544: 10
```

Note that this program is still incorrect: A `java.util.ArrayList`, which is not a thread-safe structure, is shared among threads without synchronization. However, the bug no longer manifests itself. Commenting out the print statement and running the program results again in nontermination. Such bugs, which disappear when observed, are sometimes facetiously called *Heisenbugs*.

18.4 Locking

The incorrect code examples so far in this chapter all make the same mistake: Threads share mutable data without proper synchronization. There are different approaches to solving this problem, some of which are discussed in later chapters, but locking remains one of the most commonly used techniques to synchronize thread manipulation of shared data.

The basic principle of locking is to guard portions of code (such as functions and methods) with locks that need to be acquired before running the code. The most common form of lock is the exclusive lock, which can be acquired by only one thread at a time. When a thread acquires an exclusive lock, the thread is said to own the lock. Ownership ceases when the lock is released by the thread. While a thread owns an exclusive lock, the lock is not available to other threads. Any attempt by another thread to acquire the lock is denied, usually by blocking the requesting thread until the lock becomes available.

In Listing 18.2, two threads add strings into a shared list, leading to undesirable behaviors and incorrect output. To fix the problem, one strategy could be to have each thread acquire an exclusive lock before it can add a string to the list:

```
                                                    ── pseudocode ──
exclusiveLock.lock()
shared.add(str)
exclusiveLock.unlock()
```

Because the lock is exclusive, you cannot have two threads inside the list's **add** method at the same time. Instead, one thread must complete the execution of the entire call to **add** before it releases the lock and another threads starts the method again. In effect, method **add** now appears to be atomic: It is not possible for a thread to partially run the method and have another thread come in. In particular, the intermediate states that the list can have while a thread is executing **add** are not visible to other threads— assuming the list is not used elsewhere in the application.

18.5 Intrinsic Locks

The JVM defines its own basic form of exclusive locks, called intrinsic locks. (Other types of locks are discussed in Section 23.1.) In Scala, intrinsic locks are acquired and released by a method **synchronized**, which takes its code argument by name, unevaluated (see Section 12.2):

```
                                                          ── Scala ──
lock.synchronized(shared.add(str))
```

or

```
                                                          ── Scala ──
lock.synchronized {
  shared.add(str)
}
```

(Recall that Scala lets you invoke a single argument function using braces instead of parentheses.) The lock is acquired upon entry into the specified code fragment and released when the thread exits this code, either normally or by throwing an exception. While a thread is inside the **synchronized** method, the lock is not available, and other threads attempting to acquire it will be blocked. The value `lock` must be a reference to an object. Any Java object can be used as a lock.[4]

The incorrect list sharing program of Listing 18.2 can be fixed using an intrinsic lock:

```scala
val shared = ArrayList[String]()

def addStrings(n: Int, str: String): Unit =
  n times {
      shared.synchronized(shared.add(str))
  }

val t1 = Thread(() => addStrings(5, "T1"), "T1")
val t2 = Thread(() => addStrings(5, "T2"), "T2")

t1.start(); t2.start()
t1.join(); t2.join()

println(shared.size)
```

Listing 18.5: Multiple threads share a list safely; fixed from Lis. 18.2.

Both threads need to lock the **shared** object before they can call its **add** method. Since only one thread can own the lock at any given time, it is now impossible for multiple threads to be inside the **add** method at the same time. The size of the list displayed at the end of the program is now guaranteed to be 10.

In Listing 18.5, the lock is acquired and released before and after each call to **add**. As an alternative, a thread could acquire the lock once and keep it while calling **add** multiple times:

```scala
def addStrings(n: Int, str: String): Unit = shared.synchronized {
  n times shared.add(str)
}
```

In this case, locking makes the entire function **addStrings** appear atomic: One thread adds all its strings to the list, followed by all the strings of the other thread. There will be no interleaving of "T1" and "T2" in the list.

Which function **addStrings** is right? It depends on the needs of your application. If, for instance, a list of strings is shared for the purpose of logging, and threads call the **add** method to add a logging message, locking each invocation of **add** separately might be the right choice. Conversely, if method **add** is used to add one line of a multiline logging message, you will probably have to synchronize a single block around multiple

---

[4]When using locks, you should stick to objects that you have allocated. Some objects are created implicitly by the JVM—for instance, to box primitive values—and cannot reliably be used as locks.

calls to **add**, since a log containing interleaved lines from different messages would be undesirable. You could even offer both functions as a choice to the user:

```scala
                                                                  Scala
def addStrings(n: Int, str: String): Unit =
  n times {
      shared.synchronized(shared.add(str))
  }

def addAllStrings(n: Int, str: String): Unit = shared.synchronized(addStrings(n, str))
```

Listing 18.6: Illustration of lock reentrancy.

Depending on their needs, users can now call **addStrings** for fine-grained parallelism or **addAllStrings** for coarse-grained parallelism. Note that calls to **addStrings** that originate from within **addAllStrings** already own the **shared** lock by the time they reach **shared.synchronized(shared.add(str))**. This is fine. The JVM intrinsic locks are reentrant, and a thread that owns a lock can enter other blocks of code synchronized on the same lock. A thread will release a lock only when it exits the outer block—in this example, when it finishes its call to **addAllStrings**.

You need to use locks judiciously to introduce enough atomicity for a program to be correct. If the code chunks made atomic by locking are small, they can be interleaved nondeterministically in many different ways, and all the possibilities need to be considered when asserting correctness. If the chunks are too small—three atomic steps to increment an integer, for instance—correctness might be lost. On the flip side, large atomic steps reduce parallelism because these steps must be executed sequentially, one thread at a time. This can have a negative impact on performance.

18.6 Choosing Locking Targets

The list sharing example was fixed by having threads lock the list itself, **shared**, before they could add strings to it. Locking was necessary, but the lock did not have to be the list. The only thing that matters is that a lock object is shared among threads and that all the threads synchronize by locking the same object.

Consider this variant of the program as a stand-alone application:

```scala
                                                                  Scala
object SharedListApplication:
  @main def run(msg: String, count: Int) =

      val msg1 = msg + "1"
      val msg2 = msg + "2"

      val shared = ArrayList[String]()
```

```scala
    class Adder(str: String):
      def addStrings(n: Int): Unit =
        n times {
          [          ].synchronized(shared.add(str))
        }

    val t1 = Thread(() => Adder(msg1).addStrings(count), "T1")
    val t2 = Thread(() => Adder(msg2).addStrings(count), "T2")

    t1.start(); t2.start()
    t1.join(); t2.join()

    println(shared.size)
end SharedListApplication
```

The object on which method `synchronized` is invoked is not specified. Several potential objects could be used. The lock could be the list `shared`, as before. But you could also use `SharedListApplication`, the object that defines the entire application, or `msg1`, the string used by the first thread, or even `scala.collection.immutable.Nil`, the object that represents an empty list. All these choices would result in a correct program.

Obviously though, some choices make more sense than others. In this example, using `shared` or `SharedListApplication` is reasonable. Using `msg1` would be confusing. Using `Nil` would be downright bizarre. The question of which objects to use as locks is revisited in more detail in Chapter 19. Note that if you choose `msg1`, the program works because both threads lock the same object, not each thread its own string. It is essential that all threads compete for the same lock to achieve the desired mutual exclusion. A possible mistake here would be to use `this` as the target of synchronization—that is, to simply write `synchronized(shared.add(str))`. In that case, each thread would lock its own `Adder` instance when writing into the shared list. Both instances could be locked at the same time, allowing the threads to enter the `add` method of the list together. In other words, setting code inside a synchronized block is not a guarantee that this code cannot be executed by multiple threads at the same time. It all depends on which object you use as the locking target.

In some cases, there is no obvious object to lock on. In these situations, you can create an additional object for this purpose. The program in Listing 18.4 is incorrect because of a non-atomic `if-then-else`. It can be fixed with an intrinsic lock:

```scala
                                                          Scala

private var userCount = 0

private val lock = Object()

def getRank(): Option[Int] = lock.synchronized {
  if userCount < 5 then
    userCount += 1
```

```
        Some(userCount)
    else None
}
```

Listing 18.7: Atomic check-then-act using locking; fixed from Lis. 18.4.

Because locking is necessary to make the `if-then-else` atomic, there is no issue with incrementing a regular integer and `AtomicInteger` is not needed.

Depending on the circumstances, you can choose to protect data with a single lock, or decide to split data in chunks guarded by separate locks. Assume, for instance, that the registered users of Listing 18.7 are players, and a function `play` can be called by a registered user to act in the game:

```scala
                                                            ─ Scala ─
def getRank(): Option[Int] = X.synchronized {
    // register user
}

def play(rank: Int): Unit = Y.synchronized {
    // act in the game
}
```

Depending on the internal design of the class, new user registration may or may not interfere with playing. If X and Y are references to the same object—X `eq` Y is true—the `getRank` and `play` functions are mutually exclusive: A thread inside one of the functions prevents other threads from entering the other function. If, however, X and Y refer to two distinct objects, a thread can be executing function `getRank` with the X lock owned, while another thread executes function `play` with the Y lock owned. Whether X and Y are the same object or two different objects, no two threads can execute `getRank` at the same time, and no two threads can execute `play` at the same time. Our next case study, in Chapter 20, explores different choices of the object used as a single lock and also discusses a two-lock variant of the same structure.

18.7 Summary

- JVM objects are allocated in a shared heap that all threads can access. If multiple threads have a reference to the same object, they can use it at the same time. However, the nondeterministic scheduling of threads makes it possible for them to be interrupted in the middle of an operation, possibly leaving data in a state that is not suitable for other threads to use. Mutable structures that were not designed with thread-safety in mind cannot be shared among threads without additional coordination, or they will fail in unpredictable ways. In particular, this is true of most collections from `java.util`.

- These failures are the result of an unpredictable interleaving of instructions in the executing code. Even conceptually simple operations, such as an integer increment, are implemented in terms of several smaller instructions. To prevent undesirable interleaving, a group of instructions can be made atomic. When an atomic operation is executed by a thread, either all of its effects or none at all are visible to other threads.

- Different data types offer different atomicity commitments. Writing an `Int`, incrementing an `AtomicInteger`, and calling `putIfAbsent` on a `ConcurrentHashMap`, for instance, are all guaranteed to be atomic in the presence of multiple threads. However, compound actions that use atomic operations may still involve unpredictable interleaving of elementary steps—incrementing an `Int`, incrementing an `AtomicInteger` only if less than a bound, and adding multiple key–value pairs to a `ConcurrentHashMap` are not atomic operations.

- The most common way to create atomic units of code is by locking. Exclusive locks, which are available to only one thread at a time, can be used to guarantee that blocks of code are mutually exclusive. Threads that need to execute code guarded by a lock need to acquire the lock first and may be blocked waiting for it to become available before they can proceed.

- Inside the JVM, any object can be used as an exclusive lock. These intrinsic locks are available at the language level, either as a function (Scala, Kotlin, Clojure), an annotation (Groovy), or a keyword (Java). Intrinsic locks are reentrant: A thread that owns a lock is not blocked when trying to acquire it again.

- Locked sections of code must be chosen carefully to ensure enough atomicity, as necessary for correctness, while not overly limiting parallelism. Large locked sections of code result in big atomic operations, which are easier to reason about, but concurrency is reduced because each locked section is executed sequentially.

- Locking targets—the locks themselves—must also be selected wisely. Code sections guarded by different locks can be executed in parallel, which may or may not be desirable depending on the details of an application. On the one hand, the same lock used for multiple purposes can prevent threads from making progress on independent tasks and can create a synchronization bottleneck. On the other hand, threads that synchronize on different locks can still interfere with each other when accessing shared data, with potentially undesirable outcomes.

Chapter 19

Thread-Safe Objects

The most common way threads interact is by sharing objects. Objects that can be freely shared without the need for threads to coordinate accesses are said to be thread-safe. Immutable objects are naturally thread-safe, but mutable objects need to rely on internal strategies to ensure thread-safety, often by locking. Different locking designs allow thread-safe objects to expose more or less of their synchronization strategy, resulting in a trade-off between flexibility and risk of misuse.

19.1   Immutable Objects

Earlier examples have shown that programs can easily behave incorrectly when data is shared by multiple threads. What all these examples have in common is that the data being shared is mutable: an integer variable declared as `var`, an instance of `AtomicInteger`, or a mutable list backed by an array.

Indeed, many of the difficulties of concurrent programming stem from sharing mutable data. Mutable objects are not naturally thread-safe because of unpredictable *write/write* and *read/write* concurrent accesses. By contrast, immutable objects are readable but not writable and can be freely shared among threads without additional synchronization.

The following example uses three threads to run a collection of tasks stored in an immutable data structure:

```scala
val tasksA: List[Runnable] = ...
val tasksB: List[Runnable] = ...

val duties: Map[Int, List[Runnable]] = Map(1 -> tasksA, 2 -> tasksB, 3 -> tasksB)

def runTasks(id: Int): Unit = for task <- duties(id) do task.run()

val t1 = Thread(() => runTasks(1), "T1")
val t2 = Thread(() => runTasks(2), "T2")
val t3 = Thread(() => runTasks(3), "T3")

t1.start(); t2.start(); t3.start()
```

Listing 19.1: Example of threads freely sharing immutable objects.

Tasks are stored in immutable lists, and the lists in an immutable map. As they run, all three threads access the map concurrently, and threads T2 and T3 also safely share the list `tasksB`. This is done without any locking or other synchronization.

You can greatly simplify the design of your multithreaded programs by avoiding shared mutable data, first by minimizing sharing—when possible, threads are better off working on their own data—and second by making shared data immutable as often as possible. In Part I of the book, we considered some of the advantages of immutability in the context of functional programming. Immutable objects are also tremendously beneficial to concurrent programming.

On the JVM, there is technically a difference between immutable objects and objects that are never mutated, due to a special treatment of final fields. Non-final fields (`var` fields in Scala) may require some form of initial synchronization before they can be freely read by any thread. This synchronization tends to happen naturally in clean, simple designs.[1] Still, it is good practice, when dealing with threads, to prefer `val` over `var`—or to add the `final` modifier in Java—for fields that are not intended for mutation. To decide if a non-final field of a never-mutated object can safely be read by a thread requires an understanding of the Java Memory Model (JMM), a somewhat advanced topic (see Section 22.5).

19.2   Encapsulating Synchronization Policies

You can freely share immutable objects among threads, but mutation of shared data requires that threads coordinate through synchronization, often in the form of exclusive locks. In Listing 18.5, for example, two threads were able to correctly share—and modify—a mutable list by locking the list before every access to it. As described in Section 18.6, the choice of locking the list itself is arbitrary. You could use any other object as a lock, as long as the object is shared and all the threads agree that this is the object to lock when accessing the list.

Relying on such an agreement is error-prone. It requires that user code always locks a specific lock before accessing an object, which can be checked only by considering all uses of the object throughout a code base. This is an onerous task if done manually.[2] It is like requiring that all modifications to an object's public fields maintain some invariant. This is not practical. Instead, good designs rely on data encapsulation, a key feature of object-oriented programming: Mutable fields tend to be private, and public methods are available to modify them.

You can use the same principle—encapsulation—to control inter-thread synchronization. Instead of specifying a synchronization policy that code needs to follow to

[1] For instance, the program in Listing 19.1 is still correct if the map is mutable and all the `val` are replaced with `var`, as long as the map is never mutated and the variables never reassigned.

[2] Indeed, some static analyzers do exactly this: When a value is almost always accessed with the same object locked, any access to the value without this lock is flagged as suspicious code.

access an object, you make the object itself encapsulate its own policy. Objects capable of enforcing their policy internally are thread-safe: The required thread coordination is implemented inside the object's methods, and threads can freely call these methods without further synchronization.

As an illustration, let's rewrite the list-sharing example with an encapsulated locking strategy:

```scala
                                                              ─ Scala ─
class SafeStringList:
  private val contents = ArrayList[String]()

  def add(str: String): Unit = synchronized(contents.add(str))
  def size: Int = synchronized(contents.size)
end SafeStringList

val shared = SafeStringList()

def addStrings(n: Int, str: String): Unit = n times shared.add(str)
```

Listing 19.2: Safe list that encapsulates synchronization; contrast with Lis. 18.5.

The array-based list, which is not thread-safe, is encapsulated inside a `SafeStringList` class. The inner list `contents` is private and accessed only via methods `add` and `size`. These methods implement the necessary synchronization by always locking `this` before they use the array list. You can now write function `addStrings` without any explicit synchronization.

Inside class `SafeStringList`, *both* methods use locking to access the inner list—not only `add`, which modifies the list, but also `size`, which just queries its size. This is extremely important: When mutable data is protected by a lock, *all* accesses to the data *must* go through the lock. This includes both writing and reading accesses.[3]

There are two main reasons for this requirement. First, locking when reading prevents undesirable *read/write* interactions. If read accesses are not locked, you could possibly observe intermediate, inconsistent states of a structure. Though unlikely in an array-based list, method `size` could be implemented by using a loop that traverses the list, and a list that is in the middle of a modification by a thread may not be in a state that is safe for another thread to perform this iteration. The second reason is more technical. It is a consequence of the Java Memory Model: Without locking when reading, there is no guarantee that a thread will see all the modifications to a structure that were made earlier by other threads, including data written with locks owned. The details are not essential, and the rule is simple: When locking, all accesses—writing *and* reading—must go through the same lock.

---

[3]Listing 18.5 correctly queries the size of the list at the end without locking, because the query is done after checking that both worker threads are terminated.

19.3   Avoiding Reference Escape

The encapsulation of synchronization in `SafeStringList` works because there is a corresponding encapsulation of data. You can ensure that all accesses to `contents` use the proper lock because there is no way to reach the data other than to go through method `add` or method `size`.

If a reference to `contents` were to escape encapsulation, threads could start reading and writing the list without locking:

```
                                                              ─ Scala ─

  // DON'T DO THIS!
  def getAll: List[String] = synchronized(contents)
```

With this method added, `SafeStringList` ceases to be thread-safe:

```
                                                              ─ Scala ─

  shared.getAll.add(...) // adds to the list without locking!
```

A thread that executes this code acquires the lock to obtain a reference to the inner list `contents`. However, the lock is released at the end of method `getAll`, *before* the thread calls `add`. In other words, the thread is now adding to the array-based list without the lock.

Of course, reference escape is often harmful in object-oriented designs and needs to be avoided even in single-threaded programs. However, multithreading tends to complicate the issue. This next variant of method `getAll` shares the `contents` list in a way that would be harmless in a single-threaded context but will still cause problems when multiple threads are involved:

```
                                                              ─ Scala ─

  // DON'T DO THIS!
  def getAll: List[String] = Collections.unmodifiableList(synchronized(contents))
```

The Java function `Collections.unmodifiableList` creates a wrapper that disables all the mutating methods of a list. It is often used to provide external code with read-only access to an internal list without breaking data encapsulation: User code can use the wrapper to query the list but cannot modify it. However, a thread that calls `shared.getAll.get(...)` would still be reading the list without locking. As discussed at the end of Section 19.2, this is unsafe because other threads might lock the list and modify it at the same time, causing concurrent *read/write* conflicts (in addition to memory model issues).

In short, some of the techniques you could use to maintain data encapsulation in a single-threaded context are inadequate in the presence of multiple threads. You can still write a thread-safe variant of method `getAll`, but at the cost of a full copy of the list:

```scala
                                                                    ── Scala ──
def getAll: List[String] = ArrayList(synchronized(contents))
```

Such defensive copies can often be avoided by implementing mutable objects in terms of immutable data structures. This was discussed in Section 3.8, and Section 19.5 will revisit the topic in the context of multiple threads.

19.4 Public and Private Locks

In the implementation of `SafeStringList` in Listing 19.2, the wrapper itself is used as the lock. This design choice makes the lock public—code that uses a `SafeStringList` can access the lock directly—and offers the benefit of client-side locking.

For instance, you can write a function to add elements up to a maximum size:

```scala
                                                                    ── Scala ──
val shared: SafeStringList = ...

def addStringIfCapacity(str: String, bound: Int): Boolean = shared.synchronized {
    if shared.size >= bound then false
    else
        shared.add(str)
        true
}
```

Listing 19.3: Example of client-side locking.

This function adds a string to the `shared` list only if the size of the list remains within a given bound. It is similar to function `getRank` in Listing 18.7 and requires locking for the same reason—atomicity of check-then-act. Such locking is made possible by the fact that the lock used internally in the implementation of methods `add` and `size` has been made public (and is reentrant).

Three main difficulties must be considered when using public locks. First is the issue of documentation: It needs to clearly state which lock is used and becomes binding afterwards, preventing future implementations from using another (public or private) lock instead. As an example, the documentation of Java's `Collections.synchronizedList`—a standard library function similar to `SafeStringList`—specifies that "It is imperative that the user manually synchronize on the returned list when traversing it," thus indicating that the wrapper itself is the lock that is used internally.

Second, public locks involve a risk of being misused by code that locks the list when it should not. A thread that executes code of the form

```scala
shared.synchronized {
    // lengthy computation, or I/O, or other blocking calls...
}
```

prevents other threads from accessing the **shared** list in any way, even just to query its size, possibly for a long time.

Third and finally, public locking is viable only when using simple synchronization policies—**SafeStringList** uses a single lock. It ceases to be workable with more complex strategies, such as lock striping (e.g., `java.util.concurrent.ConcurrentHashMap`) and lock-free algorithms (e.g., `java.util.concurrent.ConcurrentLinkedQueue`).

To circumvent these difficulties, locks can be kept private:

```scala
class SafeStringList:
    private val contents = ArrayList[String]()

    def add(str: String): Unit = contents.synchronized(contents.add(str))
    def size: Int = contents.synchronized(contents.size)
```

Listing 19.4: Safe list based on a private lock; contrast with Lis. 19.2.

This implementation of **SafeStringList** is just as thread-safe as before but uses a private object, the inner list, as a lock. The drawback, of course, is that external functions that require an atomic iteration or an atomic check-then-act cannot be written. A function like **addStringIfCapacity** from Listing 19.3 is no longer possible because it has no access to **contents** for locking. As an alternative, you can enrich **SafeStringList** to offer additional atomic operations, but users will be limited to what the class defines.

19.5   Leveraging Immutable Types

This chapter began with the observation that immutable structures are naturally thread-safe. It is also true that mutable objects can often be implemented in terms of immutable data stored in reassignable fields (see Section 4.1 for an example). This dual observation yields the following thread-safe `SafeStringList` implementation:[4]

```scala
                                                              ─ Scala ─
class SafeStringList:
   private var contents = List.empty[String]

   def add(str: String): Unit = synchronized(contents ::= str)
   def size: Int = synchronized(contents.size)
   def getAll: List[String] = synchronized(contents)
```

Listing 19.5: Safe list based on an immutable list; contrast with Lis. 19.2 and 19.4.

The `List` type refers here to Scala's lists, and `contents` is now an immutable list. Instead of a `val`, the list is stored into a `var` field so it can be reassigned. You add elements by setting `contents` to a new list—`contents ::= str` is the same as `contents = str :: contents`. An interesting aspect of this implementation is that `getAll` simply returns a reference to the internal list, avoiding the copy that would be needed if you used a mutable list. The internal list ends up being shared among threads but, because the list is immutable, this sharing is harmless.[5]

Of course, locking is still needed to read and write variable `contents`. This variant uses a public lock, the wrapper itself (`this`). If a private lock is preferred, locking on the underlying list, as in Listing 19.4, is not an option:

```scala
                                                              ─ Scala ─
// DON'T DO THIS!
class SafeStringList:
   private var contents = List.empty[String]

   def add(str: String): Unit = contents.synchronized(contents ::= str)
   ...
```

---

[4]I assume here that threads obtain references to objects from other threads through proper synchronization, as is typically the case. Otherwise, the subtleties of the Java Memory Model again come into play, and the `contents` field would need to be initialized while owning the lock:

```scala
private var contents: List[String] = uninitialized
synchronized {
   contents = List.empty
}
```

[5]Because values are always added to the front of the list, they are returned in reverse order. If order is relevant, an immutable type other than a list, such as an immutable queue, can be used.

This approach does not work. A thread that calls **add** needs to read the value of **contents** first, before it can use it as a lock. This reading is done without locking and is incorrect.

A peek at the bytecode for method **add** helps make the issue more tangible:

```
                                                              ──── bytecode ────
 0: aload 0
 1: getfield #38 // Field contents:Lscala/collection/immutable/List;
 4: dup
 5: astore 2
 6: monitorenter
 7: aload 0
 8: aload 0
 9: getfield #38 // Field contents:Lscala/collection/immutable/List;
12: aload 1
13: invokevirtual #51 // Method scala/collection/immutable/List.$colon$colon: ...
16: putfield #38 // Field contents:Lscala/collection/immutable/List;
...
```

Field **contents** is read on line 1, without any locking. It is then locked on line 6—**monitorenter** is the JVM locking instruction—and read again on line 9. Between lines 1 and 6, variable **contents** could be written by another thread that invokes method **add**, in which case the list that is read here on line 9 is different from the list that is locked on line 6. A scenario, in simplified bytecode, is shown in Figure 19.1. After three calls to method **add**, the list contains only two values. Note how, at some point, the two threads end up locking two different objects—an empty list and a list that contains only "B"—and proceed inside their synchronized code in parallel.

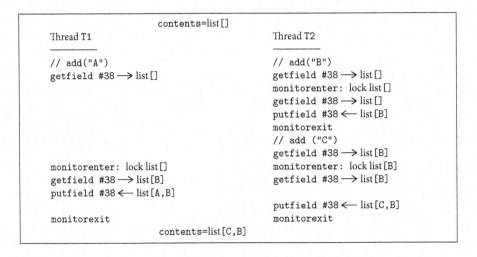

Figure 19.1 Possible interleaving of three `SafeStringList.add` **operations.**

You can use a val field as a lock to guard itself, as in Listings 18.5 and 19.4, but you cannot do that with a reassignable var field. (The same applies to final and non-final fields in Java.) Instead, you need to create an additional locking target, as in Listing 18.7:

—— *Scala* ———

```scala
class SafeStringList:
  private var contents = List.empty[String]

  private val lock = Object()

  def add(str: String): Unit = lock.synchronized(contents ::= str)
  def size: Int = lock.synchronized(contents.size)
  def getAll: List[String] = lock.synchronized(contents)
```

Listing 19.6: Safe list with an immutable list/private lock; contrast with Lis. 19.5.

19.6   Thread-Safety

Both this chapter and Chapter 18 include examples of flawed programs that behave incorrectly in the presence of multiple threads. We also saw how correctness can be brought back through locking, resulting in thread-safe objects that can handle concurrent accesses. So far in this discussion, however, "safe" (or "unsafe") and "correct" (or "incorrect") have only been loosely defined.

Some programs are clearly incorrect, like the program in Listing 18.2 that blows with an exception when trying to add a string to a list. But what does it mean exactly for a program to be correct in the presence of concurrency? The program in Listing 18.5 is correct because a list of strings has length 10 in the end. But why is the value 10 expected? You could answer that the runs 5 `times shared.add("T1")` and 5 `times shared.add("T2")` in sequence produce a list of size 10, and thus that this should also be the case when the two computations are executed in parallel. But the sequential execution also produces all five "T1" values together and all five "T2" values together, and this is not expected of the parallel version, which can produce an arbitrary interleaving of "T1" and "T2" values. So, a parallel program might produce a list that is impossible in its sequential counterpart, yet not be considered incorrect because of that. A more detailed explanation is needed.

When you add a string to a list, there is an expectation that method add is atomic in its effects. The list first exists without the string, then with the entire string—there is no state of the list where a string is "half added." The very definition of a list—the semantics of what it means to be a list—is expressed in terms of such atomic operations. The "thread-safe" expectation is that these atomic operations are preserved—in other words, that a list continues to be a list when accessed by multiple threads.

Concurrency can be formally defined in terms of interleaving of atomic operations. If A and B are atomic operations on a shared structure—like add or get on a list—and a thread executes A in parallel with another thread that executes B, denoted as $A \parallel B$, the outcome of the computation must be the same as A followed by B (denoted $A; B$) or B followed by A—nothing more, nothing less. Put differently, when A and B are executed on an object, the object is subjected to the effects of A and B. When A and B happen in parallel, the order ($A; B$ or $B; A$) is unknown, but both A and B (and nothing else) have to take place.

Figure 19.2 illustrates this concept visually. When two atomic operations A and B are executed concurrently, it is valid for a thread-safe implementation to behave as if A follows B or B follows A. Anything else is invalid. Your responsibility, as a developer, is to assert that $A; B$ and $B; A$ are the only two possible outcomes.[6] Thread-safety is thus defined in terms of a parallel execution being equivalent to some ordering of atomic operations.

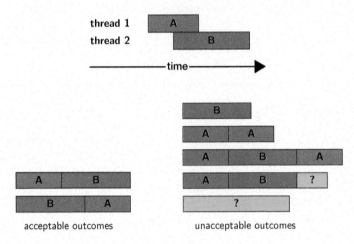

Figure 19.2 Semantics of concurrency as interleaving of atomic actions.

The same principle can be generalized to more than two threads and to compound operations. If A, B, C, and D are atomic operations, and three threads execute A, $(B; C)$, and D concurrently—$A \parallel (B; C) \parallel D$—the outcome, after all operations are finished, should be the same as $A; B; C; D$ or $A; B; D; C$ or $A; D; B; C$ or $B; A; C; D$ or $B; A; D; C$ or $B; C; A; D$ or $B; C; D; A$ or $B; D; A; C$ or $B; D; C; A$ or $D; A; B; C$ or $D; B; A; C$ or $D; B; C; A$. As long as a program produces one of these outcomes, it is behaving correctly. Note how B must always come before C because B and C are executed by the same thread, sequentially.

As an illustration, consider a list that contains only X and Y, and three threads that call `add(Z)`, `remove(Z)`, and `clear()` in parallel.[7] If the list is thread-safe, then after

---

[6]Note that it could happen in an execution of $A \parallel B$ that half (or more) of action A has already been executed by the time B starts, but $B; A$ is still a valid outcome. Indeed, when non-locking strategies are involved, such as those explored in Sections 27.1 and 27.2, $B; A$ can be the more likely outcome of a run of $A \parallel B$ in which A starts first and B interferes.

[7]I assume here that method `clear` is atomic, but no other outcome is acceptable, even under the assumption that it is not.

all three operations are completed, it can either be empty or contain only Z. These are the only possible outcomes of the three calls in any order, and thus the only acceptable outcome of a parallel execution.

Going back to the program in Listing 18.5, if a thread calls `add("T1")` on a list while another thread calls `add("T2")`, the list must behave as if both calls happened sequentially, in some order. In particular, after both calls are completed, both strings were added to the list and nothing else was added or removed. This is the reason you can rightfully expect a size of 10 after two threads perform five `add` operations each: The list should be the same as if all ten operations had happened sequentially, in some order.

This discussion of thread-safety is based on atomic operations. What is and is not atomic depends on the structure under consideration. For instance, many thread-safe structures from `java.util.concurrent` include an `addAll` method. The method is guaranteed to be safe—no value will be lost—but not necessarily atomic. Therefore, a concurrent execution of `add(T)` and `addAll(X,Y,Z)` on an empty structure can potentially produce `[X,Y,T,Z]`, which is not equivalent to both methods invoked in sequence.

19.7 Summary

- Many—if not most—of the difficulties of concurrent programming arise from threads sharing mutable data. In your concurrent applications, you should strive to minimize sharing; when sharing is necessary, you should prefer sharing of immutable objects.

- Immutable objects are inherently thread-safe. Any thread that obtains a reference to an immutable object can freely read this object in parallel with other threads. The design of concurrent applications can be greatly simplified by maximizing the use of immutable objects.

- When sharing mutable objects, you need a well-defined synchronization policy, such as guarding data with an exclusive lock. Encapsulation makes it easier to check that all accesses to shared data are performed in accord with the chosen policy. For this purpose, both the data and the synchronization steps need to be properly encapsulated. Once an object encapsulates its own synchronization, it is said to be thread-safe and can be freely shared among threads.

- All accesses to shared mutable data must go through the proper synchronization steps. This includes not only code that modifies the data, but also all reading accesses. Without the necessary synchronization, reading data that is modified by other threads can lead to unpredictable behavior.

- You must also maintain data encapsulation by making sure that references to internal data do not escape. Escaping references could allow threads to access data without going through the proper synchronization steps. Be aware that some single-threaded techniques—such as sharing a read-only view on internal data—cease to be valid when multiple threads are involved.

- Users of an object can sometimes participate in its synchronization policy. This can be achieved by sharing the locks used internally, a technique known as client-side locking. A benefit of this approach is that external code can lock the state of an object to implement multistep atomic operations, like iterations. A drawback is that code may also misuse the synchronization policy, such as by unnecessarily holding locks and thus creating synchronization bottlenecks. A safer—but more limiting—strategy keeps the synchronization fully encapsulated, such as by only using private instances as locks.

- Mutable objects can rely on immutable types internally. A major benefit of this approach is that references to internal immutable data can safely be shared among threads. This is often a viable alternative to read-only views (which are unsafe with multiple threads) or defensive copies (which are expensive).

- When immutable types are used to implement a mutable object, they are stored in reassignable variables. To guarantee thread-safety, these variables must be read and assigned using proper synchronization. It is crucial never to use a reassignable field itself as a lock: The object in the field would have to be read without locks first—and thus possibly concurrently with other threads writing the field—before the necessary locking can take place.

- When designing a concurrent program, you must first decide which operations on mutable objects should be perceived externally as atomic. You then achieve thread-safety by making sure that atomic actions executed in parallel by multiple threads always have the same effect as some sequential ordering of the same actions.

Chapter 20

Case Study: Thread-Safe Queue

This first concurrent programming case study discusses several possible lock-based implementations of a thread-safe first-in-first-out queue. Of particular interest are the contrasts between public and private locks and between single and multiple locks.

20.1 Queues as Pairs of Lists

One classic design of a first-in-first-out queue uses two functional lists. The idea is to store the state of a queue into two lists: in and out. List out represents the front of the queue, in order, and list in is the back of the queue, in *reverse* order (Figure 20.1). Accordingly, the head of out is the oldest (first-inserted) element of the queue; the head of in is the youngest (last-inserted). Queue elements are removed from the front of list out and added to the front of list in. This way, both lists are used from the head, avoiding inefficient tail-end accesses. When out runs out of elements, you need to reverse in and make it the new out (the new in is then empty). This reversal is amortized over multiple queue operations, resulting in constant-time insertion and removal on average.

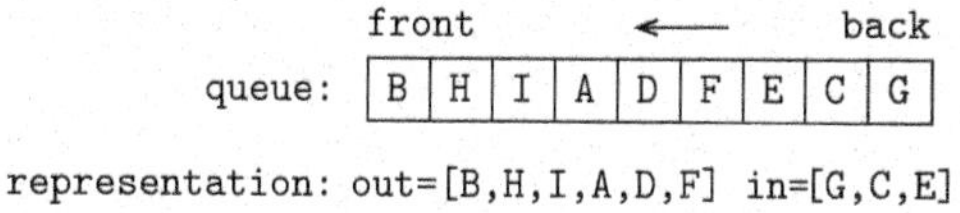

```
               front        ←——        back
      queue:   B  H  I  A  D  F  E  C  G

representation: out=[B,H,I,A,D,F]  in=[G,C,E]
```

Figure 20.1 FIFO queue implemented as two LIFO lists.

In this chapter, the goal is to write a version of this queue that is safe for multi-threaded usage. The resulting queue will be non-blocking: Adding elements is always possible (unbounded capacity), and elements taken from the queue are returned as options so that taking from an empty queue can return None.[1]

---

[1] The alternative is to block a thread on a full queue until elements are removed by other threads and on an empty queue until elements are added by other threads. This requires the use of synchronizers, which are discussed in Chapters 22 and 23. See possible blocking queue implementations in Listings 23.6 to 23.8.

20.2   Single Public Lock Implementation

The simplest way to make the traditional two-list queue thread-safe is to use the queue itself as an exclusive lock and to only access either list with the lock owned:

```scala
class ConcurrentQueue[A]:
  private var in, out = List.empty[A]

  def isEmpty: Boolean = synchronized(out.isEmpty && in.isEmpty)

  def put(value: A): Unit = synchronized(in ::= value)

  def take(): Option[A] = synchronized {
    if isEmpty then None
    else
      if out.isEmpty then
        out = in.reverse
        in = List.empty
      val first = out.head
      out = out.tail
      Some(first)
  }
```

Listing 20.1: Thread-safe queue (single public lock); see also Lis. 20.5 and 20.7.

A queue is empty when both lists are empty. You add a value to the queue by prepending it to the `in` list—`in ::= value` is the same as `in = value :: in`. You remove a value from the queue by reducing list `out` to its tail and returning its head. An empty list `out` needs to be handled as a special case: Reverse list `in`, make it the new `out`, and reset `in` to an empty list. The resulting code is basically a standard two-list queue implementation, except that the entire body of each method is executed with a lock.

Note that `isEmpty` is called from within `take` with the lock already owned. There is no harm in that, as intrinsic locks are reentrant. However, the following variant, which calls `isEmpty` before acquiring the lock, is incorrect:

```scala
// DON'T DO THIS!
def take(): Option[A] =
  if isEmpty then None
  else
    synchronized {
      if out.isEmpty then
        out = in.reverse
        in = List.empty
      val first = out.head
```

```
        out = out.tail
        Some(first)
    }
```

This method always reads and writes both variables in and out with the lock owned, but this is not sufficient. The mistake here is that take now relies on a non-atomic check-then-act: The lock is acquired when entering isEmpty, *released* at the end of this method, and acquired *again* in the else branch. Between the moment the queue is unlocked and when it is locked again, it could be acquired by another thread, resulting in the scenario depicted in Figure 20.2. You should always be wary of a non-atomic check-then-act and take into account anything that might happen between releasing a lock and reacquiring it.

```
                            in=list[], out=list[X]
    Thread T1                                        Thread T2
    ─────────                                        ─────────

    // take()                                        // take()
    lock
    isEmpty ⟶ false
    unlock

                                                     lock
                                                     isEmpty ⟶ false
                                                     unlock

    lock
    out.isEmpty ⟶ false
    out ⟵ list[]
    return Some(X)
    unlock

                                                     lock
                                                     out.isEmpty ⟶ true
                                                     out ⟵ list[]
                                                     in ⟵ list[]
                                                     out.head ⟶ NoSuchElementException!
```

Figure 20.2 **Possible interleaving of two** ConcurrentQueue.take **operations.**

Listing 20.1 uses the queue itself as the lock, enabling client-side locking. For instance, you can write a function to add a batch of values to a queue without intervening elements:

```scala
──────────────────────────────────────────────────────────── Scala ─
def putAll[A](queue: ConcurrentQueue[A], values: A*): Unit =
    queue.synchronized {
        for value <- values do queue.put(value)
    }
```

Listing 20.2: Batch insertions by client-side locking on a concurrent queue.

This relies again on the fact that locks are reentrant, and the outer locking guarantees that the queue is not modified between successive calls to put. Batch removal can be implemented as a drain function that dumps the entire contents of a queue into a list:

```scala
                                                                    Scala
def drain[A](queue: ConcurrentQueue[A]): List[A] =
    val buffer = List.newBuilder[A]
    queue.synchronized {
        while !queue.isEmpty do buffer += queue.take().get
    }
    buffer.result()
```

Listing 20.3: Batch extraction by client-side locking on a concurrent queue.

Synchronization is necessary to avoid another scenario like that shown in Figure 20.2: After a queue is tested to be non-empty at the beginning of the while-loop, it is emptied by another thread before the code reaches take, and get then throws an exception.

Alternatively, you can write a different function drain without explicit synchronization, as long as it does not rely on isEmpty:

```scala
                                                                    Scala
def drain[A](queue: ConcurrentQueue[A]): List[A] =
    val buffer = List.newBuilder[A]
    var option = queue.take()
    while option.nonEmpty do
        buffer += option.get
        option = queue.take()
    buffer.result()
```

Listing 20.4: Batch extraction without synchronization; contrast with Lis. 20.3.

The strategy here is different: Instead of testing the queue for emptiness, you blindly call take and test the resulting option. This implementation repeatedly calls take on the queue until it returns None.

Observe that the two implementations of drain are not equivalent. If a thread attempts to add (or remove) a value while another thread is in the middle of draining a queue, this value is excluded from (or included in) the list according to the implementation in Listing 20.3, but not in the Listing 20.4 variant. In practice, this makes little difference: If a call to drain runs concurrently with calls to put or take, whether the drained list contains the added/removed values is unpredictable anyway.[2]

[2]Another difference is that the first implementation locks the queue once for an entire drain, while the second variant locks and unlocks the queue each time it removes a value. The impact on performance is hard to predict. A standard compiler optimization—lock coarsening—could skip any number of unlock/relock pairs when running the second variant.

20.3 Single Private Lock Implementation

As an alternative design for a concurrent queue, you could decide that there is little value in client-side locking and use a private lock instead:

```scala
                                                                    ─── Scala ───
class ConcurrentQueue[A]:
  private var in, out = List.empty[A]
  private val lock    = Object()

  private def isEmpty: Boolean = lock.synchronized(out.isEmpty && in.isEmpty)

  def put(value: A): Unit = lock.synchronized(in ::= value)

  def take(): Option[A] = lock.synchronized {
    if isEmpty then None
    else
      if out.isEmpty then
        out = in.reverse
        in = List.empty
      val first = out.head
      out = out.tail
      Some(first)
  }
```

Listing 20.5: Thread-safe queue (single private lock); see also Lis. 20.1 and 20.7.

Not much of the code is changed. Instead of **this**, a private object—created for this purpose—is used as the lock.

Note that, as a design decision, method **isEmpty** has become private. Without client-side locking, keeping **isEmpty** public is not essential because, in general, the value returned by the method is useless in the presence of other threads calling **put** and **take** on the queue. A public **isEmpty** method is an invitation to write incorrect code:

```scala
                                                                    ─── Scala ───
// DON'T DO THIS!
if queue.isEmpty
then ... // no guarantee that the queue is empty here
else ... // no guarantee that the queue is non-empty here
```

There are scenarios in which a public method **isEmpty** would be usable—for instance, the value returned by **isEmpty** cannot switch from true to false if all the tasks liable to add to the queue are terminated—but you can usually deal with these situations by relying on `take` (as in Listing 20.4).

As before, `isEmpty` acquires the lock to access fields `in` and `out`. Given that the method is private, this is not strictly necessary: `isEmpty` is called only from within method `take`, after the lock has been acquired, and therefore a thread that enters `isEmpty` already has the necessary lock. You could write the method as follows:

```scala
private def isEmpty: Boolean =
   assert(Thread.holdsLock(lock))
   out.isEmpty && in.isEmpty
```

An assertion is used to ensure that the necessary lock is indeed held. It can help catch a mistake, by which other paths to `isEmpty` have been overlooked. In practice, there is little value in this alternative implementation. Going through a lock that is already acquired is extremely fast.

Due to private locking, functions `putAll` and `drain` from Listings 20.2 and 20.3 can no longer be written. If needed, you can implement them within class `ConcurrentQueue`:

```scala
// inside ConcurrentQueue
def putAll(values: A*): Unit = lock.synchronized {
   for value <- values do in ::= value
}

def drain(): List[A] =
   val (in, out) = lock.synchronized {
      val i = this.in
      val o = this.out
      this.out = List.empty
      this.in = List.empty
      (i, o)
   }
   out ++ in.reverseIterator
```

Listing 20.6: Batch processing from queue with a private lock.

Method `drain` is written in such a way that the lock is held for as little time as possible, enough to grab the `in` and `out` lists and to reset them to empty lists. The more costly iteration and list building are performed after the lock has been released, with the queue already available to other threads. In general, it is good practice to avoid keeping locks longer than necessary and to perform lengthy operations after all unnecessary locks have been released.

20.4   Applying Lock Splitting

A drawback of the queue implementations of Listings 20.1 and 20.5 is that threads that add to the queue and threads that take from the queue are competing for the same lock, even though, most of the time, they end up accessing different lists—in when adding and out when taking. This is undesirable, as contention for exclusive locks can be a major cause of performance loss in concurrent applications.

You can improve the thread-safe queue by applying lock splitting: Split the single lock into two locks, and use one to guard list in and the other to guard list out. This results in the following implementation of ConcurrentQueue:

```scala
class ConcurrentQueue[A]:
  private var in, out        = List.empty[A]
  private val inLock, outLock = Object()

  def put(value: A): Unit = inLock.synchronized(in ::= value)

  def take(): Option[A] =
    outLock.synchronized {
      out match
        case first :: others => out = others; Some(first)
        case Nil =>
          val in = inLock.synchronized {
            val i = this.in
            this.in = List.empty
            i
          }
          in.reverse match
            case first :: others => out = others; Some(first)
            case Nil             => None
    }
```

Listing 20.7: Thread-safe queue (two private locks); see also Lis. 20.1 and 20.5.

Two private objects, inLock and outLock, are created to serve as locks.[3] Inside method put, which is based solely on list in, you acquire inLock, but leave outLock free for threads that call method take. Method take is a little more intricate. You start by using outLock to access list out. If the list is non-empty, this is enough: outLock is the only lock you need, and the call to take proceeds without any interference with concurrent calls to put. If, however, list out is empty, you have to acquire the second lock, inLock,

---

[3]In Scala, val x, y = expr evaluates expr twice, once to initialize x and once to initialize y.

to retrieve and reset list `in`. You then reverse it and use it as the new `out` list. The code is written to hold `inLock` to read and update list `in`; the list is reversed after the lock is released, so that calls to `put` can take place concurrently with this reversal. You also want to avoid any initial `isEmpty` test, because it would require locking both lists. Between occasional reversals, multiple calls to `put` and `take` can proceed fully in parallel, without lock contention.[4]

In this implementation of `ConcurrentQueue`, the locks are private and not exported. Client-side locking is not available, but you can implement `addAll` and `drain` as part of the class if needed:

```scala
// inside ConcurrentQueue
def putAll(values: A*): Unit = inLock.synchronized {
  for value <- values do in ::= value
}

def drain(): List[A] =
  val (in, out) =
    outLock.synchronized {
      inLock.synchronized {
        val i = this.in
        val o = this.out
        this.out = List.empty
        this.in = List.empty
        (i, o)
      }
    }
  out ++ in.reverseIterator
```

Listing 20.8: Batch processing from a queue with a split lock.

Like `put`, method `putAll` needs to acquire only `inLock`. Method `drain` acquires both locks, and then proceeds as in Listing 20.6. The order in which the two locks are acquired is very important. This variant is incorrect:

```scala
// DON'T DO THIS!
def drain(): List[A] =
  val (in, out) =
    inLock.synchronized {
      outLock.synchronized {
        val i = this.in
        val o = this.out
        this.out = List.empty
        this.in = List.empty
```

[4]Lock splitting can be generalized to more than two locks, a strategy known as lock striping. It is used, for instance, in the current implementation of `java.util.concurrent.ConcurrentHashMap`.

```
            (i, o)
        }
    }
out ++ in.reverseIterator
```

The only difference is that `inLock` is acquired before `outLock`. The change may seem innocent enough—after all, both locks are needed anyway—but could result in a major failure if two threads call `take` and `drain` concurrently.

Consider the scenario from Figure 20.3. A thread T1 invokes method `take` at the same time a thread T2 enters method `drain`. T1 acquires lock `outLock` and T2 acquires lock `inLock`. If list `out` is empty, thread T1 now needs `inlock`—held by T2—and thread T2 needs `outLock`—held by T1. However, T1 will not release `outLock` until it locks `inLock`, and T2 will not release `inLock` until it locks `outLock`. Both threads are stuck waiting for a lock that will never be available. This situation is known as a deadlock—a set of threads waiting for each other in a cyclical way. Multiple threads acquiring the same set of locks in different orders is a common cause of deadlock. Deadlocks are discussed in Section 22.3.

	in=list[X] , out=list[]	
Thread T1		Thread T2
`// take()`		`// drain()`
`lock outLock`		`lock inLock`
`out.isEmpty ⟶ true`		`// blocks trying to lock outLock`
`// blocks trying to lock inLock`		

Figure 20.3 Possible deadlock due to an incorrect `drain` implementation in `ConcurrentQueue`.

20.5   Summary

First-in-first-out queues can be implemented in terms of two lists and the implementation made thread-safe by locking. The simplest approach is to use a single lock to guard both lists. The lock can be public—enabling client-side locking—or private. A possible mistake is to release and then reacquire the lock in the middle of a compound operation, like check-then-act, thus breaking atomicity. Instead, you want to hold the lock for the duration of the entire operation.

However, unnecessarily holding locks that are not needed can prevent other threads from performing operations that could potentially be done in parallel. In general, code should strive to release locks as soon as they are not needed, especially before starting lengthy operations.

Querying methods like `isEmpty` are of limited use on concurrent data structures without client-side locking: By the time the value they return is used, the lock has been released and the state of the structure may have changed. In particular, an `isEmpty` test cannot guarantee, in general, that the structure is or is not empty.

Since a queue uses two lists internally, an alternative to using a single lock is to have each list guarded by its own lock. A two-lock variant of the queue allows for more parallelism between the `put` and `take` operations, albeit at the cost of increased code complexity. In particular, operations that require acquiring both locks at the same time must be implemented with care to avoid possible deadlocks.

Chapter 21
Thread Pools

For performance reasons, threads are often pooled. Pooling helps reduce thread creation by reusing threads and makes it easier to place a bound on the number of active threads. A thread pool consists of generic workers that collectively execute the tasks submitted to the pool. Different types of thread pools exist, characterized by various properties: fixed or flexible number of workers, bounded or unbounded queue of tasks, scheduling and delaying facilities, and so on. Applications can use thread pools explicitly by submitting tasks directly to workers. Additionally, some languages define structures that can process their contents in parallel by submitting internal tasks to a thread pool. In functional and hybrid languages, this typically takes the form of parallel implementations of higher-order functions.

21.1 Fire-and-Forget Asynchronous Execution

Our discussion of concurrent programming began with a consideration of how threads can be created to introduce concurrency in an application. In all the examples so far, threads have been created with specific tasks that they run in parallel with other threads—such as printing a letter on the terminal or adding a string into a list. In practice, however, applications rarely start threads on a per-task basis. Instead, generic worker threads are pooled together, and tasks are submitted to them for execution.

This decoupling of threads and tasks has two main benefits. First, it makes it easier to control the number of threads created by an application. For instance, if a server creates a new thread with each incoming request, there is no upper bound on the number of threads that might be created, which can lead to poor performance and/or resource exhaustion. Second, thread creation and tear-down are not free. They tend to have a non-negligible runtime cost, which thread pools help amortize.

Instead of creating three threads to print the letters A, B, and C, as in Listing 17.1, you can create a thread pool first, and then submit letter-printing tasks to it:

```scala
                                                          Scala
println("START")

class LetterPrinter(letter: Char) extends Runnable:
  def run(): Unit = println(letter)

val exec = Executors.newFixedThreadPool(4)
```

```
exec.execute(LetterPrinter('A'))
exec.execute(LetterPrinter('B'))
exec.execute(LetterPrinter('C'))

println("END")
```

Listing 21.1: Example concurrency from a thread pool; contrast with Lis. 17.1.

A thread pool is created with four worker threads. Letter-printing tasks are submitted to it using method `execute`. The output is similar to that of Listing 17.1, except for the names of the threads:

```
main at XX:XX:38.670: START
pool-1-thread-1 at XX:XX:38.694: A
pool-1-thread-2 at XX:XX:38.694: B
main at XX:XX:38.694: END
pool-1-thread-3 at XX:XX:38.694: C
```

A thread that calls `execute` with a task typically does not run the task but only submits it for execution. Method `execute` returns immediately, and the task is executed later, asynchronously. The task is actually run when one of the available workers grabs it and starts its execution. If all the workers are busy, the task might be queued or rejected, depending on the thread pool configuration.

Method `execute` does not return anything useful—it is a **void** method in Java. Using it leads to a "fire-and-forget" programming style: Submit a task and let in run. You can also use thread pools in more controlled ways by creating handles on running tasks, known as futures. Futures are discussed in Chapter 25.

In the preceding run, notice that the main thread terminates before all the tasks are finished. Earlier examples relied on the thread method `join` to force the main thread to wait for the other threads to be done before terminating. When using thread pools, you can achieve a similar behavior by waiting for all the worker threads to be done:

```
                                                          Scala
...
exec.shutdown()
exec.awaitTermination(5, MINUTES)

println("END")
```

Method `shutdown` is used to indicate to the pool that no new task will be submitted (it disables method `execute`). Once a pool is shut down, you can wait for its termination.

This will happen after all remaining tasks have been executed[1] and the worker threads are terminated. Method `awaitTermination` waits for all the worker threads to finish, or for a timeout to have elapsed, whichever happens first. This variant of the program guarantees that the END print statement comes last, as in Listing 17.4.

In many scenarios, you often need to wait for the completion of one or more specific tasks instead of the termination of an entire thread pool. This requires the use of synchronizers, which are discussed in Chapter 22.

You can use thread pools as a convenient mechanism to create threads, have them run a set of tasks concurrently, and terminate them. For instance, class `SafeStringList` from Listing 19.5 can be tested for thread-safety by using tasks run by a thread pool:

```scala
val exec   = Executors.newCachedThreadPool()
val shared = SafeStringList()

for i <- 1 to N do exec.execute(() => 5 times shared.add(i.toString))

exec.shutdown()
exec.awaitTermination(5, MINUTES)

assert(shared.size == 5 * N)
assert((1 to N).forall(i => shared.getAll.count(_ == i.toString) == 5))
```

Listing 21.2: Using a thread pool to create threads and wait for their termination.

This program creates N numbered tasks. Each task writes its number five times into a shared list. All the tasks are executed by a thread pool to introduce concurrency. After all the tasks are completed, you can check the length of the list (it should be `5 * N`) as well as its contents (each task number should appear in the list exactly five times).

Method `newCachedThreadPool` creates a pool with no upper bound on the number of threads: As tasks come in, the pool creates more threads if none is available. Given that one reason for using thread pools is to keep a bound on the number of threads created, such an unbounded pool is rarely well suited to production code.

21.2   Illustration: Parallel Server

Thread pools are very convenient, even when they are used in a simple fire-and-forget style. As an illustration, consider this implementation of a server:

---

[1]A method `shutdownNow` can be used to discard queued tasks without starting them.

```scala
                                                    ──── Scala ────
def handleConnection(socket: Socket): Unit = ...

val server = ServerSocket(port)

while true do
   val socket = server.accept()
   handleConnection(socket)
```

Listing 21.3: A server that processes requests sequentially; contrast with Lis. 21.4.

This server starts to listen on a given port number and processes all incoming requests sequentially. There is only one thread involved. It is blocked on method **accept** until a request comes in. When a client connects to the server, **accept** returns a socket, which can be used as a bidirectional channel between the client and the server. While the thread is inside method **handleConnection**, handling a request by reading from and writing into the socket, no further connections are accepted.

You can easily make this server multithreaded to handle multiple clients in parallel:

```scala
                                                    ──── Scala ────
val server = ServerSocket(port)
val exec    = Executors.newFixedThreadPool(16)

while true do
   val socket = server.accept()
   exec.execute(() => handleConnection(socket))
```

Listing 21.4: A server that processes requests concurrently; contrast with Lis. 21.3.

In this variant, when a request comes in, the thread that was blocked on method **accept** does not process it. Instead, it creates a task—as a lambda expression—and hands it over to a thread pool. The call to method **execute** is instantaneous, and the thread immediately goes back to method **accept** to listen for more incoming connections, possibly starting new handling tasks in the thread pool, which can run in parallel. Listening and accepting connections is all the thread does, which is why it is commonly called the listening thread. All the actual work of processing requests from clients is done in the thread pool.

An easy mistake you need to avoid is the temptation to "inline" the **socket** variable:

```scala
                                                    ──── Scala ────
// DON'T DO THIS!
while true do
   exec.execute(() => handleConnection(server.accept()))
```

Such an inlining would be harmless in the sequential server of Listing 21.3, but it is unacceptable in the parallel server of Listing 21.4. The behavior would fundamentally change. Because method `execute` is asynchronous—it does not stop to execute a task— the loop now creates an unbounded number of tasks, all listening for connections. All the calls to `accept` take place in the thread pool. There is nothing blocking in the body of the loop, which will quickly exhaust resources and crash the server.

On multicore or multiprocessor hardware, the use of a thread pool improves server throughput: By handling connections in parallel, more work is being done per unit of time. Using a thread pool can also improve latency, even on single-processor systems. A drawback of the sequential server is that a single lengthy request can delay multiple smaller requests. By contrast, the thread pool makes it possible to process large and small requests together on separate threads, even on a single processor. Of course, these benefits don't come for free. In particular, you now need `handleConnection` to be implemented in a thread-safe manner, as it can end up being executed concurrently by multiple threads from the pool.

In addition to offering better performance, the parallel variant of the server is more robust than the sequential one. In a sequential implementation, requests that come in while the thread is busy processing a connection are stored in one of the internal queues managed by the operating system and/or the networking library. These queues are typically small—up to a dozen requests stored—and further attempts to connect to the server will be rejected with a "connection refused" error. By contrast, if all the worker threads in Listing 21.4 are busy processing connections, new requests are placed in the queue of the thread pool, which is stored in heap memory and typically quite large.[2]

A parallel server based on a thread pool is also more robust than the following variant:

```scala
                                                                       ─ Scala ─
// DON'T DO THIS!
while true do
   val socket = server.accept()
   Thread(() => handleConnection(socket)).start()
```

This implementation also processes connections in parallel by creating and starting a new thread with each incoming request. The main drawback of this approach— besides the overhead of thread creation and tear-down—is that there is no upper bound on the number of threads created. A burst of activity, with many requests coming in at the same time, could create hundreds or thousands of threads, which may have an adverse impact on performance and even possibly cause a crash due to running out of resources. By contrast, the server in Listing 21.4 is limited to 17 threads—1 listener and 16 workers—no matter how many requests come in.

---

[2]In the thread pool used in Listing 21.4, the queue is actually unbounded, and could potentially fill up the entire memory. However, more tasks can normally be stored in memory than sockets can be created. When overloaded, the server would likely fail at the level of the listening thread calling `accept`.

21.3   Different Types of Thread Pools

Conceptually, a thread pool consists of a queue of tasks and a set of worker threads. We have already seen `newCachedThreadPool`, which uses an unlimited number of threads and no queue,[3] and `newFixedThreadPool`, with a fixed number of threads and an unbounded FIFO queue. JVM thread pools are implemented in a class `ThreadPoolExecutor`, which is highly customizable. In particular, you can specify a factory for thread creation, a minimum number of active threads before tasks are queued, a maximum number of additional threads created when the queue is full, how long before these extra threads are removed from the pool when not needed, the type of queue to use (e.g., bounded or unbounded, FIFO or priority), and how to handle resource depletion when a queue is full of tasks and a maximum number of active threads has been reached. You can also use various "hooks" to specify custom code to run when a task starts or ends, or when the thread pool is shut down.

As an illustration, the next example customizes several thread pool elements:

```scala
                                                              ── Scala ──
object exec extends ThreadPoolExecutor(
    4,
    16,
    3, MINUTES,
    ArrayBlockingQueue(128),
    ThreadPoolExecutor.CallerRunsPolicy()
):
    override def beforeExecute(thread: Thread, task: Runnable): Unit =
        logger.info(() => s"${thread.getName} starts task $task")
```

The pool maintains a minimum of four worker threads, ready to run tasks. If all four threads are busy, tasks are queued in an array-based queue with a capacity of 128. If this queue gets full, up to 12 additional threads are created, for a maximum pool size of 16. Later, these extra threads are terminated after they have been idle for 3 minutes. If all 16 threads are busy, the queue is full, and a new task is submitted, the thread that submits the tasks runs it. (`CallerRunsPolicy` is a convenient way to bring in an extra worker and reduce task creation rate at the same time; in the server example, this would make the listening thread run connection-handling code for a while.) Finally, information is logged every time a task starts to run.

For convenience, a default thread pool is often made available to task-creating code. You can access it as `scala.concurrent.ExecutionContext.global` in Scala and as `java.util.concurrent.ForkJoinPool.commonPool` in Java. Its size is typically based on (but not necessarily equal to) the number of available cores in the runtime. Because

---

[3]More accurately, the pool uses a zero-capacity queue, which is always empty.

this thread pool is not shut down, its threads are started in daemon mode so as not to prevent JVM termination (see Chapter 17, footnote 3).[4]

In addition to standard thread pools, class `ScheduledThreadPoolExecutor` extends `ThreadPoolExecutor` with mechanisms for scheduled tasks. It defines several methods to delay and/or repeat task execution so it can be used as a timer. For instance, you can modify the letter printing example to use a scheduled thread pool:

Scala

```scala
println("START")
val exec = Executors.newScheduledThreadPool(2)

exec.schedule((() => println('A')): Runnable, 5, SECONDS)
exec.scheduleAtFixedRate(() => println('B'), 3, 10, SECONDS)
exec.scheduleWithFixedDelay(() => println('C'), 3, 10, SECONDS)

println("END")
```

Listing 21.5: Example of scheduled execution using a timer pool.

Letter A is scheduled to be displayed after 5 seconds.[5] Letters B and C are scheduled to be displayed after 3 seconds, and then repeatedly every 10 seconds afterward. A typical output looks something like this:

```
main at 09:23:41.514: START
main at 09:23:41.517: END
pool-1-thread-1 at 09:23:44.518: B
pool-1-thread-2 at 09:23:44.518: C
pool-1-thread-1 at 09:23:46.517: A
pool-1-thread-2 at 09:23:54.521: B
pool-1-thread-1 at 09:23:54.521: C
pool-1-thread-2 at 09:24:04.517: B
pool-1-thread-1 at 09:24:04.522: C
...
```

The execution starts at 09:23:41. Three seconds later, at 09:23:44, letters B and C are printed. Two seconds later—5 seconds from the beginning—letter A is printed. At 09:23:54, 10 seconds after they were first displayed, letters B and C are printed again, and so on, repeatedly.

The slight time difference between the next display of B and C illustrates the difference between `scheduleAtFixedRate` and `scheduleWithFixedDelay`. A display of letter B is initiated every 10 seconds (fixed rate), while a display of letter C is initiated

---

[4]This approach tends to make the default pool unsuitable for small illustrative examples due to early termination of the JVM. For this reason, I don't use it much in this book and rely instead on customized pools of non-daemon threads.

[5]A type ascription `:Runnable` is necessary because of another overloaded `schedule` method.

10 seconds after the previous occurrence of the same event (fixed delay). Since displaying a letter takes time, letter C is printed a few milliseconds after letter B. This difference accumulates over time. Letter B is always displayed at time 09:23:44 plus a multiple of 10 seconds; letter C is always printed 10 seconds after the previous display, with no tie to the starting time. The output at a later time shows that the time difference between B and C has increased:

```
...
pool-1-thread-2 at 10:15:14.524: B
pool-1-thread-1 at 10:15:15.526: C
pool-1-thread-2 at 10:15:24.521: B
pool-1-thread-1 at 10:15:25.531: C
...
```

Fifty-two minutes after the program started, letter C is a full second behind letter B. You might also observe the difference between fixed-rate scheduling and fixed-delay scheduling when a task takes an unusual amount of time to complete. If, for instance, printing a single B was delayed for some reason and took a full minute to complete, multiple displays of B would take place in rapid succession afterward to maintain the desired rate. By contrast, if a printing of C is delayed, missed runs are skipped and the next display takes place 10 seconds later.

21.4   Parallel Collections

The parallel server in Listing 21.4 is an example of effortless concurrent programming, with the caveat that method `handleConnection` must be thread-safe. This is more easily achieved if requests to the server are independent and have no need to interact with each other. As usual, the less sharing, the easier the parallelization.

In this spirit, concurrency libraries offer services that go one step further by processing independent data in parallel, while hiding the underlying thread pool entirely. Consider this example as an illustration:

```scala
                                                              Scala
println("START")

def distinctWordsCount(url: URL): Int =
   println(s"start $url")
   val count =
      Using.resource(Source.fromURL(url)(UTF8)) { source =>
         source
            .getLines()
            .flatMap(line => line.split("""\b"""))
            .map(word => word.filter(_.isLetter).toLowerCase)
            .filter(_.nonEmpty)
            .distinct
```

```
            .size
      }
    println(s"end $url")
    count

  val urls: List[URL] = ...

  val counts = urls.map(distinctWordsCount)
  println(counts.max)

  println("END")
```

The idea of this program is to apply function `distinctWordsCount` to a list of URLs to find the maximum value produced. The function calculates the number of distinct words in a source, and the details of its implementation are unimportant (see Section 12.6 for more examples of such pipelined computations).

A run of this program on a list of ten classic books produces an output of the following form:[6]

```
main at XX:XX:03.586: START
main at XX:XX:03.620: start https://gutenberg.org/files/13951/13951-0.txt
main at XX:XX:09.000: end https://gutenberg.org/files/13951/13951-0.txt
main at XX:XX:09.000: start https://gutenberg.org/files/2650/2650-0.txt
main at XX:XX:12.715: end https://gutenberg.org/files/2650/2650-0.txt
main at XX:XX:12.715: start https://gutenberg.org/files/98/98-0.txt
main at XX:XX:15.634: end https://gutenberg.org/files/98/98-0.txt
main at XX:XX:15.635: start https://gutenberg.org/files/1342/1342-0.txt
main at XX:XX:18.336: end https://gutenberg.org/files/1342/1342-0.txt
main at XX:XX:18.336: start https://gutenberg.org/files/76/76-0.txt
main at XX:XX:20.840: end https://gutenberg.org/files/76/76-0.txt
main at XX:XX:20.841: start https://gutenberg.org/files/4300/4300-0.txt
main at XX:XX:26.460: end https://gutenberg.org/files/4300/4300-0.txt
main at XX:XX:26.460: start https://gutenberg.org/files/28054/28054-0.txt
main at XX:XX:33.829: end https://gutenberg.org/files/28054/28054-0.txt
main at XX:XX:33.829: start https://gutenberg.org/files/6130/6130-0.txt
main at XX:XX:37.955: end https://gutenberg.org/files/6130/6130-0.txt
main at XX:XX:37.955: start https://gutenberg.org/files/2000/2000-0.txt
main at XX:XX:45.789: end https://gutenberg.org/files/2000/2000-0.txt
main at XX:XX:45.789: start https://gutenberg.org/files/1012/1012-0.txt
main at XX:XX:48.152: end https://gutenberg.org/files/1012/1012-0.txt
main at XX:XX:48.155: 29154
main at XX:XX:48.155: END
```

All the sources are processed sequentially by the main thread. The entire computation takes about 45 seconds. However, counting words in a URL is completely independent

---

[6]This application is I/O-bound, and computers are fast. In the sample outputs of this section, word processing has been artificially slowed down to observe more meaningful and predictable timings.

from other URLs, which suggests that all URLs could be processed in parallel. Indeed, achieving this parallelism can be as easy as adding `.par` to a list:

```scala
import scala.collection.parallel.CollectionConverters.ImmutableSeqIsParallelizable

val counts = urls.par.map(distinctWordsCount)
println(counts.max)
```

Listing 21.6: Example of parallel evaluation of higher-order function `map`.

The sequence `urls.par` is not of type `List` but rather of type `ParSeq`, a type of collection that implements some of its higher-order methods in parallel. This small change to the code results in an entirely different output:

```
main at XX:XX:16.571: START
scala-global-21 at XX:XX:16.642: start https://gutenberg.org/files/2000/2000-0.txt
scala-global-18 at XX:XX:16.642: start https://gutenberg.org/files/6130/6130-0.txt
scala-global-15 at XX:XX:16.642: start https://gutenberg.org/files/13951/13951-0.txt
scala-global-16 at XX:XX:16.642: start https://gutenberg.org/files/4300/4300-0.txt
scala-global-20 at XX:XX:16.642: start https://gutenberg.org/files/1012/1012-0.txt
scala-global-19 at XX:XX:16.642: start https://gutenberg.org/files/2650/2650-0.txt
scala-global-22 at XX:XX:16.642: start https://gutenberg.org/files/28054/28054-0.txt
scala-global-17 at XX:XX:16.642: start https://gutenberg.org/files/98/98-0.txt
scala-global-20 at XX:XX:19.754: end https://gutenberg.org/files/1012/1012-0.txt
scala-global-20 at XX:XX:19.754: start https://gutenberg.org/files/1342/1342-0.txt
scala-global-17 at XX:XX:20.370: end https://gutenberg.org/files/98/98-0.txt
scala-global-17 at XX:XX:20.372: start https://gutenberg.org/files/76/76-0.txt
scala-global-19 at XX:XX:21.335: end https://gutenberg.org/files/2650/2650-0.txt
scala-global-18 at XX:XX:21.653: end https://gutenberg.org/files/6130/6130-0.txt
scala-global-20 at XX:XX:22.644: end https://gutenberg.org/files/1342/1342-0.txt
scala-global-15 at XX:XX:22.648: end https://gutenberg.org/files/13951/13951-0.txt
scala-global-17 at XX:XX:23.149: end https://gutenberg.org/files/76/76-0.txt
scala-global-16 at XX:XX:23.222: end https://gutenberg.org/files/4300/4300-0.txt
scala-global-22 at XX:XX:24.960: end https://gutenberg.org/files/28054/28054-0.txt
scala-global-21 at XX:XX:25.469: end https://gutenberg.org/files/2000/2000-0.txt
main at XX:XX:25.472: 29154
main at XX:XX:25.472: END
```

Sources are now being processed by the eight[7] threads of the default thread pool. Eight computations start immediately, in parallel. The remaining two start after two worker threads—numbered 20 and 17—have become available—at times 19.754 and 20.370, respectively. Overall, the computation takes about 9 seconds.

Not apparent in the output is the fact that method `map` on `ParSeq` still computes the same list: The numbers in the list are in the order of their URLs, not in the order in which the parallel computations terminate. In other words, `List(1, 2, 3).par.map(_ * 10)` is guaranteed to be the list `[10, 20, 30]`, in this order.

---

[7]This is the size of Scala's default thread pool on an eight-core computer.

In Listing 21.6, sources are processed in parallel, but each source is still processed sequentially. This could be changed by creating a parallel collection of lines and having lines from the same source processed concurrently:

```scala
                                                            ──────── Scala ────────
    source
       .getLines()
       .to(ParSeq)
       .flatMap(line => line.split("""\b"""))
       ...
```

By inserting the stage `to(ParSeq)`, you create a parallel collection of lines, allowing later computations triggered by `flatMap`, `map`, and `filter` to proceed on multiple threads.

In this word counting example, parallelization has been achieved at very little cost in code complexity. In general, though, you need to be careful when using parallel collections. For instance, you cannot replace the call to `counts.max` with the following code:

```scala
                                                            ──────── Scala ────────
// DON'T DO THIS!
var max = Int.MinValue
for count <- counts do if count > max then max = count
```

Some runs do produce value 29,154 in variable `max`, but others do not, in an unpredictable manner. The issue here is that `for-do` in Scala is syntactic sugar for a call to higher-order method `foreach` (see Section 10.9), and method `foreach` is not sequential on a parallel collection. The `if-then` expression ends up being evaluated by multiple threads from the pool at the same time, with the adverse consequences already discussed in Section 18.3 (non-atomic check-then-act). Instead, you should call method `max`—correctly implemented on parallel sequences—directly on `counts`.

If you need to process a sequence one element at a time, for instance to compute something more complicated than `max`, you can convert a parallel sequence into a sequential one using method `seq`, which has the opposite effect of method `par`. The following computation of the maximum is correct, albeit sequential:

```scala
                                                            ──────── Scala ────────
var max = Int.MinValue
for count <- counts.seq do if count > max then max = count
```

Another aspect of parallel collections you need to be aware of is that not all higher-order methods are implemented in parallel. For instance, in the sequential word counting application, the intermediate list of numbers can be avoided by using `foldLeft` (see Section 10.4):

```scala
─────────────────────────────────────────────────── Scala ───
val max = urls.foldLeft(Int.MinValue)(_ max distinctWordsCount(_))
```

However, this approach to parallelization does not work:

```scala
────────────────────────────────────────────────── Scala ───
// DON'T DO THIS!
val max = urls.par.foldLeft(Int.MinValue)(_ max distinctWordsCount(_))
```

Method `foldLeft` is implemented sequentially, from left to right, even on parallel collections.[8] Avoiding the intermediate list of numbers while processing sources in parallel calls for the slightly more complicated method `aggregate`:

```scala
────────────────────────────────────────────── Scala ───
val max = urls.par.aggregate(Int.MinValue)(_ max distinctWordsCount(_), _ max _)
```

Method `aggregate` takes two function arguments: the main computing function, as in `foldLeft`, and a second function used to combine the intermediate results computed in parallel.

21.5 Summary

- Instead of creating a new thread whenever a task needs to be executed, pools of generic worker threads are often set up first, and tasks are then submitted to the pools for execution.

- Using thread pools has two major benefits: It makes it easier to keep the total number of threads for an application under control, and it helps amortize the cost of creating and terminating threads, which is typically non-negligible.

- Thread pools can be shut down, allowing their threads to terminate. Creating a temporary thread pool to run tasks in parallel, shutting it down after all the tasks have been submitted, and waiting for the pool to terminate can often be a simple way to implement the fork-join pattern mentioned in Section 17.4, in which a primary thread creates worker threads and then waits for them to complete their tasks.

- Thread pools can be used in a fire-and-forget style, in which tasks are submitted and let run to completion, with the submitting thread having no further interaction with them. A server that processes independent or mostly independent requests can be implemented as a single listening thread that submits request-handling

---

[8]In contrast to `foldLeft` and `foldRight`, method `fold` is implemented in parallel but cannot be used to count words from a list of URLs because of limitations in its signature.

tasks to a thread pool. Bursts of activity are then managed by temporarily storing requests in the queue of the thread pool.

- Thread pools are often available in variants that allow task execution to be delayed and/or repeated, as with a timer. Repeating tasks can be scheduled at a fixed rate, or with a fixed delay between successive runs of the task.

- Thread pools are sometimes used implicitly by mechanisms that hide the parallelism in their implementation. Scala, for instance, offers parallel collections that execute some of their higher-order methods in parallel. The functional behavior is the same as their sequential counterpart—`map` is still `map`, `filter` is still `filter`—but parallel processing can produce a performance improvement. Java implements a similar mechanism in its `Stream` class.

Chapter 22

Synchronization

Thread cooperation requires coordination, typically via synchronization. Waiting for a thread or a thread pool to terminate is an example of such synchronization. More generally, different types of synchronizers can be used to block one or more threads until the state of an application allows them to make progress. When misused, synchronization that unnecessarily blocks threads may cause a program to slow down, or even to come to a halt in the case of a deadlock. Snapshots of the states of threads—whether they are blocked, and on which synchronizer—can be used to debug these situations. Synchronization is also leveraged by runtime systems to optimize the memory usage of parallel tasks. These optimizations are specified in a memory model.

22.1   Illustration of the Need for Synchronization

In an earlier example of a concurrent program, two threads were adding strings into an unsafe list, causing the program to break. The list was then made safe through locking, and thread pools were introduced as a way to manage and reuse threads. Putting everything together, we can now write the list-sharing example as follows:

```scala
val exec   = Executors.newCachedThreadPool()
val shared = SafeStringList()

def addStrings(n: Int, str: String): Unit = n times shared.add(str)

exec.execute(() => addStrings(5, "T1"))
exec.execute(() => addStrings(5, "T2"))

exec.shutdown()
exec.awaitTermination(5, MINUTES)

assert(shared.size == 10)
```

Listing 22.1: Threads from a pool share a safe list.

For the assertion at the end of the program to be valid, you need to wait until both string-adding tasks are completed before querying the size of the list. This is achieved here by shutting down the thread pool and by waiting for termination of all its activities.

There are numerous situations in actual applications where this approach will not be practical. Perhaps the thread pool is shared with other components of the application, so it cannot be shut down; or maybe you need to wait for completion of a subset of tasks only, while leaving other activities running in the thread pool. What is needed is a mechanism for threads to wait for completion of specific tasks, and more generally to coordinate with other thread activities. *Synchronization* is such a mechanism, and *synchronizers* are its building blocks.

Before applying a valid synchronization technique to the string-adding example, let's spend some time detailing two incorrect strategies that you should avoid in general: sleeping and busy-waiting. Together—and they are often combined—they probably constitute the most common mistake in designing concurrent programs.

Let's start with sleeping. To guarantee that all strings have been added before using the list, one of the first and simplest ideas that comes to mind is to just wait "long enough":

```scala
...

exec.execute(() => addStrings(5, "T1"))
exec.execute(() => addStrings(5, "T2"))

// DON'T DO THIS!
MILLISECONDS.sleep(10)

assert(shared.size == 10)
```

The obvious flaw in this approach is that the sleeping time is arbitrary. Why 10 milli-seconds? Why not 5 or 30? You cannot choose a "long enough" sleeping time without knowing beforehand how long the tasks will take. If it is too small, the tasks may not be finished by the time you trigger the next computing stage—here, calling method `size`—and the application will break. If it is too large, you end up waiting for no reason after data is ready, which artificially slows down your application and makes it less responsive.

This is especially true of tasks with running times that follow a long-tailed distribution: Tasks are short most of the time, but can occasionally be very long. If you choose a sleeping value large enough to accommodate the longest runs, much time is wasted when runs are shorter. But if you reduce the sleeping time to improve performance, the application will fail with the rare occurrences of unusually long tasks.

In short, the sleeping approach does not work because there is no right amount of sleeping time in general. Still, it is enormously tempting,[1] when you know that a bug is caused by code that finishes a little too early, to want to solve it by inserting a well-adjusted delay. Don't do it.

---

[1] As the joke goes, there are only two kinds of concurrent programmers: those who have used a well-adjusted delay in their code and those who lie about it.

The other common—but mistaken—strategy you want to avoid is busy-waiting. In this pattern, a thread continuously polls the state of the activity it is waiting on. For instance, a counter could be introduced to keep track of tasks as they terminate:

```scala
val shared     = SafeStringList()
var terminated = 0

def addStrings(n: Int, str: String): Unit =
   n times shared.add(str)
   terminated += 1

exec.execute(() => addStrings(5, "T1"))
exec.execute(() => addStrings(5, "T2"))

// DON'T DO THIS!
while terminated < 2 do ()

assert(shared.size == 10)
```

Based on our earlier discussion of shared accesses and locks, we already know that this program is flawed: Mutable variable `terminated` is shared by multiple threads without locking. In particular, both threads could finish their task at the same time and execute `terminated += 1` concurrently, which we know to be unsafe.

However, adding the necessary locking is not the solution:

```scala
val shared     = SafeStringList()
var terminated = 0
val lock       = Object()

def addStrings(n: Int, str: String): Unit =
   n times shared.add(str)
   lock.synchronized(terminated += 1)

exec.execute(() => addStrings(5, "T1"))
exec.execute(() => addStrings(5, "T2"))

// DON'T DO THIS!
while lock.synchronized(terminated) < 2 do ()

assert(shared.size == 10)
```

Variable `terminated` is now always accessed with a lock. As written, the program does guarantee that the main thread waits for both tasks to finish before calling method `size` on the shared list, but the implementation is still unacceptable. The real flaw of the busy-waiting approach is that the main thread keeps running while the tasks are being executed. This is wasteful of computing resources—CPU cycles—and cannot scale to real-size applications, especially when waiting for long-running tasks. To make things worse, the main thread is not only wasting CPU time, it is also interfering with the running tasks by repeatedly acquiring the shared lock—about a hundred thousand times in this small illustrative program—thus potentially delaying the completion of the task it is waiting for!

Sleeping and busy-waiting are sometimes combined in a mixed approach:

Scala

```
// DON'T DO THIS!
while lock.synchronized(terminated) < 2 do MILLISECONDS.sleep(5)
```

While this alleviates some weaknesses of each individual approach—less CPU time is wasted in the main thread, and smaller sleeping times can safely be used—it still won't make your code as efficient and responsive as a properly synchronized solution.

These approaches—sleeping, busy-waiting, or a combination thereof—are a major source of bugs and poor performance in concurrent programs and should be avoided. Instead, you want to rely on synchronizers, which can efficiently suspend threads (no CPU wasted) until the exact moment a desired condition is established (no time wasted sleeping).

22.2   Synchronizers

Fundamentally, synchronizers are stateful objects, capable of blocking threads. A synchronizer has a mutable state and defines operations to modify it. Moreover, some of these operations may block the threads that call them until the synchronizer is transitioned into an acceptable state by another thread. You can think of synchronizers as smart traffic lights for thread coordination: They stop threads or let them go and use the threads' own actions to change the lights.

To help illustrate the concept, consider exclusive locks, which we discussed in Chapters 18 and 19. Locks are synchronizers. A lock has a two-valued state—`free` or `owned`—and defines operations to modify this state—`lock`, which changes the state from `free` to `owned`, and `unlock`, which changes it from `owned` to `free`. The `lock` operation can be blocking if a lock is in the `owned` state. The `unlock` operation never blocks: An owned lock can always be freed, and freeing a free lock is invalid.

As another example, consider thread pools. In some of the earlier examples, they were used as synchronizers. A thread pool can transition from one state where it is active and accepting tasks, to another state where it is shut down and all its tasks are terminated. Method `awaitTermination` is used to block a thread until a pool is in the terminated state.

The focus of this chapter is inter-thread synchronization via shared memory. In systems that communicate via messages instead, a channel is also a synchronizer. Sending and receiving messages are operations that modify the state of a channel, and that can be blocking if a channel is full or empty. Synchronization of non-thread entities, such as actors and coroutines, and the use of messages are briefly discussed in Chapter 27.

Locks are primarily used for non-interference, but other synchronizers are better suited to cooperation. Chapter 23 gives an overview of the most common synchronizers. For now, let's solve the list-sharing problem with a simple but useful synchronizer: the countdown latch. It is implemented in the `java.util.concurrent` library as a `CountDownLatch`:

```scala
val shared = SafeStringList()
val latch  = CountDownLatch(2)

def addStrings(n: Int, str: String): Unit =
  n times shared.add(str)
  latch.countDown()

exec.execute(() => addStrings(5, "T1"))
exec.execute(() => addStrings(5, "T2"))

latch.await()

assert(shared.size == 10)
```

Listing 22.2: Waiting for task completion using a countdown latch synchronizer.

The state of a countdown latch is a counter. Method `countDown` decrements this counter if it is positive, and method `await` blocks any calling thread until the latch's counter is 0. In this example, a latch is created with a state equal to 2. The main thread waits for the latch state to be 0 before querying the size of the list. The other two threads each decrement the state by 1 as they finish, thus bringing it to 0 when they are both done. By calling `latch.await`, you avoid the drawbacks of sleeping or busy-waiting: The main thread is blocked efficiently and does not use CPU time while waiting, and it is notified to resume execution as soon as the latch opens, without additional sleeping delay.

22.3 Deadlocks

When a program uses synchronizers, threads are blocked until the synchronizer reaches a desired state. Synchronization carries a danger—namely, it makes threads wait for a condition that may never be satisfied. Some errors are easy to catch. For instance, a thread calls `await` on a latch, but nowhere is `countDown` ever called in the code. Other mistakes can be trickier, such as waiting for more countdowns than can possibly happen in a program.[2]

---

[2]Though not the focus of this section, waiting for *fewer* countdowns is also a synchronization mistake, resulting in a thread that uses data too early.

Deadlocks are a rather common situation in which threads end up waiting for a condition that is never established. In a deadlock, multiple threads wait for each other in a cycle. As an illustration, consider the following implementation of a thread-safe box:

```scala
class SafeBox[A]:
  private var contents = Option.empty[A]
  private val filled   = CountDownLatch(1)

  // DON'T DO THIS!
  def get: A = synchronized {
    filled.await()
    contents.get
  }

  def set(value: A): Boolean = synchronized {
    if contents.nonEmpty then false
    else
      contents = Some(value)
      filled.countDown()
      true
  }
```

Listing 22.3: Deadlock-prone implementation of a box; fixed in Lis. 22.4.

A box is created empty, and can be filled only once, using method **set**. Further attempts to invoke **set** simply return false. A latch is open when the box is filled. Threads that need access to the contents of a box are blocked on this latch until **set** is called. A box is designed so that **set** and **get** can be called by different threads concurrently. All accesses to variable **contents** go through a lock, the box itself.[3]

This all sounds very reasonable, but the implementation of **get** is incorrect. It starts by locking the box. Then, if the box is still empty, the calling thread is blocked on the latch. This thread, however, still owns the lock on the box, making it impossible for any other thread to run **set** to fill the box. This is a deadlock situation, as shown in Figure 22.1. Thread T1 owns the lock on the box and waits for T2 to fill the box. Thread T2 waits for T1 to release the lock so T2 can set the contents of the box. The two threads are waiting for each other, permanently.

---

[3]Such a box is typically made available in concurrency libraries as a *future* or a *promise* and does not need to be reimplemented. Futures and promises are discussed in Chapter 25.

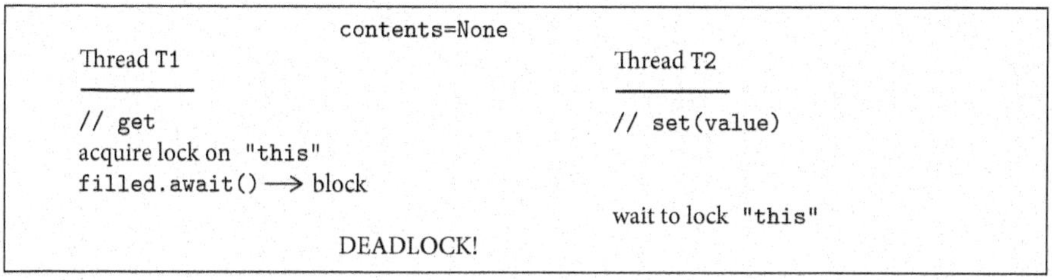

```
                        contents=None
    Thread T1                                    Thread T2
    ──────────                                   ──────────
    // get                                       // set(value)
    acquire lock on "this"
    filled.await() ──→ block
                                                 wait to lock "this"
                        DEADLOCK!
```

Figure 22.1 Possible deadlock of the incorrect box implementation in Lis. 22.3.

This problem is easy to fix. There is no need for a thread inside method `get` to access the contents of the box until the latch is open. Therefore, the thread should wait on the latch first. (As a synchronizer, a latch is obviously thread-safe and can be accessed without locking.) Then, after the latch is open, the thread can lock the box to access its contents:

```scala
                                                              ─ Scala ─
class SafeBox[A]:
  private var contents = Option.empty[A]
  private val filled   = CountDownLatch(1)

  def get: A =
    filled.await()
    synchronized(contents.get)

  def set(value: A): Boolean = synchronized {
    if contents.nonEmpty then false
    else
      contents = Some(value)
      filled.countDown()
      true
  }
```

Listing 22.4: Thread-safe box with a latch; fixed from Lis. 22.3; see also Lis. 27.2.

The implementation of **set** is left unchanged. Since `countDown` is a fast, non-blocking operation, you can call it while holding the lock.

Developers who are new to concurrent programming might think it strange, but you can also implement method **set** in this way:

```scala
                                                            ── Scala ──
def set(value: A): Boolean = synchronized {
   if contents.nonEmpty then false
   else
      filled.countDown()
      contents = Some(value)
      true
}
```

Listing 22.5: First variant for method set from Lis. 22.4.

This variant opens the latch *before* variable contents is set, while the box is still empty. It might seem like a mistake, but thanks to locking, this latch opening is harmless: A thread inside get might go through the latch at this point, but it will still be blocked by the lock until the box contents are actually set.

If you want to access the latch outside the locked section, as in get, you can write the set method slightly differently:

```scala
                                                            ── Scala ──
def set(value: A): Boolean =
   val setter = synchronized {
      if contents.nonEmpty then false
      else
         contents = Some(value)
         true
   }
   if setter then filled.countDown()
   setter
```

Listing 22.6: Second variant for method set from Lis. 22.4.

In this variant, you first lock the box to check that it is still empty. If so, the box contents are set, and setter is true. You can then release the lock before opening the latch. Releasing the lock is harmless: It simply lets another thread call set and find the box already filled.

22.4   Debugging Deadlocks with Thread Dumps

Programming with synchronizers is error-prone, and deadlocks are a common problem. Deadlocks can be devastating—threads hang and the system halts—but they are not the worst kind of concurrency bug. What makes deadlocks somewhat easier to investigate compared to other situations is the fact that the threads involved in a waiting cycle are not running, and you can examine them at your leisure.

A Java virtual machine (JVM) can usually provide information on its threads, typically in the form of a thread dump. How you trigger a thread dump depends on the JVM—the HotSpot JVM used in this book reacts to a SIGQUIT signal—and the exact format of the output may vary.

As an illustration, you can cause the incorrect box implementation from Listing 22.3 to deadlock by using the following two-thread program:

```scala
val exec = Executors.newCachedThreadPool()
val box  = SafeBox[Int]()
exec.execute(() => box.set(0))
println(box.get)
```

A secondary thread attempts to set a box with zero while the main thread invokes get. On some runs, this program terminates properly. On others, it gets stuck. A thread dump reveals the following information (slightly edited for clarity):

```
"pool-1-thread-1" #15 prio=5 os_prio=31 cpu=3.79ms elapsed=121.29s
   java.lang.Thread.State: BLOCKED (on object monitor)
     at chap22.Box1$SafeBox.set
     - waiting to lock <0x000000061f1f6a68> (a chap22.Box1$SafeBox)

"main" #1 prio=5 os_prio=31 cpu=223.28ms elapsed=121.51s
   java.lang.Thread.State: WAITING (parking)
     at jdk.internal.misc.Unsafe.park
     - parking to wait for <0x000000061f1f99e8>
       (a java.util.concurrent.CountDownLatch$Sync)
     at java.util.concurrent.locks.LockSupport.park
     at java.util.concurrent.locks.AbstractQueuedSynchronizer.acquire
     at java.util.concurrent.CountDownLatch.await
     at chap22.Box1$SafeBox.get
         - locked <0x000000061f1f6a68> (a chap22.Box1$SafeBox)
```

(The dump includes many more threads not displayed here. These are internal to the JVM and are used for just-in-time compilation, garbage collection, and other operations.)

The output shows that the two threads of interest are not running. The worker thread from the pool, pool-1-thread-1, is blocked on an object monitor—JVM's terminology for its intrinsic locks—at the beginning of method set. It is trying to lock object 0x000000061f1f6a68, an instance of SafeBox. Meanwhile, the main thread is blocked on method await from CountDownLatch. (All the synchronizers in java.util .concurrent are implemented in terms of an AbstractQueuedSynchronizer class and use a low-level operation park to suspend threads.) You can see on the last line that the main thread owns the lock on the same SafeBox instance that the worker thread is waiting for, object 0x000000061f1f6a68. The deadlock state is exactly that shown in Figure 22.1 (main is T1 and pool-1-thread-1 is T2).

22.5   The Java Memory Model

A memory model defines the semantics of operations that utilize memory—in particular, reading and writing variables. You may be thinking that what happens when writing and reading variables is pretty clear and does not need to be explained in a four-page section. If so, it is only because you have in mind the simple memory model used in single-threaded programs. When multiple threads are involved, the story becomes more complicated.

As an illustration, Figure 22.2 displays reading and writing operations on two variables, x and y, in a single-threaded program as they occur over time. The notation Wx(v) represents the action of writing variable x with value v, and Rx is a reading of variable x. In this scenario, reading x produces the value v3, and both reads of y produce the value v4. Nothing surprising there: Reading a variable produces the last value written to this variable, a property known as sequential consistency.

Figure 22.2 Single-threaded executions are sequentially consistent.

In the presence of multiple threads, however, memory models are often *not* sequentially consistent—in other words, reading a variable may not produce the last value written into it. The reason is that sequential consistency is typically not needed in multithreaded applications, and hardware can be more efficient by not implementing it. In particular, weaker consistency models facilitate hardware optimizations such as core-level caching, instruction reordering, and speculative execution. To improve performance, hardware manufacturers make consistency commitments that are not sequential, and programmers need to be aware of them (especially when implementing compilers and operating systems). To ensure portability across different hardware and operating systems, Java defines its own memory model, the Java Memory Model (JMM), common to all languages running on the JVM. And to better leverage hardware performance, the JMM is not sequentially consistent.[4]

Figure 22.3 shows the same operations as Figure 22.2, but executed by two different threads, T1 and T2. While sequential consistency would ensure that when variable x is read by T1 its value is v3, there is no such guarantee under the JMM, even through v3

---

[4]The memory model of .NET languages is very similar to the JMM; the C/C++ model is more complex.

is the last value written into x. Similarly, the reading of variable y by T2 is not guaranteed
to produce v4.

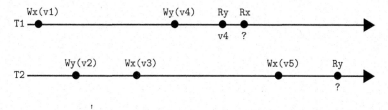

Figure 22.3 Multithreaded executions are not sequentially consistent.

So, what do we know about the reading of x in T1 and the reading of y in T2? In
the absence of synchronization, the JMM does not guarantee much. We know that the
reading of variable y by T1 does produce v4, the last value written into y by thread T1
itself. The reading of variable x by T1, however, may produce v1, or v3, *or a mixture
of* v1 *and* v3, such as an object in which some fields are as in v1 and others are as in v3.
Similarly, the value of variable y read by T2 could be v2, or v4, or a combination of
both. Clearly, writing correct programs under such assumptions is next to impossible.

Fortunately, threads tend to coordinate their actions via synchronization to ensure
that some operations take place before others, and the JMM makes stronger guarantees when synchronization is involved. This is why a sequentially consistent model is not
needed: Most multithreaded programs require some form of synchronization, and a memory model that guarantees consistency for properly synchronized programs is enough.

The JMM is defined in terms of a *happens-before* ordering of events (thread actions).
Events include reading and writing variables, but also starting threads and synchronization operations such as locking and unlocking. The precise semantics of the happens-
before relation are defined in Section 17.4 of the Java Language Specification and in the
documentation of concurrency libraries such as `java.util.concurrent`. The details are
beyond the scope of this book, and it is usually sufficient that you keep in mind three
characteristics of the happens-before relation:

- Intra-thread code is sequentially consistent: An action taken by a thread happens-
  before a subsequent action by the same thread. This is why in Figure 22.3,
  thread T1 is guaranteed to read v4 in variable y.

- Synchronization operations—locking, unlocking, inserting into a thread-safe queue,
  opening a latch, and so on—connect events from different threads in terms of
  happens-before.

- The happens-before relation is transitive: If A happens-before B and B happens-
  before C, then A happens-before C.

For example, in Listing 17.3, we saw a pattern for thread termination that uses a volatile Boolean variable to request termination of another thread. It is reproduced here:

```scala                                                            Scala
@volatile private var continue = true

def terminate() = continue = false

def run() =
   while continue do
      // perform task
   end while
   // cleanup
```

The defining property of volatile variables is that writing a volatile variable happens-before the next read of that variable. From this, you know that the first time a thread in `run` reads the shared variable `continue` after method `terminate` has been called, it will read the value false written in `terminate`. If the shared Boolean flag is not volatile, there is no happens-before connection between its writing and subsequent reading, and the runner thread is at risk of still reading true after false was written, and thus of continuing to run.

As another illustration, consider a three-thread program:

```scala                                                            Scala
def run1() = // behavior of thread t1
   SECONDS.sleep(4)
   println(x)
   SECONDS.sleep(5)
   y.synchronized {
      SECONDS.sleep(1)
      println(x)
      SECONDS.sleep(2)
   }

def run2() = // behavior of thread t2
   x = v1
   SECONDS.sleep(2)
   t3.start()
   SECONDS.sleep(3)
   y.synchronized {
      SECONDS.sleep(2)
      x = v2
      SECONDS.sleep(1)
   }
```

```
def run3() = // behavior of thread t3
  SECONDS.sleep(1)
  println(x)
  SECONDS.sleep(11)
  println(x)
```

Listing 22.7: Example of events tied and not tied by happens-before; see Fig. 22.4.

The three threads start running at the same time, and the graph in Figure 22.4 shows how their actions are connected according to the happens-before relation. Ly and Uy represent the locking and unlocking of object y, respectively. Of particular interest are the edges between t3.start and t3.Rx (starting a thread happens-before the first action taken by that thread) and between t2.Uy and t1.Ly (releasing a lock happens-before the next acquiring of that lock). The other edges are the consequence of in-thread program ordering. Calls to method sleep do not create happens-before links—another reason why you should not use sleeping for synchronization purposes in addition to the reasons discussed in Section 22.1.

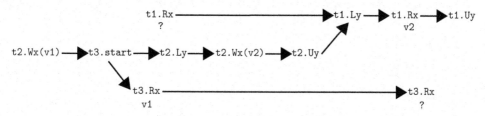

Figure 22.4 Happens-before graph for actions in Lis. 22.7.

The first read of variable x by thread t3 produces v1, the last value written into x, because t2.Wx(v1) happens-before t3.Rx (by transitivity). Similarly, the second read of variable x by thread t1 produces v2, the last value written into x, because t2.Wx(v2) happens-before the second t1.Rx, by transitivity. Note that t2.Wx(v1) happens before (no dash, as in "takes place earlier than") the first t1.Rx in terms of real time, but it does not happen-before it (with dash, according to the relation that defines the JMM). This is also true of t2.Wx(v2) and the second t3.Rx. As a result, the first t1.Rx and the second t3.Rx are free to produce values other than v1 and v2.

Roughly speaking, you can think of concurrent programs as belonging to one of three groups:

- **Group 1:** fully synchronized programs in which all the necessary happens-before relations exist and are obvious due to locking, submitting to thread pools, or other forms of explicit synchronization.

- **Group 2:** fully synchronized programs in which the necessary happens-before relations exist but are not necessarily obvious. For instance, the implementation of

`CountDownLatch` guarantees that calls to `countdown` happen-before the unblocking of `await`. Therefore, it is not necessary to lock inside method `get` in some of the earlier box implementations:

```scala
def get: A =
  filled.await()
  contents.get
```

Listing 22.8: Possible implementation of **get** in Lis. 22.4 and 22.6.

This variant of `get` can be used in Listings 22.4 and 22.6. What makes it work is the fact that the thread that runs `set` writes variable `contents` *before* opening the latch, and the thread that runs `get` continues from waiting on the latch *before* reading the contents. Figure 22.5 shows that, by transitivity of the happens-before relation, writing variable `contents` happens-before reading it, guaranteeing that the thread that calls `get` sees the value written by the thread that previously called `set`.[5] Note that this implementation of `get` *cannot* be used in Listing 22.5: In this variant, the latch is opened *before* the box contents are set. In that case, locking remains necessary inside method `get`.

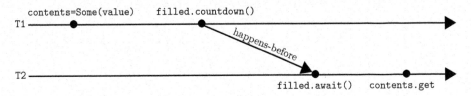

Figure 22.5 Happens-before without explicit synchronization.

- **Group 3:** programs that do not have enough synchronization to guarantee that writing a variable always happens-before the next read of that variable but that are nonetheless correct. The implementation of some standard library components, such as `ReentrantLock`, contains such code.

This book targets an introductory to intermediate level and focuses on programs in group 1. For those, you usually don't need to think too much about the JMM. You are expected to further study concurrent programming before attempting to write programs from group 2. Group 3 is the domain of experts. Stay away from it, or be ready to lie awake at night wondering if you really got that tricky code right...

---

[5]In this figure, `filled.await()` denotes the point in time when T2 returns from the call to `await`, not when that call was initiated.

22.6 Summary

- When parallel tasks are not fully independent, threads need to coordinate with other threads. A common need is for a thread to pause its computation and wait until other threads have made the state of a system suitable to continue.

- When facing this problem, two courses of actions are as tempting as they are unsuitable in general. The first mistaken approach is to make a thread sleep for a set amount of time. No matter how careful you are in the selection of a sleeping time value, there is no correct choice when the activities of other threads have unpredictable duration. Too short, and the state of an application may not be ready by the time a thread resumes after sleeping. Too long, and time is wasted sleeping while a thread could make progress instead, thus hurting an application's performance and responsiveness.

- The other misguided strategy is for a thread to constantly poll the state of the system until it is suitable for that thread to continue, a programming style known as spinning or busy-waiting. This approach is wasteful in several ways and does not scale with large numbers of threads and/or lengthy activities. First, polling threads continually use computing resources and need to repeatedly be scheduled for execution, thus taking CPU time away from the threads they are waiting on. Second, repeatedly querying the state of an application while other threads are updating it necessitates thread-safe mechanisms—such as locks—which tend to be costly when used frequently, as in a continuously checking loop.

- Instead of sleeping and busy-waiting, concurrent programs should rely on proper synchronization. Synchronizers are designed to block threads efficiently (no busy-waiting) until other threads establish a desired condition (no guessing of a suitable sleeping duration). In shared memory systems, synchronizers maintain a state and offer methods to block one or more threads until other threads set the synchronizer to the required state.

- The best known synchronizer is the exclusive lock, which blocks acquiring threads until the lock is freed by another thread and becomes available. Concurrency libraries typically implement many other types of synchronizers, some of which are discussed in Chapter 23.

- Using synchronizers is error-prone. Threads can be made to wait indefinitely for conditions that will never be established, possibly causing an entire application to halt. Deadlocks are a common cause of indefinite waiting. They are the result of threads waiting for each other in a cyclical way. Invoking blocking methods on synchronizers while holding locks is a sure way to cause a deadlock.

- Deadlocks are made easier to investigate by the fact that the threads involved are blocked, so they can be examined at the programmer's convenience. A JVM can produce a snapshot of information on its threads, known as a thread dump. This information typically includes whether threads are blocked or running, which synchronizers they are blocked on, which locks they currently own, and so forth.

- Single-threaded programs are sequentially consistent: Reading a memory location produces the last value written into that location. For performance reasons, processors, operating systems, and virtual machines are often not sequentially consistent in the presence of multiple threads. Though not sequentially consistent in general, the Java Memory Model is defined in such a way that properly synchronized programs can expect sequential consistency.

Chapter 23
Common Synchronizers

Concurrency libraries often contain extensive tools for inter-thread synchronization. This chapter describes some of the most common synchronizers, along with typical usage patterns.

23.1 Locks

The best-known synchronizer is the exclusive lock, which we have already seen in several code illustrations in previous chapters. What was used through `synchronized` is the so-called intrinsic locking mechanism of the JVM—every object can be used as a lock. The Java standard library defines three types of locks in addition to intrinsic locks. Two forms are of particular interest and are briefly discussed in this section. The third, `StampedLock`, is rarely used and reserved for advanced usage.

First is the class `ReentrantLock`. This class implements an exclusive lock, like `synchronized`, but one richer in features. For instance, threads can attempt to acquire a lock with a timeout or allow themselves to be interrupted while waiting for a lock. You can use `ReentrantLock` to write a variant of the `getRank` method from Listing 18.7 in which threads give up trying to register after 100 milliseconds if the lock is not available:

```scala
                                                                    ─ Scala ─
private var userCount = 0
private val lock = ReentrantLock()

def getRank(): Option[Int] =
  if lock.tryLock(100, MILLISECONDS) then
    try
      if userCount < 5 then
        userCount += 1
        Some(userCount)
      else None
    finally lock.unlock()
  else None
```

Listing 23.1: Variant of Lis. 18.7 with a timeout.

Like `synchronized`, method `tryLock` blocks the calling thread until the lock is available but gives up and returns false if the lock is still unavailable after the specified delay. If the method returns true, the lock has been acquired, and the code proceeds as before with an `if-then-else` before freeing the lock. You can also use `tryLock` without a timeout to acquire a lock if it is available, or give up immediately without blocking the thread.

`ReentrantLock` is typically used within a `try-finally` block to ensure that the lock is properly released, even in the presence of exceptions. In this particular example, not much could go wrong between `tryLock` and `unlock`, but a `try-finally` construct makes it easier to release the lock when a value is returned, without having to store this value in a local variable.

When acquiring a lock without a timeout, you can use `lock` to wait uninterruptibly, or use `lockInterruptibly` to make the blocked thread responsive to interrupts. The behavior of `lock` is the same as `synchronized`: Interrupting a thread does not make the thread give up trying to acquire a lock. By contrast, `lockInterruptibly` throws an `InterruptedException` when a thread is interrupted while waiting for a lock. Using `lockInterruptibly` makes it easier to write lock-using tasks that can be canceled.

Besides its more flexible locking methods, the other major benefit of `ReentrantLock` over intrinsic locks is that you can create multiple conditions on the same lock. Conditions are discussed in Section 23.4, and Listing 23.8 uses a lock with two conditions.

In addition to this reimplementation of *exclusive* locks, a second class from the standard library, `ReentrantReadWriteLock`, implements *non-exclusive* locks. The defining characteristic of these locks is that you can acquire them in two separate modes: *write* (exclusive) and *read* (shared). When acquired in write mode, a lock is owned by a single thread, as with exclusive locks. By contrast, a lock acquired in read mode can be shared among multiple threads in that mode.

You can use read-write locks to guard structures that are frequently read but rarely modified. Threads can read concurrently by acquiring the lock in read mode, whereas writing the structure requires exclusive access and necessitates that threads acquire the lock in write mode. Note, however, that the name *read-write* is historical and can be somewhat misleading. A read-write lock is really a shared-exclusive lock, whether the shared mode is used while writing or while reading.

Suppose, for instance, that an application relies on a thread-safe structure, with no additional synchronization necessary to read or write, but also occasionally needs to read the entire state of the structure to get a snapshot:

Scala

```scala
import scala.collection.concurrent.TrieMap // thread-safe

private val users = TrieMap.empty[String, UserInfo]

private val (rlock, wlock) =
    val lock = ReentrantReadWriteLock()
    (lock.readLock, lock.writeLock)

def register(username: String): Option[UserInfo] =
    val info = UserInfo(username)
```

```
    rlock.lock()
    try if users.putIfAbsent(username, info).isEmpty then Some(info) else None
    finally rlock.unlock()

def saveToFile(filename: String): Unit =
    wlock.lock()
    try Using.resource(Files.newBufferedWriter(Path.of(filename))) { out =>
        for (user, info) <- users do out.write(s"$user:$info\n")
      }
    finally wlock.unlock()
```

Listing 23.2: Example use of a read-write lock.

Class `TrieMap` implements a thread-safe map. You can read and write it concurrently from multiple threads without locking. Its `putIfAbsent` method is used here to register a new user. It returns `None` if a key–value pair is actually added and or a non-empty option if the key was already in the map. Inside `saveToFile`, you need to create a snapshot of the map. To prevent new registrations from taking place during an iteration over all the keys and values, the map is locked exclusively, using `wlock`. By contrast, method `register` uses `rlock` to allow multiple threads to call `putIfAbsent` concurrently, since the method is thread-safe. Note how the lock is acquired in "write" mode to read the map, and in "read" mode to write the map.

23.2   Latches and Barriers

Latches are simple synchronizers, which were used in earlier examples for termination detection (Listing 22.2) and to implement a thread-safe box (Listing 22.4). Latches are versatile. They are often used to implement fork-join (scatter-gather) patterns, such as in Listing 22.2 but also have other purposes. I often use latches in writing tests of concurrent programs. For instance, a latch can represent a simulated activity—the latch opens when the activity terminates. Another use of latches in testing is to synchronize activities to maximize concurrent accesses to a shared structure, and thus better assess its thread-safety.

As an illustration, let's revisit the test of a thread-safe list in Listing 21.2. As written, this code suffers from the fact that N tasks begin to access the shared list in a staggered manner: Task k might already be using the list while a thread is still being started to run task $k + 1$ (starting a thread takes time). This reduces the amount of actual concurrency applied to the list. You can add a latch to make all tasks start accessing the list at about the same time, after all the threads have been created and started:

```
                                                              ── Scala ──
val exec   = Executors.newCachedThreadPool()
val shared = SafeStringList()
val start  = CountDownLatch(N + 1)
val finish = CountDownLatch(N)
```

```scala
for i <- 1 to N do
  exec.execute { () =>
    start.countDown()
    start.await()
    5 times shared.add(i.toString)
    finish.countDown()
  }

start.countDown()
start.await()
val time1 = System.nanoTime()
finish.await()
val time2 = System.nanoTime()

exec.shutdown()

assert(shared.size == 5 * N)
assert((1 to N).forall(i => shared.getAll.count(_ == i.toString) == 5))
assert((time2 - time1) / 1E9 <= 0.01)
```

Listing 23.3: Add latches to Lis. 21.2 for increased concurrency and precise timing.

The purpose of the **start** latch, which is initialized with N + 1, is to make sure that all the pool threads start adding to the list *and* the main thread starts recording time at the same instant. First, this makes it more likely that threads will attempt to call method **add** on the list at the same time, thus increasing your chances of finding a bug if the list is not thread-safe. Second, it's a way to measure how long it takes for all the **add** operations to complete. By waiting on the **start** latch before you start keeping time, you can ignore the time needed to activate threads. The second latch, **finish**, opens when all the list insertions have taken place, at which point you can record the end time. In addition to checking the final state of the shared list, the test asserts that all the list operations were completed in less than 1/100th of a second.

Latches can transition from "closed" to "open" one time, and one time only. They cannot transition from "open" to "close" and so are not reusable—**countdown** and **await** have no effect on an open latch. When threads need to use a synchronization point repeatedly, they can use a cyclic barrier instead. A cyclic barrier automatically opens when the last thread reaches the barrier, and it closes again immediately. Instead of two latches, you could write the list testing example with a single reusable barrier:

Scala

```scala
val exec    = Executors.newCachedThreadPool()
val shared  = SafeStringList()
val startEnd = CyclicBarrier(N + 1)
```

```
for i <- 1 to N do
  exec.execute { () =>
    startEnd.await()
    5 times shared.add(i.toString)
    startEnd.await()
  }

startEnd.await()
val time1 = System.nanoTime()
startEnd.await()
val time2 = System.nanoTime()

exec.shutdown()

assert(shared.size == 5 * N)
assert((1 to N).forall(i => shared.getAll.count(_ == i.toString) == 5))
assert((time2 - time1) / 1E9 <= 0.01)
```

Listing 23.4: Replace two latches from Lis. 23.3 with a single barrier.

In this variant of the test, all the threads reach the barrier a first time, at which point the pool threads start adding to the list and the main thread starts keeping track of time. After all the add operations are completed, all the threads reach the barrier again, and the main thread records the finish time. Cyclic barriers are often used in the implementation of iterative algorithms.

23.3 Semaphores

A semaphore is a synchronizer that maintains a count of virtual permits as its state. Threads can acquire and release permits, and when no permit is available, the acquiring method becomes blocking.

Semaphores are very versatile, but rather low-level synchronizers. You can implement many other synchronizers using semaphores. (Concurrency libraries typically rely on more efficient, non-semaphore-based implementations.) For instance, you can write a simple, exclusive, non-reentrant lock using a semaphore:

```scala
class SimpleLock:
  private val semaphore      = Semaphore(1)
  @volatile private var owner = Option.empty[Thread]

  def lock(): Unit =
    semaphore.acquire()
    owner = Some(Thread.currentThread)
```

```
def unlock(): Unit =
    if !owner.contains(Thread.currentThread) then
        throw IllegalStateException("not the lock owner")
    owner = None
    semaphore.release()
```

Listing 23.5: Simple lock implementation using a semaphore.

In this lock implementation, a semaphore is created with a single permit. The lock is locked by acquiring this permit and unlocked by releasing the permit. The lock is not reentrant: A thread that owns the lock and attempts to lock it again will get stuck on an empty semaphore. To prevent threads from attempting to unlock a lock that they do not own, a reference is kept on the current lock owner, as an option.

Because of their notion of permits, semaphores are often used to enforce bounds. For example, you can implement a bounded queue using two semaphores:

Scala

```
class BoundedQueue[A](capacity: Int):
    private val queue   = mutable.Queue.empty[A]
    private val canTake = Semaphore(0)
    private val canPut  = Semaphore(capacity)

    def take(): A =
        canTake.acquire()
        val element = synchronized(queue.dequeue())
        canPut.release()
        element

    def put(element: A): Unit =
        canPut.acquire()
        synchronized(queue.enqueue(element))
        canTake.release()
```

Listing 23.6: Bounded queue based on two semaphores; see also Lis. 23.7 and 23.8.

The number of permits in semaphore `canTake` equals the number of elements in the queue, initially zero. A permit from `canTake` is needed to take an element out of the queue, thus ensuring that the queue is not empty. If the queue is empty, method `take` blocks the calling thread. A permit for semaphore `canTake` is created inside method `put` when an element is added to the queue, so the number of permits always reflects the number of elements in the queue. Semaphore `canPut` is used in a symmetrical way: Its number of permits equals the number of available slots in the queue, initially set to the queue's capacity. Permits from `canPut` are acquired to insert elements—thus guaranteeing that the queue is not full—and created when elements are removed—in other words, when empty slots are created.

Observe that, to avoid deadlocks, semaphore permits are acquired first, before locking the internal queue (see the discussion in Section 22.3). Note also that permits *acquired* by some threads may be *released* by other threads (semaphore permits are virtual), hence my choice of the word "created" instead of "released."

This implementation of a bounded queue suffers from the fact that operations on a non-empty and non-full queue—which are non-blocking—still need to go through two semaphore operations. This inefficiency is avoided in a better bounded queue implementation in Listing 23.8.

23.4   Conditions

Conditions are another low-level synchronizer that you can use to implement other synchronizers. Conceptually, a condition maintains a set of waiting threads, which are blocked. A condition defines methods for a thread to notify another thread from the set that it can continue, to notify all the threads in the set that they can continue, or to add itself to the set. Notification has no effect if no thread is currently waiting.

Conditions have been available on the JVM since the beginning: Every Java object is a condition, in the same way that every Java object is a lock. Conditions and locks work hand-in-hand: You typically need to lock a shared state to decide whether waiting is needed. If a thread needs to wait, it must release this lock before waiting so that other threads can lock and modify the shared state. Note that an object needs to maintain two separate sets of waiting threads: those waiting to acquire the lock and those waiting to be notified from the condition.

Before the advent of `java.util.concurrent` in Java 5, you had to write all your synchronizers in terms of these basic Java conditions. As an illustration, the blocking queue from Section 23.3 could be reimplemented using a condition:

```scala
class BoundedQueue[A](capacity: Int):
  private val queue = mutable.Queue.empty[A]

  def take(): A = synchronized {
    while queue.isEmpty do wait()
    notifyAll()
    queue.dequeue()
  }

  def put(element: A): Unit = synchronized {
    while queue.length == capacity do wait()
    notifyAll()
    queue.enqueue(element)
  }
```

Listing 23.7: Bounded queue with a single condition; see also Lis. 23.8.

The bounded queue itself is used as the lock and condition—all calls to methods `synchronized`, `wait`, and `notifyAll` are made on `this`. In `take`, you make the calling thread wait on the condition if the queue is empty; in `put`, you make it wait if the queue is full. After any successful element insertion or removal, you notify the entire set of waiting threads that the state of the queue has changed.

This code has a few peculiarities that deserve to be discussed in detail:

- The blocking method `wait` is called within the synchronized block of code, even though I stated earlier that you should never invoke a blocking method while holding a lock because it results in deadlocks. First, let's understand why this is necessary. The issue is a non-atomic check-then-act: In `take`, for instance, a thread could see that a queue is empty and release the lock in anticipation to calling `wait`. But before this thread reaches `wait` and is actually added to the set of waiting threads, another thread invokes `put` and calls `notifyAll`. By the time the taking thread reaches the waiting set, `notifyAll` has already happened, and the thread gets stuck, even though the queue is now non-empty. (Listing 23.6 does not suffer from this problem because a semaphore permit can always be safely created, whether a thread is waiting for it or not.)

  Calling method `wait` within the synchronized block avoids this problem, but what about the deadlock issue? Things work correctly only because `wait` *internally* releases the lock after a thread is added to the waiting set (and it is invalid for a thread to invoke `wait` on an object that is not locked by the thread). So, the first rule to remember is simple: Code should always use `X.wait` inside an `X.synchronized` block on the same object X.

- In both `take` and `put`, the check that a queue is not empty or not full is performed inside a loop. This is essential, and it is a consequence of the locking issues discussed earlier. When a thread calls `wait`, it owns a lock that is automatically released. This lock needs to be reacquired after the thread is notified for the thread to continue executing the synchronized block. Several threads—notified from the set of waiting threads, or initiating new calls to method `take` or `put`—compete for this lock, and any thread that ends up acquiring the lock can modify the state of the queue. A taking thread, for instance, could be notified that a queue is non-empty, but the queue could become empty again by the time the thread manages to reacquire the lock. So, once the lock has been reacquired, a thread needs to test the state of the queue again and go back to waiting again if the state is not suitable. The second rule is as simple as the first: Always invoke `wait` in a loop that reevaluates the condition you are waiting for.

- All the waiting threads are notified—using `notifyAll`—after a queue element is added or removed. This is wasteful: If you are adding one element in an empty queue, why notify ten threads to come and get it? However, method `notify`, which notifies only one of the waiting threads, cannot be used in this example. When multiple threads are waiting, method `notify` does not specify which thread is notified. In this implementation, threads waiting to add to the queue and threads waiting to take from the queue are waiting on the same condition. Therefore, a call to `notify` within method `take`, for instance, would run the risk of notifying another taking thread instead of a thread waiting to put an element into the queue.[1]

By using `notifyAll`, more threads may end up being notified than can make progress, but all the threads reevaluate the state of the queue in a loop anyway and will wait again if needed. For instance, if an element is added to an empty queue, all the threads waiting to take from the queue are notified, even though only one will be able to get the element. All the others will observe that `isEmpty` is true and block again. The implementation is correct but inefficient. See Listing 23.8 for an alternative implementation that avoids this problem.

Methods `wait`, `notify`, and `notifyAll` treat Java objects as intrinsic conditions associated with intrinsic locks. If you use `ReentrantLock` as an alternative implementation of exclusive locks, you can use its own implementation of conditions. The main advantage of `ReentrantLock` over intrinsic locks, at least in that regard, is that *multiple* conditions can be associated with the *same* lock. You can write a better bounded queue by having the threads that need the queue to not be empty, and the threads that need the queue to not be full, wait on two separate conditions. This is difficult to do with `wait` and `notify` because then two conditions would require two locks, and `wait` would release only one of them. With `ReentrantLock`, you can create multiple conditions on the same lock, using method `newCondition`:[2]

```scala
                                                              ─── Scala ───
class BoundedQueue[A](capacity: Int):
  private val queue        = mutable.Queue.empty[A]
  private val lock         = ReentrantLock()
  private val canPut, canTake = lock.newCondition()

  def take(): A =
    lock.lock()
    try
      while queue.isEmpty do canTake.await()
      canPut.signal()
      queue.dequeue()
    finally lock.unlock()
```

---

[1]The issue is subtle. It is not immediately obvious that threads that add to the queue and threads that take from the queue can end up in the set of waiting threads *at the same time*, but it can happen if the number of threads sharing the queue is more than double the queue capacity (see the aside on model checking at the end of this section). In such a scenario, replacing calls to `notifyAll` with `notify` could result in a deadlock.

[2]In Scala, `val x, y = expr` evaluates `expr` twice, once to initialize `x` and once to initialize `y`.

```
def put(element: A): Unit =
  lock.lock()
  try
    while queue.length == capacity do canPut.await()
    canTake.signal()
    queue.enqueue(element)
  finally lock.unlock()
```

Listing 23.8: Bounded queue based on two conditions.

Methods `await`, `signal`, and `signalAll` correspond to methods `wait`, `notify`, and `notifyAll` on intrinsic conditions. This implementation has better performance than Listing 23.7 because inserting or removing an element triggers the notification of at most one thread—using `signal`, not `signalAll`. Standard blocking queues from `java.util.concurrent` rely on a similar strategy—an instance of `ReentrantLock` and two conditions.

Aside on Verification by Model Checking

Footnote 1 mentioned that using `notify` instead of `notifyAll` in Listing 23.7 could lead to a deadlock situation. This deadlock is not as systematic as it was in Listing 22.3—most runs proceed correctly to completion—and the steps it takes to make it happen are not entirely obvious. As an illustration of techniques that can be used to complement runtime testing, this aside applies model checking to the incorrect queue implementation—`notifyAll` replaced with `notify`—to discover the deadlock.

The formalism used here is TLA^+, the Temporal Logic of Actions. It is a mathematical notation based on set theory, with some temporal logic elements added. A model of method `put` from a blocking queue can be written in TLA^+ as follows:

$$\text{Put}(t, m) \triangleq \text{IF Len(queue)} < \text{Capacity}$$
$$\text{THEN queue}' = \text{Append(queue}, m) \land \text{Notify}$$
$$\text{ELSE Wait}(t) \land \text{UNCHANGED queue}$$

The details are not essential, but it can be seen that the model uses the same strategy as in Listing 23.7, except that `notify` is used instead of `notifyAll`.[a] In particular, if the queue is not full, an element is added and method `notify` is called; otherwise, the thread calls method `wait` and the queue is unchanged. Method `take` is modeled similarly.

---

[a]The models uses IF instead of `while` because of an implicit loop in the TLA^+ model, but the condition is being rechecked as in Listing 23.7.

Methods `wait`, `notify`, and `notifyAll` can also be modeled according to their Java semantics:

$$\text{Wait}(t) \triangleq \text{waitSet}' = \text{waitSet} \cup \{t\}$$
$$\text{Notify} \triangleq \text{IF waitSet} = \{\} \text{ THEN UNCHANGED waitSet}$$
$$\text{ELSE } \exists\, t \in \text{waitSet} : \text{waitSet}' = \text{waitSet} \setminus \{t\}$$
$$\text{NotifyAll} \triangleq \text{waitSet}' = \{\}$$

Again, the details are beyond the scope of this note, but you can see that `wait` adds a thread t to the set of waiting threads—in TLA^+, the notation $\text{waitSet}' = \cdots$ means "the new value of waitSet is ...." Similarly, `notifyAll` removes all the threads from the waiting set, making the set empty. The representation of method `notify` is a little more complex. It basically says that if the set of waiting threads is empty, nothing happens and the set is unchanged. Otherwise, a thread t is removed from the set. The existential quantifier is used to represent the fact that method `notify` does not specify which thread is being removed—*some* thread is taken out of the set.

Given these mathematical definitions—and a few other elements omitted here—a model-checker can be run. A basic model-checker simply tries to enumerate all possible ways threads might interleave their actions until all possibilities have been checked or an error is found.

On the blocking queue, a model-checker can produce the deadlock scenario shown Figure 23.1. In this scenario, a queue has a capacity of two and is shared among three producing threads—p1, p2, and p3—and two consuming threads—c1 and c2. Initially, the queue is empty and all the threads are running. The producers start calling method `put` until the queue is full (state 3). The next three calls to `put` result in producers calling `wait` and being added to the set of waiting threads (state 6). Consumers start calling method `take`, notifying a producer each time, until the queue is empty (state 8). They keep calling `take` until they are all added to the waiting set (state 10). Interestingly, at this point, the set contains both producing and consuming threads.

In state 11, a producer—p2 or p3—adds an element into the queue, and as a result calls `notify`. The intent of this call to `notify` is to let a consumer know that a value has been added to the queue. However, thread p1—a producer—is taken out of the set instead. The queue is again filled (state 12), resulting in the producers being blocked in the waiting set (state 15). At this point, thread c1 is the only running thread. It consumes a first element from the queue and notifies p1 (state 16). It then takes the second element from the queue but notifies consumer c2 instead of a producer (state 17). Both consumers then block on the empty queue, leaving only thread p1 to run (state 19). This thread puts a value in the queue but notifies p2 instead of a consumer.

State 1: <Initial predicate>
 waitSet = {}
 queue = <<>>

State 2: <Put>
 waitSet = {}
 queue = <<m>>

State 3: <Put>
 waitSet = {}
 queue = <<m, m>>

State 4: <Put>
 waitSet = {p1}
 queue = <<m, m>>

State 5: <Put>
 waitSet = {p1, p2}
 queue = <<m, m>>

State 6: <Put>
 waitSet = {p1, p2, p3}
 queue = <<m, m>>

State 7: <Take>
 waitSet = {p1, p2}
 queue = <<m>>

State 8: <Take>
 waitSet = {p1}
 queue = <<>>

State 9: <Take>
 waitSet = {p1, c1}
 queue = <<>>

State 10: <Take>
 waitSet = {p1, c1, c2}
 queue = <<>>

State 11: <Put>
 waitSet = {c1, c2}
 queue = <<m>>

State 12: <Put>
 waitSet = {c2}
 queue = <<m, m>>

State 13: <Put>
 waitSet = {p1, c2}
 queue = <<m, m>>

State 14: <Put>
 waitSet = {p1, p2, c2}
 queue = <<m, m>>

State 15: <Put>
 waitSet = {p1, p2, p3, c2}
 queue = <<m, m>>

State 16: <Take>
 waitSet = {p2, p3, c2}
 queue = <<m>>

State 17: <Take>
 waitSet = {p2, p3}
 queue = <<>>

State 18: <Take>
 waitSet = {p2, p3, c1}
 queue = <<>>

State 19: <Take>
 waitSet = {p2, p3, c1, c2}
 queue = <<>>

State 20: <Put>
 waitSet = {p3, c1, c2}
 queue = <<m>>

State 21: <Put>
 waitSet = {c1, c2}
 queue = <<m, m>>

State 22: <Put>
 waitSet = {p1, c1, c2}
 queue = <<m, m>>

State 23: <Put>
 waitSet = {p1, p2, c1, c2}
 queue = <<m, m>>

State 24: <Put>
 waitSet = {p1, p2, p3, c1, c2}
 queue = <<m, m>>

Figure 23.1 Deadlock scenario of a blocking queue, as discovered by a model-checker.

In the next step, a producer—p1 or p2—adds to the queue, and (mistakenly) notifies p3. At this point, in state 21, the situation is hopeless: The queue is full and all the consumers are blocked. The two remaining producers then invoke method put and are added to the waiting set. In state 24, a deadlock is reached: All the threads are blocked inside the set.

Figure 23.1 shows an actual output from the model-checker—slightly edited to refer to the Put and Take method names. The power of model checking is this capacity to produce traces that describe the states leading to a problem. A deadlock of the incorrect blocking queue may or may not be observed while running tests, but even when it happens, looking at a thread dump shows only the final deadlock state, not the steps that the threads took to get there. It should be noted that the model-checker used here explores states in a breadth-first manner. As a consequence, a deadlock scenario is guaranteed to have minimal length.

The main limitation of model-checking techniques is the rapid growth of the number of states that need to be explored, a phenomenon known as the *combinatorial state space explosion*. For instance, a queue of capacity 10 requires at least 21 threads to reach a deadlock. The shortest scenario takes 431 steps, and has the model-checker explore 23,011,357 distinct states to discover it.

23.5 Blocking Queues

The bounded queues implemented in Listings 23.6 to 23.8 are not just data structures: They are themselves synchronizers. Their methods can block threads based on the state of the queue, empty or full. Concurrency libraries often implement two types of queues: concurrent queues, which are thread-safe data structures, but may not have blocking methods, and blocking queues, which are synchronizers. Blocking queues are always concurrent queues because they need to be thread-safe, but not all concurrent queues are blocking queues. The queues implemented in Chapter 20, for instance, are concurrent, non-blocking queues. Within each type, several variants exist. Queues can be bounded or not; they can be backed by an array or a list or some other structure; they can rely on locks or lock-free algorithms; they are often first-in-first-out but can also use other orderings, based on priorities or on time; and so on.

Blocking queues are typically used in a *producer–consumer* pattern: Producing activities add to a shared queue while consuming activities concurrently take from the queue. This pattern, which is widely used, offers multiple benefits. First, it decouples data creation from data use, in a pattern similar to the application of streams in Section 12.5. Second, you can sometimes use a single-producer or single-consumer pattern to mix concurrent and sequential activities, as in 23.9. Third, producer–consumer patterns are somewhat naturally self-balancing: When a queue is full, producing tasks are blocked, freeing resources for consuming tasks to catch up, and vice versa when a queue is empty.

As an illustration, consider again the problem of searching files in parallel. Each task consists of two stages: Find targeted data in files and store the search results. An implementation could proceed as follows:

```scala
                                                        ─── Scala ───
val exec: ExecutorService          = ...
def isMatch(line: String): Boolean = ...
val files: ConcurrentLinkedQueue[Path] = ...
val out: Writer                    = ...

def searchFile(path: Path): Unit =
  Using.resource(Source.fromFile(path.toFile)(UTF8)) { in =>
    for line <- in.getLines() do
      if isMatch(line) then out.synchronized { out.write(line); out.write('\n') }
  }

val searchTask: Runnable = () =>
  var file = Option(files.poll())
  while file.nonEmpty do
    searchFile(file.get)
    file = Option(files.poll())

N times exec.execute(searchTask)
```

In this code, the files to search are stored in a concurrent queue. The queue needs to be thread-safe because all the searching tasks obtain files from it in parallel. Each searching task keeps taking files from the queue until the queue is empty, at which point the task terminates. The queue does not need to be blocking: It is filled with files initially and is not used after it is empty. You need to use poll—which returns null[3] on an empty queue—to extract a file from the queue: if !files.isEmpty then file = files.take() would not work because of a non-atomic check-then-act. Each file is searched sequentially, and matching lines are added to a shared output file. You need to lock accesses to this file because, even though instances of type Writer tend to be thread-safe in Java, line contents and newline separators could be improperly interleaved otherwise.[4]

Instead of making all the searching tasks add their results to a shared output, you could refactor the code into a producer–consumer pattern in which producers create matching lines from files, and a single consumer stores these lines into the output file:

---

[3]To deal with null, values are wrapped into options, as was done in Section 12.2.

[4]Class PrintWriter defines an atomic println method, which I could have used here. However, it is implemented as two calls to method write in a synchronized block, just as in my searchFile method.

```scala
                                                            ─ Scala ─
val queue = ArrayBlockingQueue[String](capacity)

def searchFile(path: Path): Unit =
  Using.resource(Source.fromFile(path.toFile)(UTF8)) { in =>
    for line <- in.getLines() do if isMatch(line) then queue.put(line)
  }

val writeTask: Runnable = () =>
  while  ?  do
    out.write(queue.take())
    out.write('\n')

N times exec.execute(searchTask)
exec.execute(writeTask)
```

In this code, a blocking queue is created as a buffer of lines. As a file is searched, matching lines are added to a queue instead of being directly written into the output file. A single `writeTask` activity retrieves lines from the queue and stores them into the file. Locking on `out` is no longer needed because the file is now accessed by just one thread. Of course, locking is still likely taking place within the implementation of the blocking queue, but calls to `put` and `take` are fast, and no lock is held during I/O operations. The code for task `searchTask` is unchanged and can still be run by multiple threads in parallel. Each thread takes files from a (concurrent) queue and puts matching lines into a (concurrent, blocking) queue. Note how the program now uses both types of queues, blocking and non-blocking.

   A piece of code is missing in function `writeTask`: the condition to terminate the line writing loop. Termination issues tend to be subtle in producer–consumer patterns. First, let's convince ourselves that the following approach does not work:

```scala
                                                            ─ Scala ─
// DON'T DO THIS!
while !queue.isEmpty do ...
```

The blocking queue could be temporarily empty—all matching lines found so far have been written into the output file—but that doesn't mean the search is finished. Searching tasks are still potentially opening and reading files and could find more matches. If the writing task terminates because the queue was empty, these new matches will never be saved to file.

The next idea is to keep track of how many searching tasks are still active. The count of active tasks has to be thread-safe—it is decremented by the searching tasks themselves and queried by the file writing task. If N searching tasks are used, you could be tempted to modify the code as follows:

```
——————————————————————————————————————— Scala ———
val active = AtomicInteger(N)


...
active.decrementAndGet() // at the end of each searching task

// DON'T DO THIS!
while active.get() > 0 do ...
```

However, this could still result in early termination of the loop: All the searching tasks have terminated, the `active` count reaches zero, and the file writing task is allowed to terminate without processing the lines that might possibly remain in the queue. This would result again in matches missing from the output file.

Now you might think: No problem, let's combine both termination conditions—no active searching tasks, empty queue of matches—to make sure that the writing task drains the queue after all searching tasks are done:

```
——————————————————————————————————————— Scala ———
// DON'T DO THIS!
while active.get() > 0 || !queue.isEmpty do ...
```

This still doesn't work, but the issue here is more subtle. Suppose you take the last matching line from the queue but searching tasks are still running. At this point, the queue is empty, but the condition `active.get() > 0` is true, so the file writing task does not terminate. Instead, it reenters its loop, calls `queue.take`, and blocks. However, if no further matches are found, the searching tasks terminate without adding any more lines to the queue. The `active` count becomes zero, and the termination condition is established—the count is zero and the queue is empty. But the consuming thread remains blocked on `take` indefinitely, with no opportunity to evaluate this condition again.

A common technique to properly terminate producer–consumer applications is to insert special values—called *poison pills*—into the queue as a way for producers to indicate that consumers should terminate. There are two ways you can apply a poison pill strategy to the file searching example. First, you can keep a thread-safe count of running producers, as before, and make the last producer to terminate insert a single poison pill into the queue. Alternatively, you can make each producer insert a special value upon termination and have the consuming thread count these values until they are all received. The first approach still requires a thread-safe count of active tasks; the second approach, used in the following code, does not:

```scala
                                                              ── Scala ──
val queue = ArrayBlockingQueue[Option[String]](capacity)

def searchFile(path: Path): Unit =
  Using.resource(Source.fromFile(path.toFile)(UTF8)) { in =>
    for line <- in.getLines() do if isMatch(line) then queue.put(Some(line))
  }

val searchTask: Runnable = () =>
  var file = Option(files.poll())
  while file.nonEmpty do
    searchFile(file.get)
    file = Option(files.poll())
  queue.put(None)

val writeTask: Runnable = () =>
  var active = N
  while active > 0 || !queue.isEmpty do
    queue.take() match
      case None => active -= 1
      case Some(line) =>
        out.write(line)
        out.write('\n')
```

Listing 23.9: Searching files and storing results as a producer–consumer pattern.

The queue of matching lines is changed into a queue of options: Some(line) represents a match, and None is the poison pill. Each searching task inserts a single None in the queue at the end of its search. The file writing task counts these None values and knows to terminate when all have been received *and* the queue is empty. Counting is internal to the task and does not entail the use of a thread-safe atomic integer. Indeed, producers and consumers coordinate entirely through the queue and rely on no other shared synchronization mechanism. (The total number of producing tasks, N does need to be known by the consumer, though.)

23.6   Summary

- The Java standard library offers a flexible implementation of exclusive locks through class ReentrantLock, which can be used as an alternative to intrinsic locks. It provides users with the same basic locking properties but defines additional methods for threads to be interrupted or to time out (or even not block at all) when a lock is not available.

- The library also defines non-exclusive locks, commonly known as read-write locks. These locks can be acquired in shared mode or in exclusive mode; that is, a lock that is not free can either have a single exclusive-mode owner or one or more shared-mode owners. Concurrency can be increased by replacing a regular exclusive lock with a read-write lock and having multiple threads work in parallel with the lock acquired in shared mode.

- Latches are simple synchronizers that block threads until the latch is open. Java implements countdown latches, which open after their `countDown` method is called a specific number of times.

- Latches cannot be reused because once open, they cannot be closed again. By contrast, cyclic barriers open and close repeatedly and automatically. Barriers are set up for a fixed number of participating threads. They open—and close again immediately—every time all the threads reach the barrier. (In other words, the arrival of the last thread is the event that triggers opening.) Barriers are often used in iterative algorithms to guarantee that no thread can begin its kth iteration until all threads have completed $k - 1$ iterations.

- Semaphores are a classic type of synchronizer, defined in terms of virtual permits. Permits can be acquired (or consumed) by threads and released (or created) by other threads. When a semaphore runs out of permits, its acquiring method becomes blocking. Semaphores are versatile, and they have been used historically to implement other synchronizers.

- Conditions maintain a set of waiting threads and offer methods to block threads (add them to the set) or notify threads (remove them from the set). Conditions are always used within locked sections of code. Threads that block on a condition automatically—and atomically—release the corresponding lock. Threads that are notified reacquire the necessary lock automatically, but this is not atomic—other threads may run code with the lock after a thread has been notified and before it can itself reacquire the lock. The JVM's intrinsic locks supports only a single condition; the later class `ReentrantLock` permits multiple conditions to be created on the same lock.

- Blocking queues are both (thread-safe) data structures and synchronizers. In addition to standard queue semantics, they define methods to synchronize threads based on the state of the queue: Taking from an empty queue is blocking and, if the queue is bounded, adding to a full queue is also blocking. Blocking queues are often used in producer–consumer patterns to decouple data-producing activities from data-consuming activities. Useful patterns can be defined by using a single producer (scattering data), a single consumer (gathering data), or multiple producers and consumers on the same blocking queue.

Chapter 24

Case Study: Parallel Execution

This chapter investigates, as a case study, the problem of performing a collection of independent tasks in parallel. Tasks are represented as executions of an impure function, run for its side effects. (Value-returning tasks are the focus of the next few chapters.) Different strategies are explored that rely on explicit thread creation (bounded or unbounded), thread pools (bounded or unbounded, dedicated or shared), or parallel collections. The last section uses conditions and semaphores to implement a variant in which additional tasks can be submitted after the computation has already started.

24.1 Sequential Reference Implementation

You can implement a reference sequential runner as follows:

```scala
class Runner[A](comp: A => Unit):
  def run(inputs: Seq[A]): Unit = for input <- inputs do comp(input)
```

A runner is created from a function of type `A => Unit`. Method `run` is given a sequence of inputs and executes the function on each input in turn. To better demonstrate parallelism, we will use a function `sleepTask`, of type `Int => Unit`, throughout the chapter. This function takes the number of seconds to run as its input value and displays a message on the terminal when it starts and when it stops. You can use it in a sequential run:

```scala
println("START")

val runner = Runner(sleepTask)
runner.run(Seq(2, 1, 3))

println("END")
```

The run would proceed as follows:

```
main at XX:XX:47.521: START
main at XX:XX:47.550: begin 2
main at XX:XX:49.551: end 2
main at XX:XX:49.552: begin 1
main at XX:XX:50.552: end 1
main at XX:XX:50.552: begin 3
main at XX:XX:53.552: end 3
main at XX:XX:53.553: END
```

All the work is performed by the thread that calls method `run`. The entire execution takes 6 seconds, the sum of the duration of the three tasks.

This chapter discusses several strategies for parallelization. Parallel runners are required to run all the tasks to completion within a synchronous call to method `run`—all the tasks must be finished before the END message—but they can use additional threads to execute multiple tasks in parallel and speed up the computation. The tasks are assumed to be independent and to not interfere with each other.

24.2   One New Thread per Task

The simplest—but somewhat old-fashioned—strategy for parallelization is to create a new thread for each task:

Scala

```scala
class Runner[A](comp: A => Unit):
    def run(inputs: Seq[A]): Unit =
        val threads = inputs.map(input => Thread(() => comp(input)))
        for thread <- threads do thread.start()
        for thread <- threads do thread.join()
```

Listing 24.1: Parallel execution: one new thread per task.

Higher-order method `map` is used to create a sequence of threads, one per input. It is followed by two iterations—one to start all the threads and another to wait for their termination—using method `join`. If you process the same 2, 1, 3 sequence as before, you get an output of the following form:

```
main at XX:XX:06.593: START
Thread-0 at XX:XX:06.623: begin 2
Thread-2 at XX:XX:06.623: begin 3
```

```
Thread-1 at XX:XX:06.623: begin 1
Thread-1 at XX:XX:07.623: end 1
Thread-0 at XX:XX:08.623: end 2
Thread-2 at XX:XX:09.623: end 3
main at XX:XX:09.624: END
```

All three tasks run in parallel. The execution takes about 3 seconds, the duration of the longest of the tasks.

The order in which you call `join` on the threads doesn't matter—the code needs to wait for all the threads to terminate—but it is essential that all the threads are started before the calls to `join` begin. A possible mistake would be to try to combine the last two iterations into a single loop:

—— *Scala* —

```scala
// DON'T DO THIS!
for thread <- threads do
   thread.start()
   thread.join()
```

Even though you still execute each task in a separate thread, the tasks now run sequentially because you start a thread only after the previous thread has terminated. Processing a 2, 1, 3 sequence takes 6 seconds, as with the sequential runner:

```
main at XX:XX:06.235: START
Thread-0 at XX:XX:06.263: begin 2
Thread-0 at XX:XX:08.264: end 2
Thread-1 at XX:XX:08.265: begin 1
Thread-1 at XX:XX:09.265: end 1
Thread-2 at XX:XX:09.266: begin 3
Thread-2 at XX:XX:12.266: end 3
main at XX:XX:12.267: END
```

24.3 Bounded Number of Threads

A major drawback of Listing 24.1 is that the runner creates an unreasonable number of threads if the sequence of inputs is large. For instance, if your computer has eight cores and an input sequence contains 1000 values, you end up with 1000 threads sharing eight processors, which is unlikely to be the most efficient way to process the inputs in parallel.

To limit the number of threads created by a runner to a specified bound, you can rely on a queue-based approach similar to Listing 23.9:

```scala
class Runner[A](bound: Int)(comp: A => Unit):
  def run(inputs: Seq[A]): Unit =
    val queue = ConcurrentLinkedQueue(inputs.asJava)

    val task: Runnable = () =>
      var input = Option(queue.poll())
      while input.nonEmpty do
        comp(input.get)
        input = Option(queue.poll())

    val threads = Seq.fill(bound min inputs.length)(Thread(task))
    for thread <- threads do thread.start()
    for thread <- threads do thread.join()
```

Listing 24.2: Parallel execution: bounded number of threads.

All the given inputs are placed inside a thread-safe queue. The minimum between the desired bound on threads and the number of inputs is the number of threads created. The threads all run the same task. This task uses a loop to extract inputs from the queue and apply the runner's function to them. It terminates when the queue is empty.

You can create a runner as `Runner(2)(sleepTask)` to limit the number of threads to two. A typical output, when applied to the list of inputs 2, 1, 3, is shown here:

```
main at XX:XX:15.696: START
Thread-1 at XX:XX:15.731: begin 1
Thread-0 at XX:XX:15.731: begin 2
Thread-1 at XX:XX:16.733: end 1
Thread-1 at XX:XX:16.733: begin 3
Thread-0 at XX:XX:17.732: end 2
Thread-1 at XX:XX:19.734: end 3
main at XX:XX:19.734: END
```

The runner uses two threads; they immediately pull inputs 2 and 1 from the queue. After 1 second, `Thread-1` completes the first task and pulls input 3 from the queue. One second later—2 seconds into the run—`Thread-0` finishes task 2, finds the queue empty, and terminates. Two seconds later, `Thread-1` finishes task 3 and also terminates. The entire run takes about 4 seconds.

24.4 Dedicated Thread Pool

Chapter 21 discussed several reasons why per-task thread creation is often avoided in favor of thread pools. Instead of individual threads, method **run** could create a thread pool. If you think about it, Listing 24.2 actually reimplements its own mini thread pool. You might as well use an actual thread pool, which already implements its own queue and looping task:

```scala
class Runner[A](bound: Int)(comp: A => Unit):
   def run(inputs: Seq[A]): Unit =
      val exec = Executors.newFixedThreadPool(bound)

      for input <- inputs do exec.execute(() => comp(input))

      exec.shutdown()
      exec.awaitTermination(Long.MaxValue, NANOSECONDS)
```

Listing 24.3: Parallel execution: dedicated thread pool.

You start a thread pool with a fixed number of threads. The thread pool maintains an internal queue of tasks, which you can use to replace the queue of inputs used in Listing 24.2: Create a task for each input and add it to the queue. The thread in charge of the run then shuts down the pool and blocks until all submitted tasks have been executed.[1] By default, Java's fixed thread pools create worker threads on demand, up to the bound. Therefore, this variant creates a number of threads no larger than the minimum between the bound and the number of inputs, as in Listing 24.2. Except for the names of the threads, the output of the sample run is the same, but the implementation is much simpler:

```
main at XX:XX:33.200: START
pool-1-thread-2 at XX:XX:33.231: begin 1
pool-1-thread-1 at XX:XX:33.231: begin 2
pool-1-thread-2 at XX:XX:34.233: end 1
pool-1-thread-2 at XX:XX:34.233: begin 3
pool-1-thread-1 at XX:XX:35.232: end 2
pool-1-thread-2 at XX:XX:37.233: end 3
main at XX:XX:37.234: END
```

---

[1]There is no variant of `awaitTermination` without a timeout. `Long.MaxValue` nanoseconds add up to more than 292 years, which is infinite in practice.

24.5   Shared Thread Pool

One of the motivations for using thread pools is to keep a bound on the number of threads, as in the preceding example. Another is thread reuse, as applications often benefit from sharing pools across multiple components.

Listing 24.3 creates a new thread pool, with fresh new threads, for each run of a runner; thus, thread reuse is limited in that example. As an alternative, you could implement a runner that uses an existing thread pool instead of creating its own. This change impacts the design because you cannot shut down a shared thread pool. Instead, the thread that calls method `run` needs to wait for all the tasks to finish, whether the threads from the pool are still running or not. This is a problem that we already faced in Listing 22.2, and the same approach—a countdown latch—can be applied to solve it:

```scala
                                                              Scala

class Runner[A](exec: Executor)(comp: A => Unit):
  def run(inputs: Seq[A]): Unit =
    val done = CountDownLatch(inputs.length)

    for input <- inputs do
      val task: Runnable = () =>
        try comp(input)
        finally done.countDown()
      exec.execute(task)

    done.await()
```

Listing 24.4: Parallel execution: shared thread pool.

A latch is created with a count equal to the number of input values. The tasks submitted to the thread pool are extended to count down the latch at the end of each computation. The `try-finally` construct ensures that the latch is counted down even if the execution of the function fails. The thread that calls `run` does not shut down the pool but simply waits on the latch.

Using a pool with two threads produces the same 4-second run as before. Note, however, that multiple, concurrent runs of the same runner execute tasks on the same pool, whereas they would run on separate, independent pools with the Listing 24.3 implementation.

Other synchronizers could be used to wait for task completion. For instance, you can create a semaphore with no permits, have each completing task create a permit, and make the waiting thread block until it can acquire a number of permits equal to the length of the sequence of inputs. Also, the thread pool may already implement methods for this purpose. If argument `exec` is given as a value of type `ExecutorService` instead of `Executor`—all the standard Java thread pools implement this type—its method `invokeAll` can also be used directly to wait for completion of a list of tasks.

24.6   Bounded Thread Pool

In Listing 24.3, you can place a bound on the number of tasks that run concurrently, which can be beneficial in some circumstances. This feature is lost in Listing 24.4 because you have no control over the number of worker threads in the shared pool.

A best-of-both-worlds implementation would rely on a shared thread pool *and* implement an additional constraint on how many tasks may run concurrently inside the pool. You can achieve this with a semaphore, created with as many permits as the desired level of parallelism:

```scala
class Runner[A](exec: Executor, bound: Int)(comp: A => Unit):
  def run(inputs: Seq[A]): Unit =
    val canStart = Semaphore(bound)

    for input <- inputs do
      val task: Runnable = () =>
        try comp(input)
        finally canStart.release()

      canStart.acquire()
      exec.execute(task)
    end for

    canStart.acquire(bound)
```

Listing 24.5: Parallel execution: shared thread pool with a bound.

The thread that invokes method `run` acquires a permit from the semaphore before submitting each task for execution. When a task finishes, it releases the permit so another task can be submitted. This guarantees that the maximum number of tasks running at any point in time is bounded by the initial number of permits in the semaphore. After all tasks have been submitted, `canStart.acquire(bound)` is used to wait for task completion: Once all the permits are back inside the semaphore, you know that all the tasks are finished. No additional countdown latch is needed.

A runner created as `Runner(exec, 2)(sleepTask)` where `exec` is an unlimited thread pool may produce the following output:

```
main at XX:XX:04.870: START
pool-1-thread-1 at XX:XX:04.901: begin 2
pool-1-thread-2 at XX:XX:04.901: begin 1
pool-1-thread-2 at XX:XX:05.901: end 1
pool-1-thread-3 at XX:XX:05.902: begin 3
pool-1-thread-1 at XX:XX:06.901: end 2
pool-1-thread-3 at XX:XX:08.902: end 3
main at XX:XX:08.903: END
```

The run ends up using three different threads—the thread pool is unlimited—but there are never more than two tasks active at the same time. The overall run takes about 4 seconds, as before.

24.7   Parallel Collections

For a final—and simpler—variant of the runner, recall the discussion of parallel collections in Section 21.4. Indeed, given our assumption that the concurrent invocations of the shared function are independent, parallel collections are a perfect match. You can trivially modify the one-line sequential runner implementation used at the beginning of the chapter to introduce parallelism in the execution of the tasks:

```scala
class Runner[A](comp: A => Unit):
   def run(inputs: Seq[A]): Unit = for input <- inputs.par do comp(input)
```

Listing 24.6: Parallel execution: parallel collections.

In Scala, `for-do` is syntactic sugar for a call to higher-order method `foreach`, and the body of method `run` could be written as `inputs.par.foreach(comp)`. On parallel collections, `foreach` is implemented using a common thread pool.[2] The runner in Listing 24.6, on the same 2, 1, 3 example, produces an output of the following form:

```
main at XX:XX:26.201: START
scala-execution-context-global-16 at XX:XX:26.275: begin 1
scala-execution-context-global-17 at XX:XX:26.275: begin 3
scala-execution-context-global-15 at XX:XX:26.275: begin 2
scala-execution-context-global-16 at XX:XX:27.276: end 1
scala-execution-context-global-15 at XX:XX:28.276: end 2
scala-execution-context-global-17 at XX:XX:29.277: end 3
main at XX:XX:29.277: END
```

24.8   Asynchronous Task Submission Using Conditions

Section 24.7 makes concurrent programming look easy—and it sometimes is. However, you should be ready for scenarios that do not quite fit the canned patterns as nicely.

As an illustration, consider a variation of the runner problem that allows more inputs to be added after a run has started. The `Runner` type is extended with a method `addInput` that can be used to add one or more input values to an ongoing run. This small change brings a host of problems and design challenges:

[2]Mechanisms are available that can make parallel collections run on your own thread pool, but they are a bit awkward in Scala.

- The thread that initiates a computation is stuck inside method run for the duration of the run. Adding tasks can happen only in other threads. Accordingly, runner instances now need to be safe when shared by multiple threads.

- There is an inherent race condition between a finishing run and an attempt to add inputs to this run. A method to test the state of a runner—is it running?—would be useless because of a non-atomic check-then-act: A runner could become passive right after it is checked for being active. Instead, method addInput should be expected to fail to add an input to the current run if it comes too late, and it needs a way to indicate such a failure to its caller.

- Waiting for run completion is harder because new tasks can be added after waiting has begun. In particular, the simple approach used earlier, based on a countdown latch created from a known number of tasks, becomes insufficient.

- If runs are allowed to overlap—a new run can be started by another thread before the previous run is finished—and further inputs are added while multiple runs are ongoing, to which run should they be added?

- Alternatively, overlapping runs can be prohibited by making sure that method run is not allowed to start until the previous run is completed. This choice requires that the method behaves differently depending on the state of a runner—active versus passive. All the runners implemented so far have been stateless—not counting the thread pool, which is obviously thread-safe. A stateful runner must be designed more carefully when shared among threads.

This section focuses on implementations that share two design choices. First, runs cannot overlap. Method run blocks until the previous run is terminated, then submits a new set of inputs (and blocks again until this new computation is finished). Second, addInput indicates success or failure by returning a Boolean value. (Some of Java's concurrent collections use the same approach, such as method offer on queues.)

You can implement blocking in method run by combining conditions with a count of active tasks. With this approach, a run finishes—and a new run may begin—when all the tasks in a runner have completed, including tasks that were added after the run started:

```scala
                                                             ── Scala ──
class Runner[A](exec: Executor)(comp: A => Unit):
    private var active = 0
    private var runs   = 0

    def run(inputs: Seq[A]): Unit = synchronized {
        while active != 0 do wait()
        val myRun = runs + 1
        runs = myRun
        active = inputs.length
```

```scala
      for input <- inputs do exec.execute(task(input))
      while runs == myRun && active != 0 do wait()
   }

   def addInput(input: A): Boolean = synchronized {
      if active == 0 then false
      else
         active += 1
         exec.execute(task(input))
         true
   }

   private def task(in: A): Runnable = () =>
      try comp(in)
      finally synchronized {
         active -= 1
         if active == 0 then notifyAll()
      }
```

Listing 24.7: Extensible parallel execution using a single condition.

A variable `active` is used to count the number of tasks still active in the current run. It is incremented when new tasks are submitted to the executor (inside `run` and `addInput`) and decremented by the tasks themselves as they terminate. All accesses to this variable are guarded by using `synchronized` to lock the runner itself.

When trying to add a new input, the code needs to check whether the current run is still ongoing. If `active == 0`, method `addInput` returns false immediately. Variable `active` needs to be zero to start a new run (first line of method `run`) and also to complete the current run (last line of method `run`). The last task of a run, when the active count reaches zero, notifies waiting threads that the run is terminated using `notifyAll`.

The role of variables `runs` and `myRun` is subtle and deserves a detailed explanation. Consider first a simpler but incorrect implementation of method `run`, without these variables:

Scala

```scala
// DON'T DO THIS!
def run(inputs: Seq[A]): Unit = synchronized {
   while active != 0 do wait()
   active = inputs.length
   for input <- inputs do exec.execute(task(input))
   while active != 0 do wait()
}
```

Method `run` waits for the active count to be zero to start a run, and again to terminate the run. Consider now a scenario in which a thread T1 initiates a run and is blocked waiting for the run to terminate and a thread T2 is blocked at the beginning of method `run` waiting to start a second run. Both threads wait for `active` to be zero. When the last task of the first run finishes, both threads are notified. At this point, they compete to relock the runner so as to continue their execution of method **run**. If thread T2, which is waiting to start a run, gets the lock first, it will submit new tasks to the executor and make the active count non-zero. It will then release the lock and wait for this second run to finish. Thread T1 can then obtain the lock, but it will test **active != 0** to be true and will go back waiting—now waiting for the completion of the *second* run, instead of simply being done with its own run.

This is a difficulty that is actually not uncommon in concurrent programming. You often need to distinguish between separate repetitions of the same state—here, a runner with a positive count of active tasks. For instance, cyclic barriers face a similar challenge when they need to differentiate between two closed states in a *closed–open–closed* sequence. A common strategy, used here, is to number iterations as a mechanism to distinguish between states that otherwise would be equivalent: *Closed–open–closed* becomes $closed_1$–$open_1$–$closed_2$, where $closed_2$ is somehow different from $closed_1$.

In the runner example, each run is assigned a unique number,[3] and threads that have started a run wait for the active count of their own run to be zero. If a new run has already started—which implies that the active count must have reached zero—those threads are free to terminate their execution, even if the active count has already become non-zero again.[4]

To conclude this section, I will make two final comments on this implementation. First, locking is necessary to manipulate fields **active** and **runs**: You need to read and write them within **synchronized** blocks. However, it is essential that when the tasks apply the runner's function, they do it without the lock owned. If the code **comp(in)** is placed inside the synchronized block, all parallelism is lost.

Second, it is necessary to use **notifyAll** when you wake waiting threads because you need to notify not only the thread that initiated the run that its run is finished, but also possibly another thread that is waiting to start a new run. Two successive calls to **notify** won't work because they might notify two threads waiting to start a run, and not the thread that is finishing. In contrast, by using **notifyAll**, you can notify all the waiting threads, including multiple threads waiting to start a new run, even though only one of them can initiate a run at a time.

Ideally, you would like to notify the thread waiting for its run to finish as well as *one* of the threads waiting to start a new run. For this, you need to use two separate conditions, one to start a run and another to finish a run:

---

[3]Strictly speaking, **runs** can wrap and reuse a value, but the number of runs needed is so large that it is not an issue in practice: A run will have terminated long before its number is being reused.

[4]To avoid getting stuck because the active count quickly transitions from non-zero to zero and back to non-zero, you might be tempted to implement method **run** as follows (assuming **inputs** is not empty):

```
// DON'T DO THIS!
def run(inputs: Seq[A]): Unit = synchronized {
    while active != 0 do wait()
    active = inputs.length
    for input <- inputs do exec.execute(task(input))
    wait()
}
```

This is incorrect because the JVM allows for spurious wake-ups: A thread blocked on **wait** may—rarely—unblock and continue without having been notified. For this reason, it is important to always stick to the pattern of invoking **wait** inside a loop that reevaluates the condition a thread is waiting for.

Scala

```scala
class Runner[A](exec: Executor)(comp: A => Unit):
  private var active       = 0
  private var runs         = 0
  private val lock         = ReentrantLock()
  private val start, finish = lock.newCondition()

  def run(inputs: Seq[A]): Unit =
    lock.lock()
    try
      while active != 0 do start.await()
      val myRun = runs + 1
      runs = myRun
      active = inputs.length
      for input <- inputs do exec.execute(task(input))
      while runs == myRun && active != 0 do finish.await()
      start.signal()
    finally lock.unlock()

  def addInput(input: A): Boolean =
    lock.lock()
    try
      if active == 0 then false
      else
        active += 1
        exec.execute(task(input))
        true
    finally lock.unlock()

  private def task(in: A): Runnable = () =>
    try comp(in)
    finally
      lock.lock()
      try
        active -= 1
        if active == 0 then finish.signal()
      finally lock.unlock()
```

Listing 24.8: Extensible parallel execution using two conditions.

An instance of `ReentrantLock` is used to obtain two conditions on the same lock, which plain `synchronized` doesn't support. Inside `run`, a thread waits first on the `start` condition, then on the `finish` condition. When the last task of a run finishes, it notifies one thread on the `finish` condition—there is only one waiting, the thread that initiated the current run. This thread, in turn, notifies one thread on the `start` condition that a new run can begin. Although multiple threads could be waiting on the `start` condition, only one is notified to begin a new run. The remainder of the implementation is unchanged,[5] except for the awkwardness of having to use `ReentrantLock` instead of `synchronized`.

24.9   Two-Semaphore Implementation

Section 24.8 illustrated the use of conditions, a fundamental construct of concurrent programming, as well as the common issue of repeated states that need to be distinguished through a generation counter (variable **runs** in Listings 24.7 and 24.8). In reality, for this particular example, you can achieve a simpler design by not using conditions at all.

What complicates the earlier implementations is the fact that both threads that need to begin a run and threads that need to end a run are waiting for the same state of the application (`active == 0`) even when using two separate conditions. You can avoid that by using two completely separate waiting criteria. The following implementation shows the power and versatility of semaphores:

Scala

```scala
class Runner[A](exec: Executor)(comp: A => Unit):
   private var active = 0
   private val start  = Semaphore(1)
   private val finish = Semaphore(0)

   def run(inputs: Seq[A]): Unit =
      if inputs.nonEmpty then
         start.acquire()
         synchronized {
            active = inputs.length
            for input <- inputs do exec.execute(task(input))
         }
         finish.acquire()
         start.release()

   def addInput(input: A): Boolean = synchronized {
      if active == 0 then false
      else
         active += 1
         exec.execute(task(input))
         true
   }
```

---

[5]The `runs` variable is still necessary to handle the case of a thread that calls method `run` just as the current run finishes and gets the lock before the thread that is about to terminate its own run.

```
   private def task(in: A): Runnable = () =>
      try comp(in)
      finally synchronized {
           active -= 1
           if active == 0 then finish.release()
      }
```

Listing 24.9: Extensible parallel execution using two semaphores.

The `start` semaphore is used to make sure that runs do not overlap. It has only one permit, which is needed to execute the `run` method. A second semaphore, `finish`, is used for termination. It is initially empty, and the very last task to finish creates a single permit for it.[6] The thread that initiated the run waits for this permit. Before it returns from the `run` method, it releases the permit of the `start` semaphore to allow another thread to begin a new run.

24.10 Summary

In most applications, concurrent programming need not take the form of individual threads created on a per-task basis and coordinated using low-level synchronizers such as locks. Abstractions such as thread pools and parallel collections (more will be explored in the following chapters) can be used to hide intricate synchronization details and achieve parallelism with relatively simple code. The old proposition that concurrent programming is hard remains true in many cases, but parallelism can also often be achieved with code that is safe and straightforward by leveraging suitable high-level constructs.

When do-it-yourself levels are warranted—for instance, while implementing generic libraries—code complexity can increase rapidly. This case study developed several implementations of a parallel runner of independent tasks. Some, like Listing 24.6, are trivially simple. Others, while not as trivial, can be written in terms of a single synchronizer, without explicit threads or locks. Still others combine multiple synchronizers in complex ways, and their correctness can be asserted only after all sneaky scenarios have been taken into account.

---

[6] As a result, and by contrast to the earlier variants, this implementation works properly only if the sequence of inputs is not empty.

Chapter 25

Futures and Promises

One of the major themes of Part I was that functional programming involves a shift from actions and mutability to functions and immutability, a major benefit of which is easier sharing of data across program components. In Part II, we have already seen in Chapters 22 to 24 that sharing mutable data among threads—and the resulting need for synchronization—is a great source of complexity in concurrent programming. This chapter and the next aim to show that concurrent code can be greatly simplified by leveraging functional programming principles. As before, it all begins with the use of pure functions as units of computation but is now executed by separate threads. Futures are a standard programming language construct used to manipulate concurrently executed functions. At a basic level, a future combines the characteristics of a function and a synchronizer. Chapter 26 considers futures in an even more functional way.

25.1 Functional Tasks

Most of the tasks used so far to illustrate concurrent programming have been instances of the Runnable interface. Its run method returns nothing and is used to apply modifications to some shared data. For instance, Listing 22.1, reproduced here, uses two tasks to add strings to a shared list:

```scala
val exec   = Executors.newCachedThreadPool()
val shared = SafeStringList()

def addStrings(n: Int, str: String): Unit = n times shared.add(str)

exec.execute(() => addStrings(5, "T1"))
exec.execute(() => addStrings(5, "T2"))

exec.shutdown()
exec.awaitTermination(5, MINUTES)

assert(shared.size == 10)
```

To ensure this approach would work, the shared list was designed to be thread-safe—in this case, by relying on locks. Note, however, that this thread-safety gives us more than we need: The list remains in a valid state after each call to its add method by any thread. In this particular example, these intermediate states, while valid, are not needed. The list is used only after the tasks that added to it are finished—when it already contains all ten strings.

If all you need is to build a collection of all the strings produced together by the two tasks, you don't care about the state of the list as it evolves during this computation. Instead, you can have each task produce its own collection of strings, and then put the two collections together at the end:

```scala
                                                              ──── Scala ────
val exec = Executors.newCachedThreadPool()

def makeStrings(n: Int, str: String): List[String] = List.fill(n)(str)

var strings1: List[String] = null
var strings2: List[String] = null

exec.execute(() => strings1 = makeStrings(5, "T1"))
exec.execute(() => strings2 = makeStrings(5, "T2"))

exec.shutdown()
exec.awaitTermination(5, MINUTES)

val strings: List[String] = strings1 ::: strings2
assert(strings.size == 10)
```

This variant of the program proceeds differently from before. Instead of sharing a single list, each task creates its own list. These per-task lists are not shared and do not need to be thread-safe.[1] No locks are involved. After the tasks have terminated, the main thread puts the two lists together, again without a need for synchronization.

The program works but lacks elegance. It uses two mutable variables, initialized with arbitrary values, and runs the risk that these values may be used by mistake, resulting in a `NullPointerException`. What brings about this convoluted structure is a discrepancy between the purpose of each task—to create a list—and the fact that the tasks are still implemented as *actions*—instances of `Runnable` that modify mutable data. It would be more sensible for the tasks to be *functions*—value-producing tasks, or *functional tasks*—instead of actions that set external variables.

All of the mechanisms used so far to create concurrent activities—the `Runnable` interface, the constructor of `Thread` class, the `execute` method of a thread pool—focus on actions. They are inadequate to handle functional tasks. This chapter and the next discuss *futures*, an established device tailored to value-producing tasks.

---

[1] As immutable lists, they *are* thread-safe in this example, but they don't need to be.

25.2 Futures as Synchronizers

NOTE

The Java standard library defines an interface Future, introduced in Java 5. The Scala standard library also defines a trait by the same name. The Scala type includes many functionalities not found in the Java interface. Various third-party libraries—most notably Google's Guava—developed types of future that were closer to Scala's Future trait until a class CompletableFuture was introduced in Java 8. Java's CompletableFuture and Scala's Future now offer similar mechanisms (CompletableFuture has a bit more), which are explored in Chapter 26. This chapter focuses on using futures as synchronizers, which you can do with all three types. Code illustrations in this section and the next use Java's earlier Future for simplicity. Section 25.4 introduces the other two implementations.

So far, we have used thread pools through a method execute, which takes an argument of type Runnable. In addition to Runnable, Java defines a Callable interface. In contrast to the run method in Runnable, the call method in Callable can return values.[2] Java thread pools define a method submit that takes a Callable argument. While execute returns nothing—it's a void method—submit returns a future:

```scala
                                                              ── Scala ──
val exec: ExecutorService = ...

def makeStrings(n: Int, str: String): List[String] = List.fill(n)(str)

val f1: Future[List[String]] = exec.submit(() => makeStrings(5, "T1"))
val f2: Future[List[String]] = exec.submit(() => makeStrings(5, "T2"))

val strings: List[String] = f1.get() ::: f2.get()
assert(strings.size == 10)
```

Listing 25.1: Value-producing tasks handled as futures.

As with Runnable, you often create values of type Callable as lambda expressions. In this example, two tasks are handed to a thread pool for execution using method submit. Each task invokes function makeStrings; no assignment statement is involved. You can then use the futures returned by submit to retrieve the lists created by the tasks using method get, and concatenate the lists as before.

---

[2]Another difference is that call can throw checked exceptions. This is something that neither run (in Runnable) nor apply (in Function) is allowed to do.

Several noteworthy aspects of this program should be pointed out:

- Method `submit`, like `execute`, typically triggers an asynchronous execution of its argument and returns immediately.

- The method returns a future, parameterized by the type of the value produced by a task—here, a list of strings. You can think of a future as a handle on a task, or even as the task itself (which it sometimes is, as the later discussion of `FutureTask` describes).

- Futures define mechanisms that you can use to retrieve the value produced by a task. On a Java future, this is method `get`.

- If a task is not finished—it is still running or not yet started—its return value is not available, and method `get` is blocking: `f1.get` blocks until the first task completes, and so does `f2.get` with the second task. This feature is used here by the main thread to wait for both tasks to finish, without the code shutting down the pool or using a latch as before.

- The mutable variables `strings1` and `strings2` of the previous program, which were assignable and arbitrarily initialized, have been replaced with functional, non-reassignable variables—the two futures.[3]

You can see from this example that futures are synchronizers: They can block a thread—using method `get`—based on the finished/unfinished state of a task. Like blocking queues, futures are both synchronizers and data structures. After a task terminates, a future contains the value produced by that task. Method `get` stops being blocking and can be used to simply access this value. In the previous example, if the main thread invokes `f1.get` or `f2.get` a second time, it will not block.

Futures are extremely powerful, and much concurrent programming can be simplified by leveraging them. Consider, for instance, a simple server similar to Listing 21.4:

Scala

```scala
val exec   = Executors.newFixedThreadPool(16)
val server = ServerSocket(port)

def handleConnection(connection: Connection): Unit =
    val request = connection.read()   // get request from client
    val data = dbLookup(request)      // search the database
    addToLog(data)                    // log the results of the search
    val ad = fetchAd(request)         // fetch a customized ad
    val page = makePage(data, ad)     // create a page
    connection.write(page)            // reply to the client
    connection.close()                // close the socket
    updateStats(page)                 // record some statistics
```

---

[3]This transformation is similar to the transition from imperative to functional programming discussed in Part I—for instance, between Listing 3.2 and Listing 3.3.

```
while true do
  val socket = server.accept()
  exec.execute(() => handleConnection(Connection(socket)))
```

This server uses a thread pool to handle incoming connections in parallel, up to 16 requests concurrently. Each connection, however, is processed sequentially through a series of operations: First read the request, then retrieve data from a database, then fetch a customized ad, and so on.

Instead of happening in sequence, some of these steps could be executed concurrently. For instance, the server could be made faster and more responsive by fetching the ad in parallel with the other operations:

```
                                                              Scala
val exec1  = Executors.newFixedThreadPool(12)
val exec2  = Executors.newFixedThreadPool(8)
val server = ServerSocket(port)

def handleConnection(connection: Connection, exec: ExecutorService): Unit =
  val request = connection.read()
  val futureAd = exec.submit(() => fetchAd(request))
  val data = dbLookup(request)
  addToLog(data)
  val page = makePage(data, futureAd.get())
  connection.write(page)
  connection.close()
  updateStats(page)

while true do
  val socket = server.accept()
  exec1.execute(() => handleConnection(Connection(socket), exec2))
```

Listing 25.2: A parallel server with parallelism within responses; see also Lis. 26.8.

After a request has been read from a socket, a task is created to fetch a customized ad. The call to method `submit` returns immediately with a future, and the thread handling the request continues with the database lookup. After the data has been retrieved and logged, the ad is needed to assemble the page. You obtain it by calling `get` on the future. There are two possibilities at this point. If the ad-fetching task is still running, method `get` blocks. Once the ad becomes available, `get` unblocks, and the page is assembled. If, however, the ad-fetching task is already finished by the time you reach `makePage`, method `get` does not block and simply returns the ad, which you use to assemble the page. In other words, fetching the ad and querying the database now happen in parallel, and the same code handles all cases, whether ad fetching is faster or slower than database querying.

In addition to the no-argument method `get`, futures in Java define a method `isDone` to query the status of a task without blocking. It can be used to implement more complex strategies that involve combinations of polling and blocking. Note that the server in Listing 25.2 uses two thread pools. Using the same executor to run `handleConnection` and `fetchAd` would run a risk of deadlock. This topic is discussed in detail in Section 26.1.

25.3   Timeouts, Failures, and Cancellation

A future carries the result of a functional task after the task has completed. But what happens if the task fails? In this case, the future must still be completed—there is no point in waiting on `get` for a result that will never come. Instead of the task's result, the future then contains the cause of the failure. In Java, method `get` rethrows the exception that caused a task to fail but wraps it first inside an `ExecutionException`.

As with almost all synchronizers, you can set an upper limit on the amount of time a thread might be blocked. Java's method `get` accepts an optional timeout argument. If the timeout is reached before a task produces a value, this variant of `get` throws a `TimeoutException`.

As an illustration, you can modify the server from Listing 25.2 to use a fallback ad if loading a customized ad fails and to replace a customized ad with a default ad if loading takes more than 0.5 second after database lookup and logging have been completed:

```scala
val futureAd = exec.submit(() => fetchAd(request))
... // DB lookup and logging
val ad =
   try futureAd.get(500, MILLISECONDS)
   catch
      case _: ExecutionException => failedAd
      case _: TimeoutException   => futureAd.cancel(true); timeoutAd
val page = makePage(data, ad)
...
```

Listing 25.3: Dealing with a future's timeout and failure.

Variable `ad` is set with one of three values: (1) a customized ad, if loading finishes within the 0.5-second timeout; (2) a failed ad if loading fails within 0.5 second; or (3) a default ad if loading is still running after 0.5 second. In this last case, the ad that is still being loaded will never be used, and loading can be interrupted. This is the purpose of the call `cancel(true)`.[4]

---

[4]The Boolean argument in `cancel` affects tasks that have already started to run. If it is true, there is an attempt to terminate the execution. This is often implemented by interrupting the running thread, which may or may not stop the task. If the Boolean is false, no attempt is made to stop a running task, but the future is still marked as canceled. Java's newer futures implement only `cancel(false)` semantics, and Scala's futures have no cancellation mechanism. (The rationale is that, as a cancellation mechanism, interruption works adequately only with tasks designed to respond to it. Tasks that perform non-interruptible I/O, for instance, will not react to `cancel(true)`.) Canceling running tasks is difficult in general. The case study in Chapter 28 requires the need to cancel tasks after they have begun to run and implements an ad hoc cancellation strategy independent of futures.

25.4 Future Variants

The code examples in Sections 25.2 and 25.3 rely on `java.util.concurrent.Future`, the oldest of Java's two `Future` types. Java 8 introduced `java.util.concurrent .CompletableFuture`, which is created slightly differently. For instance, the future `f1` in Listing 25.1 could be created as a `CompletableFuture` as

```scala
val f1 = CompletableFuture.supplyAsync(() => makeStrings(5, "T1"), exec)
```

or

```scala
val f1 = CompletableFuture.supplyAsync(() => makeStrings(5, "T1"))
```

The second form uses a common thread pool instead of a user-specified thread pool.

Scala uses its own futures and specifies the thread pool to use as an implicit argument. This allows you to write

```scala
given ExecutionContext = exec

val f1 = Future(makeStrings(5, "T1")) // uses exec
```

or

```scala
val f1 = Future(makeStrings(5, "T1")) // uses the default thread pool in scope
```

Note that Scala relies on an unevaluated, by-name argument, thereby avoiding the use of a lambda expression as an explicit thunk (see the discussion in Section 12.2).

With both Scala's `Future` and Java's `CompletableFuture`, the future that is returned implements a richer interface that supports a form of functional-concurrent programming, as discussed in Chapter 26.

25.5 Promises

Promises are the internal mechanism by which futures are created. A promise represents the (yet-to-come) value of a future. In some sense, it is the data part of the data/synchronizer combination that constitutes a future.

A promise can be fulfilled with either a value or an error, at which point the future is complete. Promises are often—but not always—created by one thread and completed by another. For instance, this is how futures are created by thread pools: The thread that submits a task creates a promise, and a worker from the pool fulfills it.

As an illustration, consider function `apply`, from the `Future` companion object. It was used earlier to create future `f1`—recall that `Future(makeStrings(5, "T1"))` is `Future.apply(makeStrings(5, "T1"))` in Scala. You could implement `apply` using a promise:

```Scala
import scala.concurrent.{ Future, Promise }

def apply[A](code: => A)(using exec: ExecutionContext): Future[A] =
    val promise = Promise[A]()
    exec.execute(() => promise.complete(Try(code)))
    promise.future
```

Listing 25.4: Possible implementation of `Future.apply`; see also Lis. 25.5 and 25.6.

Function `apply` is curried and its first argument—the code to be executed—is passed by name, unevaluated. The function creates a promise and returns the future associated with it. It also schedules on the thread pool a task that evaluates the code argument and fulfills the promise with its output. Method `complete` is used to fulfill the promise. It uses an argument of type `Try` (see Section 13.3), which allows it to handle both the successful and failure cases. As an alternative, Scala promises define methods `success` and `failure` if you want to handle both cases separately.

If you want to write a similar `apply` function that produces a Java future instead, you have a choice between using the older or newer implementation of `Future`:

```Scala
import java.util.concurrent.{ CompletableFuture, Future }

def apply[A](code: => A)(using exec: ExecutionContext): Future[A] =
    val promise = CompletableFuture[A]()
    exec.execute { () =>
        try promise.complete(code)
        catch case ex: Exception => promise.completeExceptionally(ex)
    }
    promise
```

Listing 25.5: Future creation from a `CompletableFuture` promise.

This variant uses the newer `CompletableFuture`. As before, a promise is created and a task is scheduled to fulfill it. One difference from Listing 25.4 is that `CompletableFuture` doesn't use a `Try` type, so you need to treat the successful and error cases separately. Another difference is that the promise is itself the future being returned—type `CompletableFuture` plays both parts.[5]

Alternatively, you could implement `apply` by using Java's older futures:

```scala
                                                                   ─ Scala ─
import java.util.concurrent.{ Future, FutureTask }

def apply[A](code: => A)(using exec: ExecutionContext): Future[A] =
  val promise = FutureTask(() => code)
  exec.execute(promise)
  promise
```

Listing 25.6: Future creation from a `FutureTask` promise.

The type `FutureTask` is both a `Runnable` and a `Future`, so the promise itself is being executed in the thread pool and returned as a future. If its `run` method fails, the future is completed exceptionally.

25.6   Illustration: Thread-Safe Caching

In Listings 25.4 to 25.6, promises are used in conjunction with thread pools to provide a user with a future, but there are many other useful patterns that involve promises. This section uses promises to implement a thread-safe variant of our memoization example from Chapter 12. No thread pools are involved, and futures are only used internally and are not publicly visible.

Recall that the problem is to cache the values computed by a function. In Listing 12.2, function `memo` uses a closure to store a mapping of input–output pairs of known outputs for given inputs. Given a function `f`, function `g = memo(f)` computes the same values as `f`, but with additional caching. Function `g`, however, contains a mutable state—the mapping inside the closure—and is not thread-safe, even if function `f` is.

---

[5] JavaScript also implements a promise and a future as a single object but calls it a *promise*, while Java refers to it as a *future*. As it happens, because of the way promises are currently implemented in Scala, `promise.future` is also the same object as `promise`—method `future` simply returns `this`—but is used through two distinct types, `Future` and `Promise`.

To make it thread-safe, a naive idea could be to replace the regular `mutable.Map` with a thread-safe map:

─── *Scala* ───

```
// DON'T DO THIS!
def memo[A, B](f: A => B): A => B =
  val store = TrieMap.empty[A, B]
  x => store.getOrElseUpdate(x, f(x))
```

Class `TrieMap`, which was used in Chapter 23 in a read-write lock example, implements a thread-safe map. As a result, `memo(f)` is now thread-safe if function `f` is. However, the implementation suffers from a major drawback.

Consider the following scenario: Suppose function `f` is such that it takes 10 seconds to compute $f(x_0)$ for some value x_0. Function `g` is created as `memo(f)`. A thread T_1 calls $g(x_0)$ and starts to calculate $f(x_0)$. Nine seconds later, a thread T_2 also calls $g(x_0)$. At that time, thread T_1 is still inside its computation of $f(x_0)$, and the `store` map is still empty. Accordingly, method `getOrElseUpdate` triggers a second computation of $f(x_0)$ within thread T_2. It will take 10 seconds from this moment for thread T_2 to obtain the value $f(x_0)$, which is 9 seconds after it is added to the map by thread T_1 (Figure 25.1).

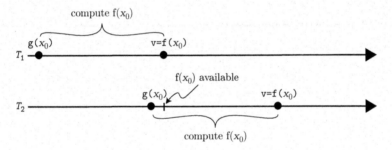

Figure 25.1 Flaw in a naive thread-safe memoization strategy.

Instead of starting another 10-second computation, it would be better for thread T_2 to wait just 1 second for thread T_1 to finish and then get the value from the `store` map. You can achieve this behavior by using promises and futures.

The key idea is to add a future into the `store` map when a thread begins a computation so that other threads that need the same value know that a computation is already ongoing. They can then wait for this future to complete, instead of starting a new computation of their own. The following variant implements this strategy using Java's older futures, but you could also do so with `CompletableFuture` or Scala's `Future`:

```scala
                                                        ─── Scala ───
def memo[A, B](f: A => B): A => B =
  val store = TrieMap.empty[A, Future[B]]
  x =>
    val future = store.get(x) match
      case Some(future1) => future1
      case None =>
        val task = FutureTask(() => f(x))
        store.putIfAbsent(x, task) match
          case Some(future2) => future2
          case None =>
            task.run()
            task
    future.get()
```

Listing 25.7: A thread-safe memoization function, using promises and futures.

Variable `store` now maps inputs of type `A` to *futures* of outputs of type `Future[B]`. When a thread needs the value `f(x)`, you start by querying the map. If you find a future—`future1`—you use it, rather than recompute `f(x)`. If `x` is not in the map, you create a promise/future as an instance of `FutureTask` named `task`. You then attempt to add it to the map. If in the meantime—right after the call to method `get`—some other thread already started a computation of `f(x)`, method `putIfAbsent` does not add `task` to the map, but instead returns a future on this other computation—`future2`. In that case, use it (and forget about `task`). If method `putIfAbsent` succeeds in adding `task` to the `store` map, the current thread is now in charge of computing `f(x)`. Other threads that need this value will find `task` in the map and possibly block on it until the computation of `f` is complete. You then call `task.run`, which triggers an evaluation of `f(x)`. After this run completes, any subsequent lookup for `x` in the `store` map will find a completed future and will retrieve value `f(x)` from it without invoking `f` or blocking on method `get`.

Note that `task` is referred to as a promise/future. Indeed, it is both. It is completed as a promise by the thread that created it, and it is used as a future by any thread that needs the computed value. Note also that `future1` handles the case of a computation started some time before this current call to the memoized function, while `future2` handles the case of two threads that call the memoized function on the same input at the same time: Both threads fail to find a key in the `store` map, both attempt to add a promise to the map, and only one succeeds.

25.7 Summary

- Tasks that produce values can be implemented as actions—typically, instances of interface `Runnable`. In that case, they need to modify shared data to store these values, and concurrent access to shared mutable data requires that they implement their own synchronization. Futures are an alternative synchronization mechanism specifically designed for tasks to retrieve values produced by other tasks.

- Futures are well suited to functional tasks—that is, tasks that invoke a function to produce a value. If the function is pure, all the synchronization that is needed can be embedded into a future.

- Thread pools can create a future when a task is submitted for execution. The future then acts as a handle on the task. It can be used to query the status of the task or as a synchronizer to wait for task completion. After the task finishes, the future also serves as a container for the value—or the error—produced by the task.

- Different types of futures vary in the functionalities they offer. This chapter focused on the basic mechanisms defined by Java's older `Future` type. Scala's `Future` is richer, and Java's `CompletableFuture` is richest. Their additional features are explored in Chapter 26.

- Futures are created from promises. A promise is a container, initially empty, that can be fulfilled by setting a value or, in case of failure, an exception. A promise can be fulfilled by the thread that created it (as in Listing 25.7), or by some other thread, such as from a thread pool (as in Listings 25.4 to 25.6).

- Promises and futures are tightly coupled and are often the same object, playing two roles. Terminology can be a bit confusing, as some sources refer to this object as a promise and others as a future.

Chapter 26

Functional-Concurrent Programming

Functional tasks can be handled as futures, which implement the basic synchronization needed to wait for completion and to retrieve computed values (or exceptions). As synchronizers, however, futures suffer from the same drawbacks as other blocking operations, including performance costs and the risk of deadlocks. As an alternative, futures are often enriched with higher-order methods that process their values asynchronously, without blocking. Actions with side effects can be registered as callbacks, but the full power of this approach comes from applying functional transformations to futures to produce new futures, a coding style this book refers to as *functional-concurrent programming*.

26.1   Correctness and Performance Issues with Blocking

In Chapter 25, we looked at futures as data-carrying synchronizers. Futures can be used to simplify concurrent programming, especially compared to error-prone, do-it-yourself, lock-based strategies (e.g., Listings 22.3 and 22.4).

However, because they block threads, all synchronizers suffer from the same weaknesses—and that includes futures. Earlier, we discussed the possibility of misusing synchronizers in such a way that threads end up waiting for each other in a cycle, resulting in a deadlock. Synchronization deadlocks can happen with futures as well and can actually be quite sneaky—running the server of Listing 25.2 on a single thread pool is a mistake that is easy to make.

Before going back to this server example, consider first, as an illustration, a naive implementation of a parallel quick-sort:

```scala
// DON'T DO THIS!
def quickSort(list: List[Int], exec: ExecutorService): List[Int] =
  list match
    case Nil => list
    case pivot :: others =>
      val (low, high) = others.partition(_ < pivot)
      val lowFuture   = exec.submit(() => quickSort(low, exec))
```

```
      val highSorted  = quickSort(high, exec)
      lowFuture.get() ::: pivot :: highSorted
```

Listing 26.1: Deadlock-prone parallel quick-sort; see also Lis. 26.5.

This method follows the same pattern as the previous implementation of quick-sort in Listing 10.1. The only difference is that the function uses a separate thread to sort the low values, while the current thread sorts the high values, thus sorting both lists in parallel. After both lists have been sorted, the sorted low values are retrieved using method `get`, and the two lists are concatenated around the pivot as before. This is the same pattern used in the server example to fetch a customized ad in the background except that the task used to create the future is the function itself, recursively.

At first, the code appears to be working well enough. You can use `quickSort` to successfully sort a small list of numbers:

```
                                                        ── Scala ──
val exec = Executors.newFixedThreadPool(3)
quickSort(List(1, 6, 8, 6, 1, 8, 2, 8, 9), exec) // List(1, 1, 2, 6, 6, 8, 8, 8, 9)
```

However, if you use the same three-thread pool in an attempt to sort the list [5,4,1,3,2], the function gets stuck and fails to terminate. Looking at a thread dump would show that all three threads are blocked on a call `lowFuture.get` in a deadlock.

Figure 26.1 displays the state of the computation at this point as a tree. Each sorting task is split into three branches: `low`, `pivot`, and `high`. The thread that first invokes `quickSort` is called `main` here. It splits the list into a `pivot` (5), a `low` list ([4,1,3,2]), and a `high` list ([]). It quickly sorts the empty list itself, and then blocks, waiting for the sorting of list [4,1,3,2] to complete. Similar steps are taking place with the thread

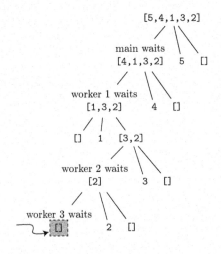

Figure 26.1 Deadlock as a result of tasks created by tasks.

in charge of sorting list [4,1,3,2], and so on, recursively. In the end, the three workers from the thread pool are blocked on three sorting tasks: [1,3,2], [2], and []. This last task—sorting the empty list at the bottom left of Figure 26.1—sits in the queue of the thread pool, as there is no thread left to run it.

This faulty implementation of quick-sort works adequately on computations with short low lists, even if the high lists are long. You can use it to sort the already sorted list [1,2,...,100] on a three-thread pool, for instance. However, the function fails when low lists are long, even if high lists are short. On the same three-thread pool, it cannot sort the list [5,4,1,3,2], or even the list [4,3,2,1].

Tasks that recursively create more tasks on the same thread pool are a common source of deadlocks. In fact, that problem is so prevalent that special thread pools were designed to handle it (see Section 27.3). Recursive tasks will get you in trouble easily, but as soon as tasks wait for completion of other tasks on the same thread pool, the risk of deadlock is present, even without recursion. This is why the server in Listing 25.2 uses two separate thread pools. Its handleConnection function—stripped here of code that is not relevant to the discussion—involves the following steps:

```scala
val futureAd: Future[Ad] = exec.submit(() => fetchAd(request)) // a Java future
val data: Data           = dbLookup(request)
val page: Page           = makePage(data, futureAd.get())
connection.write(page)
```

Listing 26.2: Ad-fetching example; contrast with Lis. 26.3, 26.6, and 26.7.

With a single pool of N threads, you could end up with N simultaneous connections, and thus N concurrent runs of function handleConnection. Each run would submit an ad-fetching task to the pool, with no thread to execute it. All the runs would then be stuck, forever waiting on futureAd.get.

Avoiding these deadlock situations is typically not easy. You may have to add many threads to a pool to make sure that deadlocks cannot happen, but large numbers of threads can be detrimental to performance. It is quite possible—likely, even—that most runs will block only a small subset of threads, nowhere near a deadlock situation, and leave too many active threads that use CPU resources. Some situations are hopeless: In the worst case, the naive quick-sort example would need as many threads as there are values in the list to guarantee that a computation remains free of deadlock.

Even if you find yourself in a better situation and deadlocks can be avoided with a pool of moderate size, waiting on futures still incurs a non-negligible cost. Blocking—on any kind of synchronizer, including locks—requires parking a thread, saving its execution stack, and later restoring the stack and restarting the thread. A parked thread also tends to see its data in a processor-level cache overwritten by other computations, resulting in cache misses when the thread resumes execution. This can have drastic consequences on performance.

Avoiding deadlocks should, of course, be your primary concern, but these performance costs cannot always be ignored. Thus, they constitute another incentive to reduce thread blocking. Several strategies have been proposed to minimize blocking, and some are described in detail in Chapter 27. For now, we will focus on a functional-concurrent programming style that uses futures through higher-order functions without blocking. It departs from the more familiar reliance on synchronizers and as such takes some getting used to. Once mastered, it is a powerful way to arrange concurrent programs.

26.2 Callbacks

NOTE

The code illustrations in this chapter rely mostly on Scala's futures for the same reason the book uses Scala in the first place: They tend to be cleaner than (though not always as rich as) Java's CompletableFuture. Listings 26.10 and 27.9 and some of the code in Chapter 28 make use of CompletableFuture, with more examples in Appendix A. Note also that callback mechanisms and other higher-order functions on futures often require an execution context—typically a thread pool in concurrent applications. How this context is specified varies from language to language. It can also become a distraction when presenting more important concepts. Most functions in this chapter assume a global execution context, which is left unspecified. One exception is Listing 26.5 (for consistency with Listing 26.1); other functions could use a similar pattern—that is, add a "(using ExecutionContext)" argument instead of assuming a global context.

A callback is a piece of code that is registered for execution, often later (asynchronous callback). Modern implementations of futures—including Scala's Future and Java's CompletableFuture—offer a callback-registration mechanism. On a Scala future, you register a callback using method onComplete, which takes as its argument an action to apply to the result of the future. Because a future can end up with an exception instead of a value, the input of a callback action is of type Try (see Section 13.3).

On a future whose task is still ongoing, a call to onComplete returns immediately. The action will run when the future finishes, typically on a thread pool specified as execution context:

```scala
println("START")
given ExecutionContext = ... // a thread pool

val future1: Future[Int]    = ... // a future that succeeds with 42 after 1 second
val future2: Future[String] = ... // a future that fails with NPE after 2 seconds
future1.onComplete(println)
future2.onComplete(println)

println("END")
```

This example starts a 1-second task and a 2-second task and registers a simple callback on each. It produces an output of the following form:

```
main at XX:XX:33.413: START
main at XX:XX:33.465: END
pool-1-thread-3 at XX:XX:34.466: Success(42)
pool-1-thread-3 at XX:XX:35.465: Failure(java.lang.NullPointerException)
```

You can see that the main thread terminates immediately—callback registration takes almost no time. One second later, the first callback runs and prints a Success value. One second after that, the second callback runs and prints a Failure value. In this output, both callbacks ran on the same thread, but there is no guarantee that this will always be the case.

You can use a callback in the ad-fetching scenario. Instead of waiting for a customized ad to assemble a page, as in Listing 26.2, you specify as an action what is to be done with the ad once it becomes available:

```
                                                          ── Scala ──
val futureAd: Future[Ad] = Future(fetchAd(request))
val data: Data          = dbLookup(request)
futureAd.onComplete { ad =>
  val page = makePage(data, ad.get)
  connection.write(page)
}
```

Listing 26.3: Ad-fetching example with a callback on a future.

After the connection-handling thread completes the database lookup, it registers a call-back action on the ad-fetching task, instead of waiting for the task to finish. The callback action extracts a customized ad from the Try value (assuming no error), assembles the data and ad into a page, and sends the page back as a reply as before. The key difference from Listing 26.2 is that no blocking is involved.

26.3   Higher-Order Functions on Futures

By using a callback to assemble and send the page, you avoid blocking, and thus eliminate the risk of deadlock. However, because the function argument of onComplete is an action, which is executed for its side effects, some of the earlier functional flavor is lost. Recall that in the full version of the server in Listing 25.2, the assembled page is also used in a statistics-keeping function. If a value produced as a future is needed in multiple places, handling these uses with callbacks can get complicated. If the value

is used asynchronously, you may even need callbacks within callbacks, which are difficult to write and even more difficult to debug. A better solution would be to bring the
non-blocking nature of callbacks into code that maintains a more functional style.

Before we revisit the ad-fetching example in Section 26.5, consider this callback-
based function:

```scala
─────────────────────────────────────────────────────── Scala ───

def multiplyAndWrite(futureString: Future[String], count: Int): Unit =
    futureString.onComplete {
        case Success(str) => write(str * count)
        case Failure(e)   => write(s"exception: ${e.getMessage}")
    }
```

Somewhere, an input string is being produced asynchronously. It is passed to function `multiplyAndWrite` as a future. This function uses a callback to repeat the
string multiple times and to write the result—in Scala, `"A" * 3` is `"AAA"`. This approach requires that you specify in the callback action everything you want to do
with the string `str * count`, which does not exist outside this callback. This is a
source of possible complexity and loss of modularity. It could be more advantageous to
replace `multiplyAndWrite` with a `multiply` function that somehow returns the string
`str * count` and makes it available to any code that needs it.

Within this `multiply` function, however, the string to multiply may not yet be
available—its computation could still be ongoing. You also cannot wait for it because you
want to avoid blocking. Instead, you need to return the multiplied string itself as a future.
Accordingly, the return type of `multiply` is not `String`, but rather `Future[String]`.
The future to be returned can be created using a promise, as in Listing 25.4:

```scala
─────────────────────────────────────────────────────── Scala ───

def multiply(futureString: Future[String], count: Int): Future[String] =
    val promise = Promise[String]()
    futureString.onComplete {
        case Success(str) => promise.success(str * count)
        case Failure(e)   => promise.failure(e)
    }
    promise.future
```

You create a promise to hold the multiplied string and a callback action to fulfill the
promise. If the future `futureString` produces a string, the callback multiplies it and
fulfills the promise successfully. Otherwise, the promise is failed, since no string was
available for multiplication.

Now comes the interesting part. Conceptually, the preceding code has little to do
with strings and multiplication. What it really does is transform the value produced by
a future so as to create a new future. Of course, we have seen this pattern before—for
instance, to apply a function to the contents of an option—in the form of the higher-

order function `map`. Instead of focusing on the special case of string multiplication, you could write a generic `map` function on futures:

```scala
def map[A, B](future: Future[A], f: A => B): Future[B] =
  val promise = Promise[B]()
  future.onComplete {
    case Success(value) => promise.complete(Try(f(value)))
    case Failure(e)     => promise.failure(e)
  }
  promise.future
```

This function is defined for generic types A and B instead of strings. The only meaningful difference with function `multiply` is that `f` might fail and is invoked inside `Try`. Consequently, the promise could be failed for one of two reasons: No value of type A is produced on which to apply `f`, or the invocation of function `f` itself fails.

The beauty of bringing up `map` is that it takes us to a familiar world, that of higher-order functions, as discussed in Chapters 9 and 10 and throughout Part I. Indeed, the `Try` type itself has a method `map`, which you can use to simplify the implementation of `map` on futures:

```scala
def map[A, B](future: Future[A], f: A => B): Future[B] =
  val promise = Promise[B]()
  future.onComplete(tryValue => promise.complete(tryValue.map(f)))
  promise.future
```

Listing 26.4: Reimplementing higher-order function `map` on futures.

Note how error cases are handled transparently, thanks to the `Try` type (see Section 13.3 for the behavior of `map` on `Try`).

Functions as values and higher-order functions constitute a fundamental aspect of functional programming. Chapter 25 introduced futures as a way to start making concurrent programming more functional by relying on a mechanism adapted to value-producing tasks. Once you choose to be functional, you should not be surprised to see higher-order patterns begin to emerge. But the story doesn't end with `map`. Various higher-order functions on futures give rise to a powerful concurrent programming style that is both functional and non-blocking.

You don't need to reimplement `map` on futures: Scala futures already have a `map` method. You can simply write function `multiply` as follows:

```scala
def multiply(futureString: Future[String], count: Int): Future[String] =
  futureString.map(str => str * count)
```

A thread that calls `multiply` does not block to wait for the input string to become available. Nor does it create any new string itself. It only makes sure that the input string will be multiplied once it is ready, typically by a worker from a thread pool.

26.4   Function flatMap on Futures

In function `multiply`, the string argument is given asynchronously, as a future, but the count is already known at call time and is passed as an integer. In a more general variant, the multiplying count itself could be the result of an asynchronous computation and be passed to `multiply` as a future. In that case, you need to combine `futureString`, of type `Future[String]`, and `futureCount`, of type `Future[Int]`, into a `Future[String]`. The expression

`futureString.map(str => futureCount.map(count => str * count))`

would have type `Future[Future[String]]`, which is not what you want. Of course, we have had this discussion before (with options, in Section 10.3) and used it to introduce the fundamental operation `flatMap`. Scala futures also have a `flatMap` method:

```scala
                                                        Scala
def multiply(futureString: Future[String], futureCount: Future[Int]): Future[String] =
    futureString.flatMap(str => futureCount.map(count => str * count))
```

There is nothing blocking in this function. Once both futures—`futureString` and `futureCount`—are completed, the new string will be created.

You can use other functions to achieve the same purpose. For instance, you can combine the two futures into a `Future[(String,Int)]` using `zip`, then use `map` to transform the pair:

```scala
                                                        Scala
def multiply(futureString: Future[String], futureCount: Future[Int]): Future[String] =
    futureString.zip(futureCount).map((str, count) => str * count)
```

You can even use `zipWith`, which combines `zip` and `map` into a single method:

```scala
                                                        Scala
def multiply(futureString: Future[String], futureCount: Future[Int]): Future[String] =
    futureString.zipWith(futureCount)((str, count) => str * count)
```

The last two functions may be easier to read than the `flatMap/map` variant. Nevertheless, you should keep in mind the fundamental nature of `flatMap`. Indeed, `zip` and `zipWith` can be implemented using `flatMap`.

An experienced Scala programmer might write `multiply` as follows:

```scala
def multiply(futureString: Future[String], futureCount: Future[Int]): Future[String] =
  for str <- futureString; count <- futureCount yield str * count
```

Recall from Section 10.9 that `for-yield` in Scala is implemented as a combination of `map` and `flatMap` (and `withFilter`). This code would be transformed by the compiler into the earlier `flatMap/map` version. The `for-yield` syntax is very nice, especially when working with futures. I encourage you to use it if you are programming in Scala. However, as mentioned in an earlier note, I will continue to favor the explicit use of `map` and `flatMap` in this book's examples for pedagogical reasons.

By combining two futures into one—using `flatMap`, `zip`, or `zipWith`—you can rewrite the parallel quick-sort example of Listing 26.1 as a non-blocking function:

```scala
def quickSort(list: List[Int])(using ExecutionContext): Future[List[Int]] = list match
  case Nil => Future.successful(list)
  case pivot :: others =>
    val (low, high) = others.partition(_ < pivot)
    val lowFuture   = Future.delegate(quickSort(low))
    val highFuture  = quickSort(high)
    lowFuture.flatMap(lowSorted =>
      highFuture.map(highSorted => lowSorted ::: pivot :: highSorted)
    )
```

Listing 26.5: Non-blocking implementation of parallel quick-sort.

To avoid blocking, the return type of the function is changed from `List[Int]` to `Future[List[Int]]`. As before, the task of sorting the low values is delegated to the thread pool. You could equivalently write it as `lowFuture = Future(quickSort(low))` `.flatten`. A direct recursive call is used to sort the high values, and the two futures are combined, following the same pattern as in function `multiply`. This variant of quick-sort involves no blocking and, in contrast to Listing 26.1, cannot possibly deadlock.[1]

---

[1]This implementation remains inefficient. Its main weakness is that it creates separate sorting tasks for very small lists down to the empty list. More realistic implementations would stop the parallelization at some point and sort short lists within the current thread instead. Java's `Arrays.parallelSort` function, for instance, stops distributing subarrays to separate threads once they have 8192 or fewer elements.

26.5   Illustration: Parallel Server Revisited

Equipped with standard higher-order functions on futures, we can now go back to the
server example. First, you can replace the callback action in Listing 26.3 with a call to
map to produce a Future[Page] out of a Future[Ad]:

```scala
val futureAd: Future[Ad]     = Future(fetchAd(request))
val data: Data               = dbLookup(request)
val futurePage: Future[Page] = futureAd.map(ad => makePage(data, ad))
futurePage.foreach(page => connection.write(page))
```

Listing 26.6: Ad-fetching example with map and foreach on futures.

You use map to transform an ad into a full page by combining the ad with data already
retrieved from the database. You now have a Future[Page], which you can use wherever
the page is needed. In particular, sending the page back to the client is a no-value action,
for which a callback fits naturally. For illustration purposes, this code registers the
callback with foreach instead of onComplete. The two methods differ in that foreach
does not deal with errors: Its action is not run if the future fails.

In Listing 26.6, the database is queried by the connection-handling thread while
a customized ad is fetched in the background. Alternatively, database lookup can be
turned over to another thread, resulting in a value of type Future[Data]. You can then
combine the two futures using flatMap/map:

```scala
val futureAd: Future[Ad]     = Future(fetchAd(request))
val futureData: Future[Data] = Future(dbLookup(request))
val futurePage: Future[Page] =
   futureData.flatMap(data => futureAd.map(ad => makePage(data, ad)))
futurePage.foreach(page => connection.write(page))
```

Listing 26.7: Ad-fetching example with flatMap and foreach on futures.

What is interesting about this code is that the thread that executes it does not
perform any database lookup, ad fetching, or page assembling and writing. It simply
creates futures and invokes non-blocking higher-order methods on them. If you write
the remainder of the connection-handling code in the same style, you end up with a
handleConnection function that is entirely asynchronous and non-blocking:

```scala
given exec: ExecutionContextExecutorService =
   ExecutionContext.fromExecutorService(Executors.newFixedThreadPool(16))
```

```
val server = ServerSocket(port)

def handleConnection(connection: Connection): Unit =
  val requestF = Future(connection.read())
  val adF      = requestF.map(request => fetchAd(request))
  val dataF    = requestF.map(request => dbLookup(request))
  val pageF    = dataF.flatMap(data => adF.map(ad => makePage(data, ad)))
  dataF.foreach(data => addToLog(data))
  pageF.foreach(page => updateStats(page))
  pageF.foreach(page => { connection.write(page); connection.close() })

while true do handleConnection(Connection(server.accept()))
```

Listing 26.8: A fully non-blocking parallel server.

The `handleConnection` function starts by submitting to the thread pool a task that reads a request from a socket and produces a future, `requestF`. From then on, the code proceeds by calling higher-order functions on futures. First, using `map`, an ad-fetching task is scheduled to run once the request has been read. This call produces a future `adF`. A database lookup future, `dataF`, is created in the same way. The two futures `dataF` and `adF` are combined into a future `pageF` using `flatMap` and `map`, as before. Finally, three callback actions are registered: one on `dataF` for logging, and two on `pageF` for statistics recording and to reply to the client.

No actual connection-handling work is performed by the thread that runs function `handleConnection`. The thread simply creates futures and invokes non-blocking functions on them. The time it takes to run the entire body of `handleConnection` is negligible. In particular, you could make the listening thread itself do it, in contrast to Listing 25.2, where a separate task is created for this purpose.

The various computations that need to happen when handling a request depend on each other, as depicted in Figure 26.2. The server implemented in Listing 26.8 executes a task as soon as its dependencies have been completed, unless all 16 threads in the pool are busy. Indeed, the 16 threads jump from computation to computation—fetching ads, logging, building pages, and so on—as the tasks become eligible to run, across request boundaries. They never block, unless there is no task at all to run. This implementation maximizes parallelism and is deadlock-free.

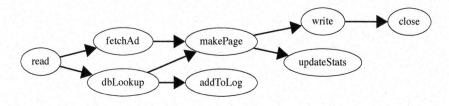

Figure 26.2 Activity dependencies in the server example.

Instead of Scala futures, you could implement the server of Listing 26.8 using Java's `CompletableFuture` (see Appendix A.14 for a pure Java implementation). Note, however, that `CompletableFuture` tends to use less standard names: `thenApply`, `thenCompose`, and `thenAccept` are equivalent to `map`, `flatMap`, and `foreach`, respectively.

There is one aspect of concurrent programming that a non-blocking approach tends to make more difficult: handling timeouts. For instance, you could decide that it is undesirable to have the server wait for more than 0.5 second for a customized ad after data has been retrieved from the database. In a blocking style, you can achieve this easily by adding a timeout argument when invoking `futureAd.get`, as in Listing 25.3. It can be somewhat more challenging when using a non-blocking style.

Here, `CompletableFuture` has the advantage over Scala's `Future`. It defines a method `completeOnTimeout` to complete a future with an alternative value after a given timeout. If the future is already finished, `completeOnTimeout` has no effect. You can use it to fetch a default ad:

Scala

```scala
val adF: CompletableFuture[Ad] = ...
...
adF.completeOnTimeout(timeoutAd, 500, MILLISECONDS)
```

Scala's `Future` type has no such method, which makes the implementation of a timeout ad more difficult. You can follow a do-it-yourself approach by creating a promise and relying on an external timer to complete it if needed. First, you create a timer as a scheduling thread pool:

Scala

```scala
val timer = Executors.newScheduledThreadPool(1)
```

Then, you create a promise when the database lookup finishes:

Scala

```scala
val pageF = dataF.flatMap { data =>
   val safeAdF =
      if adF.isCompleted then adF
      else
         val promise = Promise[Ad]()
         val timerF =
            timer.schedule(() => promise.trySuccess(timeoutAd), 500, MILLISECONDS)
         adF.foreach { ad =>
            timerF.cancel(false)
            promise.trySuccess(ad)
         }
         promise.future
   safeAdF.map(ad => makePage(data, ad))
}
```

This code runs when future `dataF` completes—when data from the database becomes available. If, at that point, the ad is ready—`adF.isCompleted` is true—you can use it. Otherwise, you need to make sure that an ad will be available quickly. For this purpose, you create a promise, and you use the timer to fulfill this promise with a default ad after 0.5 second. You also add a callback action to `adF`, which tries to fulfill the same promise. Whichever runs first—the timer task or the customized ad task—will set the promise with its value.[2] The call `timerF.cancel` is not strictly necessary, but it is used to avoid creating an unnecessary default ad if the customized ad is available in time.

As part of the last case study, Listing 28.4 uses a similar strategy to extend Scala futures with a `completeOnTimeout` method.

26.6 Functional-Concurrent Programming Patterns

Both futures, on the one hand, and higher-order functions, on the other hand, are powerful abstractions. Together, they form a potent combination, though one that can take some effort to master. Even so, it is a worthwhile effort. This section illustrates a few guidelines you should keep in mind as you venture into functional-concurrent programming.

flatMap as an Alternative to Blocking

Higher-order functions are abstractions for code you don't have to write. They are convenient but could often be replaced with handwritten implementations. If `opt` is an option, for instance, `opt.map(f)` could also be written:

```scala
opt match
  case Some(value) => Some(f(value))
  case None        => None
```

In the case of futures, however, higher-order functions are an alternative to computations that would be hard to implement directly. If `fut` is a future, what can you replace `fut.map(f)` with? A future cannot simply be "opened" to access its value, since the value may not yet exist. Short of creating—and blocking—additional threads, there is no alternative to using higher-order functions to act inside a future.

You can leverage your functional programming skills with higher-order functions when working with futures. Earlier, for instance, we used `flatMap` on options to chain computations that may or may not produce a value. You can use `flatMap` in a similar way on futures to chain computations that may or may not be asynchronous. Instead of "optional" stages, from `A` to `Option[B]`, you define asynchronous stages, as functions from `A` to `Future[B]`.

---

[2]Method `trySuccess` is used because method `success` fails with an exception when invoked on an already completed promise.

As an illustration, the three optional functions used in Section 10.3 can be changed to represent asynchronous steps:

```scala
def parseRequest(request: Request): Future[User] = ...
def getAccount(user: User): Future[Account] = ...
def applyOperation(account: Account, op: Operation): Future[Int] = ...
```

The steps can then be chained using `flatMap`:

```scala
parseRequest(request)
   .flatMap(user => getAccount(user))
   .flatMap(account => applyOperation(account, op))
```

Listing 26.9: A pipeline of futures using `flatMap`.

The expression in Listing 26.9 is *exactly* the same as that in Listing 10.5, except that it produces a value of type `Future[Int]` instead of `Option[Int]`.

Uniform Treatment of Synchronous and Asynchronous Computations

You could mix synchronous and asynchronous operations by combining steps of type `A => B`—using `map`—and steps of type `A => Future[B]`—using `flatMap`. Instead, it is often more convenient to use only steps of the form `A => Future[B]` combined with `flatMap`. When needed, synchronous steps can be implemented as already completed futures. This design increases flexibility: It makes it easier to replace synchronous steps with asynchronous steps, and vice versa.

For instance, if accounts are simply stored in a map, the `getAccount` function from the earlier example can be implemented synchronously, within the calling thread:

```scala
val allAccounts: Map[User, Account] = ...
def getAccount(user: User): Future[Account] = Future.successful(allAccounts(user))
```

This function returns an already completed future and does not involve any additional thread. If a need to fetch accounts asynchronously then arises, you can reimplement the function without modifying its signature, and leave all the code that uses it—such as Listing 26.9—unchanged.

Functional Handling of Failures

Exceptions are typically thrown and caught within a thread. They don't naturally travel from thread to thread, and they are ill suited for multithreaded programming. Instead, you are better off following the functional approach to error handling discussed in Chapter 13.

An added benefit of relying on computations of type `A => Future[B]` instead of `A => B` is that futures can also carry failures—in Scala, you can think of `Future` as an asynchronous `Try`. For example, you can improve the `getAccount` function by making sure it always produces a future, even when a user is not found:

```scala
                                                          ———— Scala ————
def getAccount(user: User): Future[Account] = Future.fromTry(Try(allAccounts(user)))
```

This way, an expression like `getAccount(user).onComplete(...)` still executes a callback action, which is not true if `getAccount` throws an exception. Failed futures can be handled functionally, using dedicated functions such as `recover` in Scala or `exceptionally` in Java.

For simplicity, the connection-handling function from Listing 26.8 does not deal with errors. You could use standard future functions to add robustness to the server. For instance, failure to create a page could be handled by transforming the `pageF` future:

```scala
                                                          ———— Scala ————
val safePageF: Future[Page] = pageF.recover { case ex: PageException => errorPage(ex) }
```

or by adding a failure callback:

```scala
                                                          ———— Scala ————
pageF.failed.foreach { ex =>
    connection.write(errorPage(ex))
    connection.close()
}
```

Either the callback actions specified using `pageF.foreach` or those specified using `pageF.failed.foreach` will run, but not both.

Non-Blocking "Join" Pattern

In the server example, `pageF` is created by combining two futures, `dataF` and `adF`, using `flatMap`. You can use the same approach to combine three or more futures:

```scala
                                                          ———— Scala ————
val f1: Future[Int]    = ...
val f2: Future[String] = ...
val f3: Future[Double] = ...

val f: Future[(Int, String, Double)] =
    f1.flatMap(n => f2.flatMap(s => f3.map(d => (n, s, d))))
```

This won't scale to larger numbers of futures, though. An interesting and not uncommon case is to combine N futures of the same type into a single one, for an arbitrary number N. In the server example, a client might obtain data from N database queries, which are executed in parallel:

```scala
                                                          ─── Scala ───
def queryDB(requests: List[Request]): Future[Page] =
  val futures: List[Future[Data]] = requests.map(request => Future(dbLookup(request)))
  val dataListF: Future[List[Data]] = Future.sequence(futures)
  dataListF.map(makeBigPage)
```

The first line uses `map` to create a list of database-querying tasks, one for each request. These tasks, which run in parallel, form a list of futures. The key step in `queryDB` is the call to `Future.sequence`. This function uses an input of type `List[Future[A]]` to produce an output of type `Future[List[A]]`. The future it returns is completed when all the input futures are completed, and it contains all their values as a list (assuming no errors). Invoking `Future.sequence` serves the same purpose as the "join" part of a fork-join pattern, but does so without blocking. The last step uses a function `makeBigPage` from `List[Data]` to `Page` to build the final page.

As of this writing, there is no standard `sequence` function for `CompletableFuture`, but you can implement your own using `thenCompose` (equivalent to `flatMap`) and `thenApply` (equivalent to `map`):

```scala
                                                          ─── Scala ───
def sequence[A](futures: List[CompletableFuture[A]]): CompletableFuture[List[A]] =
  futures match
    case Nil => CompletableFuture.completedFuture(List.empty)
    case future :: more =>
      future.thenCompose(first => sequence(more).thenApply(others => first::others))
```

Listing 26.10: Joining a list of `CompletableFuture`s into one without blocking.

This function uses recursion to nest calls to `thenCompose` (`flatMap`). In the recursive branch, `sequence(more)` is a future that will contain the values of all the input futures, except the first. This future and the first input future are then combined using `thenCompose` and `thenApply` (`flatMap` and `map`), according to the pattern used earlier to merge two futures (as in Listings 26.5, 26.7, and 26.8).

Non-Blocking "Fork-Join" Pattern

Function `queryDB` uses a fork-join pattern in which `sequence` implements the "join" part without blocking. Fork-join is a common enough pattern that Scala defines a function `traverse` that implements both the "fork" and "join" parts of a computation. You can use it for a simpler implementation of `queryDB`:

```scala
                                                          ─── Scala ───
def queryDB(requests: List[Request]): Future[Page] =
  Future.traverse(requests)(request => Future(dbLookup(request))).map(makeBigPage)
```

Instead of working on a list of futures, as `sequence` does, function `traverse` uses a list of inputs and a function from input to future output. It "forks" a collection of tasks by applying the function to all inputs, and then "joins" the tasks into a single future, as in `sequence`, without blocking.

26.7 Summary

- When used as a synchronizer, a future requires a thread to potentially block and wait to access the value being computed. Parking and unparking threads has a non-negligible performance cost. Worse yet, tasks that block to wait on other tasks running on the same group of threads can easily result in deadlocks. It is not always possible to avoid these deadlocks by increasing the number of threads in a pool, and larger pool sizes tend to cause inefficiencies even when it can be done.

- Callbacks can be used as an alternative to blocking. They trigger a computation when a future is ready, without having to explicitly wait for this future to finish. Callbacks can be complex—future values can be used in arbitrary ways—and can lead to intricate code, especially when callbacks within callbacks are involved.

- By defining non-blocking higher-order functions on futures, you can bring to the world of concurrent programming the same shift from actions to functions that is at the core of functional programming. Instead of using effect-based callbacks, future values are handled functionally, as when using functions, but asynchronously.

- The resulting functional-concurrent programming style does not use futures as synchronizers—thereby avoiding many deadlock scenarios and performance costs associated with blocking—and also sidesteps the inherent complexity of callbacks.

- Higher-order functions on futures can be used to transform values, combine multiple computations asynchronously, or recover from failures. The same higher-order functions that proved hugely beneficial to functional programming—particularly, `map`, `flatMap`, `foreach`, and `filter`—provide developers with tools to orchestrate complex concurrent computations according to patterns that maximize concurrency while avoiding blocking.

- Functions `flatMap` and `map`, in particular, can be used to combine in a uniform way computations that may be synchronous or asynchronous, failed or successful. They can also be used to implement, without blocking threads, patterns that (conceptually) wait for tasks to finish, such as fork-join.

- Adjusting to functional-concurrent programming requires a shift in program design, away from locks and synchronizers. This can initially require some effort, similar to casting aside assignments and loops when moving from imperative to functional programming. Once you become accustomed to it, though, this programming style is often easier and less error-prone than the alternatives.

Chapter 27

Minimizing Thread Blocking

Chapter 26 advocates the functional use of futures in a programming style that minimizes thread blocking. Over the years, much effort has been spent trying to avoid unnecessary thread blocking, often for performance reasons.[1] This chapter provides a quick overview of some popular techniques that strive not to block threads and often abstain from using locks and other synchronizers.

27.1 Atomic Operations

As a first illustration, consider the case of class `java.util.concurrent.AtomicInteger`, used in some earlier examples. It is straightforward to implement a thread-safe mutable integer in Java[2] using locks:

```
                                                                  Java
// THIS IS NOT java.util.concurrent.AtomicInteger!
private int value = 0;

public synchronized int get() {
  return value;
}

public synchronized int incrementAndGet() {
  value += 1;
  return value;
}
```

This code is correct and thread-safe, but not necessarily efficient. If two threads share such an integer, and both invoke `incrementAndGet` at the same time, one thread successfully acquires the object's intrinsic lock and the other thread is blocked. This is undesirable because it will take a lot more time to park and unpark this thread than is needed for the other thread to execute `value += 1`. When the lock is not available, it

---

[1]This process is still ongoing. On the JVM, in particular, see `https://openjdk.org/jeps/425`, known as *Project Loom*.

[2]The first code examples are in Java because the standard `AtomicInteger` is a Java class, and also because it uses constructs—atomic updaters—that are not available in Scala.

would be better for a thread to waste a few CPU cycles spinning instead of blocking,[3] until another thread is done incrementing the integer.

The actual class `AtomicInteger` does not use a lock. Conceptually, it is implemented as follows:

─── *Java*

```
public class AtomicInteger {

  private static final AtomicIntegerFieldUpdater<AtomicInteger> updater
    = newUpdater(AtomicInteger.class, "value");

  private volatile int value;

  public int get() {
    return value;
  }

  public int incrementAndGet() {
    while (true) {
      int current = value;
      int next = current + 1;
      if (updater.compareAndSet(this, current, next))
        return next;
    }
  }
}
...
```

Listing 27.1: Conceptual implementation of class `AtomicInteger` in Java.

No method is synchronized, and the implementation does not rely on any locking mechanism. Instead, variable `value` is volatile and accessed without locking.

Reading the integer is not a problem: Method `get` simply reads and returns `value`. Method `incrementAndGet`, however, presents an atomicity challenge. You need to avoid the scenario in which two threads that enter the method concurrently overwrite each other's updates (see the discussion in Section 18.1).

The implementation relies on a compare-and-set (CAS) operation:

compare-and-set(target, expectedValue, newValue)

This expression sets a target to a new value, but only if the target equals an expected value. If the target is different from the expected value, the CAS operation does not modify it. Semantically, this is equivalent to `if (target == expected) target = newValue`, except that the check-then-act is performed atomically. A CAS returns true if the target is successfully updated, and false otherwise.[4]

───────────────

[3]For this reason, modern JVM implementations often do not park a thread right away when a lock is not available, but instead spin for a while first, in case the lock becomes available quickly.

[4]Compare-and-set is sometimes also called *compare-and-swap*. The difference is that compare-and-swap returns the value of a variable before the swap, while compare-and-set returns a Boolean.

The role of `updater` in Listing 27.1 is to provide a CAS operation on the `value` field of the class.[5] This gives you an atomic check-then-act that is sufficient to safely implement `incrementAndGet`. First, you read the number in `value` into a local variable `current`. Then, you use CAS to update `value`: If it is still equal to `current`, it is replaced with `next`, which is `current + 1`. If the CAS fails and returns false, it is an indication that another thread has modified `value` after it was read. In that case, you use a loop to read the new contents of `value`, and you attempt the increment operation again.

One way to think about this implementation is that, instead of using locks to guard against interference, a thread proceeds under an optimistic assumption that no other thread will interfere with its operation. If, however, interference does take place, it is detected from the failure of CAS, and the operation is restarted.

When two threads modify an atomic integer at the same time, it is possible that a thread ends up computing `next = current + 1` twice, but the cost of the additional increment is negligible compared to the time it takes to park and unpark a thread. Even if more than two operations are involved and some threads end up repeating the loop multiple times before a CAS is successful, this non-locking strategy tends to outperform a lock-based one, unless the number of threads is extreme.

The Java standard library defines other types with atomic operations, such as `AtomicLong` and `AtomicBoolean`. As an illustration of the latter, you can rewrite the thread-safe box from Listing 22.4 without using any lock:

Scala

```scala
class SafeBox[A] :
  private var contents: A = uninitialized
  private val filled      = CountDownLatch(1)
  private val isSet       = AtomicBoolean(false)

  def get: A =
    filled.await()
    contents

  def set(value: A): Boolean =
    if isSet.get || isSet.getAndSet(true) then false
    else
      contents = value
      filled.countDown()
      true
```

Listing 27.2: Thread-safe box with a latch and no lock.

Method `get` is implemented by simply reading `contents` after the latch has been opened (as in Listing 22.8). Inside `set`, you can use an atomic Boolean to make sure that the box is successfully set by only one thread. The Boolean is false initially and can be flipped from false to true only once using `getAndSet`. The implementation of `AtomicBoolean`

---

[5]The actual `AtomicInteger` class from `java.util.concurrent` uses a different updater, but the principle is the same.

guarantees that if several threads call `getAndSet(true)` on a false Boolean, the method returns false for exactly one thread and true for all the other threads. Internally, `getAndSet` is implemented as a loop, using CAS.

The test `isSet.get` is not strictly necessary: It's a performance optimization to avoid the more costly `getAndSet` if the Boolean is already true. The `nonEmpty` test on an option, which was necessary in Listing 22.4, is no longer used. The useless option is removed for performance reasons, and variable `contents` has now type `A` instead of `Option[A]`.

27.2 Lock-Free Data Structures

Compare-and-set operations are not limited to primitive types such as integers and Booleans. Indeed, they are also available on references to objects as methods of the `AtomicReference` class. This makes it possible to update pointers atomically without locking, which is the basis of lock-free algorithms.

As an illustration, consider this lock-based implementation of a thread-safe stack:

Scala

```scala
private class Node[A](val value: A, val next: Node[A])

final class Stack[A]:
  private var top: Node[A] = null

  def peek: Option[A] = synchronized {
    if top == null then None else Some(top.value)
  }

  def push(value: A): Unit = synchronized {
    top = Node(value, top)
  }

  def pop(): Option[A] = synchronized {
    if top == null then None
    else
      val node = top
      top = node.next
      Some(node.value)
  }
```

You need locking to bring atomicity to `push` and `pop`. Without synchronization, two concurrent calls to `push`, for instance, could read the same `top` value and create two nodes, V_1 and V_2, that both refer to it (Figure 27.1). Then, if you update `top` to point to node V_1, you lose the V_2 value, and vice versa.

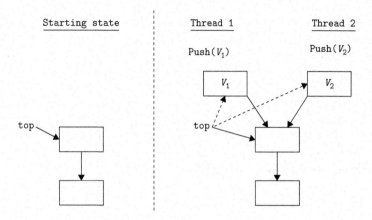

Figure 27.1 Possible loss of value from concurrent calls to push on a stack.

To avoid locking, you can change top to be an atomic reference and update it using CAS. This way, a failed CAS can be used to detect attempts to modify the stack concurrently:

```scala
import java.util.concurrent.atomic.AtomicReference

private class Node[A](val value: A, var next: Node[A])

final class Stack[A]:
   private val top = AtomicReference[Node[A]]()

   def peek: Option[A] = top.get match
      case null => None
      case node => Some(node.value)

   def push(value: A): Unit =
      val node = Node(value, top.get)
      while !top.compareAndSet(node.next, node) do node.next = top.get

   @tailrec
   def pop(): Option[A] = top.get match
      case null => None
      case node => if top.compareAndSet(node, node.next)
                   then Some(node.value) else pop()
```

Listing 27.3: Lock-free implementation of a thread-safe stack (Treiber's algorithm).

Method `peek` is not much different from before: It reads the top node and, if it is not null, returns its value. No atomicity is needed, and `top` is used as if it were a plain volatile variable. The other two methods are more involved.

In `push`, you start by creating a new node that refers to the current value of `top` as its own `next` pointer. You then need to update `top` to point to this new node (move `top` pointer up in Figure 27.2). You do this with a CAS, in case another thread is modifying `top` concurrently (inside `push` or pop). If the CAS fails, you update the node's `next` pointer to refer to the new value of `top` and attempt to update `top` again. Similarly, pop uses a CAS to try to update `top` to `top.get.next` (move the `top` pointer down in Figure 27.2) and retries the pop operation if the CAS fails.[6]

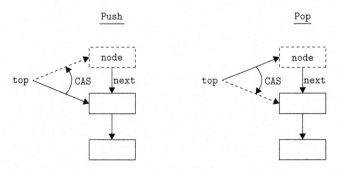

Figure 27.2 Compare-and-set to push/pop a lock-free stack.

In this stack example, you can see that the lock-free algorithm is noticeably more complex than one that uses locks. Many thread-safe data structures in `java.util` `.concurrent` rely on lock-free algorithms, including structures used internally to implement synchronizers, such as queues of waiting threads. Some of them are quite tricky due to the fact that an operation needs to update *multiple* references, which is not an atomic operation, even when using `compareAndSet` on instances of `AtomicReference`.

A limitation of CAS is that it can be successful, even if the target value has been modified concurrently, as long as it was modified back to its expected value—a scenario known as the ABA problem. For instance, `compareAndSet(false, true)` on an `AtomicBoolean` can fail to notice concurrent interactions that changed the Boolean from false to true, then back to false. If it is necessary for an algorithm to detect such a change, class `AtomicStampedReference` can be used. This class adds an integer counter to references as a way to distinguish between identical values.[7]

---

[6]Method pop uses tail recursion for retries; method push uses a loop because it makes it easier to reuse the same node across CAS attempts—using recursion would require introducing an additional method.

[7]Modern processors offer an alternative to CAS known as *load-linked/store-conditional* (LL/SC), a pair of bracketed instructions that detect interference between a load and a store independently from the values being loaded and stored, and, therefore, are not sensitive to the ABA problem.

27.3   Fork/Join Pools

NOTE

Sections 27.3 to 27.6 rely on the ad-fetching example from Chapter 26 to illustrate various frameworks. This example is not necessarily the best illustration of the strengths of these frameworks. Instead, the goal here is to make it easier to compare approaches and to emphasize that they can all be used to achieve the same non-blocking computation.

In Chapter 26, I started my discussion on the dangers of blocking with an example of a recursive task: A quick-sort task starts another quick-sort task and waits for its completion (Listing 26.1). This results in threads waiting on tasks, while tasks wait for threads for execution, leading to possible deadlocks.

To better handle the common pattern of tasks that create other tasks, the Java concurrency library defines a special form of thread pool called `ForkJoinPool`. This pool implements the same functionalities as regular pools but also has a dedicated mechanism that enables tasks to create tasks (`fork`) and to wait for their completion (`join`) *without blocking a worker thread*. Method `join` is implemented in such a way that if the task being joined is not finished, a worker thread instead retrieves and starts another one of the tasks scheduled for execution.[8] This keeps the thread active, and progress keeps being made on the tasks as a whole, thus avoiding deadlocks—as long as tasks are not set up to wait for each other in a cycle.

To illustrate the use of this non-blocking `join`, let's use `ForkJoinPool` to rewrite our solution to the example of fetching a customized ad in parallel with a database lookup:

```scala
import java.util.concurrent.ForkJoinTask

val futureAd: ForkJoinTask[Ad]       = ForkJoinTask.adapt(() => fetchAd(request)).fork()
val futureData: ForkJoinTask[Data]   = ForkJoinTask.adapt(() => dbLookup(request)).fork()
val data: Data                       = futureData.join()
val ad: Ad                           = futureAd.join()
val page: Page                       = makePage(data, ad)
```

Listing 27.4: Example of non-blocking concurency using `ForkJoinPool`.

---

[8]The `ForkJoinPool` class implements a work-stealing pattern in which each worker thread maintains its own queue of tasks and "steals" from other workers when it runs out of work. In contrast to a single queue model, this approach has the benefit that newly created tasks can be added to the queue of the current worker for later processing without interfering with other threads. This became such a popular feature that Java later introduced a `newWorkStealingPool` method that makes this pattern available independently from the fork/join mechanism.

The calls `futureData.join()` and `futureAd.join()` do not block the thread, even if the ad or the data is not yet available. Contrast this implementation with Listing 25.2, in which method `get` of a regular future is used to retrieve the ad, possibly causing a worker thread to block if the ad-fetching task is still running.

For all practical purposes, the implementation in Listing 27.4 is equivalent to Listing 26.7, which uses `flatMap` and `map` to combine the ad with database data in a non-blocking way. Its main benefit is that it is closer in style to familiar (but blocking) variants like that seen in Listing 25.2.

With `fork` and `join`, you have a mechanism for a task to wait for another task without blocking a thread. However, if you use a lock, or a semaphore, or a blocking queue, you can still block a thread. To truly leverage the advantages of `ForkJoinPool`, you need to refrain from using synchronizers. If you absolutely need to block a thread, the framework defines a `ManagedBlocker` interface, which you can use to indicate that a thread is about to block. This makes it possible for the pool to create additional threads appropriately to maintain a desired level of parallelism.

27.4   Asynchronous Programming

The idea of waiting without blocking, as in Listing 27.4, is also found in other programming models. These tend to focus on making code asynchronous—as opposed to concurrent—but can also typically be configured to support concurrency. In Scala, for instance, you can use an experimental asynchronous framework to implement the parallel ad-fetching and database lookup example in a standard-looking style:

```scala
import cps.compat.sip22.{ async, await }

async {
    val futureAd: Future[Ad]     = Future(fetchAd(request))
    val futureData: Future[Data] = Future(dbLookup(request))
    val ad: Ad                    = await(futureAd)
    val data: Data                = await(futureData)
    val page: Page                = makePage(data, ad)
}
```

Listing 27.5: Example of non-blocking concurrency with an *async/await* construct.

Method `await` suspends the execution of the `async` block until its target future is completed, but it does not block the thread, which continues to run code elsewhere. The implementation again follows a conventional blocking style but is pretty much equivalent in behavior to Listing 26.7 (with `flatMap/map`) or Listing 27.4 (with `ForkJoinPool`).[9]

---

[9]This example uses a non-standard library by Ruslan Shevchenko, which actually transforms `async/await` code into corresponding calls to `map/flatMap` at compile time.

Because it already defines an elegant `for-yield` construct to deal with `flatMap` and `map`, Scala has not focused on this programming style as much as some other languages. Kotlin, for instance, offers richer constructs through its coroutines. You can use coroutines to implement the ad-fetching example:

```
                                                                  Kotlin
import kotlinx.coroutines.*

coroutineScope {
  val futureAd: Deferred<Ad>     = async { fetchAd(request) }
  val futureData: Deferred<Data> = async { dbLookup(request) }
  val data: Data                 = futureData.await()
  val ad: Ad                     = futureAd.await()
  val page: Page                 = makePage(data, ad)
}
```

Listing 27.6: Example of non-blocking concurrency using Kotlin coroutines.

In Kotlin, the `async` construct is used to launch a coroutine and produces a `Deferred` object. Like `ForkJoinTask`, this is a kind of future. It implements a method `await`—similar to `join` on a `ForkJoinTask`—that you can use to wait for future completion without blocking the current thread. The code is very similar to that of Listings 27.4 and 27.5.

One strength of Kotlin coroutines is that they implement other non-blocking synchronization, besides task completion. For instance, `Mutex` implements an exclusive lock in which the `lock` method suspends code execution without blocking the thread, and `Semaphore` implements a semaphore in which the `acquire` method suspends code execution without blocking the thread.

For message-passing applications, `Channel` defines methods to send and receive messages that are conceptually waiting (if the channel is full or empty) but do not block the current thread. Go is another popular language that emphasizes this programming style. Its "goroutines" can wait on channels for an incoming message, for instance, without blocking the thread that executes them. Coroutines that communicate using channels (or other synchronizers designed not to block threads) have become a popular means of achieving non-blocking concurrency.

27.5 Actors

Actors is a classic message-based model that has been revived through languages such as Erlang and libraries such as Akka. Actors do not typically share mutable data, but instead communicate by sending and receiving (immutable) messages. Within an actor, all messages are processed sequentially, allowing actors to rely on internal data structures that are not thread-safe. When an actor has no message to process, it remains passive, but no thread is blocked. Instead, threads are available to run other actors, making it possible for a small number of threads to handle a large number of actors, as with coroutines.

You could use Akka actors to reimplement the parallel ad-fetching and database lookup example:

```scala
import akka.actor.typed.{ ActorRef, Behavior }
import akka.actor.typed.scaladsl.Behaviors

case class RequestMsg(replyTo: ActorRef[PageMsg], request: Request)
case class AdMsg(ad: Ad)
case class PageMsg(page: Page)

def requestHandling(): Behavior[RequestMsg] =
  Behaviors.receivePartial {
    case (context, RequestMsg(replyTo, request)) =>
      val dbQueryingActor = context.spawnAnonymous(dbQuerying(replyTo, request))
      context.spawnAnonymous(adFetching(dbQueryingActor, request))
      Behaviors.same
  }

def adFetching(replyTo: ActorRef[AdMsg], request: Request): Behavior[Nothing] =
  Behaviors.setup { context =>
    val ad = fetchAd(request)
    replyTo ! AdMsg(ad)
    Behaviors.stopped
  }

def dbQuerying(replyTo: ActorRef[PageMsg], request: Request): Behavior[AdMsg] =
  Behaviors.setup { context =>
    val data = dbLookup(request)

    Behaviors.receiveMessagePartial {
      case AdMsg(ad) =>
        val page = makePage(data, ad)
        replyTo ! PageMsg(page)
        Behaviors.stopped
    }
  }
```

Listing 27.7: Example of non-blocking concurrency using actors.

Listing 27.7 defines a `requestHandling` actor to handle messages of type `RequestMsg`, which contain a request and an address `replyTo` indicating where to send the final page. Upon receiving a request, this actor spawns two new actors: `adFetching`, to fetch a customized ad, and dbQuerying, to query the database. You give adFetching the address of dbQuerying so it can send the ad after it has been fetched. (The method "!" is used to send a message in Akka, a notation that has its origins in CSP.) The behavior of dbQuerying starts with a database query and continues by handling the message sent by adFetching, which contains the ad. The actor then assembles the page and sends it back to the entity that made the initial request (replyTo). Figure 27.3 shows the flow of messages in this actor system. By running actors on a pool with multiple threads, you achieve the same parallel, non-blocking ad fetching and database querying as in Listings 26.7, 27.4, 27.5, and 27.6.

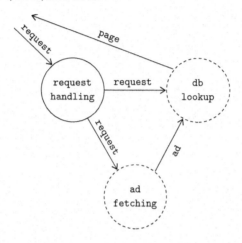

Figure 27.3 Message flow of actors in Lis. 27.7.

After it spawns two new actors—which takes very little time—the requestHandling actor is finished with the request. However, it continues to exist, with the same behavior as before, Behaviors.same, remaining ready to handle more requests. By contrast, adFetching and dbQuerying are transient actors. They terminate, using Behaviors.stopped, after they have completed their task.

You can achieve great flexibility by choosing to reuse one or more existing actors, or by deciding instead to spawn new ones. If you are implementing the full server from Listing 26.8, for instance, you could decide to use a single actor for logging, thus guaranteeing that all logging is done sequentially. Instead of spawning a new actor to fetch an ad for each request, you could dedicate a fixed number of actors to the task of fetching ads, and even dynamically change this number based on server activity.

Finally, relying on message-based protocols makes it easier to deploy actors in a distributed system—as long as messages can be serialized for network communication. Akka is often used to implement computations over a network and offers many features to support distributed computing, including actor migration and load balancing.

As a side note, actors have the interesting property that they can switch behaviors, and thus process subsequent incoming messages differently. This can be leveraged to implement state machines in terms of actors:

```scala
                                                                    Scala
trait Command
case class Start(replyTo: ActorRef[Number]) extends Command
case class Number(value: Int)               extends Command
case object Stop                            extends Command

def reset(): Behavior[Command] =
  Behaviors.receiveMessagePartial {
      case Start(replyTo) => add(replyTo, Behaviors.same)
  }

def add(replyTo: ActorRef[Number], reset: Behavior[Command]): Behavior[Command] =
  var sum = 0
  Behaviors.receiveMessagePartial {
      case Number(value) =>
          sum += value
          Behaviors.same
      case Stop =>
          replyTo ! Number(sum)
          reset
  }
```

Listing 27.8: Example of a state machine as an actor that switches behavior.

This example implements a counter by starting an actor with a **reset** behavior. This actor waits for the **Start** command. When **Start** is received, the actor changes its behavior to **add**, passing its current behavior as an argument so it can be used later to switch back. Messages are then processed according to the new behavior. When a message of type **Number** is received, its value is added into an accumulator **sum**, and the behavior of the actor remains the same. When the **Stop** message is received, the actor replies with the accumulated sum and reverts to its initial behavior, waiting for another **Start** message. As a state machine, the actor transitions between states as follows:

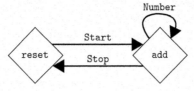

Method **add** is implemented in an imperative style, with a mutable variable **sum**. This is done on purpose, to emphasize the fact that, within an actor, messages are processed sequentially. The actor may receive numbers concurrently and still add them correctly, even though no lock is used and the assignment **sum += value** is not thread-safe.

27.6   Reactive Streams

Listings 27.4 to 27.7 all end with a single page having been constructed. In an actual application, you would then need to operate on the page in some fashion. This pattern works well if all the pages are used independently from each other, as in the server example: Each page is sent back to a client via a socket. But if you need to handle all the pages, as a whole, within a larger component, a scattering of asynchronously created pages—a collection of `Future[Page]` values, for instance—becomes inadequate. As an alternative, you can use a *stream* of asynchronous pages.

Reactive streams are an abstraction that combines the asynchronous characteristics of futures with the manifold nature of iterators. Several implementations exist, in a variety of languages—for example, RxJava, RxSwift, RxAndroid, Akka Streams, and Vert.x—including a bare-bones variant as `java.util.concurrent.Flow`. The next example uses Reactor, a popular Java implementation:

```scala
                                                            ─ Scala ─
import reactor.core.publisher.{ Flux, Mono }

def makePages(requests: Flux[Request]): Flux[Page] =
  requests.flatMap { request =>
    val adF   = CompletableFuture.supplyAsync(() => fetchAd(request), exec)
    val dataF = CompletableFuture.supplyAsync(() => dbLookup(request), exec)
    val pageF = dataF.thenCombine(adF, makePage)
    Mono.fromFuture(pageF)
  }
```

Listing 27.9: Example of non-blocking transformation using reactive streams.

Instead of creating a single page from a single request, this variant transforms a stream (called `Flux` in Reactor) of requests into a stream of pages. The code is asynchronous: A call to method `makePages` on a stream of requests completes immediately and returns a stream of pages. Later, as requests are added to the input stream, corresponding pages appear in the output stream. As before, ad fetching and database lookup are executed in parallel on a thread pool.[10] The two futures are combined into a future page asynchronously (`thenCombine` is `CompletableFuture`'s version of `zipWith`, which was used in Section 26.4). The future page is transformed into a short stream of one value, called `Mono` in Reactor.

The power of reactive streams lies in their mechanisms for managing back pressure (slowing upstream computations until downstream can catch up), error handling, and time-based processing. These mechanisms are beyond the scope of this book, but as a brief illustration of time-based processing, consider this example:

---

[10]I use `CompletableFuture` instead of Scala's `Future` because this is the type that `Mono.fromFuture` expects.

```scala
                                                              ── Scala ──
val pages: Flux[Page] = ...

val largestPastHour: Flux[Int] =
  pages
      .map(_.length)
      .window(Duration.ofHours(1), Duration.ofMinutes(5))
      .flatMap(lengths => lengths.reduce(0, Integer.max))
```

The expression uses overlapping windows to report every 5 minutes the length of the longest page created in the previous hour, as a stream of numbers. Think of how you would implement this directly in terms of individual futures of pages, without ever blocking a thread. This is a nontrivial problem.

27.7   Non-blocking Synchronization

This chapter and Chapter 26 present several techniques that avoid blocking threads. In this last section, I want to clear up a misconception I have encountered several times. It is the idea that because threads are never blocked when using these approaches, synchronization mistakes such as deadlocks are impossible. This is not the case. Yes, some common deadlock-prone situations can be avoided by not blocking threads—see, for instance, the discussion of recursive tasks in Section 26.1. But it does not follow that synchronization mistakes—including deadlocks—cannot happen.

You need to distinguish between a future, task, coroutine, or actor "waiting" for some event—which does not involve blocking a thread—and a thread being parked. In particular, you can still end up with a deadlock by having futures, tasks, coroutines, or actors wait for each other in a cycle, independently from the status of the threads that run them. As an illustration, this (contrived) example has two futures waiting for each other:

```scala
                                                              ── Scala ──
lazy val future1: Future[Int] = Future.delegate {
  println("future 1 starts")
  val future2: Future[String] = Future.delegate {
    println("future 2 starts")
    future1.map(n => n.toString)
  }
  future2.map(str => str.length)
}
```

When executed on a pool with multiple threads, this program prints the two statements "future 1 starts" and "future 2 starts", and then hangs. To complete, future2 needs a number from future1, and future1 needs a string from future2. This is a deadlock of futures, not of threads. A thread dump would reveal that all the threads from the pool are idle, waiting for tasks to execute.

You might object that this example is artificial (it is), but complex applications, especially when you use promises explicitly, can face this type of situation. It is also easy to end up deadlocked in a message-oriented framework by having a set of entities wait for messages in a cycle. For instance, you can use Kotlin coroutines to wait for a message on a channel without blocking a thread:

```kotlin
val strings = Channel<String>()
val ints = Channel<Int>()

suspend fun task1() = coroutineScope {
  launch { task2() }
  println("waiting for a string")
  val str = strings.receive()
  ints.send(str.length)
}

suspend fun task2() = coroutineScope {
  println("waiting for an int")
  val n = ints.receive()
  strings.send(n.toString())
}
```

This program also prints two messages and then stops, even though method receive is not blocking threads and all threads are idle. You face the same difficulty with actors. It is a common pattern for an actor to need N messages before it can issue a response—similar to using a countdown latch in a blocking variant. If you wait for $N-1$ messages instead, you may produce an incomplete response; if you wait for $N+1$ messages, you may end up in a deadlock, with no response being sent at all.

Besides performance considerations, which are important, a major benefit of non-blocking strategies is that they help programmers shift their attention from non-interference to cooperation. Non-interference synchronization—typically using locks—is not needed, but the patterns that would require a cooperating synchronizer—such as a blocking queue or a countdown latch—are still there. You just implement them differently—for instance, as an actor or a coroutine waiting for messages, or by combining several futures through zip or flatMap. The fact that threads are not blocked, however, does not necessarily prevent these patterns from being implemented incorrectly. Concurrent programming is still hard.

27.8   Summary

- When programming with synchronizers, such as locks, latches, and futures, threads can be temporarily blocked while other threads perform an operation, which often results in non-negligible performance loss. Chapter 26 presented a programming style that uses futures in a functional way, without blocking threads. Some other techniques minimize thread blocking, as discussed in this chapter.

- Compare-and-set (CAS) is a hardware instruction that implements an elementary atomic check-then-act operation. It is also available on language-level types like `AtomicInteger` and `AtomicReference` as a `compareAndSet` method. It can be used to implement other thread-safe operations, such as `incrementAndGet` and `getAndSet` in class `AtomicInteger`.

- In particular, class `AtomicReference` and atomic updaters make it possible to manipulate pointers atomically without going through locks. This is the basis for various lock-free algorithms that implement thread-safe data structures without locking, albeit at the cost of increased code complexity.

- Lock-free algorithms tend to follow a similar pattern. Computation proceeds without locking, and thus with no guarantee that other threads will not interfere. Work is performed speculatively and then committed using CAS. A failed CAS is an indication that interference from other threads did take place, in which case the operation can be reattempted.

- Functional-concurrent programming avoids blocking threads by using futures through callbacks and higher-order functions. An alternative approach is to make it possible for code to explicitly wait for completion of a future, but without blocking a thread. Many different implementations of this principle are possible. Java's `ForkJoinTask`, for instance, implements a kind of future with a `join` method that suspends code execution until the future terminates, but does not block the running thread, leaving it free to execute other tasks in the pool. This results in a programming style that often feels more natural—resembling a blocking variant—than one that relies on callbacks and scheduled transformations.

- This idea of waiting without blocking is sometimes extended beyond futures and made available in other flavors, such as *async/await* constructs and coroutines. In addition to waiting for a value produced by a task, these constructs offer non-blocking ways to wait for a message from a channel, or to acquire an exclusive lock, for instance.

- Actors are a model of concurrent and distributed programming centered on messages. Actors send and receive messages, which are handled sequentially within an actor, making it possible to use non-thread-safe code during message processing. Passive actors, with no pending messages, use no computing resources. They do not block threads, which remain available to run active actors.

- Frameworks also exist to process streams of data in parallel while avoiding thread blocking when data is not available. Reactive streams complement futures—which eventually either produce a single value or fail—by being able to produce zero or more values before they terminate. A generic reactive streams specification (www.reactive-streams.org) has been implemented in a variety of programming languages.

- When code does not block threads, performance often improves, and many synchronization mistakes common to programming with locks are avoided. Non-blocking approaches, however, are not fool-proof. Concurrent entities still need to correctly coordinate to achieve overall computational objectives. In particular, synchronization mistakes can still result in deadlocks—of futures, coroutines, or actors—even if the underlying threads are not blocked.

Chapter 28

Case Study: Parallel Strategies

Our final case study expands on the previous one by focusing on the parallel execution of functions—as opposed to the actions examined in Chapter 24. It considers a scenario in which several functions are applied to the same input, each with a different likelihood of succeeding. The implementation leverages the concurrency constructs explored in earlier chapters—promises, futures, higher-order functions—and uses their features to address failure, timeout, cancellation, and caching issues.

28.1 Problem Definition

NOTE

This case study was inspired by a problem I faced, a long time ago, while working on static analysis of programs. I was implementing a tool that worked by generating proof obligations—that is, logical formulas that need to be valid to show that a program satisfies a desirable property. The formulas were typically large, numerous, and costly to verify. My tool used automatic theorem provers to check the validity of the formulas, but different theorem provers—and different configurations of the same theorem prover—would often perform very differently on the same formula. With no way to predict which prover would work best, several theorem provers were started in parallel on each formula and stopped as soon as one prover found the formula to be valid or invalid. Some of the assumptions made in this chapter reflect the particulars of this theorem-proving scenario.

This last case study investigates a scenario in which a series of problems need to be solved using a variety of heuristics. For a given problem, you don't know which heuristic will work, so you would like to try several heuristics in parallel until one succeeds. In this chapter, heuristics are represented in terms of a `Strategy` interface:

```scala
trait Strategy[A, B]:
  trait Task:
    def run(): Option[B]
    def cancel(): Unit

  def apply(input: A): Task
```

Strategies are parameterized by an input type A and an output type B. (In the program verification problem, type A would represent logical formulas, and type B would be Boolean.) When applied to a given input, a strategy produces a task, which can be run in an attempt to calculate the corresponding output. A task may succeed or fail, and thus returns an option. A task can also be canceled—for instance, because it has exceeded its time quota, or because another strategy has already solved the problem. The code developed in this chapter hinges on several assumptions:

- A strategy can only succeed with a value, fail by returning an empty option, or keep running forever. In particular, we assume that strategies do not fail with exceptions. This is not a significant limitation. You can always replace a function f of type A => Option[B] that might throw an exception with the function x => Try(f(x)).getOrElse(None), which returns None instead.

- For a given input, all the strategies that produce a successful value produce the same value. (In my original context, if a theorem prover can show that a formula is valid, other provers cannot show that it is not, and vice versa.) There is no notion of "better" value. This makes it possible—and even desirable—to ignore the output of all the other strategies once a strategy has terminated successfully.

- Tasks are canceled by invoking their cancel method, which is customized for each strategy. This makes it easier for strategies to use code that is not responsive to thread interrupts—the default cancellation mechanism used by Java thread pools—such as socket I/O. (My verification tool ran theorem provers on remote computers.)

- Cancellation may be implemented on a "best effort" basis: A task may continue to run for some time after it has been canceled. Calling cancel on a task does not guarantee that a thread inside its run method completes this call immediately.

- Canceling a task before it runs prevents this task from ever running; if invoked, its run method returns None immediately. Canceling a task that is already finished has no effect.

For reference, a simple sequential implementation would try all the strategies in turn until either one produces a non-empty option or all the strategies have been exhausted:

```
                                                            ──────── Scala ────────
{runner-seq}
class Runner[A, B](strategies: Seq[Strategy[A, B]]):
  def compute(input: A): Option[B] =
    strategies.view.flatMap(strategy => strategy(input).run()).headOption
```

A runner is created from a collection of strategies. Its compute method iterates over all the strategies, using a view. For each strategy, it creates and runs a task, until either one task produces a non-empty option or all the strategies fail. The use of a view guarantees that compute terminates as soon as a strategy is successful, without needlessly evaluating the remaining strategies.[1] (See Sections 12.8 and 12.9 for an introduction to using views and iterators in this programming style.)

28.2   Sequential Implementation with Timeout

The implementation just described ignores strategies that return an empty option, but it does not handle strategies that fail by continuing to run—a common behavior with theorem provers and other searches based on heuristics. In particular, `compute` may keep running forever if it gets stuck with a non-terminating strategy.

You can write a better implementation that takes an additional argument as a timeout, in seconds:

```scala
                                                               ──── Scala ────
class Runner[A, B](strategies: Seq[Strategy[A, B]]):
  def compute(input: A, timeout: Double): Option[B] =
    val exec  = Executors.newSingleThreadExecutor()
    val tasks = strategies.map(strategy => strategy(input))

    val future: Future[Option[B]] = exec.submit { () =>
      tasks.view.flatMap(task => task.run()).headOption
    }
    exec.shutdown()

    try future.get((timeout * 1E9).round, NANOSECONDS)
    catch
      case _: TimeoutException =>
        for task <- tasks do task.cancel()
        None
```

Listing 28.1: A sequential runner of strategies with timeout.

You cannot afford to use the thread that invokes `compute` to directly evaluate strategies because it could get stuck—possibly uninterruptibly—inside a `run` method that does not terminate before the timeout. Instead, you can create a separate thread—as a single-thread executor—and use it to run all the strategies, sequentially. This run produces a future of type `java.util.concurrent.Future`, which the first thread can use to retrieve the result.

You implement the desired timeout by using a variant of the `get` method that throws an exception if the future is not completed before a specified amount of time has elapsed. Note that the time it takes to create the tasks and to start the second thread is assumed to be negligible and is not taken into account: The entire timeout duration is spent on the `get` method. Other runner implementations in this chapter will refine this assumption.

---

[1]You could implement this approach as a loop with a `break` statement in an imperative language. I use a functional style here because Scala has no `break` statement.

After you catch a timeout exception but before `compute` returns `None`, it can be desirable to cancel the run that is still ongoing, since it is now wasting computing resources to calculate data that will never be used, as well as all the runs that follow. The easiest way to do so is simply to cancel all the tasks, including tasks that have already completed with a failure: In this case study, we assume that canceling a finished task is harmless. This approach to cancellation is used in all runner implementations throughout the chapter.[2]

Despite the use of a second thread, the runner implementation in Listing 28.1 remains sequential: One thread is blocked while the other thread applies strategies one at a time. In particular, the (single) computing thread might potentially spend all the allowed time running an early strategy, even though other strategies further down the list could produce a result more quickly.

With no a priori knowledge of which strategies are more likely to be successful, and assuming enough computing resources, a better approach is to start all the strategies in parallel and use the result of the first strategy that succeeds. It is straightforward to modify Listing 28.1 to use a multithreaded pool and to create multiple tasks that each evaluate a single strategy. The difficulty is to wait exactly until the first successful strategy terminates or the elapsed time has reached the timeout value.

A "do-it-yourself" solution is certainly possible. For instance, you could use an approach that combines:

- A shared mutable variable to store the result of the first successful strategy, if any.

- A counter of how many strategies are actively running.

- A latch to wait, with a timeout, for the first available result. The latch is opened by a task if it is successful *or* if it is the last task to finish.

- A lock, to guard the variable used to store the result and the count of active tasks.

Instead of a low-level programming style, which we exercised in Chapter 24, the remainder of this chapter uses futures—and related standard mechanisms—to derive simpler or richer implementations.

28.3   Parallel Implementation Using invokeAny

A first possible approach to achieving a simpler runner implementation is to rely on method `invokeAny`, available on Java thread pools. You can use this method to run a collection of tasks in parallel, to wait for the completion of the first task that terminates successfully, and then to cancel all other tasks. This pattern nicely fits the requirements for a parallel runner of strategies:

---

[2]Even if you try to cancel only running (and yet to run) tasks, you face the inherent race condition that a task you are about to cancel might terminate at any time, and therefore the possibility that `cancel` is applied to a finished task needs to be addressed anyway.

```scala
                                                            ─ Scala ─
class Runner[A, B](strategies: Seq[Strategy[A, B]], exec: ExecutorService):
  def compute(input: A, timeout: Double): Option[B] =
    val deadline = System.nanoTime() + (timeout * 1E9).round

    val tasks = strategies.map(strategy => strategy(input))
    val calls = tasks.map(task => (() => task.run().get): Callable[B])

    try Some(exec.invokeAny(calls.asJava, deadline - System.nanoTime(), NANOSECONDS))
    catch case _: ExecutionException | _: TimeoutException => None
    finally for task <- tasks do task.cancel()
```

Listing 28.2: A parallel runner of strategies based on invokeAny.

The first argument of invokeAny is a list of tasks to execute in parallel. The method submits all the tasks for execution and blocks until one task finishes successfully, ignoring failed ones. Here, each task has type Callable[B] and is created as a lambda expression () => task.run().get. The call to get is necessary because invokeAny defines "failure" as throwing an exception, while strategies in this case study fail by returning None (but None.get will throw an exception). Method invokeAny throws a TimeoutException if no task completes successfully before the timeout, or an ExecutionException if all the tasks fail. Both exceptions are caught, and None is returned instead. Upon completion (successfully or by timeout), invokeAny cancels the remaining computations. However, it does so by interrupting threads, which could be insufficient in the case of strategy tasks. Instead, all tasks are explicitly canceled in a finally block.

The timeout value is handled slightly differently than in Listing 28.1. Instead of assuming that the time it takes to start threads and create tasks is negligible, you can subtract it from the initial timeout value. You do this by calculating an absolute deadline as the very first step of compute and then by having invokeAny wait for only the amount of time left before the deadline: deadline - System.nanoTime().

28.4 Parallel Implementation Using CompletionService

Method invokeAny perfectly fits the needs of a parallel runner of strategies, except for the minor inconvenience that failures are defined in terms of exceptions instead of empty options. However, this method is available only in the ExecutorService interface. If instead you need to work with an instance of Executor (in Java) or ExecutionContext (in Scala), you cannot use invokeAny.

The Java concurrency library defines a notion of completion service, which you can use to fulfill the requirements of a parallel runner—it is actually used internally to implement invokeAny. The CompletionService interface lets you submit tasks to a thread pool, and wait for them in the order in which they terminate. You can use it to implement a runner on a thread pool specified as an instance of `Executor`:

```scala
class Runner[A, B](strategies: Seq[Strategy[A, B]], exec: Executor):
  def compute(input: A, timeout: Double): Option[B] =
    val deadline = System.nanoTime() + (timeout * 1E9).round

    val tasks = strategies.map(strategy => strategy(input))
    val queue = ExecutorCompletionService[Option[B]](exec)
    for task <- tasks do queue.submit(() => task.run())

    @tailrec
    def loopQueue(pending: Int): Option[B] =
      if pending == 0 then None
      else
        queue.poll(deadline - System.nanoTime(), NANOSECONDS) match
          case null                          => None
          case future if future.get().nonEmpty => future.get()
          case _                             => loopQueue(pending - 1)

    try loopQueue(tasks.length)
    finally for task <- tasks do task.cancel()
```

Listing 28.3: A parallel runner of strategies based on `CompletionService`.

A completion service `queue` is created from the thread pool, and tasks are submitted to it. The queue forwards them to the pool for execution. You can then use `poll` to wait for the earliest task that finishes—`poll` blocks until one of the tasks is ready, but not necessarily the first that was submitted. If this task was successful, you are done. Otherwise, you need to keep polling the queue for the next task. Recursive function `loopQueue` implements this iteration. Each call to `poll` uses a smaller timeout value as you are getting closer to the deadline. Recursion terminates when `pending == 0` (all tasks have failed), `poll` returns null (the deadline has been reached), or `future.get` is a non-empty option (a task has produced a successful value). All tasks are canceled when `compute` terminates, as before.

As tasks terminate, their results are returned as completed futures. This is done to handle tasks that fail with an exception and produce no value. (A Scala equivalent could use type `Try` for that, but Java has no such type in its standard library.) All the `future.get` calls in Listing 28.3 are guaranteed to be non-blocking.

28.5 Asynchronous Implementation with Scala Futures

Instead of blocking the calling thread while the strategies are running, a runner's `compute` method could have the following signature:

```scala
                                              ─────── Scala ───
def compute(input: A, timeout: Double): scala.concurrent.Future[Option[B]] = ...
```

A call to `compute` returns immediately. Later, the future is completed when a strategy succeeds, all the strategies have failed, or the specified timeout is reached, whichever comes first. An asynchronous runner is more flexible than the blocking variant: You can choose to use the returned future asynchronously, by means of higher-order functions, or to block until the future is complete, which brings you back to the behavior of the previous (blocking) `compute` methods.

The implementation of an asynchronous runner using Scala futures faces two difficulties. First, you need a mechanism to complete a future after a timeout. You can reuse the approach described in Section 26.5, based on a promise and a timer, to implement a generic `completeOnTimeout` extension to futures:

```scala
                                              ─────── Scala ───
extension [A](future: Future[A])
  def completeOnTimeout(timeout: Long, unit: TimeUnit)(fallbackCode: => A)(
      using exec: ExecutionContext, timer: ScheduledExecutorService
  ): Future[A] =
    if future.isCompleted then future
    else
      val promise    = Promise[A]()
      val complete   = (() => promise.completeWith(Future(fallbackCode))): Runnable
      val completion = timer.schedule(complete, timeout, unit)

      future.onComplete { result =>
        completion.cancel(false)
        promise.tryComplete(result)
      }
      promise.future
```

Listing 28.4: Extending Scala futures with `completeOnTimeout`.

If the future is not already completed, a promise is created, and a task is scheduled on a timer to complete this promise with a default value after a timeout delay. Using `onComplete`, a callback action is registered with the original future, which also tries to complete the same promise, using the future's own result. If this action runs before the timeout, the timer task is not needed and is canceled—`completion` is a Java future with a `cancel` method. In all cases, the promise is eventually completed either by the timer task, after a timeout delay, or when the initial future terminates, if this happens before the timeout.

You may be wondering about the initial `if-then-else` because no locks are used, which results in a non-atomic check-then-act. Could this be a problem? The answer is that the test is not strictly necessary: The code still works even if all it does is follow the `else` branch. The early test is merely an optimization that avoids creating a new promise if `completeOnTimeout` happens to be called on a completed future. If a future completes right after you test it to be incomplete, the `else` branch is applied to a finished future and unnecessarily creates a promise and a timer task. But everything still works.

The default value, `fallbackCode`, is not needed if the timeout is not triggered and is passed by name, unevaluated. If the timeout is triggered, `fallbackCode` is evaluated on the thread pool `exec` to avoid running unknown code in a timer thread—timer tasks are typically expected to be short. This is the reason `completeWith` is used instead of `tryComplete` to complete the promise from the timer. Except for the fact that the fallback code is passed unevaluated, this extension behaves like the `completeOnTimeout` method of Java's `CompletableFuture`.

The second difficulty in implementing a non-blocking runner is the need to complete the future returned by method `compute` exactly when the first successful strategy terminates—assuming no timeout. Scala defines a function `firstCompletedOf`, which is a kind of non-blocking `invokeAny`: Given a list of futures, it creates a future that is completed when the first future from the list terminates. At first glance, this would seem to be exactly what we need. However, while `invokeAny` returns the first future to terminate *successfully*, `firstCompletedOf` returns (a future equivalent to) the first future that terminates either *successfully or unsuccessfully*. This is a problem because a direct application of `firstCompletedOf` on a list of running strategies will produce a future that contains the result of the first strategy that terminates, even if this strategy returns `None`. That's not what you want.

What you do want is a `findFirst` function that finds from a list the earliest future to terminate with a value that satisfies a given predicate—a non-empty option, for instance. You can use `firstCompletedOf` to implement `findFirst`,[3] with a mixture of `flatMap` and recursion, reminiscent of Listing 26.10:

Scala

```scala
def findFirst[A](futures: Seq[Future[A]], test: A => Boolean)(
    using ExecutionContext
): Future[Option[A]] =
  if futures.isEmpty then Future.successful(None)
  else
    Future.firstCompletedOf(futures).flatMap { _ =>
      val (finished, running) = futures.partition(_.isCompleted)
      finished.flatMap(_.value.get.toOption).find(test) match
        case None  => findFirst(running, test)
        case found => Future.successful(found)
    }
```

Listing 28.5: Earliest Scala future that satisfies a condition; see also Lis. 28.7.

Function `findFirst` does nothing blocking. Its responsibility is to create a future that will eventually contain the value you are looking for. It achieves this by using `flatMap` to trigger computations when a future finishes. First, you use `firstCompletedOf` to create a future that is completed when the first future from the list terminates. At this

---

[3]You don't have to. You can also implement `findFirst` directly with callbacks and a promise, as in Listing 28.7.

point—when this future terminates—you know that at least one future is completed. You separate finished futures from those that are still running and look inside the finished futures for a successful outcome that passes the test.[4] If one is found, it is the value you are looking for. You return it as a completed future, and you are done. Otherwise, you keep waiting for the remaining running futures with a recursive call. If the list runs out of futures without finding one with a value that satisfies the test, you return None as a completed future. Note that finished is necessarily non-empty (one future has to finish to trigger the evaluation of the body of flatMap), so running is a smaller list than futures, as is needed for recursion to work.

With methods completeOnTimeout and findFirst implemented, you can finally write an asynchronous runner of strategies:

```scala
class Runner[A, B](strategies: Seq[Strategy[A, B]], exec: ExecutionContext)
                  (using ScheduledExecutorService)(using ExecutionContext):
  def compute(input: A, timeout: Double): Future[Option[B]] =
    val deadline = System.nanoTime() + (timeout * 1E9).round

    val tasks   = strategies.map(strategy => strategy(input))
    val futures = tasks.map(task => Future(task.run())(using exec))

    val first = findFirst(futures, _.nonEmpty)
      .map(_.flatten)
      .completeOnTimeout(deadline - System.nanoTime(), NANOSECONDS)(None)

    first.onComplete(_ => for task <- tasks do task.cancel())
    first
```

Listing 28.6: A parallel asynchronous runner of strategies using Scala futures.

Tasks are created as before and started as a list of futures. Using findFirst, you extract from that list the earliest future that produces a successful result (as a non-empty option). You then use completeOnTimeout to add a suitable timeout.[5] Before the future is returned, you use onComplete to add a callback that cancels all the remaining strategies when the future finishes. Thanks to the use of findFirst and completeOnTimeout, the future that is produced terminates when a strategy succeeds, all strategies have failed, or the timeout is reached, whichever happens first.

This runner relies on three separate thread pools. Here, exec is the main pool on which the strategies are run. Two additional pools are used to run the various callbacks needed for timeout and cancellation. No lengthy computation is ever run on these pools, and two single-thread pools would be sufficient, or even a single pool with a single thread if it implements both the ScheduledExecutorService and ExecutionContext interfaces.

---

[4]The expression that implements this search applies value to a future, get to an option, and toOption to a Try, and uses flatMap to ignore None values.

[5]A map(_.flatten) step is needed because strategies return options, as does method findFirst. Thus, the result from the earliest successful strategy is returned as an option of option.

28.6 Asynchronous Implementation with CompletableFuture

Instead of Scala futures, you can base a parallel asynchronous implementation on Java's `CompletableFuture`. This class already implements a `completeOnTimeout` method, so no additional code is needed to deal with timeouts. However, you still need a `findFirst` function to retrieve the result of the earliest successful strategy.

Java defines a function `anyOf` that returns (a future equivalent to) the first finished `CompletableFuture` from an array. It is similar in purpose to Scala's `firstCompletedOf`, but differs in the fact that the input array can contain futures of different types, and the resulting future loses all type information—it is a `CompletableFuture[Object]`. To avoid the awkwardness of working without types, and as an excuse to illustrate a different approach, the following implementation bypasses `anyOf` and uses a promise instead:

```scala
def findFirst[A](futures: Seq[CompletableFuture[A]],
                 test: A => Boolean): CompletableFuture[Option[A]] =
  if futures.isEmpty then CompletableFuture.completedFuture(None)
  else
      val promise = CompletableFuture[Option[A]]()
      val active  = AtomicInteger(futures.length)

      for future <- futures do
        future.handle { (value, ex) =>
          if !promise.isDone then
            if (ex eq null) && test(value) then promise.complete(Some(value))
            else if active.decrementAndGet() == 0 then promise.complete(None)
        }
      promise
```

Listing 28.7: Earliest `CompletableFuture` that satisfies a condition.

Unless the list of futures is empty, a promise is created as an incomplete instance of `CompletableFuture`. The idea is to fulfill this promise with the first future from the list that produces a value that satisfies the given test. However, if no future produces such a value, the promise still needs to be finished. Therefore, a counter `active` is introduced to keep track of how many futures are still running. This way, the last future that terminates can still complete the promise with `None` if no suitable value was found. This counter is shared among threads and needs to be thread-safe—an instance of `AtomicInteger` is used here. With this counter in place, you then add a callback to each future, using method `handle`, which is `CompletableFuture`'s equivalent of Scala's `onComplete`. If the promise is still open and a future produces a value that satisfies the test, this value is used to fulfill the promise. Otherwise, the `active` counter is decremented, and if the future is the last to terminate, it fulfills the promise with `None`.

(The code stops updating the `ative` counter after the promise has been fulfilled, since it will not be needed at this point.)

The action used to create the callbacks begins with a non-atomic check-then-act. It is harmless for the same reason that the initial, non-atomic test in Listing 28.4 is harmless: The test if `!promise.isDone` is included here only as a performance optimization. The case of multiple threads attempting to fulfill the promise at the same time is handled by method `complete`, which internally uses an atomic if-then. The worst thing that can happen is that threads needlessly evaluate `test(value)` or decrement `active` after the promise has already been completed.

With method `findFirst` written, you can easily implement an asynchronous runner:

```Scala
class Runner[A, B](strategies: Seq[Strategy[A, B]], exec: Executor):
  def compute(input: A, timeout: Double): CompletableFuture[Option[B]] =
    val deadline = System.nanoTime() + (timeout * 1E9).round

    val tasks   = strategies.map(strategy => strategy(input))
    val futures =
      tasks.map(task => CompletableFuture.supplyAsync(() => task.run(), exec))

    val first = findFirst(futures, _.nonEmpty)
      .thenApply(_.flatten)
      .completeOnTimeout(None, deadline - System.nanoTime(), NANOSECONDS)

    first.handle((_, _) => for task <- tasks do task.cancel())
    first
```

Listing 28.8: Asynchronous runner variant based on `CompletableFuture`.

This code is practically the same as that in Listing 28.6. The main difference is that Scala futures are replaced with `CompletableFuture`, which uses different method names: `map` becomes `thenApply` and `onComplete` becomes `handle`. These methods use existing threads according to their own design and do not need the two additional thread pools used in Listing 28.6.[6]

28.7   Caching Results from Strategies

A premise of this case study is that applying a strategy can be an expensive computation, worthy of our effort to introduce parallelism. Therefore, it could be desirable for a runner to cache the results of previous strategy runs.

We could potentially reuse the generic memoization mechanism implemented in Listing 12.2, or its thread-safe variant from Listing 25.7. Instead, we will develop an improved version that continues to be thread-safe but also takes timeout values into

---

[6]Alternatively, Listings 28.7 and 28.8 could rely on methods `thenApplyAsync` and `handleAsync`, which take a thread pool argument, for an implementation closer to the Scala variants.

account. This design is based on the assumption that failed strategy runs might have succeeded with more time, but not with less.[7] As before, the cache is organized as a thread-safe mapping from inputs to futures of outputs (see the rationale in Section 25.6) but also stores a timeout value associated with each future.

When a thread calls `compute` with an input value and a timeout, the mapping is searched for the input, and the outcome of this search is handled as follows:

1. *The input is not found.* In this case, the design from Listing 25.7 is reused: Put a promise into the mapping, and invoke strategies to complete it.

2. *A completed future with a value other than* `None` *is found.* This implies that a strategy was successful in the past. The desired output is taken from the future, and no further computation is necessary.

3. *A future is found but has no usable output.* This is either an incomplete future or a future completed with `None`. In this situation, there are two cases to consider:

    (a) If the timeout associated with this earlier computation is larger than the timeout now specified, you have no hope of improving the result, due to the assumption stated earlier; don't start a new computation, and use the future from the mapping.

    (b) If the future in the mapping corresponds to a computation with a smaller timeout, you could use it in hopes that it produces a successful outcome, but there is also a chance that it has failed (or will fail) where a lengthier computation would have succeeded.

    This is the interesting case. If the cached future is completed (with `None`), you can ignore it. But if it is still running, you need to consider it: It may soon produce a successful output. However, you cannot commit to it because it may still fail. Furthermore, the future can also switch from incomplete to complete at any moment while you are considering it.

    You handle this case by initiating a new computation, with a larger timeout, and by using the first successful result available, either from this new computation or from the future already in the cache. Note that this approach works whether the cached future is completed or not, so it correctly handles the case where the cached future suddenly finishes in the middle of these steps, successfully or not.

Using Scala futures for a change—Listing 25.7 uses `CompletableFuture`—a possible implementation is as follows:

Scala
```
class Runner[A, B](strategies: Seq[Strategy[A, B]], exec: ExecutionContext)
                  (using ScheduledExecutorService)(using ExecutionContext):
```

[7]This may not be true in practice, as computing resources may fluctuate, making it possible for shorter runs to use more actual CPU time than longer runs did.

```scala
private val cache = TrieMap.empty[A, (Double, Future[Option[B]])]

def compute(input: A, timeout: Double): Future[Option[B]] =
  val deadline = System.nanoTime() + (timeout * 1E9).round

  def hasResult(future: Future[Option[B]]): Boolean =
    future.value.flatMap(_.toOption).flatten.nonEmpty

  def searchCache(): Future[Option[B]] = cache.get(input) match
    case None => // case 1
      val promise = Promise[Option[B]]()
      if cache.putIfAbsent(input, (timeout, promise.future)).isEmpty
      then doCompute(None, promise)
      else searchCache()

    case Some((_, future)) if hasResult(future) => // case 2
      future

    case Some(cached @ (time, future)) => // case 3
      if time >= timeout then // case 3(a)
        future.completeOnTimeout(deadline - System.nanoTime(), NANOSECONDS)(None)
      else // case 3(b)
        val promise = Promise[Option[B]]()
        if cache.replace(input, cached, (timeout, promise.future))
        then doCompute(Some(future), promise)
        else searchCache()
  end searchCache

  def doCompute(future: Option[Future[Option[B]]],
                promise: Promise[Option[B]]): Future[Option[B]] =
    val tasks   = strategies.map(strategy => strategy(input))
    val futures = tasks.map(task => Future(task.run())(using exec)) ++ future

    findFirst(futures, _.nonEmpty)
      .map(_.flatten)
      .completeOnTimeout(deadline - System.nanoTime(), NANOSECONDS)(None)
      .onComplete { result =>
        promise.complete(result)
        for task <- tasks do task.cancel()
      }
    promise.future
  end doCompute

  searchCache()
end compute
```

Listing 28.9: Asynchronous runner with thread-safe caching.

This is the very last code illustration of the book, but certainly not its simplest. You can follow it step by step. A cache is allocated as a thread-safe mapping from inputs to pairs. Each pair contains a future and the timeout associated with it. Method `compute` simply returns the future produced by `searchCache`, which proceeds with the cases outlined earlier, in the same order.

In the first case, no future is found in the cache. Therefore, you must initiate a new computation. You create a promise and try to add it to the cache. If the promise is added, you use `doCompute` to start the computation. The `else` branch deals with the case where another thread added a promise to the cache before you could (see discussion of Listing 25.7 in Section 25.6), in which case you need to consider it with a recursive call to `searchCache` [the same thing happens in case 3(b)].

The next case in `searchCache` finds a successful completed future and returns it unchanged. (Function `hasResult` is hard to read: It returns true if a future is finished, its computation didn't throw an exception, and the option it produced is non-empty.)

The third case deals with a future that is either failed or incomplete. If the future is associated with a timeout value larger than what the current invocation of `compute` is allowed [case 3(a)], you use it without starting a new computation. You simply add a timeout to the existing future in case its remaining run is longer than the timeout argument used in the call to `compute`.

This leaves case 3(b): You find a future—failed or incomplete, it doesn't matter—but its timeout is smaller than what you can afford to spend in the current call to `compute`. In this case, you create a promise for a new computation, as in case 1, and use it to replace the existing cached future. Once the new future is in the cache, you initiate its computation. The only difference from case 1 is that, to the list of futures created from the strategies, you add the older future that you found in the cache (this is done with `++ future` at the beginning of function `doCompute`).

To implement function `doCompute`, used in cases 1 and 3(b), you proceed as in Listing 28.6: Use `findFirst`, flatten, add a timeout, and cancel all remaining tasks upon completion. However, instead of returning the future produced by `findFirst` directly, you use it to complete the promise that is already in the cache.

In summary, this caching runner treats existing futures in the cache in one of two ways. If a future cannot possibly be improved—it is finished with a successful value or it is based on a larger timeout—it is used. Otherwise, it is replaced by a future that cannot possibly be worse.[8] This new future is completed as soon as the existing future terminates successfully or later based on new strategy calls. It is no worse than the previous future, because it produces a successful outcome at the same time if the original future is successful or keeps running and may still produce a successful value after the original future has failed.

---

[8]Ignoring the possibility that starting new computations slows down existing ones given limited computing resources.

28.8 Summary

While the case study in Chapter 24 focused on tasks as actions, executed for their side effects, this variant considered functional—value-producing—tasks instead. It used futures, a common handler of functional tasks, either as synchronizers (Lis. 28.1), or jointly with other synchronizers (Lis. 28.2 and 28.3), or through non-blocking higher-order functions (Lis. 28.4 to 28.9). Special attention was given to issues of time-outs and cancellation. To contrast two standard future implementations, we implemented the asynchronous runner twice, first with Scala futures and then with Java's `CompletableFuture`. Finally, a thread-safe, timeout-aware cache was added to asynchronous runners using Scala futures and promises.

Appendix A

Features of Java and Kotlin

This appendix reviews many of the concepts and features discussed in the book, using an older language, Java, and a newer language, Kotlin, instead of Scala. Several examples written earlier in Scala are rewritten in Java or in Kotlin (or both). Code illustrations use Kotlin 1.7 and Java 19 (with some "preview" features enabled).

A.1 Functions in Java and Kotlin

Java and Kotlin both define methods—both are languages with an object-oriented leaning—and functions (see discussion in Section 9.4). Somewhat confusingly, Kotlin methods are called functions.

Methods and functions are introduced by the keyword `fun` in Kotlin, whereas Java uses no keyword:

—————————————————————————— Java ———
```java
int abs(int x) {
  if (x > 0) return x;
  else return -x;
}
```

—————————————————————————— Kotlin ———
```kotlin
fun abs(x: Int): Int = if (x > 0) x else -x
```

You can define functions locally inside functions in Kotlin but not in Java:

—————————————————————————— Kotlin ———
```kotlin
fun abs(x: Int): Int {
  fun max(a: Int, b: Int) = if (a > b) a else b
  return max(x, -x)
}
```

Kotlin can use a simple expression as a function body, as in the first `abs` implementation. If a block is used instead, you need to use `return`—blocks are not values as they are in Scala. You can also see from the examples here that Kotlin, like Scala, omits semicolons, uses the `variable: Type` syntax, and has a functional `if-then-else` construct.

In Kotlin, you can define functions as extensions and invoke them as methods. Also, a Kotlin method declared `infix` can be invoked in infix notation. This example combines both features to define an infix extension `max` to integers:

```
                                                               ── Kotlin ──
infix fun Int.max(that: Int): Int = if (this > that) this else that
```

Given this definition, you can write expressions like `x.max(y)` or `x max y` on integers `x` and `y`. There is no support for these features in Java.

Neither language supports symbolic names, but several operators can be defined in Kotlin by implementing a corresponding method:

```
                                                               ── Kotlin ──
operator fun String.times(count: Int): String {
    val builder = StringBuilder(this.length * count)
    for (i in 1..count) builder.append(this)
    return builder.toString()
}

"A" * 3 // "AAA"
```

In this example, an operator `*` similar to Scala's is added on strings by implementing an extension method `times`. Other operators have corresponding method names: "+" is `plus`, "++" is `inc`, "+=" is `plusAssign`, ".." is `rangeTo`, and so on.

A special method `invoke` plays the role of Scala's `apply`:

```
                                                               ── Kotlin ──
operator fun String.invoke(i: Int): Char = this[i]

"foo"(2) // 'o'
```

Note that `this[i]` is actually compiled into a method call `this.get(i)`. By defining your own `get`, you can set up a square bracket syntax on your own types, something that is not possible in Scala. There is no support for user-defined operators or for functions applied implicitly in Java.

In both Java and Kotlin, you can parameterize functions by types. For instance, the following function returns the first and last elements of a list as a short list:

```java
                                                         ── Java ──
<A> List<A> firstLast(List<A> list) {
  return List.of(list.get(0), list.get(list.size() - 1));
}
```

```kotlin
                                                         ── Kotlin ──
fun <A> firstLast(list: List<A>): List<A> = list.slice(listOf(0, list.size - 1))
```

In both languages, function `firstLast` is parameterized by the type of list elements: It returns a `List<String>` when applied to a `List<String>`, and a `List<Color>` when applied to a `List<Color>`.

Both languages have support for variable-length arguments:

```java
                                                         ── Java ──
double average(double first, double... others) {
  return (first + Arrays.stream(others).sum()) / (1 + others.length);
}
```

```kotlin
                                                         ── Kotlin ──
fun average(first: Double, vararg others: Double): Double =
  (first + others.sum()) / (1 + others.size)
```

Function `average` can accept a variable number of arguments: it can be called as `average(1.0, 2.3, 4.1)` or `average(10.0, 20.0)`, for instance.

Finally, Kotlin functions can use named arguments and default values:

```kotlin
                                                         ── Kotlin ──
fun write(str: String, withNewline: Boolean = true): Unit =
  if (withNewline) println(str) else print(str)

// can be called as:
write("message")
write("message", false)
write("message", withNewline = false)
```

Java has no such feature.

A.2   Immutability

Java and Kotlin functions can be either pure or impure. For actions—functions with no return value, applied for side effects—Java has a keyword `void`, whereas Kotlin uses a `Unit` return type, like Scala. Kotlin uses `var` and `val` to define reassignable and non-reassignable variables, like Scala. In Java, variables are reassignable by default but become non-reassignable when the keyword `final` is used.

Kotlin lets you defer the initialization of a `val` variable, a feature Scala does not have:

——————————————————————————————— Kotlin ———

```
fun parseVerbosity(arg: String): Int {
  val verbosity: Int
  if (arg == "-v") verbosity = 1
  else if (arg == "-vv") verbosity = 2
  else verbosity = 0
  return verbosity
}
```

Most Java collections are mutable. Kotlin defines immutable collection types, but they are mostly read-only views of underlying mutable implementations:

——————————————————————————————— Kotlin ———

```
val readOnly: List<Int> = listOf(1, 2, 3)
val cheating = readOnly as MutableList<Int>
cheating[1] = 20
val x = readOnly[1] // 20
```

In this example, variable `readOnly` is of type `List`, an immutable type in Kotlin. Internally, however, it is implemented (on the JVM) as an old-fashioned array-based list. It can even be type cast to a mutable type, and modified: The second element of list `readOnly` is changed from 2 to 20.

This makes Kotlin lists fundamentally different from lists in Scala (or in any functional programming language). In particular, Kotlin lists have no constant-time `head` and `tail` operations:

——————————————————————————————— Scala ———

```
val a: List[String] = List("A","B","C")
val b = a.tail // constant time, lists a and b share all their data
```

```kotlin
                                                        ─ Kotlin ─
val a: List<String> = listOf("A","B","C")
val b = a.drop(1) // requires a full copy, no data sharing
```

Immutable structures in Kotlin do not implement the data sharing scheme described in Section 3.7 (and shown in Figure 3.1 with Scala lists). They are more like the unmodifiable views available in Java. One difference is that they define their own types, without methods for mutation. In contrast, in Java, calling a mutating method on an unmodifiable structure throws an exception:

```java
                                                        ─ Java ─
List<Integer> nums = List.of(1, 2, 3);
nums.add(4); // throws UnsupportedOperationException
```

```kotlin
                                                        ─ Kotlin ─
val nums = listOf(1, 2, 3)
nums.add(4) // rejected at compile time
```

In both Java and Kotlin, there is only one list implementation internally. In Kotlin, you can view it as mutable or immutable, under two different types—List and MutableList. In Java, there is only one type—List, mutable—but, on some lists, mutating methods are not available at runtime.

A.3 Pattern Matching and Algebraic Data Types

As yet, neither Java nor Kotlin offers the full power of pattern matching, as found in functional languages. In particular, there is little support for algebraic data types. Nevertheless, Java is steadily catching up—pattern matching of records, which are similar to Scala's case classes, is coming as a preview in Java 19. The switch construct became an expression in Java 14:

```java
                                                        ─ Java ─
int parseVerbosity(String arg) {
  return switch(arg) {
    case "-v" -> 1;
    case "-vv" -> 2;
    default -> 0;
  };
}
```

Here, you use the whole `switch` expression as the value returned by the function. Later, Java added type testing and logical guards:

```java
                                                                    ─ Java ─
<A> String listInfo(List<A> list) {
  return switch (list) {
    case null -> "no list";
    case List<A> empty when empty.isEmpty() -> "an empty list";
    case RandomAccess seq -> "a random access list";
    default -> "some other list";
  };
}
```

Java also recently introduced pattern matching of records, which are similar to Scala's case classes (see Section 5.2):[1]

```java
                                                                    ─ Java ─
record TempRecord(String city, int temperature) {}

TempRecord rec = ...

String str = switch (rec) {
  case TempRecord(String city, int temp) -> "%d in %s".formatted(temp, city);
};
```

Some of Scala's fancier patterns, such as `case TempRecord("Phoenix", temp)` and `case TempRecord(city, temp) if temp >= 100`, are not possible in Java.

Kotlin's `when` construct offers similar but different capabilities:

```kotlin
                                                                    ─ Kotlin ─
val str: String = when (obj) {
  1 -> "One"
  2, "2" -> "Two"
  is List<*> -> "A list"
  !is String -> "Not a string"
  else -> "Unknown"
}
```

The `when` construct neither supports arbitrary guards nor the deconstruction of records as in Java and Scala.

---

[1] The last two Java examples in this section and the Java code in Section A.4 use a pattern matching syntax that is available only as a preview in Java 19.

A.4   Recursive Programming

Functions can be recursive in both Java and Kotlin. Tail recursion optimization is available in Kotlin but not in Java:

```kotlin
                                                                          Kotlin
fun factorial(n: Int): Int {
  tailrec fun loop(m: Int, f: Int): Int = if (m == 0) f else loop(m - 1, f * m)
  return loop(n, 1)
}
```

The `tailrec` keyword works differently from the `@tailrec` annotation in Scala. In Kotlin, optimization takes place only if `tailrec` is specified (and the function is indeed tail recursive).

You can define and process recursive structures in both languages, as shown here:

```java
                                                                            Java
sealed public interface BinTree {
  BinTree Empty = new Empty(); // empty tree singleton
}
record Empty() implements BinTree {}
record Node(int key, BinTree left, BinTree right) implements BinTree {}

int size(BinTree tree) {
  return switch (tree) {
    case Empty() -> 0;
    case Node(int __, BinTree left, BinTree right) -> 1 + size(left) + size(right);
  };
}
```

```kotlin
                                                                          Kotlin
sealed interface BinTree
object Empty : BinTree
data class Node(val key: Int, val left: BinTree, val right: BinTree) : BinTree

fun size(tree: BinTree): Int = when (tree) {
  is Empty -> 0
  is Node  -> 1 + size(tree.left) + size(tree.right)
}
```

The main difference with the Scala variant in Listing 6.7 is that Kotlin's when is more limited than pattern matching: You cannot use a pattern of the form Node(...) to extract the left and right children of a node, as you would in Java or Scala.

A.5   Higher-Order Functions

You can use functions as values in both Java and Kotlin. Kotlin denotes with (A) -> B the type of functions from inputs of type A to outputs of type B—that is, A => B in Scala. The story is more complicated in Java: Function<T,R> represents functions from a type T to a type R, but both T and R must refer to objects and cannot be primitive types. A function that uses an object to produce a primitive int value, for instance, has type ToIntFunction<T>, and a function that consumes an int to create an object has type IntFunction<R>. Similarly, a function that produces a bool value from an object has type Predicate<T>, while a function from int to bool has type IntPredicate, and a function from int to int has type IntBinaryOperator. Corresponding types are defined for the other primitive types.

Java does not have a Unit type like Scala and Kotlin but uses void methods instead. It also needs to accommodate functions that take no arguments. So, a function that consumes an object but does not return a value has type Consumer<T>, while a no-argument function that returns an object has type Supplier<R>. Of course, primitive types make it necessary to define types such as IntConsumer and LongSupplier. Java also lacks a pair type and instead defines specific interfaces for two-argument functions, such as BiFunction<T,U,R>, BiConsumer<T,U>, ObjIntConsumer<T>, and IntBinaryOperator. In total, the java.util.function package defines 43 functional interfaces.

Both Java and Kotlin have a lambda expression syntax for anonymous functions. As an example, you can use either language to define a function **negate** that negates a predicate:

```
───────────────────────────────────────────────────── Java ──────

<A> Predicate<A> negate(Predicate<A> f) {
  return x -> !f.test(x);
}
```

```
───────────────────────────────────────────────────── Kotlin ──────

fun <A> negate(f: (A) -> Boolean): (A) -> Boolean = { x -> !f(x) }
```

Function **negate** takes a predicate—a Boolean-valued function—as its argument and returns a predicate, defined as a lambda expression. On function f, Kotlin's invoke method is called implicitly, while Java requires method test to be called explicitly. The body of a lambda expression can be a simple expression, as in the preceding examples. If the body is a full block of code, both languages require the use of a return keyword.

Java and Kotlin offer bridges between methods and functions via method references. Kotlin also defines a shorter form for anonymous functions, where `x -> f(x)` is replaced with `f(it)`, similar to Scala's use of "`_`" for partial application:

```Kotlin
fun pos(x: Int): Boolean = x > 0

val neg: (Int) -> Boolean = negate { x -> pos(x) }
val neg: (Int) -> Boolean = negate { pos(it) }
val neg: (Int) -> Boolean = negate(::pos)
```

If `pos` were a method of an object `ref`, you would replace `::pos` with `ref::pos` in the last expression. In Java, methods are always defined within a class, so the "`::`" operator used for method reference always has a left-hand-side argument:

```Java
class Math {
  public boolean pos(int x) {
    return x > 0;
  }
}
Math m = new Math();

Predicate<Integer> neg = negate(x -> m.pos(x));
Predicate<Integer> neg = negate(m::pos);
```

In the other direction, lambda expressions can be used to implement methods. In Java, like in Scala, lambda expressions can implement SAM interfaces directly:

```Scala
val byLength: Comparator[String] = (a, b) => a.length.compareTo(b.length)
```

```Java
Comparator<String> byLength = (a, b) -> Integer.compare(a.length(), b.length());
```

By contrast, in Kotlin, you often need to mention an interface's name explicitly for a lambda expression to implement it:

```Kotlin
// rejected by the compiler:
val byLength: Comparator<String> = { a, b -> a.length.compareTo(b.length) }

val byLength = Comparator<String> { a, b -> a.length.compareTo(b.length) } // OK
```

In Java, lambda expressions actually *require* that you use a SAM interface:

```
                                                                    Java
ToIntFunction<String> len = (String str) -> str.length(); // OK

Object len = (String str) -> str.length(); // rejected by the compiler
var len = (String str) -> str.length();    // rejected by the compiler
```

This is not an issue in Scala or Kotlin:

```
                                                                    Scala
val len: Any = (str: String) => str.length // OK
val len = (str: String) => str.length       // type String => Int inferred
```

```
                                                                    Kotlin
val len: Any = { str: String -> str.length } // OK
val len = { str: String -> str.length }       // type (String) -> Int inferred
```

Recall that, in Scala, functions can be curried, and single-argument calls can use curly braces instead of parentheses:

```
                                                                    Scala
def existsOrEmpty[A](list: List[A])(test: A => Boolean): Boolean =
  list.isEmpty || list.exists(test)

val e = existsOrEmpty(List(1, 2, 3)) { num =>
  num > 1
}
```

Kotlin has no curried functions but uses a different "trick" for the same purpose. It lets you move a lambda expression—which includes its own pair of braces—outside the list of arguments if it is the last argument in a call:

```
                                                                    Kotlin
fun <A> existsOrEmpty(list: List<A>, test: (A) -> Boolean): Boolean =
  list.isEmpty() || list.any(test)

val e = existsOrEmpty(listOf(1, 2, 3)) { num ->
  num > 1
}
```

Notice how, in the last expression, the lambda expression `{ num -> num > 1 }` has been moved outside the list of `existsOrEmpty` arguments.

Kotlin's `any`, used in the preceding example, is equivalent to the Scala method `exists`. Kotlin collections define most standard higher-order functions, including `forEach`, `filter`, `map`, and `flatMap`. For instance, you can convert Fahrenheit temperatures into Celsius using `map`:

```kotlin
─────────────────────────────────────────────── Kotlin ───

temps.map { temp -> ((temp - 32) / 1.8f).roundToInt() }
```

As a more complex combination of higher-order functions, you could start from a list of strings, parse each string as a space-separated list of temperatures, ignore non-numerical values, and convert numerical values to Celsius:

```kotlin
─────────────────────────────────────────────── Kotlin ───

val SPACES = Regex("\\s+")
val strings: List<String> = ...

val celsius: List<Int> = strings
  .flatMap { SPACES.split(it) }
  .mapNotNull { it.toIntOrNull() }
  .map { ((it - 32) / 1.8f).roundToInt() }
```

This example uses the shorter syntax based on `it`. Kotlin tends to use null where Scala would use options—for instance, `toIntOrNull` instead of `toIntOption`. Method `mapNotNull` combines a mapping and filtering steps, ignoring null outputs of the mapped function.

In Java, the standard collections implement very few higher-order functions. Instead, collections are bridged into streams, which implement all the higher-order functions. A simple conversion into Celsius could be written as follows:

```java
───────────────────────────────────────────────── Java ───

List<Integer> temps = ...

List<Integer> celsius = temps.stream().map(temp -> round((temp - 32) / 1.8f)).toList();
```

This calculation forces boxing and unboxing of primitive `int` values to and from `Integer` values. To avoid it, Java also defines specialized stream classes for its primitive types:

```java
───────────────────────────────────────────────── Java ───

int[] temps = ...

int[] celsius = Arrays.stream(temps).map(temp -> round((temp - 32) / 1.8f)).toArray();
```

In this computation, `map` is invoked on an object of type `IntStream` instead of `Stream`.

You can also implement in Java the more complex transformation shown earlier, from a list of lines into a list of Celsius temperatures. There is no standard Java function to parse a string into an optional integer (or even into a nullable integer), so you need to write one first:

```
———————————————————————————————————— Java ———
Optional<Integer> parse(String str) {
  try {
    return Optional.of(Integer.valueOf(str));
  } catch (NumberFormatException ex) {
    return Optional.empty();
  }
}
```

Using this function, the code for the transformation is similar to what it would be in Scala. The key difference is that an option needs to be converted into a stream explicitly in the second call to `flatMap` (Scala uses an implicit conversion there):

```
———————————————————————————————————— Java ———
Pattern SPACES = Pattern.compile("\\s+");
List<String> strings = ...

List<Integer> celsius = strings.stream()
    .flatMap(str -> Arrays.stream(SPACES.split(str)))
    .flatMap(str -> parse(str).stream())
    .map(temp -> round((temp - 32) / 1.8f))
    .toList();
```

You could also write a variant that processes an array of strings `String[]` into an array of integers `int[]` by using `OptionalInt` instead of `Optional` and `IntStream` instead of `Stream`.

When higher-order functions return functions, closures are created in both Java and Kotlin. The memoization example of Listing 12.2 can be written in either language:

```
———————————————————————————————————— Java ———
<A, B> Function<A, B> memo(Function<A, B> f) {
  Map<A, B> store = new HashMap<>();
  return x -> store.computeIfAbsent(x, f);
}
```

```
——————————————————————————————————— Kotlin ———
fun <A, B> memo(f: (A) -> B): (A) -> B {
  val store = mutableMapOf<A, B>()
  return { x -> store.computeIfAbsent(x, f) }
}
```

In Kotlin, closures can write the captured data, as they do in Scala:

```
──────────────────────────────────────────────── Kotlin ───────
fun <A, B> single(f: (A) -> B): (A) -> B {
  var called = false
  return { x ->
    if (called) throw IllegalStateException()
    called = true
    f(x)
  }
}
```

This example creates a variant of a function f that can be invoked only once before it throws an exception—for instance, for the purpose of testing. This requires writing the Boolean variable called from the closure. By contrast, Java does not allow closures to reassign variables. This code is rejected by the compiler:

```
──────────────────────────────────────────────── Java ───────
<A, B> Function<A, B> single(Function<A, B> f) {
  var called = false;
  return x -> {
    if (called) throw new IllegalStateException();
    called = true; // rejected at compile time
    return f.apply(x);
  };
}
```

Instead, you can replace the lambda expression with an anonymous class that defines a reassignable Boolean field:

```
──────────────────────────────────────────────── Java ───────
<A, B> Function<A, B> single(Function<A, B> f) {
  return new Function<>() {
    private boolean called = false;

    public B apply(A x) {
      if (called) throw new IllegalStateException();
      called = true;
      return f.apply(x);
    }
  };
}
```

The argument f is still captured in a closure, but it is only read and not reassigned.

A.6   Lazy Evaluation

By replacing values with no-argument functions (thunks), you can delay the evaluation of function arguments in both Java and Kotlin. The fancier by-name arguments of Scala do not exist in either language.

Kotlin, however, makes the arrow of a lambda expression optional when the lambda takes no arguments or its arguments are ignored. The following Scala expressions

```
                                                                  Scala
List.tabulate(5)(i => "X" * (i + 1)) // [X, XX, XXX, XXXX, XXXXX]
List.fill(5)(Random.between(1, 11))  // 5 numbers, possibly different
```

can be written in Kotlin as

```
                                                                  Kotlin
List(5) { i -> "X".repeat(i + 1) }
List(5) { Random.nextInt(1, 11) }
```

You can use the same function `List` where you need two functions, `tabulate` and `fill`, in Scala. The Kotlin function used in this example is equivalent to `tabulate`. You could write the last line in the preceding example as

```
                                                                  Kotlin
List(5) { _ -> Random.nextInt(1, 11) }
```

but the unused argument and arrow are optional.

This makes it possible to achieve in Kotlin a form of control abstraction similar to Scala's, despite the lack of by-name arguments. For instance, you can rewrite function `timeOf` from Listing 12.3 in this way:

```
                                                                  Kotlin
fun <U> timeOf(code: () -> U): Double {
  val start = System.nanoTime()
  code()
  val end = System.nanoTime()
  return (end - start) / 1E9
}
```

It is used in exactly the same way as the Scala variant, with no explicit thunk visible:

```
                                                                ─ Kotlin ─
val time = timeOf {
  computeSomething()
}
```

Java is more limited than Scala or Kotlin. Even its `Stream` class does not define a `tabulate` function, and `Collections.fill` can only fill a list with a repetition *of the same value*. You can still create the two lists used at the beginning of this section, but in a more roundabout way:

```
                                                                  ─ Java ─
RandomGenerator random = RandomGenerator.getDefault();

IntStream.range(1, 6).mapToObj("X"::repeat).toList(); // [X, XX, XXX, XXXX, XXXXX]
random.ints(1, 11).limit(5).boxed().toList();         // 5 numbers, possibly different
```

The first list is built by mapping a stream of numbers to strings of corresponding lengths. For the second list, you can rely on the fact that Java pseudo-random generators already implement streams of random numbers (the call to `Boxed` is used to transform an `IntStream` into a `Stream`).

You can define a `timeOf` function in Java, but a thunk will be visible when the function is used:

```
                                                                  ─ Java ─
double time = timeOf(() -> {
  computeSomething();
});
```

For the same reason, alternatives to empty options—`orElse` and `getOrElse` in Scala—need to refer explicitly to a function in Java:

```
                                                                  ─ Java ─
Optional<String> maybeString = ...;

String str = maybeString.orElseGet(() -> someStringComputation());
Optional<String> optStr = maybeString.or(() -> maybeOtherString());
```

Kotlin doesn't use options, but you can achieve a similar behavior—lazily evaluated alternates—with its special handling of null (see Section A.7).

Scala's `LazyList`—a lazily evaluated, memoized sequence—has no direct equivalent in the Java or Kotlin standard libraries. Java's `Stream` and Kotlin's `Sequence` are more like Scala's views and iterators; they provide delayed evaluation without memoization. The iterator-based function from Listing 12.9 can be written in Java or in Kotlin:[2]

```java
                                                                    Java
int collatz(BigInteger start) {
  return (int) Stream.iterate(start, n ->
          n.mod(BigInteger.TWO).equals(BigInteger.ZERO) ? n.divide(BigInteger.TWO)
              : n.multiply(BigInteger.valueOf(3)).add(BigInteger.ONE))
      .takeWhile(n -> !n.equals(BigInteger.ONE))
      .count();
}
```

```kotlin
                                                                    Kotlin
fun collatz(start: BigInteger): Int =
  generateSequence(start) { n ->
    if (n % BigInteger.TWO == BigInteger.ZERO) n / BigInteger.TWO
    else n * 3.toBigInteger() + BigInteger.ONE
  }
  .takeWhile { n -> n != BigInteger.ONE }
  .count()
```

Like Scala's iterators and views, **Stream** and **Sequence** stack and delay transformations until the sequence is consumed, avoiding the creation of intermediate structures. The two functions shown here do not allocate the list of numbers from **start** to ONE.

Finally, Kotlin—but not Java—offers a mechanism similar to Scala's **lazy** for lazy initialization of variables. Scala's

```scala
                                                                    Scala
lazy val variable: Int = someComputation()
```

can be written in Kotlin as

```kotlin
                                                                    Kotlin
val variable: Int by lazy {
  someComputation()
}
```

In both cases, **someComputation** is triggered only the first time **variable** is accessed, if it is accessed at all. As in Scala, **lazy** is thread-safe by default, but thread-safety can be turned off when it is not needed.

---

[2]Both implementations could be written more simply without a **takeWhile** step. In Java, you could use a predefined "iterate while" function; in Kotlin, you could rely on the fact that **generateSequence** stops when its function argument returns null. The code here is written to mimic the Scala variant.

A.7   Handling Failures

Error handling in Java and Kotlin is still very much centered on throwing and catching exceptions. Kotlin recently introduced a `Result` type, similar to Scala's `Try`. You could rewrite in Kotlin some of Scala's `Try`-based code from Section 13.3:

```
                                                          ——— Kotlin ———
val lines: Result<List<String>> = runCatching {
   ... // a list-producing computation
}

val linesOrNull: List<String>? = lines.getOrNull()
val linesOrEmpty: List<String> = lines.getOrDefault(listOf())
val linesOrOther: List<String> = lines.getOrElse { someListComputation() }
```

Value `lines` is a successful result if the computation inside `runCatching` produces a list. If instead it throws an exception, the exception is caught and wrapped into a failed result. The value inside `Result` can be extracted and replaced with a default value or with null if it is missing. (In Kotlin, a type `A` does not contain null, which is added in type `A?`; see the later discussion.)

As with `Try`, `Result` values can be transformed using higher-order functions:

```
                                                          ——— Kotlin ———
fun compute(list: List<String>): Int = ...
fun computeOrFail(list: List<String>): Result<Int> = ...

lines.map { compute(it) }                             // of type Result<Int>
lines.mapCatching { computeOrFail(it).getOrThrow() } // of type Result<Int>
```

The second expression is simpler in Scala, but Kotlin's `Result` type does not (yet) implement a `flatMap` method.

Java only has its `Optional` type to offer, but at least it defines a `flatMap` method:

```
                                                            ——— Java ———
List<String> someListComputation() { ... }
int compute(List<String> list) { ... }
Optional<Integer> computeOrFail(List<String> list) { ... }

Optional<List<String>> lines = ...

List<String> linesOrEmpty = lines.orElse(Collections.emptyList());
List<String> linesOrOther = lines.orElseGet(() -> someListComputation());
```

```
lines.map(list -> compute(list));          // of type Optional<Integer>
lines.flatMap(list -> computeOrFail(list)); // of type Optional<Integer>
```

Beside the `Result` type, Kotlin implements a form of compile-time null-safety. It forces you to test for nullity, provide alternative values, or propagate null. It is one of the most popular features of Kotlin, as it helps programmers avoid many occurrences of the dreaded `NullPointerException`.

As a consequence, Kotlin tends to rely on null values where other languages would use options. For instance, Scala's

```
                                                            ── Scala ──
val maybeString: Option[String] = ...

val optStr: Option[String] = maybeString.map(_.toUpperCase)
val optInt: Option[Int]    = maybeString.flatMap(_.toIntOption)
```

is equivalent to Kotlin's

```
                                                            ── Kotlin ──
val maybeString: String? = ...

val optStr: String? = maybeString?.uppercase()
val optInt: Int?    = maybeString?.toIntOrNull()
```

Kotlin types `Int` and `String` do not contain null, but types `Int?` and `String?` do. Therefore, `maybeString` could be either a string or null. The call `maybeString.uppercase()` is rejected at compile time, requiring that you add a check for null in your code. Instead of relying on `if-then-else`, Kotlin defines additional syntax that makes it easier to handle null values. The operator "`?.`" applies a method to a non-null reference, or returns null, but does not throw `NullPointerException`. It replaces the use of `map` and `flatMap` on options in Scala.

On its `Option` type, Scala also define methods like `orElse` and `getOrElse` that take an unevaluated argument, to be used only when an option is empty:

```
                                                            ── Scala ──
def someStringComputation: String    = ...
val maybeString: Option[String]      = ...
def maybeOtherString: Option[String] = ...

val str: String            = maybeString.getOrElse(someStringComputation)
val optStr: Option[String] = maybeString.orElse(maybeOtherString)
```

In this example, functions `someStringComputation` and `maybeOtherString` are triggered only if `maybeString` is empty. Kotlin relies on an operator "?:" (called "Elvis")[3] instead:

```kotlin
fun someStringComputation(): String = ...
val maybeString: String?            = ...
fun maybeOtherString(): String?     = ...

val str: String = maybeString ?: someStringComputation()
val optStr: String? = maybeString ?: maybeOtherString()
```

The right-hand side of "?:" is evaluated only if the left-hand side is null.

A.8   Types

Types in Scala, Java, and Kotlin are similar in many ways. All three languages are statically typed but allow for type testing and casting at runtime. They rely on interfaces (or traits) and classes as the primary mechanism to introduce user-defined types. You can rely on type inference to various degrees—Java does not infer the return type of methods, for instance. Function names can be overloaded for ad hoc polymorphism, classes and functions can be parameterized by types for parametric polymorphism, and dynamic binding of methods implements subtype polymorphism.

Both Scala and Kotlin let you define type aliases—the same type under different names. Java does not. Scala can define opaque types—separate types with identical implementations:

```scala
// inside a package
opaque type Length = Double

def fromMeters(meters: Double): Length = meters
def wholeMeters(len: Length): Length = len.ceil

// outside the package
val oneInch: Length = fromMeters(0.0254)
val len: Length = wholeMeters(oneInch)

wholeMeters(2.3) // rejected at compile time
```

---

[3]If you wonder about the name, tilt your head left and look again at the symbol. Does it remind you of someone?

Type `Length` is implemented as a double value but is incompatible with type `Double`. Outside the defining package, you cannot call `wholeMeters` on a `Double` value.

Kotlin achieves the same type safety using inline classes (which was the approach used in earlier versions of Scala):

—————————————————————————————————— Kotlin ——————

```kotlin
@JvmInline
value class Length(val meters: Double)

fun fromMeters(meters: Double): Length = Length(meters)
fun wholeMeters(len: Length): Length = Length(ceil(len.meters))
```

As in Scala, `wholeMeters` cannot be called on a `Double` value. However, because `Length` is an inline class, `wholeMeters` is implemented internally as a function from `Double` to `Double` and does not involve the construction of objects of type `Length` at runtime. Thus, it delivers type safety without a runtime cost, as in Scala. Some standard library types, such as `Result` used earlier, are defined in terms of value classes for improved performance.

Java and Kotlin differ noticeably in regard to type variance. The case of Java was discussed in Section 15.8. By contrast, Kotlin is much closer to Scala. Most **Book/Magazine/Publication** examples from Chapter 15 could be written in Kotlin:

—————————————————————————————————— Kotlin ——————

```kotlin
fun printTitles(pubs: List<Publication>) {
  for (pub in pubs) println(pub.title)
}

val books: List<Book> = listOf(book1, book2)
printTitles(books) // prints both titles
```

This code successfully prints the titles of both books. Recall that a similar `printTitles` function in Java could not be invoked on a `List<Book>` value because lists are non-variant in Java. In Kotlin, the `List` type is covariant. It is defined as follows:

—————————————————————————————————— Kotlin ——————

```kotlin
public interface List<out E> : Collection<E> { ... }
```

The variance annotation `out` plays the same role as "+" in Scala and makes the immutable `List` type covariant. As in Scala, mutable types are non-variant. Types such as `Array` and `MutableList` are defined in this way

—————————————————————————————————— Kotlin ——————

```kotlin
public class Array<T> { ... }
public interface MutableList<E> : List<E>, MutableCollection<E> { ... }
```

without an `out` annotation. A variance annotation `in` plays the role of "-" in Scala. It is used to define contravariant types:

```kotlin
───────────────────────────────────────────── Kotlin ──
public interface Comparable<in T> { ... }
```

Accordingly, `Comparable<Publication>` is a subtype of `Comparable<Book>` in Kotlin.

As in Java and Scala, you can deal with non-variant types with use-site variance annotations:

```kotlin
───────────────────────────────────────────── Kotlin ──
fun printTitles(pubs: Array<out Publication>) {
  for (pub in pubs) println(pub.title)
}
```

Argument `pubs` has type `Array<out Publication>` instead of `Array<Publication>`. You can invoke this `printTitles` function on a value of type `Array<Book>`, even though `Array` is not covariant.

Some advanced constructs, such as type classes, higher-kinded types, and type unions, which exist in Scala, have no direct equivalent in Java or Kotlin.

A.9 Threads

NOTE

Part II of the book illustrates concurrent programming concepts using mostly Scala and Java. Like Scala, Kotlin targets platforms other than the JVM. The discussion in this appendix pertains to Kotlin's JVM incarnation.

Kotlin defines a utility function to create threads:

```kotlin
───────────────────────────────────────────── Kotlin ──
val tA = thread {
  println('A')
}

val tB = thread(name = "TB", start = false) {
  println('B')
}
tB.start()
```

By default, threads are automatically started, as with thread `tA` in the example. However, this can be disabled—for instance, thread `tB` is started after creation, explicitly.

A.10   Atomicity and Locking

When executed on the JVM, Java, Scala, and Kotlin rely on the same threads and the same bytecode, and atomicity issues are the same in all three languages. Acquiring and releasing intrinsic locks uses a similar syntax in Java and in Kotlin. Scala's Listing 18.7 could be written as follows:

Java

```java
private final Object lock = new Object();
private int userCount = 0;

OptionalInt getRank() {
  synchronized (lock) {
    if (userCount < 5) {
      userCount += 1;
      return OptionalInt.of(userCount);
    }
    return OptionalInt.empty();
  }
}
```

Kotlin

```kotlin
private val lock = Object()
private var userCount = 0

fun getRank(): Int? = synchronized(lock) {
  if (userCount < 5) {
    userCount += 1
    userCount
  } else null
}
```

Note, however, that **synchronized** is a Java keyword, while in Kotlin, it is a function whose second argument is itself a function.

Java also uses additional syntax to conveniently lock the entire body of a method:

Java

```java
synchronized OptionalInt getRank() {
  if (userCount < 5) {
    userCount += 1;
    return OptionalInt.of(userCount);
  }
```

```
    return OptionalInt.empty();
}
```

This method behaves as if using this definition:[4]

```
                                                                    Java
OptionalInt getRank() {
  synchronized (this) {
    if (userCount < 5) {
      ...
```

Kotlin achieves the same purpose using an annotation:

```
                                                                    Kotlin
@Synchronized
fun getRank(): Int? =
  if (userCount < 5) {
    ...
```

A.11   Thread-Safe Objects

By relying on intrinsic locks, you can design thread-safe objects in Java or Kotlin using the same strategies—and facing the same trade-offs—as those discussed in Chapter 19. A weakness of both languages, compared to Scala, is the lack of functional data structures in the standard library. For instance, this Scala thread-safe set

```
                                                                    Scala
class SafeSet[A]:
  private var elements = Set.empty[A] // an immutable set

  def += (elem: A): Int = synchronized {
    elements += elem // this is: elements = elements + elem
    elements.size
  }

  def all: Set[A] = synchronized(elements)
```

has no exact equivalent in Java or Kotlin. In the Scala implementation, both "+=" and all are efficient: "+=" creates a new set that shares much of its data with the current set, and all simply returns a pointer to the current set.

---

[4]If the method is static, the reflection object associated with the enclosing class is used as the lock instead of this.

By contrast, code that relies on the Java or Kotlin standard libraries requires a full copy of the set, either when adding or when returning the entire collection. In the following Java and Kotlin variants, for instance, you need to copy the entire set—with the lock owned—inside method `all`:

--- *Java* -----

```java
public class SafeSet<A> {
  private final Set<A> elements = new java.util.HashSet<>();

  public synchronized int add(A elem) {
    elements.add(elem);
    return elements.size();
  }

  public synchronized Set<A> all() {
    return Set.copyOf(elements); // full copy here
  }
}
```

--- *Kotlin* -----

```kotlin
class SafeSet<A> {
  private val elements = mutableSetOf<A>()

  @Synchronized fun add(elem: A): Int {
    elements += elem
    return elements.size
  }

  @Synchronized fun all(): Set<A> = elements.toSet() // full copy here
}
```

These implementations of `all` would be incorrect:

--- *Java* -----

```java
// DON'T DO THIS!
public synchronized Set<A> all() {
  return Collections.unmodifiableSet(elements);
}
```

--- *Kotlin* -----

```kotlin
// DON'T DO THIS!
@Synchronized fun all(): Set<A> = elements
```

Because the set being returned is (or contains) a reference to the internal set, these implementations would potentially result in unsafe interactions between a writing thread (with the lock owned) and a reading thread (without the lock).

In contrast, if you use Kotlin's immutable sets, you can make `all` efficient—but now `add` requires a full copy of the entire set:

```kotlin
                                                                    ──── Kotlin ────
class SafeSet<A> {
  private var elements = setOf<A>() // an immutable set

  @Synchronized fun add(elem: A): Int {
    elements += elem // full copy here
    return elements.size
  }

  @Synchronized fun all(): Set<A> = elements
}
```

Scala's variant uses an efficient "+" method on immutable sets—the sets `elements` and `elements + elem` share data—that is not available in Kotlin's standard library.

A.12   Thread Pools

JVM thread pools, defined in `java.util.concurrent`, can be used directly in all three languages. For instance, the Scala code in Listing 21.4 uses a thread pool in a server:

```scala
                                                                    ──── Scala ────
exec.execute(() => handleConnection(socket))
```

It could be written in Java as

```java
                                                                    ──── Java ────
exec.execute(() -> handleConnection(socket));
```

or in Kotlin as

```kotlin
                                                                    ──── Kotlin ────
exec.execute {
  handleConnection(socket)
}
```

We saw earlier that, instead of using Java thread pools directly, Scala code typically defines execution contexts that make it easier to create futures and apply higher-order methods on them:

```
————————————————————————————————————————— Scala ———

given ExecutionContext = ExecutionContext.fromExecutor(exec)

Future {
    // can use context implicitly to create futures
}
```

In a similar way, Kotlin tends to define dispatchers that you can use to run coroutines (coroutines were discussed in Section 27.4 and are revisited in Section A.15):

```
——————————————————————————————————————————— Kotlin ———

val dispatcher = exec.asCoroutineDispatcher()

withContext(dispatcher) {
    // can use context implicitly to run coroutines
}
```

Conversely, you can use Scala contexts and Kotlin dispatchers as regular Java thread pools if needed:

```
————————————————————————————————————————— Scala ———

ExecutionContext.global.execute(() => handleConnection(socket))
```

```
——————————————————————————————————————————— Kotlin ———

Dispatchers.Default.asExecutor().execute {
    handleConnection(socket)
}
```

You can use thread pools implicitly in Scala to speed up the execution of higher-order functions on parallel collections. For instance, Listing 21.6 processes URLs in parallel by first transforming a regular list into a parallel sequence, using **par**:

```
————————————————————————————————————————— Scala ———

val urls: List[URL] = ...

val counts = urls.par.map(distinctWordsCount)
```

The same mechanism exists in Java. (Kotlin has no direct equivalent in its standard library.) Java streams can be parallel or sequential, and parallel streams implement their higher-order functions on top of thread pools:

```
                                                              ─── Java ───
List<URL> urls = ...;

IntStream counts = urls.parallelStream().mapToInt(url -> distinctWordsCount(url));
```

Thread pools are used transparently in a few other places in Java. For instance, class `java.util.Arrays` defines functions `parallelSetAll` and `parallelSort` that rely on the common thread pool to initialize and sort arrays, respectively.

A.13 Synchronization

The synchronizers discussed earlier are implemented in the Java standard library and thus are available in Java, Scala, and Kotlin. As an illustration, you can implement the simple lock from Listing 23.5 in Java or in Kotlin using code very similar to the Scala variant:

```
                                                              ─── Java ───
public class SimpleLock {
  private final Semaphore semaphore = new Semaphore(1);
  volatile private Thread owner;

  public void lock() throws InterruptedException {
    semaphore.acquire();
    owner = Thread.currentThread();
  }

  public void unlock() {
    if (owner != Thread.currentThread())
      throw new IllegalStateException("not the lock owner");
    owner = null;
    semaphore.release();
  }
}
```

```
                                                              ─── Kotlin ───
class SimpleLock {
  private val semaphore = Semaphore(1)
  @Volatile private var owner: Thread? = null

  fun lock() {
    semaphore.acquire()
    owner = Thread.currentThread()
  }
}
```

```
fun unlock() {
  if (owner != Thread.currentThread())
    throw IllegalStateException("not the lock owner")
  owner = null
  semaphore.release()
}
}
```

A.14   Futures and Functional-Concurrent Programming

Earlier, we used Java's `Future` and `CompletableFuture` from within Java and Scala code. They could be used in Kotlin as well. For a functional-concurrent programming style, Scala tends to rely on its own `Future` type, while Java uses `CompletableFuture`. As an illustration, you could rewrite the parallel server from Listing 26.8 in Java:

Java

```
ExecutorService exec = Executors.newFixedThreadPool(16);

ServerSocket server = new ServerSocket(port);

void handleConnection(Connection connection) {
  var requestF = CompletableFuture.supplyAsync(connection::read, exec);
  var adF = requestF.thenApplyAsync(request -> fetchAd(request), exec);
  var dataF = requestF.thenApplyAsync(request -> dbLookup(request), exec);
  var pageF = dataF.thenCompose(data ->
      adF.thenApplyAsync(ad -> makePage(data, ad), exec)
  );
  dataF.thenAcceptAsync(data -> addToLog(data), exec);
  pageF.thenAcceptAsync(page -> updateStats(page), exec);
  pageF.thenAcceptAsync(page -> {
    connection.write(page);
    connection.close();
  }, exec);
}

while (true) handleConnection(new Connection(server.accept()));
```

Calls to `thenApply`, `thenCompose`, and `thenAccept` are non-blocking and are used to schedule future computations as data becomes available. They correspond to Scala calls to `map`, `flatMap`, and `foreach`, respectively. The thread that invokes `handleConnection` does no actual processing, and you can use the listening thread of the server.

On `CompletableFuture`, higher-order methods exist in two flavors: with or without the "Async" suffix. With the suffix, you can specify a thread pool on which to run the argument function; without the suffix, the code keeps running in an existing thread. Scala offers no such choice. (A plain `thenCompose` is used in the example because the code to run is only a call to `thenApplyAsync`, which takes no time.)

You could write a similar server in Kotlin. However, Kotlin tends to favor an asynchronous programming style that uses coroutines instead. See Listing 27.6 for a Kotlin coroutine variant of a (simpler) server.

A.15   Minimizing Thread Blocking

Chapter 27 discussed the use of `ForkJoinPool` in Java and of coroutines in Kotlin. As mentioned in Section 27.4, Kotlin defines additional coroutine-level synchronization mechanisms that do not block threads. As an illustration, consider first this Java program:

```
                                                                    ── Java ──
var exec = Executors.newFixedThreadPool(N);
var latch = new CountDownLatch(M);

for (int id = 1; id <= M; id++) {
  exec.execute(() -> {
    latch.countDown();
    try {
      latch.await();
    } catch (InterruptedException e) { /* ignored */ }
  });
}
```

In this example, a pool is created with N threads, and M tasks are submitted for execution. These tasks share a countdown latch, created with an initial count equal to M. Each task decrements the count and then waits for the latch to open.

As long as $N \geqslant M$, the tasks are able to complete. However, if $M > N$, the program gets stuck in a deadlock. After the latch count is decremented N times, all the worker threads are blocked waiting for the latch to open, and no worker is available to run the remaining decrementing tasks. The behavior would be the same in Scala or Kotlin.

In Kotlin, however, you can define a countdown latch that suspends coroutines without blocking a thread:

```
                                                                    ── Kotlin ──
class CountDownLatch(count: Int) {
  private val remaining = AtomicInteger(count)
  private val semaphore = Semaphore(permits = 1, acquiredPermits = 1)
  suspend fun await() {
    if (remaining.get() > 0) {
      semaphore.acquire()
```

```
      semaphore.release()
    }
  }

  fun countDown() {
    if (remaining.get() > 0 && remaining.decrementAndGet() == 0)
      semaphore.release()
  }
}
```

This implementation uses a semaphore. The semaphore has no permit initially, making method `await` blocking. Once the latch count reaches zero, a permit is created. This permit is then acquired by one of the tasks blocked on `await` and released again for the next task, thus allowing all the blocked tasks to go through the latch.

The semaphore used in the preceding example is an instance of `kotlinx.coroutines .sync.Semaphore`, and its `acquire` method is implemented to suspend a calling coroutine without blocking the corresponding thread. Therefore, `await` in the countdown latch can also block a task without blocking a thread. You can use the latch to implement a Kotlin coroutine variant of the Java program introduced earlier in this section:

Kotlin

```
val exec = Executors.newFixedThreadPool(N)
val latch = CountDownLatch(M)

withContext(exec.asCoroutineDispatcher()) {
  for (id in 1..M) {
    launch {
      latch.countDown()
      latch.await()
    }
  }
}
```

This program does not deadlock, even when $M > N$. When a thread reaches `await` on a closed latch, the corresponding coroutine is suspended, but the thread remains available to run another coroutine, which will perform another countdown. Eventually, all the countdowns are executed, and the latch opens.

Glossary

action An impure subroutine that relies on **side effects** to modify the state of an application but does not return a (meaningful) value; sometimes also called a procedure. See also **pure**. Discussed in Chapter 3.

algebraic data type A **type** that combines existing types through a combination of alternatives (sum) and aggregation (product). Many standard types, including **tuples**, **options**, **lists**, and **trees**, can be defined as algebraic data types. Discussed in Chapter 5.

anonymous function See **function literal**.

argument An input to a **function** or **method**, such as a **value** or a **type**. Also called *parameter*.

asynchronous, asynchronously The opposite of **synchronous, synchronously**.

callback 1. A piece of code registered for (single, multiple, or optional) execution. Callbacks may run **synchronously** (as in Chapter 9) or **asynchronously** (as in Chapter 26). 2. The action of running such code.

CAS Compare-and-set.

class In object-oriented programming, a template for the creation of **objects**.

concurrent Said of multiple code executions that happen at the same time ("concurrently"). In this book, synonymous with *parallel*. Discussed in Chapter 16.

curried, currying A curried **function** consumes its first **argument** (or argument list) and returns another function that will use the remaining arguments (or argument lists). By currying, a function that uses a list of multiple arguments can be transformed into a function that uses multiple lists of fewer arguments. See also **higher-order**. Discussed in Section 9.2.

deadlock A situation is which several entities perpetually wait for each other in a cycle due to faulty **synchronization**. Discussed in Sections 22.3 and 27.7.

exception A disruption in the flow of program execution, typically caused by a failure and possibly handled by an exception handler. Exceptions are said to be thrown (or raised) and caught (or handled). Uncaught exceptions can cause a **thread** to terminate its execution.

execution stack A **stack** that keeps track of the current nesting of subroutines executed by a **thread**: Entering a subroutine adds to the stack, exiting it removes from the stack. Also called *call stack*.

expression A code fragment that, through computation, evaluates to a **value**. In addition to expressions, programming languages may involve code without a value, evaluated for the purpose of **side effects**.

extension method A mechanism by which additional **methods** can be grafted onto an existing **type**. Discussed in Section 2.5.

FIFO First-in, first-out.

function 1. A mathematical abstraction that maps each **value** from a set to a unique value from another set. 2. A programming language subroutine parameterized by zero or more **arguments** and which produces a value. For disambiguation, see **pure**, **side effect**. Discussed in Chapter 2.

function literal An **expression** that denotes an unnamed **function**; also called *anonymous function*. **Lambda expressions** are a common syntax for function literals. Discussed in Section 9.3.

functional Variously defined by different authors, but often said of a programming style that emphasizes the use of **pure** functions, **immutability**, **recursion**, **algebraic data types**, **higher-order** functions, and/or **lazy** evaluation. Discussed in Chapter 1.

future A handle on an asynchronous computation. Futures vary in capabilities, and terminology is ambiguous. Futures are sometimes referred to as *promises*. Discussed in Chapters 25 and 26.

garbage collection A form of automatic memory management used to reclaim unused memory. The Java Virtual Machine implements a garbage collector, available to all languages that run on this platform.

happens-before The partial order that defines the Java Memory Model. Note that "happens before" and "happens-before" have a different meaning in the book. Discussed in Section 22.5.

higher-order Said of a **function** that consumes or produces other functions as values. Discussed in Chapters 9 and 10.

immutable That which cannot be changed. This term can apply to an **object** state (immutable object) or a non-reassignable **variable**. See also **mutable**. Discussed in Chapter 3.

imperative Said of a programming style centered on **actions** that modify a state, such as assignment statements. By contrast, **functional** programming is said to be more declarative. See also **pure**, **side effect**.

infix Said of a notation in which an **operator** appears between its two arguments, as in x + y. See also **prefix**, **postfix**.

instance A member **value** of a **type**. In object-oriented programming specifically, an instance of a **class**—that is, an **object** created by instantiating this class.

JMM Java Memory Model.

JVM Java Virtual Machine.

lambda expression A common syntax for **function literals,** named after λ-calculus, a theory of computable **functions**. Discussed in Section 9.3.

lazy Refers to various forms of delayed evaluation: lazy evaluation, lazy initialization, etc. Discussed in Chapter 12.

LIFO Last-in, first-out.

list 1. A generic term for an ordered collection of **values**, which can be **mutable** or not, support efficient access by indexing or not, etc. 2. A specific data structure used in **functional** programming, and characterized by its immutability and head/tail structure; sometimes referred to as *functional* list for disambiguation. Discussed in Section 3.7 and Chapter 7.

lock A basic **synchronization** mechanism used in **concurrent** programs to prevent data-sharing tasks from interfering with each other. Locks are only one of the many synchronizers a programming environment might offer. Discussed in Chapters 18 and 19 and Section 23.1.

method A **function**-like subroutine that is associated with a target **object**, which serves as one of its **arguments**.

mutable That can be changed. For instance, a mutable **object** has a state that can be modified; a mutable **variable** can be reassigned with a new **value**. See also **immutable**. Discussed in Chapter 3.

node In a graph, a vertex.

object The fundamental component of the state of an object-oriented program. An object typically encapsulates data and the operations that manipulate this data.

operator A **function** typically of one or two arguments, often with a symbolic name, and invoked in **prefix, infix,** or **postfix** notation.

option Used to represent a **value** that may or may not exist. An option either is empty or contains exactly one value. Options are often used as the return type of **functions** that do not always have a valid value to return. Discussed in Section 5.3.

parallel Said of multiple code executions that happen at the same time ("in parallel"). In this book, synonymous with **concurrent**. Discussed in Chapter 16.

pattern matching A construct, common in **functional** programming languages, that is used to select between alternatives and to separate components of an aggregate **type**. Pattern matching can be thought of as a powerful generalization of `switch`. It is especially handy when dealing with **algebraic data types**. Discussed in Chapter 5.

pattern-zipper An efficient implementation technique for an **immutable** structure that is traversable (navigatable). Discussed in Section 5.6.

postfix Said of a notation in which an **operator** follows its arguments, as in `x++`. See also **infix**, **prefix**.

prefix Said of a notation in which an **operator** precedes its arguments, as in `++x`. See also **infix**, **postfix**.

promise 1. A generator of a **future**. 2. Another name for a future. Discussed in Section 25.5.

pure Said of a programming **function** whose behavior depends only on its input, and which has no **side effects**. **Pure functions** are used to represent true (mathematical) functions. See also **action**. Discussed in Chapter 3.

queue 1. A data structure for temporary storage of **values** waiting to be processed. Queue elements are often retrieved in a predefined ordering. Common orderings are first-in-first-out (FIFO), last-in-first-out (LIFO), priority based, or time based. 2. A first-in, first-out queue.

recursion See **recursive**.

recursive Said of a **function** that invokes itself in its computation, one or more times, directly or indirectly, and of a programming style that relies on such functions. Discussed in Chapter 6.

runtime During code execution, the period in contrast to compile time—when code is compiled.

scope The fragment of a program in which a particular definition is operative. A defined entity (**variable**, **function**, **class**, etc.) can be used only within its scope.

set 1. A mathematical abstraction of an unordered collection of **values**, without duplicates. 2. A data structure that implements this abstraction, usually with efficient lookup, and possibly with ordering (ordered sets) or duplicates (multisets).

side effect A modification of the state of system. Could be intentional or not. See also **pure**, **action**. Discussed in Chapter 3.

stack 1. A data structure that stacks elements on top of each other, typically with only the top element accessible. Sometimes referred to as a last-in-first-out (LIFO) queue. 2. The **execution stack**.

stream A sequence whose **values** are created over time. A stream can potentially be endless. Discussed in Chapter 12.

`switch` A programming language construct used to pick among several alternatives. It can be seen as a generalization of `if-then-else`, which is basically a `switch` with two branches. See also **pattern matching**.

synchronization A generic term for mechanisms and techniques used by **threads** to coordinate. Discussed in Chapters 22 and 23.

synchronous, synchronously In this book, refers to a computation that takes place within the program flow ("now"), as opposed to an asynchronous computation that does not interfere with the current flow of execution. Discussed in Chapter 16.

tail recursion A particular form of **recursion** susceptible to compiler optimizations. Discussed in Section 6.5.

thread Short for *thread of execution*. A thread represents the execution (or run) of a program. A running program contains at least one thread, but programs can also be multithreaded. Discussed in Chapter 16.

tree A connected, acyclic graph, typically undirected. A *rooted* tree identifies a vertex as the root of the tree; an *ordered* tree maintains an ordering among the children of a **node** (e.g., left and right in a binary tree).

tuple An ordered aggregate of several **values**, possibly of different **types**. A 2-tuple is referred to as a pair; a 3-tuple as a triple.

type An abstract characterization of possible **values**. **Variables, expressions,** and **function** input and output can all have types that constrain the actual values they might take. Types also often constrain the operations that are available on values of that type. Discussed in Chapter 15.

value An immutable piece of data. Values can be stored in **variables** and data structures, returned by **functions**, or passed as **arguments** to functions.

varargs Short for *variable-length arguments*. Said of subroutines in which the number of **arguments** is not fixed. Discussed in Section 2.7.

variable A named reference, valid within a **scope**. The concept is more subtle than it sounds: Variables can refer to data or to code, and some variables can have their contents updated while others cannot. Discussed in Chapters 3 and 9.

Index

Register Your Product at informit.com/register

Access additional benefits and save up to 65%* on your next purchase

- Automatically receive a coupon for 35% off books, eBooks, and web editions and 65% off video courses, valid for 30 days. Look for your code in your InformIT cart or the Manage Codes section of your account page.

- Download available product updates.

- Access bonus material if available.**

- Check the box to hear from us and receive exclusive offers on new editions and related products.

InformIT—The Trusted Technology Learning Source

InformIT is the online home of information technology brands at Pearson, the world's leading learning company. At informit.com, you can

- Shop our books, eBooks, and video training. Most eBooks are DRM-Free and include PDF and EPUB files.

- Take advantage of our special offers and promotions (informit.com/promotions).

- Sign up for special offers and content newsletter (informit.com/newsletters).

- Access thousands of free chapters and video lessons.

- Enjoy free ground shipping on U.S. orders.*

* Offers subject to change.
** Registration benefits vary by product. Benefits will be listed on your account page under Registered Products.

Connect with InformIT—Visit informit.com/community

 twitter.com/informit

 Pearson

Addison-Wesley • Adobe Press • Cisco Press • Microsoft Press • Oracle Press • Peachpit Press • Pearson IT Certification • Que